CLARENDON LAW SERIES

Edited by

PAUL CRA

CLARENDON LAW SERIES

The Conflict of Laws

Fourth Edition

By

ADRIAN BRIGGS

St Edmund Hall, University of Oxford

OXFORD
UNIVERSITY PRESS

Great Clarendon Street, Oxford, OX2 6DP,
United Kingdom

Oxford University Press is a department of the University of Oxford.
It furthers the University's objective of excellence in research, scholarship,
and education by publishing worldwide. Oxford is a registered trade mark of
Oxford University Press in the UK and in certain other countries

First Edition published in 2002
Second Edition published in 2008
Third Edition published in 2013
Fourth Edition published in 2019

Impression: 3

Published in the United States of America by Oxford University Press
198 Madison Avenue, New York, NY 10016, United States of America

British Library Cataloguing in Publication Data

Data available

Library of Congress Control Number: 2019946459

ISBN 978–0–19–884523–2 (pbk.)
ISBN 978–0–19–883850–0 (hbk.)

Printed and bound by
CPI Group (UK) Ltd, Croydon, CR0 4YY

Preface to the Fourth Edition

Until recently it had been settled wisdom that private international law, as understood in England, was moving away from being a common law subject with European insertions and becoming a European subject with common law marginalia. Law, however, is never wholly insulated from politics. Three years after the *bouleversement* of the 2016 referendum, all that politics has produced is incoherence, albeit with lashings of mendacity; and along with everything else it has made a ruin of the law. Any hope that, if one were patient, the future would become clear enough to allow the state of the law to be assessed and described was dashed, dashed, and dashed again. If this is what 'taking back control' looks like, it would be better to be blind.

Even though the lunatics may have been given control of the asylum, the work of private international law, and lawyers, has not stopped. The bringing of this book up to date was already overdue, and so the nettle had to be grasped. Up to date, in this context, means two things: accounting for the law in force in England in the summer of 2019, and dealing, to the extent possible, with the various paths which the law may follow if 'Exit Day', as the legislation chillingly refers to it, arrives. In forty years of working with this wonderful subject, it had never occurred to me that it could be so hard to describe the law, or that the law could be so comprehensively trashed.

Whatever might be said elsewhere about the merits of membership or non-membership of the European Union, it was hard to find a conflicts lawyer, still in possession of his or her mind, who had been dreaming of putting the clock back to New Year's Eve 1986, just before the Brussels Convention came into effect in English private international law. It took a while, and perhaps longer than it should have, but English conflicts lawyers had come to terms with, and absorbed, this new law, and made it their own. The end result was usually an improvement on what was there before, which was hardly surprising, as the United Kingdom had been heavily and seriously involved in the creation of these new rules in the first place. Some planks of it, no doubt, can be pulled out of the wreckage, patched up, and made to function as rules of English private international law. But as is often the way with earthquakes for which no preparation had been made, much more of it will be irreparable and will be lost.

Perhaps one should not complain too much: private international law-yers have no right to an easy life, and the work required to make sense of tomorrow's law has always been as much privilege as burden. Even so, the mad vandalism of the last three years means that while the eggs have all been well and truly broken, there is still no sign of the omelette: one is left with the realization that smashed eggs is all there is ever going to be. While the only safe prediction is that if this book should regenerate into a fifth edition, it will look rather different from this, its fourth (or Brexit) edition, for now we shall just have to bear it. There is neither duty, nor the slightest reason, to grin.

Adrian Briggs
Oxford
Midsummer, 2019

Contents

Decisions of National Courts

Decisions of European Courts

United Kingdom Legislation

EU Legislation

International Agreements
and Conventions

1
Introduction

A. THE UNITED KINGDOM AND THE EUROPEAN UNION

The question on the mind of all those who care about English private international law, and to whom this book is addressed, is the effect of the unexecuted decision of the United Kingdom to leave the European Union. There are several parts to the response, though whether they make for an answer to the question is more difficult to say.

If the United Kingdom were to withdraw on the terms approved by Parliament, the resulting legal framework would in principle[1] be that put in place by the European Union (Withdrawal) Act 2018. That is to say, on 'Exit Day',[2] the European Communities Act 1972 will be repealed.[3] This will, at a stroke, remove the legal basis upon which a substantial body of private international law takes effect in the legal order of the United Kingdom. In order to prevent the vacuum which would result from this, the Act provides for EU law—whether domestic legislation derived from EU law[4] or EU legislation which was directly effective[5]—to be retained as the law of the United Kingdom law, but on the authority of, and according to the terms of, the 2018 Act.

The position in relation to legislation is the easiest to state. Legislation adopted or enacted before Exit Day and retained, in accordance with the 2018 Act, as UK law will continue in force and effect. But it may be amended where this is necessary to allow it to operate effectively in the United Kingdom.[6] It may also be revoked where that is appropriate, which it will be if, for example, the legislation is founded on or reflects a principle of reciprocity or mutual recognition which will cease to apply to (and, so far as other Member States

---

[1] In principle, because existing Acts of Parliament may always be superseded by newer legislation.
[2] European Union (Withdrawal) Act 2018, s 20.
[3] European Union (Withdrawal) Act 2018, s 1.
[4] European Union (Withdrawal) Act 2018, s 2.
[5] European Union (Withdrawal) Act 2018, s 3.
[6] European Union (Withdrawal) Act 2018, s 8.

The Conflict of Laws. Fourth Edition. Adrian Briggs, Oxford University Press (2019). © Adrian Briggs
DOI: 10.1093/oso/9780198838500.003.0001

are concerned, in relation to) the United Kingdom. The most significant revocation of legislation will be in the field of jurisdiction and judgments. The Brussels I Regulation, 44/2001, and the recast Regulation, 1215/2012, will be revoked. In addition, the Brussels and Lugano Conventions will be deleted from the Civil Jurisdiction and Judgments Act 1982 and from any other legislation in which they appear. The result of that is that the entire system of Brussels and Lugano instruments, governing jurisdiction and the enforcement of judgments, will disappear from English law.[7] Jurisdiction, and the associated powers,[8] of an English court will be left to be governed by the 'common law rules', albeit with some minor tinkering.[9] The effect of a judgment from a Member State of the EU in England will be determined by the rules of the common law or any (newly revived) bilateral treaty, though the Hague Convention on Choice of Court Agreements 2005 can be expected to enter into force for the United Kingdom at the same time as it ceases to extend to the United Kingdom as a Member State.[10] The prospect of any future development to replicate these laws, more or less completely (by adopting the Lugano Convention, which would require the assent of the other parties to it, for example), is evidently remote.

In the context of family law, the Brussels II Regulation 2201/2003 and the Maintenance Regulation 4/2009 will also be revoked.[11] The result of that will be that the rules for matrimonial causes (jurisdiction and recognition of decrees) which currently apply in non-European cases will extend to formerly European cases. The principal rules of private international law applicable to children, and to maintenance, will be those of the various Hague Conventions to which the United Kingdom was a signatory in its own right.

The Insolvency Regulation 2015/848 is for all practical purposes revoked, although the rule that the court has jurisdiction to open proceedings if it is the centre of the debtor's main interests will be retained. Otherwise the account to be taken of connections and proceedings outside the European Union will be governed by the Insolvency Act 1986, and the Model Law.[12]

The Rome I and Rome II Regulations,[13] governing the law applicable to contractual and non-contractual obligations, are retained as the law of the

---

[7] SI 2019/479, Part 5.
[8] SI 2018/1257.
[9] SI 2019/479, inserting ss 15B to 15E into the Civil Jurisdiction and Judgments Act 1982, to make provision for jurisdiction in matters concerning consumer and employment contracts.
[10] SI 2018/1124.
[11] SI 2019/519, Part 2 (amended by SI 2019/836).
[12] SI 2019/146.
[13] SI 2019/834.

United Kingdom; they are modified, but in very minor ways. The conflict of laws rules for obligations in civil and commercial matters will therefore not change overnight, though it is entirely plausible that there will be a slow drifting apart, especially if either Regulation is amended by the European Union for itself after Exit Day.

So far as case law is concerned, the jurisprudence of the European Court prior to Exit Day will continue to apply to retained legislation,[14] but the Supreme Court will not be strictly bound by it. As to the jurisprudence of the European Court after Exit Day 'regard may be had' to it to the extent that a court considers it to be relevant to the matter before it. It is reasonable to suppose that case law will include those principles of interpretation which underpin the jurisprudence, though this seems likely to be the most challenging part of working out what is and is not retained as the law of the United Kingdom. It will, naturally, no longer be possible for an English court to make references to the European Court for a preliminary ruling.

When is Exit Day and what does it mean? Though the 2018 Act defined it as 11pm on 29 March 2019,[15] the Act also empowered the government to fix and re-fix it.[16] That means that we will only know for sure what the date of Exit Day actually was when it has been enacted, been, and gone. The 2018 Act also makes provision for a Withdrawal Agreement, which may yet be concluded between the European Union and the United Kingdom, to be given effect. As at the date of writing, no one can say whether such a thing will be agreed to. It is, however, reasonable to suppose that a sensible version of a Withdrawal Agreement would provide for a transition period during which the principal European laws discussed in this book would continue to operate as though the United Kingdom were still a Member State.

In the current conditions of political imbecility, one has to take care of the law as best one can. This edition proceeds on the basis that the legislative texts in force, one way or another, in the United Kingdom will continue to be effective for some time yet. There are two reasons for this. One is that no one can currently predict, never mind set out, the terms on which the United Kingdom will walk out of the European Union. The other is that those states which have only ever been in the European Free Trade Association have long seen the sense, enshrined in the Lugano Conventions, of having

---

[14] European Union (Withdrawal) Act 2018, s 6.
[15] European Union (Withdrawal) Act 2018, s 20(1).
[16] European Union (Withdrawal) Act 2018, s 20(2)–(4). At the date of writing it is 11pm on 31 October 2019: European Union (Withdrawal) Act 2018 (Exit Day) (Amendment) (No 2) Regulations 2019, SI 2019/859.

rules governing jurisdiction and judgments in civil and commercial matters which are, in effect, those of the Brussels regime. The United Kingdom may or may not see the sense in doing likewise, but, if it does, the rules which are set out, in particular in Chapters 2 and 3, will continue to reflect the law. If the rupture is more violent, it should be possible, if tiresome, to overlook the pages on which the European strands of our law were examined; though if it ever comes to that, the fate of a modest textbook will be the very least of the nation's worries.

A very short summary of the Exit Day, and Day After, position, so far as this can be discerned and the information relied on, is given, in italics, at the beginning of each chapter except for Chapter 4, where its impact will be only patchy. These summaries are very short, but they set the general scene; and they do point the interested reader, as well as the horrified reader, to the place where the real detail can be found.

B. THE NATURE OF THE SUBJECT

The title of this book suggests that it is concerned with the conflict of laws, but this should not be taken too seriously, for the subject has little to do with conflict, legal or otherwise. Once some very important preliminaries have been dealt with, in the chapters which follow, the fields of inquiry will be three in number. First to be examined will be the rules which determine whether an English court has jurisdiction to hear a claim where one or more of the parties, or some other aspect of the story, may be foreign to England or to English law: the conflict of jurisdictions.[17] Second will be the effect of a foreign judgment in the English legal order: the conflict of judgments.[18] And third and finally, we will consider the rules and principles which tell an English court hearing a case with a foreign element whether to apply English law or a foreign law or a combination of laws to resolve the dispute: the conflict of laws.[19] But before we do, there is more to be said about the nature of this subject and the aim of this book.

The common lawyer's label for this entire collection of material was 'the conflict of laws'; and the technique by which a court determines which law

---

[17] See Ch 2.
[18] See Ch 3.
[19] See Chs 4–9.

to apply (the third category of material) the 'choice of law'. As so often with labels, none of these is very helpful.

The conflict of laws is an important part of the subject, but it appears to overlook the conflict of jurisdictions and the conflict of judgments. For this reason, some prefer to think of the subject as 'private international law', for it is concerned almost entirely with private law in cases and matters having international elements or points of contact. The drawback with that title is that it may suggest a relationship with public international law, which describes or regulates relations between states. That would also be misleading, for very little public international law infiltrates the subject. For example, when dealing with the confiscation or nationalization of private property by states, there may well be rules of public international law on whether the property of a foreign citizen may be seized, whether compensation should be paid, and so forth. But private international law has little concern with this: as long as the property was within the territory of the seizing state, title acquired by seizure will usually be effective in private international law, whatever public international law may say about the steps taken to acquire it.

As to the nomenclature of 'choice of law' to describe the process by which a *court* determines which country's laws should be applied to dispose of the matter before it, the problem with that is that a court does not choose. It applies well-established rules which direct it to the applicable law: in no real sense does a court 'choose', if by that we mean to make a free and unconstrained selection of the law to apply. The parties to a transaction may choose the law which will govern it. Their choice may or may not be effective or conclusive: the rules of the conflict of laws will decide that. But the *court* does not choose; and the rules by which it decides are not rules of choice. We will therefore try to avoid the terminology of 'choice of law' when describing the process by which the court identifies the applicable law. We will refer to the rules it uses as 'conflicts rules' rather than 'choice of law rules'.

Returning to our description of the subject overall, the nomenclature of 'conflict of laws' was appropriate when the subject confined its attention to the question of which law to apply to the issue before the court for decision: whether the obligation in question was governed by English or French law; whether the succession to an estate was governed by English or Spanish law; whether the validity of a marriage or effect of a divorce was governed by English or Italian law, and so on: such questions dominated the subject in the period of its classical development, from the 19th to the mid-20th century. All this changed when the House of Lords opened a door which allowed, or even encouraged, much closer attention to whether English courts had and would exercise jurisdiction in a given case. The law reports were suddenly filled with cases fighting the issue of jurisdiction and its exercise, while at the same time the number of trials which addressed questions of applicable law, the conflict of laws properly so called, sharply diminished. It revolutionized the subject.

This new attention to the law of jurisdiction coincided with developments in Europe. The original Treaty of Rome, establishing the European Economic Community, called upon Contracting States to bring forward legislation to secure the free movement of judgments across the Community. The Contracting States implemented the instruction they had given themselves by enacting a scheme to lay down uniform rules of jurisdiction, it being expected that this would ensure that full faith and credit be given to judgments from the courts of any contracting state. And so it proved. As the Community expanded, and then became a Union, this Convention, which then became a Regulation, on jurisdiction and judgments in civil and commercial matters, was updated and improved; and as it expanded its scope, the common law found that it had been cut back.

Jurisdiction and judgments was the start, but not the end. The European Union reckoned that if the law on civil jurisdiction and judgments could be marshalled towards uniformity, so could the rest of private international law. The result was a number of legislative instruments aimed at bringing uniformity to rules of private international law as applied in courts all across Europe. This extended to cover the entire law of obligations, large parts of family law, some aspects of the law of property, insolvency, and corporate activity, and a scattering of smaller and more specialist topics. To begin with, this was said to be necessary to bring about the completion of the internal market, but the harmonization of private international law across Europe became an end in itself.

All this produced a hybrid corpus of private international law, but one in which the threads were different and distinct. Laws which are European in origin have an aim and function quite different from the laws made at Westminster. They are not designed to amend the common law rules of private international law or to fit within the framework evolved by the common law. Just as an imperial spanner will not work with a metric bolt, so the fundamental techniques of the common law do not work with European material (and, to be sure, vice versa). For this reason, the general and introductory principles of the subject must always reflect that basic distinction.

C. PRIVATE INTERNATIONAL LAW AS COMMON LAW

This section will outline the common law's conception of private international law, in order that reference may be made to it when a particular question arises which is not dealt with by European legislation on private international law. Although the private international law of obligations (jurisdiction and applicable law) has been mostly taken over by European private international law, the process is not yet complete. The private international law of family relations and of property is still substantially within the domain of common law private international law: either because there is no European legislation on the subject or because the United Kingdom exercised its privilege to be not bound by certain legislative acts. And anyway, the techniques of the common law are not wholly alien to European private international law, which was built on the foundations of national laws, including English law; and above all, the common law of private international law is how the subject, as practised in the English courts, was made and refined. Its techniques provide a useful point of contrast with the new system of private international law devised and put in place by the European Union; but an appreciation of them makes clear why they have little part to play within the closed world which is European private international law.

1. FOREIGN LAW IN ENGLISH COURTS

The principal characteristic of the conflict of laws is that it will sometimes lead to a judge being asked to apply foreign law to an issue in dispute between the parties. In the ordinary course, an English judge will apply English domestic law: common law, equity, and statute law. He may not apply a rule of foreign law to an issue unless three conditions are satisfied. First, the conflict of laws rules which make up English private international law must confirm that a foreign law is in principle applicable to the issue in question. Second, the party who relies on foreign law and wishes the judge to apply it must plead it. Third, the party relying on foreign law must adduce evidence which proves its content to the satisfaction of the court. Meeting these three conditions means that the judge will be enabled and obliged to apply a rule of foreign law unless a supervening rule of English law tells him not to.

As regards the first point, we will consider in Chapter 4 and following the rules of the conflict of laws which may point to the conclusion that the court may apply a rule of foreign law. As regards the second point, the party or parties seeking to rely on foreign law must plead that it is applicable; it follows that if neither party does so, the judge will apply English domestic law to the issues in dispute. The judge has no power, still less a duty, to apply foreign law *ex officio*. Take for example a case of personal injury taking place overseas. The claimant may consider that the law of the place where she was injured affords her a good cause of action, whereas English domestic law would not. It will be up to her to plead the applicability of foreign law to the claim. Again, a defendant may consider that the law of the place where the alleged tort happened furnishes her with a defence which would not be available as a matter of English domestic law: it will be for her to plead the applicability of foreign law to the issue raised by way of defence. But neither party is obliged to do this, and a judge will therefore be left to apply English domestic law when the parties do not invoke foreign law. According to the English way of thinking, this is so even when an international convention or European Regulation stipulates that an issue *shall* be governed by a particular law. It is sometimes wondered if the relaxed-looking approach taken by the common law is consistent with a legislative instruction, say from the European Union, that the law arrived at by applying a statutory conflicts rule 'shall be applied'. Not everyone will consider it correct to understand this as though it actually said 'shall not be applied unless one of the parties chooses to plead and succeeds in proving it'. Yet the point has not really been taken, presumably because it would have a dramatic effect on the way English courts—which try a substantial number of cases with foreign elements—adjudicate. If a change in practice is to take place, it will require a clear and precise direction from a legislator, to say nothing of an impact assessment to explain how it is justified. So far neither such thing has happened.

As a matter of observable fact, contract and tort cases litigated in England will frequently be decided by application of English domestic law, even though conflicts rules might have indicated that a foreign law should be applied. This may reflect the practical truth that the principles of the law of obligations are all pretty similar, meaning that there is often little point in engaging with foreign law; and it may also be driven by the practical problem, and expense, of actually proving foreign law. It reinforces the perception that English courts take a pragmatic, rather than a dogmatic, view of their role: the parties are free to establish a common position on the inapplicability[20] of foreign law,

---

[20] But they do not have a corresponding freedom to agree that a foreign law shall be applied, for the application of *foreign* law depends on the conflicts rules of English private international law.

and once they have done that, it is not for a judge to think he knows better. This may be fair enough where a court is called on to adjudicate a matter in the law of obligations: the question whether a contract was valid or broken, or whether a defendant was the victim of negligence or *volens* to the risk, is a matter of interest to the two parties alone,[21] and if they agree to the application of English domestic law to their dispute, there is no third party with enough of an interest to object. But in cases where the court is called on to decide an issue which may have an effect *in rem*, such as whether B obtained good title to a car from S, or whether H and W were lawfully married, this relaxed approach to foreign law is less compelling, for a ruling on status may well have an impact on non-parties, such as a subsequent purchaser or an intending spouse. In this context the decision of the original parties to have their adjudication by reference only to English domestic law affects other interested persons who were not privy to the agreement. Yet English law has never taken the view that in questions of status the court is obliged to enquire into and insist on the application of foreign law contrary to the wishes of the litigants. The application, or not, of foreign law is in this respect entirely in the hands of the litigating parties.

As regards the third point, the existence and content of an applicable foreign law is a matter of fact, to be proved as such by the parties.[22] Every pleaded proposition of fact needs to be admitted or proved; and as the content of foreign law is a question of fact, evidence will have to be given by experts, usually one for each side and evaluated by the judge, who must then apply it: the role of the expert is to prove the rules or content of foreign law,[23] but it is the responsibility of the judge, not the expert, to decide how it applies to the issue before the court.[24]

Expertise in foreign law is easier to describe than to define. There is no register of individuals who are qualified, still less authorized, to give such evidence to an English court; there is no reliable way to evaluate the expert or her evidence; it may not be clear whether an expert's knowledge is practical and up to date, or whether her seeming uncertainty actually reflects the true state of the foreign law itself. An expert who has written books may have had

---

[21] Or, at most, them and their insurers.

[22] It might be thought to follow that a decision on foreign law is not subject to reversal on appeal, unless the primary judge's conclusion was so unreasonable that no judge could properly have reached the conclusion he did. But foreign law is a fact of a rather peculiar kind, and appeals are more frequent, and the substitution of an appellate court's own conclusion more common, than its status as a question of fact might suggest.

[23] *Vizcaya Partners Ltd v Picard* [2016] UKPC 5, [2016] 3 All ER 181.

[24] *BNP Paribas SA v Trattamento Rifiuti Metropolitani SpA* [2019] EWCA Civ 768.

little or no practical experience of how the law would be applied in a court; the fact that a lawyer is in private practice or judicial office may nevertheless leave her wholly unsuitable to give evidence in an area of law of which she has no direct experience. An English court may be more impressed by the reported decisions of a foreign court than a local court would be; it may be less persuaded by the writing of professors than a foreign court would be. Nor is it always clear that the content of a foreign law as derived from statute and code will be consistent in every respect with the outcome which would result from its application by a foreign judge; and anyway, is Ruritanian law the law as derived from the written sources of Ruritanian law, or the outcome which would be delivered by a Ruritanian judge called upon to apply it?

Even if all three conditions are satisfied, the answer may sometimes be overridden by a rule of English law which directs the court not to apply a rule of foreign law. So, for example, a contract admittedly governed by French law may contain a provision limiting the liability of, or even exculpating, the defendant in circumstances where this would not be permitted were the contract governed by English law. In such a case, English legislation may stipulate that the rules of English law on exemption clauses are to be applied even though English law is not otherwise the governing law. This being so, the judge will, to that extent, be precluded from applying foreign law.

Now if this is how it is done, it is legitimate to ask whether the approach which is taken to foreign law is fit for its purpose. There are many cases in which the judge has had to pick his way through baffling and contradictory evidence of foreign law, with the result that one may applaud the effort yet still lack confidence in the outcome; and the financial cost to the parties can be quite disproportionate to the substance of the claim. But the notion that the judge may go off on a frolic of his own and conduct a personal inquiry into foreign law has no place in an English court. A judge may not rely on his own personal recollection of a particular foreign law, even if he was trained and qualified in that system, for the law may have changed, and the judicial wig does not make memory infallible. Perhaps above all, for a judge to usurp the privilege of the parties would be to ignore the limits on judicial power: the principle that *curia novit jus*, that the court knows the law, begins and ends with English domestic law. The rest is up to the litigants themselves.

If the party seeking to rely on foreign law satisfies the judge that foreign law is in principle applicable, but fails to satisfy the judge as to its content, it is sometimes said that the judge will still apply the foreign law, but in the sense that foreign law is presumed to be the same as English law when the contrary has not been proved. Such tosh has no place in the discourse of the law.

In the absence of proof of the content of foreign law, an English judge still has to adjudicate. The default position was, and is, that English law will be applied, *faute de mieux*; but once or twice the courts have been prepared to dismiss a claim or defence as unproven if foreign law pleaded as its support has not been established by evidence.[25]

It may be thought that the practical difficulties in the English system reveal so many shortcomings that the model of other systems, in which the duty of the judge is to apply the law, local or foreign, is preferable. Not so. A national judge manifestly does not 'know' foreign law, so a report on it must be commissioned. Whether it will be possible for a court to locate a competent expert from whom to obtain a reliable report must be doubtful, at least where the law in question is specialized or exotic; and in complex cases in which the reporter will require close and detailed knowledge of the entire dispute, in order to be sure that she has seen all the issues which bear on the legal analysis, it is doubtful that a court-commissioned expert will be in a position to do this. Even if the report is signed off by an authoritative figure, the chances will be that it was prepared by an overworked and underpaid junior researcher. So despite the claims, sometimes heard, that the civilian system of establishing and applying foreign law is superior to the English one, the reality is that the application of foreign law by a judge is fraught with difficulty of a general complexity which will not go away unless the trial is made to go away. This in turn may point to the real truth, that unless the parties are content that the English court should adjudicate and do the best it can with a question of foreign law, a court should, on application, have the power to decline to hear certain cases if persuaded that a court elsewhere would be better placed to give the parties the adjudication, together with the prospect of a meaningful appeal, which they deserve.

2. COMMON LAW CONFLICT OF LAWS: TECHNIQUES

A judge may therefore be called upon to apply a foreign law in the determination of a dispute. There is a framework for the analysis, which keeps the exercise under control. We will see that the basic structure of the common

---

[25] *Damberg v Damberg* (2001) 52 NSWLR 492; *Global Multimedia International Ltd v Ara Media Services* [2006] EWHC 3107 (Comm), [2007] 1 All ER (Comm) 1160; *Iranian Offshore Engineering & Construction Co v Dean Investment Holdings SA* [2018] EWHC 2759 (Comm), [2019] 1 WLR 82.

law conflict of laws is built from propositions which connect 'issues' to a particular law. So for example, the common law says (or said) that the material validity of a contract is governed by its proper law; that liability in tort is governed in part by the law of the place where the person was when injured; that the effect of a disposition of movable property is governed by the law of the place where the thing was when transferred; that the capacity of an individual to marry another is governed by the law of his or her domicile at the time of the marriage; that the ranking of claims and distribution of assets in an insolvency is governed by the local law of the court administering the insolvency; and so on.

Four ideas are contained in this account. The first is the concept of an 'issue': how do we know whether to frame our question in terms of the material validity of a contract as opposed to its formal validity, or just its validity? How do we know whether to ask the question in terms of the capacity of persons to marry as opposed to the validity of the marriage? The answer is that we *characterize* an issue, or issues, as arising for decision.

The second is the concept of a law: how do we know whether the law we choose means the domestic law of the relevant country, or, if this is different, the national law which would be applied by the judge trying the case in the courts of that country? How do we know whether the law of the domicile means the domestic law of the country in which we consider the person to be domiciled or, if this is different, the law which would be applied by a judge trying the case in the courts of that country? The answer[26] is that the law relating to *renvoi* tells us whether our rule of decision, our conflicts rule, points to a domestic law only or allows a reference to the private international law rules of that country.

The third is this: suppose the facts are characterized as giving rise to two issues, each with its own conflicts rule, and for each of which English law and the foreign law would prescribe different solutions. Do we approach them independently, and try to combine the answers at the end, or does one play a dominant role, applying its rules to the determination of the other issue? This raises the *incidental question*, to which a solution must be found. Fourth and last is the identification of the connection, the 'law of the . . .'. These are the *connecting factors*, and once the appropriate one has been found, the rules of the conflict of laws have done their job, and the proof of foreign law may begin.

---

[26] Unless the choice of rule is a statutory one, and the statute itself answers the question.

These elements must now be elaborated. For though in several areas they have been displaced by statutory rules, they are the very foundation of the conflict of laws.

(a) Characterization: identification of issues to point to a law

If a conflicts rule is formulated by connecting issues to laws, the first step is to think about issues. This requires the facts to be accommodated within one, or perhaps more, legal categories for which a conflicts rule is provided. The definition of these legal categories and the location of facts within them comprises the process, or doctrine, of characterization.[27]

Both aspects of characterization are undertaken, in some sense at least, by reference to English law. The available categories are created and defined by English private international law; and the placing of the facts within one or more of them is done according to English private international law: for those who find analogies helpful, English law designs the pigeonholes, and an English sorter decides which facts belong in which pigeonhole. This exercise has to be undertaken by reference to English law, for at this stage we are far from having explained whether, still less which, foreign law is going to be relevant.

The definitional list of the available categories or characterizations is established in part by authority, and in part by principle.[28] As we look at different substantive areas of law we will identify them: the capacity to contract, the proprietary effect of a transfer, the formal validity of marriage, the capacity of a corporation to do an act, and so on. Although the categories are established, the list is not closed: there is no reason of principle why the law may not develop a new one, and sometimes every reason why it should. So, for example, it has been proposed that the established category of 'essential validity of marriage' should be broken down into 'capacity to marry' and the 'quintessential validity of marriage', for which separate conflicts rules would be prescribed;[29] it was once proposed that the category of 'capacity to marry' should be broken down into the capacity to contract a polygamous marriage and the remainder of capacity to marry.[30] These suggestions do not appear to have been picked up, but they provide material for thinking about the function of the conflict of laws. Elsewhere, movement is more likely. For example,

---

[27] Dicey, Morris, and Collins, *The Conflict of Laws* (15th edn, Sweet & Maxwell, 2012) Ch 2.
[28] *Raiffeisen Zentralbank Österreich AG v Five Star Trading LLC* [2001] EWCA Civ 68, [2001] QB 825.
[29] *Vervaeke v Smith* [1983] 1 AC 145.
[30] *Radwan v Radwan (No 2)* [1973] Fam 35.

the conflicts rules for the transfer of intangible movables may yet be refined so that certain complex issues, such as arise in the system for indirect holding of financial instruments, are dealt with separately from other intangibles. Unless superimposed by legislation, the process of change in this context will be slow and measured. The certainty of the law would be lost if new categories were created willy-nilly; an alternative response might be to make exceptions in individual cases, rather than new categories for general application.

Although characterization is necessarily done by reference to English law, it certainly does not follow that the structures of domestic law are mirrored in the rules of the conflict of laws. For example, it has occasionally been argued that there should be a characterization category for equitable claims, for which the applicable law might be the *lex fori*, the law of the court hearing the claim.[31] Quite apart from the point that such a rule would be undesirable in itself, it is almost impossible to believe that 'equitable claims' represents a coherent category, all of which should be disposed of by referring it to the same single law, in the first place. Similar doubts were expressed whether the common law needed a characterization category for 'receipt-based restitutionary claims'.[32] Though these ideas may be indispensable as a matter of domestic English law, it does not follow that there is room or need for them in the conflict of laws.

Whether a particular issue raised for decision in a case should be fitted into one or another of these categories is done with one eye on English domestic law, but with the other on the need to undertake the exercise 'in a broad internationalist spirit in accordance with the principles of the conflict of laws of the forum'.[33] In other words, the process should place comity above dogmatism, so as to identify the law which is most appropriate for application. So, for example, whether a promise is enforceable as a contract even though not given for consideration will raise a question of the material validity of a contract, even though English law would not see a gratuitous promise as a contract at all;[34] an action claiming damages for insult will be treated as tortious even though English domestic law knows no such tort of

---

[31] There is some support for this in Australian law.

[32] *Macmillan Inc v Bishopsgate Investment Trust plc (No 3)* [1996] 1 WLR 387 (CA).

[33] *Raiffeisen Zentralbank Österreich AG v Five Star Trading LLC* [2001] EWCA Civ 68, [2001] QB 825 [27]; *Investec Trust (Guernsey) Ltd v Glenalla Properties Ltd* [2018] UKPC 7, [2019] AC 271.

[34] *Re Bonacina* [1912] 2 Ch 394. These examples are taken from the common law. For contracts made after 1991, however, European legislation, rather than the common law, would determine the applicable law, and the process by which it did so would not be one of characterization properly so called.

insult; and a polygamous marriage will be treated as a marriage, even though English domestic law does not allow for polygamy. Occasionally this will lead to a result which looks odd. Some time after a marriage had been celebrated in England between a French man and an English woman it was alleged[35] that it was invalid because the parents of the man had not given their consent. One[36] analysis adopted by the court was that the need for third party consent raised a question of the formal validity of a marriage, which was governed by the law of the place (England) of celebration, under which law the absence of parental consent was immaterial. Some argue, by contrast, that the issue should have been treated as one of capacity to marry and as such governed by the domestic law of the person (French) alleged to lack marital capacity.[37] There is some force in the alternative view, especially if the court really did reason that as third party consent is a matter of formal validity in domestic English law it must be the same in the conflict of laws. Even so, it is hard to see why the capacity solution, which would mean the marriage was void, is intrinsically better than the formality alternative, which leads to its validity; and the truth may be that some cases are hard ones, no matter how you look at them. More novel cases can be expected as domestic laws are refashioned and reshaped to meet changing social conditions, especially, perhaps, in the field of family law and personal status.

As for what represents the object of characterization, the 'thing' character-ized, the usual understanding is that issues, rather than rules of law, are char-acterized.[38] The justification for this is that the very language of the subject is written in terms which connect categories of legal issue with a conflicts rule. It also has the immense practical advantage that a single law is identified to provide the solution to the single issue. If, by contrast, one were to try to char-acterize the individual rules of law found in the legal systems having poten-tial connection to the dispute, aiming to apply whichever was formulated to apply in the given context, and to not apply those which were not, one could end up with two contradictory solutions or none at all. Take the case of mar-riage without parental consent, discussed above. Suppose it had been held that the English rule that parental consent was not required was a rule about

---

[35] *Ogden v Ogden* [1908] P 46 (CA).

[36] The other was that if the facts raised an issue of capacity, it was still governed by English law, under the principle in *Sottomayor v De Barros (No 2)* (1879) 5 PD 94.

[37] Although under the rule in *Sottomayor v De Barros (No 2)*, this would not in fact have been the outcome.

[38] However, as will be seen in Ch 4, the rule of private international law that an English court will not enforce a foreign penal or revenue law will require characterization of the particular law, and not of an issue.

the formal validity of marriage, and hence applicable when a marriage took place in England; and the French rule requiring parental consent was held to be a rule about capacity to marry, and hence applicable to the marriage of a French domiciliary. Both rules would have been 'characterized' as applicable; the result of their combined application is an impossible contradiction. Or, taking the opposite possibility, each rule might have been characterized as being inapplicable. This does not seem sensible; the ends condemn the means. This is why we say that the judge is required to identify an issue, apply the conflicts rule devised for it, and to apply the legal rule found in the system to which the conflicts rule directed him.

In the only case to have confronted the issue directly,[39] a mother and daughter, domiciled in Germany but taking refuge in England, perished in an air raid. The court had to decide who succeeded to the estate of the mother. When it is unknown which of two people died first, both English and German laws solve the problem by applying a presumption: English law presuming that the older died first, German law that they died simultaneously. The judge deduced that he was called upon to decide an issue of inheritance or succession to the estate of the mother, which was governed by German law, rather than a question of evidence governed by English law. He therefore applied the German rule. Whether he was right or wrong about this, his technique of identifying *an* issue raised by the facts is the critical point to notice. Had he simply 'characterized' the respective rules of German and English law, blind as it were, he might have found that both applied or neither applied: this would have been so self-defeating that, whatever may be said in its defence, the solution could not be right.[40]

A final question concerns exactly what happens after characterization has pointed the court to a particular law in which to find the answer. Suppose a marriage has taken place in France, without the parental consent required by the French domiciliary law of one of the parties. An English court will characterize the issue as one of formal validity, and look to French law for its answer. But an answer to what question? If the question is 'is this marriage formally valid as a matter of French law despite the absence of parental consent?' the answer may be a rather puzzled 'yes': puzzled because, in the opinion of the French expert, this is not the right question to be asking. If, by contrast, the question is framed as 'is this marriage valid as a matter of French law

---

[39] *Re Cohn* [1945] Ch 5.
[40] Though it should also be said that if this would have been the outcome, there is no chance that the judge would have proceeded along this path.

despite the lack of parental consent?' the reasoning may be more complex, but the answer will be 'no': the French expert will explain that this issue is seen by French law as one of capacity, governed by the national (French) law of the allegedly incapable party, and according to which the marriage is invalid. It will be seen that the outcome of the case may depend on the manner in which the question is formulated: put shortly, is the question, formulated for the expert to answer, expressed in and bounded by the precise terms of the characterization which led there in the first place, or is characterization defunct and forgotten once it has served to make a connection to a law? The answer may well require an understanding of the principles of *renvoi*, and the suggested solution offered by the common law will be found at the end of the next section.

(b) *Renvoi*: the meaning of law

If an issue is to be governed by the law of a particular country, what do we mean by the word *law*? Does it mean the rules of domestic law which would apply to a case which was wholly local, or might it refer to law in a wider sense, including in particular the private international law rules of that legal system as a local judge might apply them? To ask it again: is the issue resolved by applying the domestic law, or by permitting a sending on—a *renvoi*—from that law to another, if the private international law rules of the applicable law would have directed the foreign judge to do that? The common law's answer is that there is no short answer: sometimes it will be the former, othertimes the latter. Which and when is a matter of authority more than anything else; why is more controversial.

Let us take an example. Suppose a woman has died without leaving a will, and the question arises concerning succession to her estate. Suppose she died domiciled in Spain, but still a British citizen. As a matter of English private international law, succession to her movable estate would be governed by Spanish law as the law of her domicile at death. Suppose also that according to Spanish domestic law, X would succeed to the estate, but that according to Spanish private international law, succession would be governed by the law of the nationality, which would be taken by a Spanish judge to be English; and as a matter of English domestic law, Y would succeed. What is the English judge to do?

He may have three possibilities. He may interpret his conflicts rule as pointing him to Spanish domestic law, and hold in favour of X. Or he may interpret his conflicts rule as pointing to Spanish law as including its rules of private international law, follow the path which points to English law, interpret this as meaning English domestic law, and find for Y. Or he may interpret his conflicts rule as pointing to Spanish law, follow the path by which this points to English law, interpret this as meaning 'English law including its conflicts rules', which point back to Spain, ask what the Spanish judge would do when she was informed that English law would look back to Spanish law, and accept whatever answer would then be given. As a matter of common law authority, the English judge will not, initially at least, take the second of these three possibilities. Sometimes he will take the first, and interpret the 'law' as meaning the domestic rules of the applicable law. But on other occasions, which include issues of succession, he will take the third, and interpret the 'law' as meaning that system of domestic law which the foreign judge, notionally hearing the case in the court whose law has been found to be applicable, would apply:[41] he will, so far as the evidence of the content of foreign law allows him to do so, impersonate the Spanish judge and decide as she would decide. This convoluted approach may be called the 'foreign court theory' of *renvoi*, or 'total *renvoi*'. Is this not all very difficult? Should the judge not simply have applied Spanish domestic law and left it at that?

Judges and writers have suggested so, and legislators often say so. Before weighing the authority and the arguments, it should be remembered that *renvoi* applies only in certain areas of private international law; and that, as the proof of foreign law lies primarily in the hands of the parties, a court will have neither need nor opportunity to examine the principles of *renvoi* unless the parties raise them and plead their relevance. One criticism of *renvoi*, that it can make life difficult for the parties and for the judge, may therefore be overstated. Another, that conflicts rules were formulated without any thought for *renvoi* but as pointers to a domestic system of law, is simply a rejection of the principle: it may not be true. Another, that *renvoi* subordinates English conflicts rules to those of a foreign system, is misconceived, for it is English law, and English law alone, which decides whether to follow a foreign court's pattern of reasoning. A fourth is that the English 'impersonation' approach works only if the notional foreign judge who is being impersonated would not be found to be trying to do the very thing which the English judge would do, which just goes to show that the very idea is flawed.[42] But this

---

[41]   *Re Annesley* [1926] Ch 692; *Re Ross* [1930] 1 Ch 377; *Re Askew* [1930] 2 Ch 259; *Re Duke of Wellington* [1947] Ch 506.

[42]   It is said that it is hardly a recommendation that the English doctrine of *renvoi* works only if other states reject it. This is just silly: one may as well say that one should never hold a door open for another to pass through, for if the other person is equally polite neither will make any progress at all.

creation of the febrile academic imagination has never arisen for decision.[43] Were it to do so, the rational answer is that if the foreign rules point back to English law, *renvoi* has shot its bolt, and English domestic law would apply.[44]

Some see the arguments in favour of *renvoi* as stronger. Rules of private international law are rules of a foreign legal system. If a foreign law is selected for application, it is odd that material parts of that law—the very parts which explain whether a local judge would actually apply that system's domestic law to the case!—are cut out and ignored. One may think of the rules of private international law as separate and distinct, but this is no more than a teaching convention which risks damaging the coherence and integrity of the law the English court is trying to apply. If a court is to apply foreign law, it feels intuitively right to apply all of it; and equally right to apply it in the same way, and to the same effect, so far as this is possible, as the foreign judge would. Moreover, although in our example it may not matter very much whether X or Y succeeds to the movable estate, it would seem distinctly odd that an English court could consider and declare that one person is entitled to foreign land when, as a matter of that foreign law, the register of title will not be amended to reflect that view. If it is ever open to an English court to make a judgment about title to foreign land, it should surely do so in conformity with what it understands to be the law which the local courts would themselves apply; and if this aligns English conflicts rules with those of another system, so much the better for that.

There may be another justification for the general operation of the principle of *renvoi*. When applied by an English court, its aim is to dispose of the case as it would have been if the action had been brought in the courts which are probably the closest to the dispute. After all, there will be little incentive to forum shop to England if the English court will try to determine the case in the same way as a judge of the court whose law is the applicable law. Viewed in this sense, *renvoi* is an antidote to forum shopping which works, when allowed to operate, by refining the rules of the conflict of laws.[45]

Common law conflicts rules evidently come in two designs. In one, the rule is defined as being the domestic law of the system to which the rule

---

[43] But the worry of it prompted the dissent of McHugh J in *Neilson v Overseas Projects Corpn of Victoria* [2005] HCA 54, (2005) 233 CLR 331, who was frightened by a paper tiger.

[44] *Casdagli v Casdagli* [1918] P 89, Scrutton LJ. Other answers may be imagined, but there is no sense in trying to find an answer which is impossible to work with. This, though, will be the case in which the second of the three options identified above may be selected: as a response to a problem caused by the third.

[45] *Neilson v Overseas Projects Corpn of Victoria* [2005] HCA 54, (2005) 233 CLR 331.

points the court. So at common law, the material validity of a contract was governed by the domestic law chosen by the parties or, in default of such expression, by the domestic law of the system with which the contract was most closely connected: so formulated, the conflicts rule made *renvoi* irrelevant. In other cases, the conflicts rule might be expressed indirectly, or formulaically, as directing a court to apply 'that law which would be applied by a judge holding court at the relevant place'. So a question of title to land would be governed by the law which would be applied by a judge sitting at the place where the land is; succession to movable property is governed by that law which would be applied by a judge sitting in the country where the defendant died domiciled. That does not seem conceptually challenging.

One observes, however, that *renvoi* is viewed in some quarters with a distaste which sometimes borders on mania. In European private international law[46] its exclusion is often legislated, but even in the common law it probably played no part in the conflicts rules for contract or tort. It may, in principle and if pleaded and proved by the parties, apply to questions of title to immovable property; and though it probably should apply to questions of title to movable property, there is first instance authority to contrary effect.[47] It applies to the validity and invalidity of marriage;[48] but not to divorce where the conflicts for granting and for recognizing divorces is to apply the law of the forum.[49] In broad outline, therefore, when the court is being asked to give a judgment which will have its effect only on the litigants themselves, *renvoi* will be unlikely to be part of the conflict rule. But when it is asked to give a judgment on status, such as the ownership of a thing or the marriageability of an individual, which will have a potential impact on third parties, the court will, if invited to do so, be more likely to interpret its conflicts rule in the *renvoi* sense where this will tend to increase the chance that the view reached by an English court will align with that which might be reached by a potentially involved other law.

One may now return to the point left open at the end of the examination of characterization: how to formulate the question which is to be referred to and answered by the expert on foreign law. The answer should be along the following lines. In a legal context where the principle of *renvoi* has no

---

[46] Which is a very different thing; see Section (D).

[47] *Iran v Berend* [2007] EWHC 132 (QB), [2007] 2 All ER (Comm) 132; *Blue Sky One Ltd v Mahan Air* [2009] EWHC 3314 (Comm).

[48] *Taczanowska v Taczanowski* [1957] P 301 (CA); *R v Brentwood Superintendent Registrar of Marriages, ex p Arias* [1968] 2 QB 956.

[49] See Ch 8 below.

application, there is no compelling need to reach the same answer as would be given by the foreign judge. The question may therefore be asked in terms of the English characterization: 'was the contract formally valid?' etc. But in a case where the principle of *renvoi* does apply, and where the broad aim is to reach the same conclusion as would be reached by a judge in the local court, it will impair the chances of success if the law is not interpreted in a *renvoi* sense: only by allowing the expert to use the characterization and conflicts rules of his own system will it be possible for him and for the court to produce an answer of the quality sought. So in the case of the absence of parental consent, the question put should be whether the absence of parental consent makes the marriage invalid, without regard to the way that the issue was originally characterized by the English judge or would be characterized by the foreign judge. But if the case were one concerning, say, the material validity of a contract, the question should be whether the foreign law regards the contract as materially invalid, even if the foreign law would not have regarded the issue as one of material, as opposed to, say, formal validity.

(c) Interlocking issues and incidental questions

Characterization allows us to identify an issue and attach a law to it. But a set of facts may involve more issues than one, and the conflicts rules may direct the court to separate laws for them. So, for example, a claim for damages for an alleged tort might have been defended by reference to a contractual promise not to sue; a claim for the delivery up of goods over which a seller has reserved his title may be met by a defence that they were sold to the defendant who bought them in good faith and thereby displaced the title of the claimant; the validity of a marriage may be impugned by the alleged ineffectiveness of a prior divorce. The problem arises wherever there is a clash between the laws which English conflicts rules identify for the two issues: a conflict of conflicts rules. To take the first example, characterization would have applied the *lex delicti* to a claim in tort, but the *lex contractus* to the contractual promise; how it combined them can be left for later.[50] But what if the private international law of the *lex delicti* were to have its own view, which diverges from the English view, of what the *lex contractus* is? If the intrinsic validity of the contractual defence depends on first identifying its *lex contractus*, is this done by applying English conflicts rules or those of the *lex delicti*? Again, the capacity of a person to marry will be affected by the recognition

---

[50] See Ch 6 below.

or otherwise of the earlier divorce: is the law which determines the validity of the divorce chosen by the conflicts rules of English law or by those of the law which governs the person's capacity to marry? Or is the capacity of the party to marry simply a consequence of the conflicts rules which determine the validity of the earlier divorce?

It can seem complicated, but the law reports suggest that it hardly ever comes up in practice. In the end, the considerations which underpin the doctrines of characterization and *renvoi* allow a sensible result to be reached. The prevailing view of the common law is to regard one of the issues, if possible, as the main one. The conflicts rules of the law which applies to that main question will in their turn identify the law which governs the incidental question, so that the overall result is generated by the law (including its conflicts rules) which the court applies to the main question. This assumes that a question can be identified as the main one; in many cases this will be the question which arises or occurs later in time, because in the end this is the decision which counts the most. By this reasoning, the effectiveness of the ultimate sale of the goods is the main question, the incidental issue being that of the validity and effect of a prior reservation of title; the law governing the later sale will also supply the conflicts rule to identify the law governing the earlier reservation of title. Again, personal capacity to (re)marry is the main question, the validity and effect of the prior divorce being incidental to it;[51] the law governing capacity to marry will supply the conflicts rule to identify the law which governs the validity of the earlier divorce. In neither case do the common law rules of private international law take a simple chronological approach, applying conflicts rules to the issues individually and sequentially and then seeking to combine the results.

Title to property and personal status are two areas in which the principles of *renvoi* probably apply, and where the court may aim to replicate the result which would be reached by the foreign judge if he were trying the case. Where the focus is on the final or main question, any prior or incidental questions should be dealt with as the judge in the final court would deal with them. But a different analysis may be called for in a case where the principles of *renvoi* have no part in the conflicts rules, and where the need to replicate the final judge's perspective is absent. So in the case of a contractual defence to a tort claim, the *lex delicti* would determine whether there was a claim in tort. If a contractual defence were pleaded, the first step would be to decide

---

[51] *Schwebel v Ungar* (1964) 48 DLR (2d) 644 (Ont CA), but only to the extent that statute has not provided otherwise.

whether the conflicts rules of the *lex delicti* or of English law select the *lex contractus*. There being no need to decide the overall question as a judge of the *lex delicti* would, there would be no reason to prefer the conflicts rules of the *lex delicti* to those of English law. Accordingly, the law which governs the contract and assesses the intrinsic validity of the defence would be identified by applying English conflicts rules; whether it defeats the claim would be a matter for the *lex delicti*; but the *lex delicti* will take the validity of the contract as given, rather than making that judgment for itself.

The incidental question therefore works within the common law conflict of laws. But it can be overridden by statute, for Parliament may have enacted a law in such a way that it precludes the possibility of assessing, say, the validity of a divorce by anything other than English law. To that extent the solution given above will be displaced, and the validity of the divorce conclusively determined, in accordance with Parliamentary intention, by English law.[52]

(d) Connecting factors

The identifier at the end of the 'law of the [something/somewhere]' formula is traditionally known as a 'connecting factor', on the ground that these points of contact are what connect an individual, or an issue, to a system of law which will, in principle, furnish the answer being looked for. They are almost all defined by English law, not foreign law: this is inevitable, for until the conflicts rules have identified a foreign law to apply to a dispute, there is no sensible basis for using any law other than English for definitional purposes. For example, if as a matter of English law X is domiciled in France, this is unaffected by the possibility that French law may not agree but would regard him as being domiciled in England instead.[53] If English rules of the conflict of laws find the law applicable to an obligation to be Swiss law, it is irrelevant that a Swiss court, applying rules of Swiss private international law, might have come to a different conclusion.

To be useful the connecting factor must identify a territory having *a* system of law, as opposed to a larger political unit which may have many systems of law or none. For example, an individual may be domiciled in England, but may not be domiciled in the United Kingdom: there is English law on her capacity to marry, but no 'United Kingdom law' on the point; and if a statute

---

[52] *Lawrence v Lawrence* [1985] Fam 106; Family Law Act 1986, s 50.
[53] *Re Annesley* [1926] Ch 692. But if the conflicts rules refer to French law in a *renvoi* sense, and as a matter of French law he is domiciled in England, this detail will form part of the overall decision, and will not be contradicted.

has been enacted to apply in England, Scotland, and Northern Ireland, and may in some sense be considered as the law of the United Kingdom, it will apply because it is part of English law, rather than for any other reason. In principle at least, an individual may be domiciled in Florida, but not in the United States, meaning that the law of Florida, as distinct from the law of the United States, will be applied; although where the relevant law of Florida is in fact a federal rule of the law of the United States, the federal rule will be applied as part of the law in the state of Florida. But by contrast, in true cases where a federal state has defined itself as a single legal unit for certain purposes, the connecting factor may point to that law. So a person may be regarded as domiciled in Australia for the purpose of capacity to marry, for Australia is constituted by its own legislation a single law district so far as concerns the law of marriage,[54] but in Queensland for the purpose of making a will, for the law of testamentary succession is a matter on which state law is sovereign, and state laws are several. A form of expression sometimes used to convey the sense of an area which has a law of its own is a 'law district'.

Connecting factors fall into two broad categories: those which define a law in terms of a personal connection, and those which define the law in terms of a state of affairs. For ease of exposition they need to be examined separately.

Personal connecting factors: domicile, residence, and nationality
The personal connecting factors which one may encounter are domicile, habitual (or ordinary or usual) residence, (simple) residence, and nationality. As far as the common law is concerned, domicile is the most significant, and it is the law of the domicile which, to a greater or lesser extent, determines the status and capacities of an individual. It is therefore worth examination.

According to the common law understanding of domicile, every person has a domicile and, subject to what appears below,[55] no person can have more than one domicile at any time. The domiciliary law—the *lex domicilii*—still has a significant role in family and in property law, but it may also define the capacity of persons, especially companies,[56] to make contracts; and it plays a significant part in the law of taxation.[57] From this very general introduction

---

[54] And, according to *John Pfeiffer Pty Ltd v Rogerson* [2000] HCA 36, (2000) 203 CLR 503, for all matters which fall within the federal jurisdiction.

[55] The persistence of the common law domicile of origin constitutes a general half-exception to the rule. The jurisdictional domicile forming the backbone of the Civil Jurisdiction and Judgments Act 1982, the Brussels I Regulation, and the Civil Jurisdiction and Judgments Order 2001 (SI 2001/3929) is a completely separate concept, irrelevant to and entirely independent of the common law of domicile.

[56] Where it means the law of the place of incorporation: see p 340.

[57] Where personal greed can lead to its being bent out of shape.

two points may emerge: 'domicile' is used in a wide but diverse range of matters, and it may be that its meaning should take its colour from its context. It is also desirable that it makes a rational connection to a particular law. In these two respects the English law of domicile scores rather badly. On the first, although it has been suggested from time to time that domicile should adjust its definition to its context, the courts have demurred. So a case on UK tax liability, in which it was held that a person had not acquired an English domicile despite 40 years' residence,[58] will be authoritative on whether and how a person may acquire an English domicile for the purpose of his or her capacity to marry or make a will, as also will be a decision on whether an illegal immigrant or over-stayer[59] has acquired a domicile in England. One imagines that the policies which underpin the individual decisions in these various legal contexts are not identical and may even be contradictory, but this fact, if it is a fact, is not reflected in the definition of domicile, for domicile has, as a matter of common law, one definition, not several definitions.

A telling difficulty, on which authority is surprisingly sparse, is how to determine the domicile of a person who, in some sense, belonged to a territory whose borders have moved or which has simply ceased to be. A woman formerly domiciled in Czechoslovakia or Yugoslavia would now face the impossibility of being domiciled in a non-country which is no longer a law district and has no law. At a guess, she will be held to have acquired a domicile of choice in the part in which she was resident on the date on which the country broke apart, but this will be more difficult to defend as a conclusion if she had not, on that date, made up her mind whether to remain, and hence to reside indefinitely, in the part-country. A person who was domiciled in the USSR, which disintegrated, is in much the same position; likewise one who was domiciled in East Germany, which country was swallowed up. And what do we say of the person living quietly in Crimea before this part of Ukraine was invaded, occupied, and annexed by Russia? It is probable that one can have a domicile in the *soi-disant* and illegal 'Turkish Republic of Northern Cyprus', but what of Palestine? In all these cases there are practical problems in defining domicile in terms which look backward to an earlier set of facts, but there is no easy solution to the problem created by the fact that political history and military force do not treat the conflict of laws with the respect it deserves.[60]

---

[58] *IRC v Bullock* [1976] 1 WLR 1178 (CA).
[59] *Mark v Mark* [2005] UKHL 42, [2006] 1 AC 98.
[60] *Re O'Keefe* [1940] Ch 124.

Domicile, as a common law concept, is a single species, but with three *genera*. The *domicile of origin* is the domicile of one's father (or mother, for one who is born out of wedlock or after the death of the father) at the date of one's birth. It is the first domicile of a child, and it serves as the actual domicile until superseded by the acquisition of another domicile, either of choice or of dependency. But it is only ever suppressed, with the result that if a later-acquired domicile is lost, then unless at the same moment a new domicile is acquired, the domicile of origin pops up again as the person's actual domicile. The domicile of origin can never be shaken off; and if it revives after decades of slumber it may connect the person to a legal system which may be remote from the circumstances of his present life.[61] Some regard this potential for the domicile of origin to reassert itself as showing why it should be abolished by legislation, but the truth is less clear-cut. After all, if a refugee is driven to flee from the country in which she had acquired a domicile of choice, it may be more offensive to hold that this domicile persists than to revive the domicile of origin unless and until a new domicile of choice is established somewhere less awful.

A *domicile of choice* is acquired by becoming resident in a law district with the intention of residing there indefinitely: both conditions must be satisfied in relation to the law district in which the domicile is to be established. The *intention* must be geographically specific, unconditional, and deliberate in order to meet the somewhat restrictive requirements of the law. If a person emigrates to the United States with an intention to remain there, but has not yet settled on which state she will, permanently or indefinitely, reside in, she will not have established a domicile of choice in any American state;[62] if she intends to reside in Texas but has not yet taken up residence there she will not have established a domicile in Texas. The intention must be to reside indefinitely. So an intention to reside for a term of years, or until the occurrence of a certain specific event such as retirement or the death of a spouse, is not enough,[63] although if the condition upon which the residence would come to an end is vague or implausible it may be disregarded.[64] This means that residence for many decades' length may still not establish a domicile of choice: a fact which certain overpaid foreign nationals living and working in London have shamelessly exploited and at which successive governments

---

[61] *Udny v Udny* (1869) LR 1 Sc & Div 441. See also *Re O'Keefe* [1940] Ch 124.
[62] *Bell v Kennedy* (1868) LR 1 Sc & Div 307 (England and Scotland).
[63] *IRC v Bullock* [1976] 1 WLR 1178 (CA) (unless wife died first); cf *Ray v Sekhri* [2014] EWCA Civ 119, [2014] 2 FLR 1168.
[64] *Re Fuld's Estate (No 3)* [1968] P 675; *Re Furse* [1980] 3 All ER 838.

have cravenly connived.[65] In a number of weirdly bizarre cases, the courts have assessed a person's distasteful intentions as insufficient to establish an English domicile. It is plausible that a fugitive from justice, who intends to remain only until the passing of time has prescribed her offence, will not acquire a domicile of choice,[66] but this was extended to a German terrorist who fled to England, whose intention to remain certainly appeared to be unconditional and indefinite, almost certainly because the court looked on her case with distaste.[67] A wastrel who came to England to sponge off his relatives was held to be too inert to have formed an intention to establish an English domicile;[68] and an American citizen who was advised on medical grounds to remain in Brighton, where he devoted himself to devising lunatic schemes to bring about the destruction of the British maritime empire, was held not to have the requisite intention either, even though he knew perfectly well that he would remain in England for ever.[69] It is hard to interpret these cartoon cases as instances of conditional intention, but what they add to the requirements for the acquisition of a domicile of choice is difficult to pin down.

What constitutes *residence* is hard to say; and the wordier version of being 'present as a resident' hardly advances matters very much. The view that residence in England originating in unlawful entry was incapable of sustaining an English domicile of choice has now been abandoned.[70] A person may remain resident in a country while overseas, but it is unclear whether a person coming in becomes a resident upon the instant of his arrival, or only some time after. In principle one can be resident in two countries at once, but to avoid the inadmissible result of this leading to there being two domiciles of choice, it is probable that the residence requirement identifies the principal residence if there is more than one contender.[71]

A domicile of choice can be lost by being abandoned, which means ceasing to reside and ceasing to intend to reside indefinitely—both elements must be terminated—or lost by the acquisition of a new domicile of choice on the basis of the rules set out above. But if the abandonment is not contemporaneous with the acquisition of a new domicile of choice, the domicile of origin will reassert itself to prevent any domiciliary hiatus.[72]

[65] *IRC v Bullock* [1976] 1 WLR 1178 (CA).
[66] *Re Martin* [1900] P 211.
[67] *Puttick v AG* [1980] Fam 1.
[68] *Ramsay v Liverpool Royal Infirmary* [1930] AC 588.
[69] *Winans v AG* [1904] AC 287.
[70] *Mark v Mark* [2005] UKHL 42, [2006] 1 AC 98.
[71] *Plummer v IRC* [1988] 1 WLR 292.
[72] *Udny v Udny* (1869) LR 1 Sc & Div 441.

A child's *domicile of dependency* is that, from time to time, of the parent upon whom, until the age of 16 or lawful marriage under this age, the child is dependent.[73] In principle, therefore, a child's domicile of origin may be suppressed by a domicile of dependency as soon as the cord is cut. When the age of independence is reached, it is debatable whether the domicile of dependency is lost by operation of law, so that the domicile of origin, if different, revives unless a domicile of choice be immediately acquired, or whether the domicile had as dependent continues as an imposed domicile of choice. Statute suggests that the latter is possible,[74] but principle suggests that it should not be, and that the domicile of dependence should be defunct on the attaining of majority.[75] The domicile of dependency of married women was abolished in 1974.[76]

It will have become apparent that the common law of domicile, with its peculiar rules and weirder authorities, has the potential to produce a capricious answer in a given case, and all the more so in Europe as political boundaries come and go.[77] But all proposals for reform have been spurned, and the cause is now lost. One particular consequence of this inability to rationalize the common law of domicile was that it was quite unsuitable for use in identifying a court in which a person should be liable to be sued in civil or commercial proceedings. For this reason the term 'domicile' in the Civil Jurisdiction and Judgments Act 1982 and the Civil Jurisdiction and Judgments Order 2001[78] was statutorily defined to make it separate and distinct from its common law homonym; it is examined in Chapter 2.

Residence as a connecting factor, both in its own right and in the variants of *habitual, usual,* and *ordinary residence,* is more usually found in laws which derive from international conventions. When it first appeared in the law as a personal connecting factor, the optimistic view was that it would allow a court to locate a person's home, but without needing to struggle with the technical complications of the common law of domicile: that view has proved to be quite wrong. The connecting factor of 'habitual residence' has received much attention in areas liable to generate high emotional stress, of which the law relating to children is the most notable. This has exposed the inherent tension between (on the one hand) the desire to reduce uncertainty

---

[73] Domicile and Matrimonial Proceedings Act 1973, s 3.
[74] ibid, s 1.
[75] See Wade (1983) 32 ICLQ 1.
[76] Domicile and Matrimonial Proceedings Act 1973, s 1.
[77] cf *Re O'Keefe* [1940] Ch 124.
[78] SI 2001/3929.

by precise specification of the details of the law and (on the other) the need to allow cases to be disposed of quickly and easily by treating it as a substantially factual matter:[79] if it is judged by the number of appeals to the Supreme Court in recent years the law can only be considered to be a catastrophe. In principle, whether residence is 'habitual' involves a degree of stability, the presence or absence of which may be illuminated by asking why the person is there and how he or she perceives that residence;[80] but this risks opening the door to excessive argument about disputed details, and raises acute questions about the way in which the views of adults and children of various ages are treated. It is probable that habitual residence indicates only one place, although regular absences will not, by themselves, deprive a residence of its habitual or usual character.[81] On the question whether it is possible, at least in the case of a child, for a person to be without a habitual residence, or to have more than one habitual residence, the views of the Supreme Court were sharply divided[82] and cannot now be predicted. Cases involving children are most difficult, because of the difficulty of deciding whether (and if so, when, and how) a child's habitual residence can diverge from that of its parent. The European Court has said, in the case of children, that habitual residence indicates 'the place which is in practice the centre of that child's life'.[83] That is fine and unnecessary in easy cases, and of little real help in the difficult ones:[84] although the judgment offers some guidelines, it may be that this just goes to show that there are, especially in the context of children who are pulled to and fro by their warring families, no bright lines, and that all attempts to pin down a robust test are bound to end in failure. That in turn suggests that the only way to avoid complexity is to avoid appeals, by treating the enquiry as purely factual and trusting courts of first instance. It is a bad solution, but all others are manifestly worse.

---

[79] *A v A (Children: Habitual Residence)* [2013] UKSC 60, [2014] AC 1; *Re B (A Child)* [2016] UKSC 4, [2016] AC 606. The earlier decisions, *Re J (A Minor) (Abduction: Custody Rights)* [1990] 2 AC 562; *Re S (A Minor) (Abduction: European Convention)* [1998] AC 750, must be read in the light of these decision.

[80] *Re LC (Children)* [2014] UKSC 1, [2014] AC 1038. Where the person is a child this is obviously a delicate matter, and the account to be taken of the views of young children was disputed and disagreed about.

[81] *Re R (Children)* [2015] UKSC 35, [2016] AC 76.

[82] *Re B (A Child)* [2016] UKSC 4, [2016] AC 606.

[83] Case C–512/17 *HR* EU:C:2018:513, [2018] Fam 385.

[84] For the way in which this idea quickly led to the idea of 'repudiatory retention' of a child, with all the terrible legal paraphernalia of intention, communication, interpretation and so on, see *Re C (Children)* [2018] UKSC 8, [2019] AC 1.

Nationality, as a connecting factor, plays little part in the English conflict of laws, by contrast with civilian jurisdictions where the *lex patriae* is still a common personal connecting factor. The reasons for its non-use in English private international law are pragmatic, but are also susceptible to over-statement. First, a person's status as a national of a particular country is determined by the law of the proposed state: no rule of English law can say whether someone is or is not a national of France, for example. Nationality is therefore immune to the judicial control which can be brought to bear on other connecting factors. Second, a person may retain a nationality long after losing all practical connection to the state in question, retaining it, perhaps, for emotional or other idiosyncratic reasons, or even forgetfully: in such a case it may not be the most appropriate law to serve as the person's personal law. Third, dual nationality, or nationality in a federal or complex state, such as the United States or the United Kingdom, or statelessness, would cause real difficulty for any person for whom nationality was a personal connecting factor. Yet it seems reasonable to suppose that those many jurisdictions which employ nationality as a personal connecting factor manage to deal with these practical objections, and it may be wrong to see these instances as so significant that the basic rule must be rejected: babies should not generally be thrown out with the bathwater. It is also true that a person who wishes to determine her nationality can usually just look inside her passport. By contrast, the person who needs to ascertain her habitual residence, to say nothing of her common law domicile, may be faced with the kind of question most usually encountered in university examinations. Pragmatism is, perhaps, not all one way.

Causal connecting factors

Terms which describe a connection between a fact or an event and a law are also defined by reference to English law; where the meaning is not obvious it will be explained in the particular area of the law where it is utilized. Some of those which will be encountered are mentioned here. The definitional concepts of the conflict of laws are still rendered, across Europe and the world, in classical form. The effort to try to render and refer to these in a clunky English paraphrase is silly and misguided, and it will not be made here. In addition to the *lex domicilii,* the law of the domicile, and the *lex patriae,* the law of the nationality, they include: the *lex fori,* the law of the court in which the trial is taking place; the *lex contractus,* the law which governs a contract, whether this is determined under the rules of the common law (for contracts made before 2 April 1991: the 'proper law') or the Rome Convention (for contracts made after 1 April 1991: the 'governing law') or

Rome I Regulation (for contracts made after 17 December 2009: the 'applicable law'); the *lex loci contractus*, the law of the place where the contract was made; the *lex delicti*, the law which governs liability in tort, whether determined under the rules of the common law, statute, or Rome II Regulation; the *lex loci delicti commissi*, the law of the place where the tort was committed; the *lex situs*, the law of the place where land, or other thing, is; the *lex loci actus*, the law of the place where a transaction was carried out; the *lex loci celebrationis*, the law of the place of celebration of marriage; the *lex incorporationis*, the law of the place of incorporation; the *lex protectionis*, the law which grants legal protection to an intellectual property right; the *lex concursus*, the law of the court which is administering an insolvent estate; the *lex successionis*, the law which governs the succession to a deceased estate; and the *lex causae*, which is used to refer generically to the law applicable to the issue in dispute.

(e) Statutes, and the principle of comity

By contrast with its reasonably sophisticated framework for dealing with the application of foreign law, the common law conflict of laws is not at its best when handling English statutes. Although a court will only apply a foreign statutory rule if the foreign law is the *lex causae*, the reverse is not true. An English court may apply an English statute even though its conflicts rules otherwise point to the application of a foreign law. Everything depends on the true construction of the statute, on whether Parliament has directed the judges to apply it without regard to or despite foreign elements in the overall dispute.[85] Some, such as the Human Rights Act 1998, can easily be seen to override all contrary rules for choice of foreign law and jurisdiction, but it is rarely as clear as that. It is sometimes said that there is a presumption that laws are made to be territorially limited, for this is what international comity would expect. But even if that is so, it is only a point of departure; and it will depend on the law, and the precise way in which the 'territory' or 'territorial' is defined: is it by reference to the person, or the property, or the transaction, or something else? When Parliament legislates without making any clear statement of the international reach or 'legislative grasp' of its laws, the courts have to do the best they can; and there are no easy answers. The question has arisen several times in the context of employment law disputes,[86] but the

---

[85] For example, Unfair Contract Terms Act 1977, s 27.
[86] On employee rights under the Employment Rights Act 1996, see, for example, *Serco Ltd v Lawson* [2006] UKHL 3, [2006] ICR 250; *Ravat v Halliburton Manufacturing Services Ltd* [2012] UKSC 1, [2012] ICR 389; *Foreign and Commonwealth Office v Bamieh* [2019] EWCA Civ 803.

problem may arise whenever an English statute, worded to suggest that its scope may be unlimited, is proposed to be applied to an issue which would not otherwise be governed by English law.[87]

This leads to a broader question, whether 'comity' has any discernible role in private international law. Some writers take the view that its lack of clear definition renders it unusable or useless. But other writers, and courts,[88] make reference to comity rather more often than this would suggest. If comity is understood as a rather woolly principle of judicial self-restraint, it would not be particularly useful. However, the principle may be formulated more precisely: as one which asserts positively that the exercise of jurisdiction and legislative power is territorial and that exercises of sovereign power within the sovereign's own territory are entitled to be respected, but which also accepts passively that parties may assume obligations which either may ask a court to enforce against the other without regard to such territoriality. On that basis it is capable of explaining the law on jurisdiction and foreign judgments, the interpretation and application of statutes, and certain elements of the conflict of laws. It has been observed by leading civilian commentators that comity plays a characteristic role in the common law of private international law, and there would be no reason for an English lawyer to deny it.[89]

A general principle of comity leads also to the specific conclusion that an English court may not be asked to rule on the validity of a foreign sovereign act carried out within its territory, whether the validity is said to be questionable by reference to the internal law of that state or by reason of some precept of public international law. Save for exceptional cases, the acts of states as states, carried out within their territory, are not justiciable; they are beyond the purview of municipal courts, not only because there are no judicial or manageable standards by which to judge them, but also because the intervention of the courts at the instance of private parties may contradict the work and authority of government in its conduct of the international relations of

---

[87] On Senior Courts Act 1981, s 36 (service of writ of subpoena), see *Masri v Consolidated Contractors International Co SAL* [2009] UKHL 43, [2010] 1 AC 90. On Insolvency Act 1986, s 423 (recovery of property transferred in fraud of creditors) see *Re Paramount Airways Ltd* [1993] Ch 223; *Bilta (UK) Ltd v Nazir* [2015] UKSC 23, [2016] 1 AC 1. On the scope of the Fatal Accidents Act 1967, see *Cox v Ergo Versicherung AG* [2014] UKSC 22, [2014] AC 1379. On the scope of the Civil Liability (Contribution) Act 1978, see *Roberts v SSAFA* [2019] EWHC 1104 (QB).

[88] For a recent example, see *Joujou v Masri* [2011] EWCA Civ 746, [2011] 2 CLC 566. It should be noted that US courts make much more frequent reference to the principle.

[89] See, further, Briggs, *The Principle of Comity in Private International Law* (Vol 354 *Recueil des cours* (Collected courses of the Hague Academy of International Law)Martinus Nijhoff, 2012) p 69.

the United Kingdom.[90] Though from time to time an attempt is made to trim this wise principle of abstention, perhaps by taking instruction from resolutions of the competent organs of the United Nations,[91] the general principle is as sound as it is valuable. Of course, foreign legislation may be refused effect in England in an individual case on grounds of public policy, but such a conclusion does not rest on the invalidity of the foreign act or legislation, but on the ordinary rules of the conflict of laws.

3. DOUBTING THE TRADITIONAL COMMON LAW APPROACH

It is accurate to describe the traditional approach of the common law as 'jurisdiction-selecting': the conflicts process selects a legal system—a jurisdiction—whose rule will be taken to govern the issue before the court; this legal system, more or less automatically, provides the answer. Little or no attention is paid to the question—which is not asked—whether this actually produces the 'right' answer, or the 'best' answer. Although it has proved remarkably durable in England and much of the common law world, and although it appears to be found in most civilian systems as well, it is still open to criticism. Several points may be suggested. First, the creation of characterization categories is to some extent an artificial process, an attempt to impose order on a market of conflicting legal rules and tending, unless care is taken, to be rigid and blinkered.[92] Secondly, the idea that within each of these categories—material validity of contract, personal capacity to marry—there is a conceptual unity which justifies subjecting them all to the same conflicts rule is not always plausible: should a single law really determine the age at which a person may marry, whether a blood or other relative may be married, whether polygamy or same-sex union is permitted, and the effect of inability or refusal to consummate the marriage? Is this really a single, coherent, group of issues, all properly referable to the same law? Thirdly, and tellingly, little interest is shown in whether the rule of law actually chosen for application was developed or enacted with the intention that it be applied in the instant case. Fourthly, little or no attempt is made to compare

---

[90] *Buttes Gas & Oil Co v Hammer* [1982] AC 888, 938.
[91] *Kuwait Airways Corpn v Iraq Airways Co (Nos 4 and 5)* [2002] UKHL 19, [2002] 2 AC 883.
[92] cf *Raiffeisen Zentralbank Österreich AG v Five Star Trading LLC* [2001] EWCA Civ 68, [2001] QB 825.

and evaluate the results which would be produced by the rules of law from the various systems which might connect to the facts, still less to choose between them. For these among other reasons American jurists,[93] and some others drawing their inspiration from them, have proposed a variety of alternative approaches. These are varied in their content; have received some, but not substantial, judicial support; are perhaps most prominent in litigation about inter-state torts; and are more complex, and may be more subtle, than the more mechanical traditional approach. Take for example the case of an inter-state traffic accident, involving cars registered in, and drivers and passengers resident in, different states; and suppose that the laws of some, but not all, of these states restrict the type and extent of damages which can be recovered. It is not hard to see the mechanical application of a *lex delicti*, such as the law of the place where the tort occurred, as being too insensitive to the actual and personal facts of the case.[94] A modest alternative, which is still jurisdiction-selecting, would be to apply the law having the closest and most real connection to the particular claim, and to assess this on a case-by-case basis; a variant would be to look to the law having the closest connection to the particular issue to be adjudicated, rather than to the tort as a whole. A more radical alternative, which may be thought of as 'rule-selecting', would enquire whether each of the various rules contained in the competing systems was intended by its legislator to apply to the case, or issue, currently before the court. If this analysis reveals that only one of the potentially applicable rules was designed to apply to a case such as this, there will have been a false or illusory conflict of laws, and the one and only concerned law will be applied. But if it is discovered that more than one of these laws was intended to apply to the given facts, the court will have to resolve a true conflict of laws, which it may do by applying its own domestic law if it is one of those which was designed to be applied, or by seeking to identify the 'better' or 'best' law. The scientific analysis of these alternatives to traditional conflict rules is not susceptible to concise statement, but insofar as the approach involves construing conflicting statutes to discern what they really intend, it taps into an ancient and orthodox tradition. But it also works better in a system where the majority of actual rules from which the selection must be made are contained

---

[93] Especially Cavers, *The Choice of Law Process* (Ann Arbor, University of Michigan Press 1965) and *Contemporary Conflicts Law in American Perspective* (Vol 131 *Recueil des cours*, Martinus Nijhoff, 1970) p 143; Currie, *Selected Essays on the Conflict of Laws* (Durham, Duke University Press,1963); American Law Institute, *Restatement Second of the Conflict of Laws* (1971).

[94] cf *Babcock v Jackson* 191 NE 2d 279 (1963).

in codes or statutes. For the common law has no legislator and its purpose is, in this sense, unknown and unknowable. This may be contrasted with statute law, on which *travaux préparatoires* and constitutional theory may illuminate the actual or presumed legislative intention. This process is sometimes called 'governmental interest analysis', which is unfortunate: call it instead 'searching for the intentions of the legislature' and it seems much less alien. Whether it could ever have been made to work in England is doubtful;[95] and as the conflict rules applicable in an English court are increasingly contained in European legislation, there is relatively little scope for an English judge to follow whatever he may take to be the American way ahead.

If private international law is to continue to use connecting factors which select a law to be applied, a greater challenge may yet come from those new technologies which make a 'law of the place of . . .' rule seem, at least as a matter of first impression, contrived. The use of electronic means of communication for publicity, trade, fraud, and defamation has yet to be properly examined in the context of the conflict of laws. Opinions vary. On one side are those who consider that these new media, as well as ideas like 'digital currency', mean that a reappraisal of jurisdiction, foreign judgments, and conflict of laws rules cannot be avoided, and the sooner the better; on the other, those who feel that, just as the conflict of laws came to terms with the telephone, telex, and fax, it will simply adapt its basic ideas to the facts of this new-fangled technology. It is too early to announce the death of the traditional conflict of laws; there is always a risk that conflicts rules tailor-made for new technology have their own obsolescence built into them.

If the past is any guide to the future, specific conflicts rules which have reached the end of their shelf life may be superseded by more flexible ones. A couple of examples may illustrate the point. In the private international law of restitution, there was authority for the view that the obligation to make restitution would, in certain cases, be governed by the law of the place of the enrichment.[96] But when claims result from the electronic transfer—except that nothing is actually transferred as banks electronically adjust their records—of funds by banks, the place of enrichment may be so fortuitous or so artificial that it makes no sense as a conflicts rule. In the private international law

---

[95] Kahn-Freund, *General Problems of Private International Law* (Vol143 *Recueil des cours*, Martinus Nijhoff, 1974) p 147; Fawcett, 'Is American Governmental Interest Analysis the Solution to English Tort Choice of Law Problems?' (1982) 31 ICLQ 189.

[96] Though the issue is now generally governed by the Rome II Regulation, its Art 10(3) applies the law of the country in which the unjust enrichment took place, which rule raises questions of a similar kind.

of intangible property, dealings with negotiable instruments are traditionally governed by the law of the place where the document is. But widely used, international electronic dealing or settlement systems, and the custodianship of securities, would risk being confounded by the rigid application of this antique rule of law to such novel methods of dealing. In such cases, new conflicts rules may be required if the most appropriate law to the issues raised by this new technology and markets is to be applied; it is no answer to shrug and say that those who enter into the market risk the surprises which traditional conflict of laws may spring on them; and it would be optimistic to assume that sensible rules can be developed without the need for legislation.

When contracts are made over the internet it may, as the law currently stands, be necessary to decide where a contract was made or was broken,[97] or whether a supplier directed his professional or commercial activities to the place of a consumer's domicile.[98] It is improbable that a technical analysis of the locations of the customer's computer and internet server, or of the server which hosts the supplier's website, the supplier's computer, and of the various ways in which this information is read or downloaded, etc, will yield a solution which is scientifically respectable, comprehensible for the people involved, and jurisprudentially rational. Where it is alleged that a reputation has been defamed by a statement displayed on a web page accessible by computer users from China to Peru, does it really make sense to ask where the tort or torts occurred, or where the damage occurred, or where was the event which gave rise to the damage?[99] For all these points of contact may be multiplied by the number of people who may have had access to the information. When it comes to jurisdiction[100] or the recognition of foreign judgments,[101] it may be necessary to ask whether the defendant was present (or carrying on business) in or at a particular place. The facts of modern business life may make this a surprisingly difficult question to answer. For the purposes of regulation of deposit-takers and investment businesses, it may be necessary to determine whether an individual carried on specified activities or business in the United Kingdom.[102] The conflict of laws must keep abreast of what is happening in this brave new world.

---

[97] See CPR PD 6B 3.1(6).
[98] Council Regulation (EC) 44/2001, [2001] OJ L12/1, Art 15.
[99] ibid, Art 5(3). cf *Gutnick v Dow Jones & Co Inc* [2002] HCA 56, (2002) 210 CLR 375.
[100] CPR 6.9(2).
[101] *Adams v Cape Industries plc* [1990] Ch 433 (CA).
[102] For example, Financial Services and Markets Act 2000, s 418.

In the absence of a more radical alternative, a tentative guess may be that the place where the individuals, or their day-to-day[103] office premises, are located will prove to be more significant than where the hardware is, and that both will be more significant than the notional places where links in the chain of communication may be found. After all, domestic law and the conflict of laws deal with communication and contracts made by telephone, and it appears to be assumed that the place of the telephone subscriber is decisive. It appears not to matter that the offeree left a message on an answering machine on the premises, or in a voicemail box maintained by a telephone company; or that either caller used a mobile phone. Rough-and-ready locations can be ascribed to the persons who communicate, and the legal analysis will proceed from there. For defamation, the eye of the reader is significant, rather than the place where or from which his computer receives the information in question.[104] For presence or the carrying on of business, it seems probable that this can indicate only where living, breathing, individuals do what they do, rather than a notional place where information is transferred. This is not to say coming to terms with conflicts issues presented by the new technology will be plain sailing, or that no legislation will be required. But the thoughtful reflection of commercial judges will usually bring about rational solutions.

D. PRIVATE INTERNATIONAL LAW AS EUROPEAN LAW

The system just described was developed to regulate the private international rules of the common law, making law from cases and the absence of cases, and from not much else. When it was required to accommodate statute law,[105] it generally did so by treating it as though the rules made were not so very different from rules of non-statute law. English legislation would therefore be applied when, but only when, English law was identified by English conflicts rules as the *lex causae*; foreign law would be applied when that foreign law was the *lex causae*, and so on. Although a rare English statute might be applied in a case in which the *lex causae* was not otherwise English, this happened when and because the legislative instruction to the judge was

---

[103] As distinct from a letterbox address in a tax haven or money laundry, but which pretends to be a central office.
[104] *Gutnick v Dow Jones & Co Inc* [2002] HCA 56, (2002) 210 CLR 375.
[105] That is, rules of domestic law in statutory form. There was very little legislation of conflicts rules.

understood to be so peremptory as to override the result which would have been derived from the ordinary English rules of the conflict of laws.[106] There is no doubt that such a direct instruction from the legislator may have this effect on an English judge. But this effect could be attributed only to English legislation, and then only where the terms in which the legislation was drafted made it sufficiently clear that it really was a direct instruction to the judge to override the rules of the conflict of laws. In the great majority of cases, English legislation was simply fitted into the established common law pattern for dealing with the conflict of laws.

But legislation is not only made in England, and instructions to judges do not come only from Westminster. Rules of private international law are now established by the organs of the European Union. Since 1987 the law on jurisdiction and the recognition of foreign judgments was mostly governed by European, which means pan-European, legislation: this is true for civil and commercial matters,[107] and in some areas of family law[108] and insolvency,[109] but the legislative aim of the European Union was always to extend its authority over the field of jurisdiction and judgments, as well as civil procedure.[110] The conflict of laws rules are also substantially European and legislative: the law applicable to contractual[111] and non-contractual[112] obligations was covered, as was maintenance[113] and some other aspects of family law;[114] so also insolvency.[115] The United Kingdom stood aside from European legislation governing the dissolution of marriage,[116] and that dealing with wills, succession, and the administration of estates,[117] but this did not prevent the legislation being made, and a state which opted out is permitted later to opt in. Still further, other European legislation which is not directly targeted at private international law may still impinge on issues of private international

---

[106] The traditional terminology of private international law was therefore to refer to these as 'overriding' statutes. A more modern usage is to refer to them as 'mandatory' laws.

[107] Regulation (EC) 44/2001, [2001] OJ L12/1.

[108] Regulation (EC) 2201/2003, [2003] OJ L338/1; Regulation (EC) 4/2009, [2009] OJ L7/1.

[109] Regulation (EC) 1346/2000, [2000] OJ L160/1, recast as Regulation (EU) 2015/848, [2015] OJ L141/19.

[110] Regulations also dealt with the service of process (Regulation (EC) 1393/2007, [2008] OJ L331/21), the taking of evidence for use in proceedings (Regulation (EC) 1206/2001, [2001] OJ L174/1), and a growing number of small claims and consumer procedures not listed here.

[111] Regulation (EC) 593/2008, [2008] OJ L177/6.

[112] Regulation (EC) 864/2007, [2007] OJ L199/40.

[113] Regulation (EC) 4/2009, [2009] OJ L7/1.

[114] Regulation (EC) 2201/2003, [2003] OJ L338/1.

[115] Regulation (EC) 1346/2000, [2000] OJ L160/1.

[116] Regulation (EU) 1259/2010, [2010] OJ L343/10.

[117] Regulation (EU) 650/2012, [2012] OJ L201/107.

law. For example, the freedom of establishment guaranteed by the European Treaty had a significant impact on the private international law of corporations. And quite apart from all that, the European Convention on Human Rights, made by the Council of Europe but legislated into English law by the Human Rights Act 1998, is also seeping into private international law. And to the extent that this law is retained after Brexit, it is EU law which is being retained.

Whatever else may be true, European legislation was not made to work within or amend the common law. It displaces the national laws of all Member States, both as to substance and as to legal method, in order to produce and put in their place uniform rules and principles of private international law. This will make it possible to know which courts will and will not have jurisdiction, and which country's law will be applied to the dispute, no matter where proceedings may be brought. It was helpful to think of these legislative texts as being pasted onto the pages of an album, initially blank but which, when filled up, would form the Code of Private International Law for the European Union.

This code, or these European materials, came with their own instructions for use. Let us take the rules for non-contractual obligations in civil or commercial matters arising from events giving rise to damage which occur after 11 January 2009. The conflicts rules of the Rome II Regulation apply if (i) the relationship in question is one of 'non-contractual obligation', (ii) the obligation is within the definition of 'civil or commercial matters', and (iii) events giving rise to damage occur after 11 January 2009. To decide (i) whether the relationship in question is a non-contractual obligation, and (ii) whether the matter is a civil or commercial one, the court is called upon to interpret Article 1 of the Regulation. To decide whether the events giving rise to damage occurred after 11 January 2009, the court is called upon to interpret Article 31 of the Regulation: all three are questions, or raise issues, of statutory interpretation of European statute law. The court does not 'characterize' the issue as being contractual, tortious, equitable, one of unjust enrichment, or otherwise, insofar as all of these are terms of art of the common law conflict of laws, or of the common law doctrine of characterization. This is because 'characterization', properly so called, is the key to the common law rules of the conflict of laws: it tells the court which category of issue forming the common law conflict of laws it is dealing with; it points the way to the connecting factor which the common law directs the court to apply. Where the Regulation applies, however, these rules of the common law, and all of them, are *res extincta*; the key does not fit the lock.

In short, this legislation made or makes up an entirely new, self-sufficient, system of private international law, conveniently called 'European Private International Law'. It comes with its own manual, which is written in European, not in English. Of course the transitional phase will be turbulent: they always are. If each system—common law, European—is designed to be complete, some awkwardness can be expected if a case requires a court to work with materials from each system. But things can only get better.

1. PRINCIPLES OF LEGISLATIVE INTERPRETATION

The skills required by the private international lawyer working with this European legislative material form the counterpart to the common law principles of characterization, etc. What is required in the domain of (retained) European private international law are those techniques which will lead to a clear and accurate interpretation of the various legislative texts. The applicable canons of European statutory interpretation are general and particular. Consideration of those which are particular to specific pieces of legislation can be postponed to be dealt with in the context in which they arise: they are most developed in the field of jurisdiction and the recognition of judgments.

Prime among these general principles is the requirement that terms of art in the legislation have a meaning which is autonomous, which is to say, independent of the national law of the court called upon to apply it. There would, as said before, be little point in enacting a single legislative text which meant different things in each of the 28 Member States: it would make no more sense for the Unfair Contract Terms Act 1977 to mean one thing in Yorkshire but another thing in Kent. Ideally these autonomous definitions of legislative terms will have been laid down by the European Court, on references for preliminary rulings made by national courts,[118] but where this has not yet happened, the national court may guide itself by considering how the European Court would have answered if it were to have been asked. It will also be generally accepted that terms of art have the same meaning across different legislative texts. Although each Regulation has its own economy,[119] it will be unusual, and certainly unhelpful, for a common term (such as 'damage') to be held to mean one thing in one Regulation, but something different in another.

---

[118] Under Art 267 of the Treaty on the Functioning of the European Union.
[119] Case C–45/13 *Kainz v Pantherwerke AG* EU:C:2014:7, [2015] QB 34.

Second, the interpretation adopted should contribute to legal certainty: this principle has been identified with increasing clarity, and it manifests itself in various ways. It will tend to mean that where one piece of legislation has replaced another, the interpretation given to provisions which are common to the old and the new should be consistent, so that a litigant may know where he is able to sue or liable to be sued, or know what law will be applied if the case has to be taken to court, without the need for complicated analysis or expensive advice. In principle, legal certainty should also argue for consistency of interpretation across the legislation, as described above, though at this point the principle may yield to more contextual concerns, considered below.

Third, rules of general application are interpreted broadly; rules of specific application which derogate from those general rules are interpreted as being no wider than is necessary to achieve the specific purpose for which they were made, lest the exception swallow up the rule. This does not always mean that a rule which may be regarded as *lex specialis* must be given the most restrictive interpretation imaginable, but the derogation from *lex generalis* should be no wider than the reason for the legislation requires.

Fourth, each piece of legislation, and (in principle, at least) each Article within that piece of legislation, has a natural scope which should neither overlap with others nor leave unplanned gaps. So, in principle at least, a matter is either within the Brussels I Regulation for jurisdiction in civil and commercial matters, or it is within the scope of the Insolvency Regulation, but it cannot be within both, for the scope of each is defined to prevent their overlapping. A claim based on breach of an obligation should not fall within the scope of the Rome I (contractual obligations) and Rome II (non-contractual obligations) Regulations, even if at first sight it might appear that it naturally does, such as when a contractual duty of care is said to have been broken by a defendant who has failed to exercise reasonable care. In cases in which the legislator appears to have been aware that this advice might be easier to formulate than to abide by, specific drafting of the legislation may lead to the conclusion that where legislative provisions overlap, they produce the same outcome, with the result that there is no conflict of laws.

Fifth, even where a local statute is or would be interpreted as one which Parliament had intended to apply to all cases within its scope without regard to the conflict of laws, where the issue before the court is governed by European legislation, such overriding or mandatory effect for local legislation is permitted only through the window provided by that legislation. This will normally require that the application of a local statute is 'mandatory', in a very narrow and restrictive sense which is designed to reduce this effect to the absolute minimum.[120]

It would not have been surprising if there had been a sixth: that when a Regulation directs a court to apply the law of a foreign country, the court should apply that law rather than falling back on the common law principle that foreign law is a matter of optionally provable fact. True, to require an English court to apply foreign law whenever a legislative rule tells it that a foreign law is applicable would impose far more fundamental a change to the practice of the courts than anything done to the substantive rules of the conflict of laws. So far the issue has been avoided by regarding the issue as one of procedure, which is often excluded from the scope of Regulations. But one day the argument may be made, that the scheme of European private international law is impaired when some, but not other, national courts decline to investigate foreign law for themselves, and as a result fail to apply it. If that were to have happened while the United Kingdom was still a Member State of the European Union, a fundamental change in methodology would have been forced upon the English courts. However, the development of a genuinely European private international law called for radical changes to the way English courts dealt with issues of private international law; and as is well known,[121] one cannot make an omelette without breaking eggs.[122]

---

[120] See Rome I Regulation, Art 9 (Case C–184/12 *Unamar NV v Navigation Maritime Bulgare* EU:C:2013:663); Rome II Regulation, Art 16; (Case C–149/18 *Silva Martins v Dekra Claims Services Portugal SA* EU:C:2019:84).

[121] Whether this observation is properly attributed to Delia Smith, or to the Great Stalin, or otherwise, is a matter on which opinion remains divided.

[122] Recent developments in the political history of the United Kingdom require one, in the interests of balance, to observe that the breaking of eggs does not always result in an omelette. It may just produce a terrible mess which no one can clear up.

2

JURISDICTION

In this chapter, and prior to Exit Day, the private international law of jurisdiction in civil and commercial matters was governed in part by a number of European Regulations and other instruments. These were the Brussels I Regulation 44/2001 and the recast Brussels I Regulation 1215/2012; the 1988 Lugano Convention and the 2007 Lugano II Convention; and the 1968 Brussels Convention as amended from time to time. According to the Civil Jurisdiction and Judgments (Amendment) (EU Exit) Regulations 2019, SI 2019 No 479, on Exit Day these instruments are revoked or, in the case of the Conventions given effect by the Civil Jurisdiction and Judgments Act 1982, as amended, repealed. Elsewhere in this book these instruments are sometimes referred to as '(former)', to convey the dreary message that until Exit Day they are in full force and effect, but that, unless further legislative arrangements are made, they will cease to apply after that date. In this chapter, however, to do so would crush the life out of the text, so it has not been done.

After Exit Day, any gap will be filled by the rules of common law jurisdiction (that is to say, common law, Parliamentary legislation, civil procedure rules, and judicial decisions) and (when brought into effect in the United Kingdom pursuant to SI 2018 No 1124) the Hague Convention on Choice of Court Agreements. Given the dramatic effect of revoking the greater part of the law which has framed the jurisdiction of English courts for over 30 years, SI 2019 No 479 was also required to make some more substantive changes, most notably in the context of jurisdiction over employment contract and consumer contract matters, where simple reversion to the law to be found outside the (former) Regulation would be too long a backward step and new statutory rules are provided. But the broad position is that the material examined in Sections (B) and (C) of this chapter (as well as the occasional point made in Section (D) will cease to operate in the United Kingdom: it will neither do so directly nor have an indirect influence on the law which has

The Conflict of Laws. Fourth Edition. Adrian Briggs, Oxford University Press (2019). © Adrian Briggs
DOI: 10.1093/oso/9780198838500.003.0002

hitherto operated alongside it. The relevant rules of civil procedure are amended accordingly, by SI 2019 No 521.

However, in the context of the jurisdiction of English courts, Part 6 of SI 2019 No 479 provides that these (former) instruments will continue to apply in England when dealing with the jurisdiction of a court in the United Kingdom which is seised of proceedings before Exit Day. More complex provision is made by Part 6 for the case in which an English court is seised before Exit Day but a court in another Member State is seised after that date. It follows that there will be a shortish period after Exit Day during which an English court, including an appellate court, will assess its jurisdiction on the basis of these otherwise-revoked and otherwise-repealed instruments.

A. JURISDICTION OR JURISDICTIONS?

To say that a court has jurisdiction means that the law considers it to have the power to hear and determine a matter brought before it. It must have jurisdiction over the subject matter of the claim, and personal jurisdiction over the defendant to it: at least, this is how the common law of jurisdiction organizes itself. This chapter therefore starts with six elements of the law of jurisdiction as this is understood by the common law. The first four points are exceptions; the fifth is the core provision, and the sixth a wider contextual point.

First, there are a few areas where an English court lacks jurisdiction over subject matter of a claim. Where this is so, it is irrelevant that the parties may be willing, or purport, to submit to the personal jurisdiction of the court: absence of subject-matter jurisdiction is something which lies beyond their power or control. The common law considers a court to have no jurisdiction to rule on title to foreign land, and therefore no jurisdiction to hear claims which depend on a question of such title.[1] Statute has modified this common law rule, so that a court may now hear a claim in tort which relates to foreign land unless it is principally concerned with title to that land;[2] but otherwise the rule remains in place until Parliament or the Supreme Court removes it.

---

[1] *British South Africa Co v Companhia de Moçambique* [1893] AC 602; *Hesperides Hotels Ltd v Aegean Turkish Holidays Ltd* [1979] AC 508.
[2] Civil Jurisdiction and Judgments Act 1982, s 30.

Second, as a matter of ancient authority, where there was a contract or an equity between the parties, the court did not lack jurisdiction to adjudicate on and enforce the personal obligations arising from it, even though the subject of this personal obligation was foreign land.[3] It follows that a court may determine the shares in a tenancy in common in foreign land arising from the trust of that land and order the parties to behave accordingly; it may order the specific performance of a contract to mortgage or to convey foreign land, albeit that it will not make such an order with which it would be illegal or impossible for the defendant to comply. Indeed, the statutory reform for tort cases, mentioned above, was needed because there is no contract or equity between tortfeasors, and this ancient principle could not be applied in the context of a tort committed in relation to foreign land. Authority still just about supports the conclusion that a court lacks jurisdiction at common law to adjudicate the validity of foreign patents, on the footing that the grant or extent of such rights is a matter for the foreign sovereign alone. But there is no equivalent exclusion for foreign copyright.[4]

Third, in a response to recent, rather shrill, complaints about 'defamation tourism', an English court now has no jurisdiction in defamation proceedings brought against a defendant not domiciled in a Member State of the EU unless England is, in the light of *all* the places in which the offending material was published (no matter that only part of the overall publication is complained about), clearly the most appropriate place for the proceedings.[5] This is rather a silly rule. It would have been much better for a court to be given a transparent discretion to not exercise jurisdiction, but a blank statutory removal of subject-matter jurisdiction will mean that the court has no power to act in such a case, even if the defendant is willing to defend the claim in England, or even if England is the only place in which a fair trial would be feasible.

Fourth, as to the person against whom the claim may be brought, the principles of state and diplomatic immunity limit the exercise of jurisdiction over non-commercial claims brought against states and diplomats;[6] and the principle that an English court will not rule on the legality of a foreign act of state limits it also. Indeed, in these cases it may be subject-matter jurisdiction, rather than personal jurisdiction, which is lacking, on the footing that once the

---

[3] *Penn v Baltimore* (1750) 1 Ves Sen 444.
[4] *Lucasfilm Ltd v Ainsworth* [2011] UKSC 29, [2012] 1 AC 208 (excluding copyright from the scope of any exclusionary rule about which the court was unenthusiastic).
[5] Defamation Act 2013, s 9.
[6] State Immunity Act 1978; *Holland v Lampen-Wolfe* [2000] 1 WLR 1573 (HL).

immunity is established, scrutiny of an act of or attributable to a foreign sovereign lies beyond the competence of the English court. Some rather difficult cases which have at their base an allegation of torture or other disgraceful behaviour by or on behalf of governments, not all of them foreign, have tested the limits of this immunity.[7] They are positioned on the tense boundary between the law of human rights, which a court certainly must adjudicate, and certain principles of public international law which constrain the municipal courts; but they have not been reduced to a clear statement of principle, no doubt because of the political sensitivity of the entire shady business.

Fifth, subject to these exceptions a court, as a matter of common law, has personal jurisdiction over a defendant, and therefore jurisdiction to adjudicate, when process has been or is deemed to have been[8] served on him. It follows, and it is as surprising as it is true, that rules which define jurisdiction *in personam* are, in English law, framed as rules which specify whether and when it is lawful to serve process on the defendant:[9] where there is service, there is jurisdiction. As to those rules, the common law considers that any person present within the territorial jurisdiction of the court is liable to be served with process by or on behalf of the claimant, who may do so as of right; the other side of the coin is that no person was liable to be served if she was outside England. To overcome this difficulty, rules of court permitted a claimant to apply for permission to serve process on a defendant out of the jurisdiction: the circumstances in which this may be done are currently set out in Part 6 of the Civil Procedure Rules (CPR).[10]

Sixth, in the common law scheme it does not follow that, just because a court has jurisdiction, it will always exercise it at the behest of the claimant. A characteristic of the common law of jurisdiction, especially where there is a conflict of potential jurisdictions, is the power of an English court, on application made by the defendant, to decline to exercise the jurisdiction which it has, with the consequence that the claimant may in practice have to proceed in a foreign court. There is a coherence to all of this, which results from two fundamental truths: that as a matter of common law the jurisdiction of the High Court is inherent, which is to say, its power to try claims is, save as

---

[7]   See in particular *Belhaj v Straw* [2017] UKSC 3, [2017] 2 AC 964.

[8]   Such as when a court authorizes service to be made by alternative means (eg on a fugitive defendant).

[9]   For the procedure for effecting service see CPR 6. Personal service is still the most common method.

[10]   Previously Rules of the Supreme Court, Order 11. Care must be taken to notice alterations to the wording of these provisions from one incarnation to the next.

mentioned above, unrestricted by the nature of the claim or the identity of the defendant; and that, as a matter of common law, a court has inherent power to regulate its own procedure, including the procedural power to not exercise a jurisdiction which it has. This results in the common law relating to jurisdiction being flexible, or unpredictable, according to one's vantage point.

All this changed after 1986. A succession of European legislative instruments, culminating in what is now the 'recast' Brussels I Regulation, Regulation (EU) 1215/2012, enacted a scheme of jurisdiction which was in every way separate and distinct from that which the court had as a matter of common law. The fact that this jurisdiction was legislated in Europe, rather than being native born, is terribly important. The enacted jurisdiction had the characteristics, but only the characteristics, which the legislator intended it to have. Its statutory language would be subject to the principles of interpretation described in Chapter 1 rather than any such rules taken from the common law. For example, a court has a discretion to decide whether to exercise jurisdiction only if that discretion can be shown to have been conferred on the court by this legislation: it cannot be derived from the common law, for the procedural powers which would be inherent in or associated with common law jurisdiction are, *ex hypothesi*, inapplicable to this form of non-inherent, enacted, jurisdiction. The court cannot pick and mix. Jurisdiction is no smörgåsbord.

The consequence is that a claimant, or a court, must first decide whether the jurisdiction which is applicable is common law or European. Where the European instruments are wholly inapplicable, the jurisdictional rules of the common law will apply: in this chapter, the expression 'common law jurisdiction' will be used to refer to the set of rules, including legislative rules made at Westminster, which operate in an English court when these European instruments make no claim to application. Where by contrast the jurisdiction of the court is governed by this European legislation, the court will be exercising 'Regulation jurisdiction'. To complicate matters only slightly, these European instruments occasionally refer to and rely on the jurisdictional rules developed at common law: incorporating them by reference, as it were. When this happens, the jurisdiction is still 'Regulation jurisdiction', a fact which may affect the rules thus taken in from the common law, but for this particular form of Regulation jurisdiction, the term 'residual Regulation jurisdiction' may be useful to mark the point that, in such cases, the Regulation is still the source of jurisdictional authority, if not the author of the rules.

It follows that an English court has jurisdictions rather than jurisdiction. This would not make English law unique. Many legal systems work with a distinction between, for example, federal and state jurisdictions, though they tend to do so by providing for separate courts. What is distinctive in England[11] is that the two forms of jurisdiction are exercised by the one court;[12] and on occasion, this can lead to the blurring of lines which ought to be kept polished and sharp. Still, clarity of thought is more easily maintained if 'Regulation jurisdiction' and 'common law jurisdiction' are treated separately, and in that order. This chapter tries to do just that, examining jurisdiction over defendants generally, and trying to keep the two systems of jurisdiction as unmixed as possible. But as jurisdiction in the specific contexts of family matters, the administration of estates, bankruptcy and insolvency, and so on is more conveniently treated alongside choice of law in the chapters which deal with those substantive topics, jurisdiction in such cases is postponed to be discussed in those chapters.

B. REGULATION JURISDICTION: INTRODUCTION

1. HISTORY

The interest of the European Union in civil jurisdiction stems from Article 220 of the Treaty of Rome, which committed the six original Member States of the EEC (Belgium, France, Germany, Italy, Luxembourg, and the Netherlands) to develop a system for the mutual recognition and enforcement of judgments in civil and commercial matters. It was decided that the best way to ensure the uncomplicated enforcement of sister-state judgments—creating a free market in judgments, as some call it—was to limit the power of the judge to review the judgment whose enforcement was sought; and that the proper way to achieve that result was to adopt a uniform set of rules for the taking of jurisdiction in the first place. The 1968 Brussels Convention was adopted to perform this dual function.

States which joined the European Community acceded to the Brussels Convention, which was successively amended on the accession of the United

---

[11] And in the other Member States.
[12] In this, and entirely coincidentally, it reflects the 19th-century fusion of law and equity into a single court.

Kingdom,[13] Denmark, and Ireland; Greece; Portugal, and Spain; and Austria, Finland, and Sweden. By the end of 2000, the re-re-re-amended text[14] of the Brussels Convention served as the jurisdictional statute of the 15 Member States. In addition, a parallel Convention, signed at Lugano in 1988,[15] bound the states of the European Union and of the European Free Trade Area. Of these, Austria, Finland, and Sweden later acceded to the Brussels Convention, and thereby ceased to be 'Lugano states', leaving Iceland, Norway, and Switzerland, which remained, and which remain, outside the European Union, as 'Lugano states'.

The process of amending an international convention is cumbersome, which is not helpful when adjustments to the law on civil jurisdiction and judgments prove to be necessary. The Member States therefore agreed to let the European Union legislate directly, transforming the Brussels Convention into a European Regulation, which became known, rather predictably, as the Brussels I Regulation.[16] It came into effect on 1 March 2002. It supplanted the Convention in the then-Member States, save for Denmark which for a while elected to stand aside. The 10 new states which acceded in 2004,[17] and the three which did so in 2007[18] and 2013,[19] were bound by the Regulation from the date of their accession; and Denmark came in from the cold in 2007 as well.[20] The three remaining Lugano states then agreed with the European Union to amend the Lugano Convention to bring it into line with the Brussels I Regulation, making the Lugano II Convention of 2007. And finally, in 2012 the Brussels I Regulation was 'recast', to make several improvements, the re-cast Regulation taking effect on 10 January 2015: the Lugano II Convention, however, was not recast.

The result of all this effort was that, in effect, an almost uniform legislative text governs jurisdiction and the enforcement of judgments in civil and commercial matters in the 28 Member States and the three Lugano states. At the date of writing, the recast Brussels I Regulation and the Lugano II

---

[13] Enacted as Sch 1 to the Civil Jurisdiction and Judgments Act 1982, which was amended on each subsequent accession. It will be deleted from this Act on Exit Day: SI 2019 No 479, along with all the successor instruments.

[14] SI 2000/1824, in force from 1 January 2001.

[15] Civil Jurisdiction and Judgments Act 1982, Sch 3C, as inserted by Civil Jurisdiction and Judgments Act 1991, Sch 1.

[16] Regulation (EC) 44/2001, [2001] OJ L12/1.

[17] Cyprus, Czech Republic, Estonia, Hungary, Latvia, Lithuania, Malta, Poland, Slovakia, and Slovenia.

[18] Bulgaria and Romania.

[19] Croatia.

[20] SI 2007/1655.

Convention are fully in force, across almost the whole territory of the continent of Europe. By any reckoning this was a remarkable achievement: it is very hard to find a rational voice of criticism of this common effort. In the account which follows, references to 'the Court' are to the Court of Justice of the European Union, or European Court. Though many of the reported cases were decided on the basis of earlier textual versions of the legislation, the account which follows has its focus on the recast Regulation, and terminology, and numbering of Articles, has been adjusted accordingly. It may be unhistorical, but so is life.

2. GENERAL SCHEME

The Regulation deals with jurisdiction in civil or commercial matters. It is the basic jurisdictional statute for the Member States, and national courts may make references to the European Court for a preliminary ruling on its interpretation.[21] It is drafted in many languages, although these versions are not, perhaps, in every nuance and respect, identical, and occasionally litigants may try to exploit the differences. As a matter of procedural law, where the Regulation confers jurisdiction on an English court, process may be served on the defendant as of right, whether in England or (with the appropriate certification of the court's jurisdiction under the Regulation) outside it.[22] In this context, service is the consequence of jurisdiction, not (as it is with the common law) the other way around.

Where the Regulation confers international jurisdiction upon the courts of a Member State, as distinct from the courts of a particular place,[23] it confers it on the courts of the United Kingdom, not England, for England is not a state. To deal with this, internal rules substantially resembling much of the Regulation allocate national jurisdiction as between the 'parts' of England, Scotland, and Northern Ireland. These rules of internal United Kingdom law are not part of European law, and are not the concern of the European Court.[24]

---

[21] Article 267 of the Treaty on the Functioning of the European Union (TFEU). The Court also has jurisdiction to interpret the Lugano II Convention as a Treaty to which the European Union is party.

[22] CPR 6.33.

[23] Special jurisdiction under Arts 7 and 8 is conferred directly on the courts of a place, not just a state.

[24] Case C–364/93 *Kleinwort Benson Ltd v City of Glasgow DC* [1995] ECR I–415.

Almost all definitional terms used in the Regulation have 'autonomous' meanings, distinct from those accorded to the same terms in national law: there would be little point in having a single legislative text with 28 different interpretations. These were mostly developed by the Court on references for preliminary rulings.[25] Certain canons of interpretation have also emerged over the years. First, as the basic principle is that a defendant shall be sued in the courts of the Member State where he is domiciled, a provision of the Regulation derogating from this rule will tend to receive a construction no wider than is necessary to secure its particular aim.[26] This was established by the Court in its jurisprudence on the Brussels Convention, and it continues to underpin the interpretation of the Regulation. Second, the Regulation is intended to make it possible for persons, long before they become litigants, to know where proceedings may and may not be brought, so an interpretation which leans in favour of this form of legal certainty will be favoured over one which makes less of a contribution; it also follows that the interpretation of the Regulation will be consistent with the earlier Convention where the relevant text has been handed on from the one to the other. Third, as the Regulation seeks to make judgments obtained in one Member State freely enforceable in other Member States, rules which allow non-recognition of judgments will be given a restrictive construction, whereas those which prevent parallel litigation should be construed more generously. Fourth, the courts of the Member States enjoy mutual trust and confidence, and it is absolutely impermissible to invite the courts of one Member State to conclude that the courts of another Member State erred in considering that they have or had jurisdiction.[27]

Where a claim falls within the domain of the Regulation, the court exercises 'Regulation jurisdiction'; the Regulation determines its jurisdiction. The application of the Regulation is not dependent on the claimant being domiciled in a Member State: not only is it wrong to see the Regulation as a statute available only to the fortunate few, but also, a defendant should not be in a worse or more exposed position if sued by a claimant not established

---

[25] So also, save where the provisions have been materially altered, will the expert reports on the various conventions: Jenard Report [1979] OJ C59/1; Schlosser Report [1979] OJ C59/71; Evrigenis Report [1986] OJ C298/1; Cruz Report [1989] OJ C189/35; Jenard and Möller Report [1990] OJ C189/61.

[26] Case C–25/18 *Kerr v Postnov* EU:C:2019:376 is the most recent affirmation of a well-established principle.

[27] Case C–351/89 *Overseas Union Insurance Ltd v New Hampshire Insurance Co* [1991] ECR I–3317; Case C–116/02 *Erich Gasser GmbH v Misat srl* [2003] ECR I–14693.

in the European Union.[28] If the defendant is out of the jurisdiction, service of process does not require the permission of the court, for where there is Regulation jurisdiction, service is a merely procedural notification that proceedings have been commenced.[29] Whether the jurisdiction of the court is Regulation jurisdiction depends on mapping the limits of the domain of the Regulation, to which we turn.

3. DOMAIN OF THE REGULATION: ARTICLES 1, 66–68, 71

The point of departure is to define the domain of the Regulation: its material, or subject-matter, scope; its temporal scope; and its relationship with other legal instruments.

(a) Material scope
According to Article 1, the Regulation applies in 'civil and commercial matters'. It will often be obvious whether the claim falls within this expression, but where it is not it calls for an autonomous interpretation of the terms. It will include claims made by or against public authorities where the obligations which are enforced are of a kind which may be assumed by or imposed on persons generally, no matter who is enforcing them. So for example, proceedings against a town council which has failed to pay a contractor who did work on the town hall will be a civil and commercial matter; proceedings brought to enforce a trader's obligation not to use unfair terms in consumer contracts are a civil or commercial matter, even though the party enforcing that obligation is a public body charged with the enforcement of the law.[30] Likewise, where a claim for repayment of sums advanced by way of financial assistance is founded on the ordinary law of restitution, the fact that the claim is brought by a state in relation to its administrative or public law duty of social support will not stop the claim being seen as civil or commercial.[31] If, by contrast, the obligation enforced in the proceedings is one which only the state has, which is peculiar to public law, the matter will not be a civil

---

[28] Case C–412/98 *Universal General Insurance Co v Groupe Josi Reinsurance Co SA* [2000] ECR I–5925.
[29] CPR 6.33.
[30] Case C–167/00 *VfK v Henkel* [2002] ECR I–8111.
[31] Case C–433/01 *Freistaat Bayern v Blijdenstein* [2004] ECR I–981.

or commercial one.[32] So for example, where a regulatory body has power to supervise and alter contractual rights and duties, and a significant part of its decision may not be questioned in court, its powers (and proceedings arising from them) are not civil or commercial in nature.[33] This approach to Article 1, which pays attention to the specific legal obligation which founds the claim, does mean that claims that look similar may fall within the Regulation in some systems but outside it in others; but the reason is that national legal systems draw the boundaries between public law and private law in their own individual ways. And the application of Article 1 is determined by reference to the claim: the nature of the defence to it is, at least in principle, immaterial.[34]

A claim is also outside the domain of the Regulation if it concerns customs, revenue, or administrative matters;[35] but in line with the point just made, if a state makes a claim formulated in tort against those who have wrongfully conspired to deprive it of taxes due to it, the claim arises in a civil or commercial matter.[36]

Also excluded are status or legal capacity of natural persons,[37] matrimonial property, or succession; bankruptcy and the winding up of insolvent companies or other legal persons;[38] social security; and arbitration: these are excluded, by specific language, precisely because they otherwise are civil or commercial matters.[39] It follows that that where one of these issues arises in the context of a matter which is civil or commercial in nature, the Regulation will apply unless the excluded matter forms the principal component in the dispute. This follows from the principle that exceptions to the Regulation are to be construed restrictively; it reflects the fact that the issues listed in Article 1(2) are indeed civil or commercial, and are therefore true exceptions to the

---

[32] Case C–265/02 *Frahuil SA v Assitalia SpA* [2004] ECR I–1543; Case C–308/17 *Hellenic Republic v Kuhn* EU:C:2018:911.

[33] Case C–579/17 *BUAK v Gradbeništvo Korana doo* EU:C:2019:162; see also Case C–226/13 *Fahnenbrock v Greece* EU:C:2015:383.

[34] Case C–266/01 *Préservatrice Foncière TIARD v Netherlands* [2003] ECR I–4867.

[35] Article 1(1).

[36] Case C–49/12 *HMRC v Sunico ApS* EU:C:2013:545, [2014] QB 391: a 'strange but true' decision if ever one was. See also Case C–551/15 *Pula Parking doo v Tederahn* EU:C:2017:193 (claim by town council for recovery of parking charge civil or commercial).

[37] Case C–386/12 *Re Schneider* EU:C:2013:633, [2014] Fam 80.

[38] The decisive question is whether the proceedings are based on ordinary civil law, even if brought by a claimant which is now insolvent (say where the company, acting by its liquidator, sues the thief who has stolen its assets: this is an ordinary tort claim, even if its benefit will now enure to the general body of creditors), or are based on obligations created by and arising from the particular law and regime of insolvency.

[39] Article 1(2)(a)–(c).

Regulation's application to civil and commercial matters. The point may be illustrated by examination of 'arbitration': a civil or commercial matter which is excluded from the Regulation. This obviously means that arbitrators are not bound by European law to apply Regulation, and that awards made by arbitrators are unrestricted by (but, by the same token, not enforceable under) the Regulation, and that judicial orders which, by one means or another, convert an award into a judgment or its equivalent are also unrestricted by (but not enforceable under) the Regulation.[40] A foreign judgment declaring that there is or is not a binding agreement to arbitrate is outside the scope of the Regulation; but if a court determines that there is no binding arbitration agreement and then goes on to give judgment on the substance of the claim, it has given judgment in a civil or commercial matter, and its judgment, in principle at least, comes within the scope of the Regulation. A court, asked to issue an injunction to restrain a party to an arbitration agreement from breaching it by suing in another Member State, may not make the order, because the proceedings before the other court are in a civil or commercial matter to which the principles of mutual respect naturally apply;[41] but it is entirely different if the 'injunction' is an award by the tribunal itself, whether or not converted into a court order, for the tribunal is not a court, and an award is not a judgment.[42]

Proceedings concerned with the enforcement of a judgment from a non-Member State are not within the Regulation, even when 'converted' into a local judgment; nor are ancillary or incidental procedures which arise in the course of such proceedings, such as the trial of an issue whether the judgment creditor obtained such judgment by fraud.[43] The reasoning is just the same as that which confirms the exclusion of judgments which make an order in terms of an arbitral award:[44] the effective or substantive determination from which enforcement follows, whether directly or indirectly, was not that of a judge of a Member State.

If the case falls outside the domain of the Regulation the English courts may exercise common law jurisdiction over the defendant, and the Regulation will have no part to play.

---

[40] Case C-190/89 *Marc Rich & Co AG v Soc Italiana Impianti PA* [1991] ECR I-3855.
[41] Case C-185/07 C-*Allianz SpA v West Tankers Inc* [2009] ECR I-663, I- referred by the House of Lords: [2007] UKHL 4, [2007] 1 Lloyd's Rep 391.
[42] Case C-536/13 *Re Gazprom OAO* EU:C:2015:316, [2015] 1 WLR 4937.
[43] Case C-129/92 *Owens Bank plc v Bracco* [1994] ECR I-117.
[44] Schlosser Report [1979] OJ C59/71.

(b) Temporal scope

Article 66 provides that the Regulation applies to the taking of jurisdiction by courts in legal proceedings instituted after 10 January 2015.

(c) Other conventions

As regards the relationship with other conventions, one might have expected that existing international agreements, especially those which involve non-Member States, would be untouched and unaffected by the Regulation. The reality is not quite so straightforward. Although Article 71 provides that the Regulation 'shall not affect any Conventions . . . which in relation to particular matters, govern jurisdiction' it goes on to explain that this means that if a convention allows the taking of jurisdiction, that provision continues to be effective, even though the defendant is domiciled in a Member State which is not party to it. So if another convention, such as those in maritime law which deal with the arrest of sea-going ships, and with cargo claims, authorize the taking of jurisdiction, the Regulation does not impede it. But if the particular convention makes no provision to prevent parallel litigation, the provisions of the Regulation[45] will apply 'to fill the gap', as though the particular convention were absorbed into the Regulation, with the consequence that it may then be modified in its operation.[46] This is very hard to reconcile with the proposition that the Regulation does not affect the assumption of jurisdiction under the particular convention; it comes close to saying that the other convention may operate only to the extent that it is consistent with the Regulation, which is hardly satisfactory; and it looks very much like an example of the European Court overreaching itself.

4. DOMICILE

Many of the individual provisions of Regulation jurisdiction turn upon whether a person, usually but not always the defendant, has a domicile in the United Kingdom or in another Member State. In this regard it is necessary to distinguish natural persons from companies or other legal persons or associations of persons, and from trusts, for the definition of domicile is not uniform. To decide whether an individual has a domicile in the United Kingdom,

---

[45] Articles 29–34 (see Section (C)(8) below)
[46] Case C–406/92 *The Tatry* [1994] ECR I–5439; Case C–452/12 *Nipponkoa Insurance Co (Europe) Ltd v Inter-Zuid Transport BV* EU:C:2013:858, [2014] All ER (Comm) 288.

Article 62 of the recast Regulation tells a court to apply the law of the United Kingdom. For this purpose, domicile in the United Kingdom is defined by statute[47] rather than by the common law. An individual is domiciled in the United Kingdom if he is resident in the United Kingdom and this residence indicates a substantial connection with the United Kingdom: this may be presumed from three months' residence. Similar rules, *mutatis mutandis*, determine whether an individual is domiciled in a part of the United Kingdom. But to determine whether an individual is domiciled in another Member State, Article 62 tells a court to apply the law of the Member State of the proposed domicile. So whether she is domiciled in France is a matter of French law; in Italy, a matter of Italian law, and so on. It follows that an individual may have a domicile in more than one Member State. This is unproblematic, for whereas it would be inconvenient for there to be concurrent domiciliary laws to determine capacity to marry, for example, it is unsurprising that a person's connections with each of two Member States are sufficient for either to be a proper place in which to sue her in matters of general[48] jurisdiction.

There has been pressure to provide a single autonomous definition of domicile, or to abandon it in favour of the concept of habitual residence, not least because of variation in the separate national law definitions of domicile. But it is difficult to see that this would improve the law. There will be occasional difficult cases, typically where a person maintains or has access to a residence in one country, but manages to cast a veil of secrecy over its ownership and his movements.[49] In such a case his domicile would probably be no more difficult to ascertain than his habitual residence, and it is unlikely that the change would have brought much about.

For a *company, other legal person,* or *association of natural persons,* Article 63 provides that it may have a domicile in any one or more of three places: where it has its statutory seat, or its central administration,[50] or its principal place of business. For the United Kingdom, 'statutory seat' is defined as the registered office or, where there is none anywhere, the place of incorporation or, where there is none anywhere, the place under the law of which the formation took place. The purpose of Article 63 is to nudge the law towards a more uniform definition of the domicile of a corporation or other legal person.

---

[47] Currently Civil Jurisdiction and Judgments Order 2001, SI 2001/3929, Sch 1, para 9.
[48] Chapter II, Section 1 of the Regulation is entitled 'General provisions'.
[49] cf *Canada Trust Co v Stolzenberg (No 2)* [2002] 1 AC 1.
[50] See *Young v Anglo American South Africa Ltd* [2014] EWCA Civ 1130.

To ascertain whether a *trust* is domiciled in the United Kingdom, Article 63(3) provides that the court will apply the law of the United Kingdom. Accordingly, a trust is domiciled in England if English law is that with which the trust has its closest and most real connection.[51] It is never necessary to determine whether a trust is domiciled in another Member State, for no jurisdictional rule is formulated on this basis.

C. REGULATION JURISDICTION: THE DETAIL

Where proceedings fall within the domain of the Regulation, and the jurisdiction of the court is therefore Regulation jurisdiction, the individual rules have a natural hierarchy which is not immediately apparent from the design of the Regulation itself. To obtain a reliable determination whether the court has Regulation jurisdiction, it is prudent to examine the provisions of the Regulation in the order in which they are set out below.

1. EXCLUSIVE JURISDICTION: ARTICLE 24

Article 24 of the recast Regulation[52] gives exclusive jurisdiction, regardless[53] of domicile, to the courts of a Member State, in five areas: in the rare case where it would confer exclusive jurisdiction on the courts of two Member States, Article 31 provides that the first such court seised has exclusive jurisdiction alone. Where Article 24 confers exclusive jurisdiction on a court, no other court has jurisdiction, even if both parties purport to submit to it; and a judgment which conflicts with Article 24 must, on application, be refused recognition.[54] For Article 24 to be engaged, the material connection must be to a Member State. If the land, or public register etc, is in a non-Member State, Article 24 has no application; the relevant question is whether the Regulation permits a court with jurisdiction under some other Article to decline it by reference to the connection to a non-Member State. The issue is not straightforward, and is considered below.

---

[51] 2001 Order, Sch 1, para 12, re-enacting Civil Jurisdiction and Judgments Act 1982, s 45.
[52] Section 6 of Chapter II.
[53] That is to say, whether the defendant is domiciled in any Member State or none.
[54] Article 45.

Article 24(1) covers proceedings which have as their principal[55] object rights *in rem* in, or tenancies of, immovable property in a Member State, giving exclusive jurisdiction to the state where the land is situated. To this two ancillary rules are added. First, where the proceedings have as their object a tenancy of immovable property concluded for temporary private use for no more than six consecutive months, Article 24(1) provides that the courts of the Member State in which the defendant is domiciled also[56] have exclusive jurisdiction, if the tenant is a natural person and landlord and tenant are domiciled in the same Member State: this is useful if the dispute is a small one concerned with a holiday letting in another Member State. Secondly, Article 8(4) provides for an associated contractual action to be combined with the action *in rem* against the same defendant, which is useful in a mortgage action.

It is not enough that the proceedings concern or are even fought over a tenancy, or have legal title to land as their prize. The words 'have as their object' require the claim[57] to be founded on legal title and to be concerned with the extent, content, ownership, or possession of land, rather than having a looser or a descriptive association.[58] Many Member States treat the determination of legal title to land as a matter for only the courts of the *situs*; and in any event, land law, and especially tenancy law, tends to be complicated and best left to local courts. As the Article derogates from the jurisdiction of the defendant's domicile, it will be interpreted restrictively. This last point has been taken to mean that proceedings in which a tenancy forms only part of the background to the dispute, or disputes in which occupation rights comprise a minor part of a more complex contract, such as an all-inclusive holiday[59] or timeshare club membership,[60] do not come under Article 24(1). Likewise, claims to enforce obligations contained in or associated with leases but which are not themselves peculiar to tenancies, such as a covenant to pay for the business goodwill in a lease of commercial premises,[61] fall outside it as well. By contrast, a claim in respect of unpaid rent or utility charges,[62] or for the cost of cleaning up behind departing tenants who made a ruin of the

---

[55] This word does not appear in the text of the Article, but was read in: Case C–280/90 *Hacker v Euro-Relais GmbH* [1992] ECR I–1111, and has not since been questioned.
[56] Joint exclusive jurisdiction may occasion the use of Art 31.
[57] And in principle it is the claim which determines the application of the Article.
[58] Case C–343/04 *ČEZ v Land Oberösterreich* [2006] ECR I–4557.
[59] Case C–280/90 *Hacker v Euro-Relais GmbH* [1992] ECR I–1111.
[60] Case C–73/04 *Klein v Rhodos Management Ltd* [2005] ECR I–8667.
[61] Case 73/77 *Sanders v Van der Putte* [1977] ECR 2383.
[62] Case 241/83 *Rösler v Rottwinkel* [1985] ECR 99.

premises,[63] are founded on obligations naturally inherent in a tenancy, and no matter how narrow the interpretation of Article 24(1), these fall within it.

Proceedings have been held to have rights *in rem* as their object where they seek a judicial partition of land held in co-ownership prior to sale,[64] or seek to annul another's option to purchase the land,[65] as in each case the very decision of the court will determine the title of the proprietor and, by being recorded on the land register, will directly affect third parties. But proceedings do not 'have as their object rights *in rem*' if the claimant does not assert that he is already legal proprietor who is suing as such but claims, for example as contractual purchaser, to acquire legal ownership[66] or claims, for example, as beneficiary under a resulting trust of the land already to be equitable owner of the land: proceedings founded on personal obligations are not *in rem*, even though the position of third parties may be affected. The early conclusion of the Court[67] that a beneficiary under a resulting trust has only an interest *in personam* against the trustee, not one *in rem* against any holder of legal title, may pay insufficient attention to the equitable doctrine of notice;[68] and its further holding that proceedings do not have a right *in rem* as their object when brought to acquire legal title from a resulting trustee is unconvincing: if an action brought to obtain a conveyance of legal title does not have legal title as its object, what on earth is the end it has in view?[69] However, if proceedings to dissolve a personal obligation relating to land are not within the Article,[70] proceedings to enforce one will not be either; and however that may be, the result of the trusts case, if not its reasoning, can be defended from two very different points of view. Where the substantive law which the court will apply is not specifically land law or tenancy law, there is no pragmatic need to engage Article 24(1), for the same principles would apply in a claim made against the trustee-owner of a yacht or of a parcel of shares. Moreover, the common law drew an analogous jurisdictional distinction

---

[63] Case C–8/98 *Dansommer A/S v Götz* [2000] ECR I–393.

[64] Case C–605/14 *Komu v Komu* EU:C:2015:833.

[65] Case C–438/12 *Weber v Weber* EU:C:2014:212, [2015] Ch 140.

[66] Or as contractual seller, seeking rescission of unperformed contract of sale: Case C–518/98 *Gaillard v Chekili* [2001] ECR I–2771, or as the donor seeking rescission against the donee of a contract of gift: Case C–417/15 *Schmidt v Schmidt* EU:C:2016:881, [2017] ILPr 127.

[67] Case C–294/92 *Webb v Webb* [1994] ECR I–1717.

[68] The interest of the beneficiary can be enforced against all the world except the *bona fide* purchaser for value without notice; it is unreal to see this as a *mere* right *in personam*.

[69] Not least because it is brought on the basis that the claimant beneficiary does have pre-existing (and exclusive) equitable title.

[70] This is not easy to square with Case C–438/12 *Weber v Weber* EU:C:2014:212, [2015] Ch 140, but in that case the point does not appear to have been properly addressed.

between determining legal title to foreign land, which it had no power to do, and enforcing a contract or other equity between the parties concerning foreign land, which it would.[71] This just goes to illustrate the manner in which the various policies behind Article 24(1), all sensible in themselves, can collide, and that their clinical reconciliation is not always possible.

Article 24(2) covers proceedings which have as their object the validity of the constitution, the dissolution or winding up of companies, or the decisions of their organs: exclusive jurisdiction is given to the Member State of the seat of the company. But where a company defends a contractual claim by pleading that it lacked capacity to bind itself to the contract, or that a corporate officer acted without proper authority, the Article does not apply: it does not apply to the claim, and a defence to liability cannot determine the (principal) object of the proceedings. Likewise, where the company brings pre-emptive proceedings for a declaration that it is not contractually liable to an opponent who has not yet issued his claim, relying on the absence of corporate capacity to avoid contractual liability, the Article will not apply, for the principal dispute is still contractual, and the corporate issue merely an incidental issue or a natural defence to it.[72]

Article 24(3) gives exclusive jurisdiction to the Member State in which a public register is kept if the proceedings have as their object the validity of an entry in that register. An action to alter an existing entry on a land register will be covered; and there is no rational reason to exclude any action which seeks the amendment of an entry in such a register, even if the court does not have exclusive jurisdiction over the claim (for example, for the rescission of a contract of gift on the ground of incapacity or undue influence[73]) which is advanced as the reason to rectify the register of title.

Article 24(4) works slightly differently. It gives exclusive jurisdiction to the Member State in which a patent or trade mark is registered or deposited if the proceedings have as their object the registration or validity of that right. A straightforward claim alleging infringement will not fall within the Article, but where, as frequently happens, the validity of the patent said to be infringed is challenged by way of defence to the allegation, the court seised with the infringement claim is forbidden to enter upon the question of

---

[71] *Penn v Baltimore* (1750) 1 Ves Sen 444.
[72] Case C–144/10 *BVG v JP Morgan Chase Bank NA* [2011] ECR I–3961; *Akçil v Koza Ltd* [2019] UKSC 40.
[73] Case C–417/15 *Schmidt v Schmidt* EU:C:2016:881, [2017] ILPr 127 (in fact, the title claim was held to fall under Article 24(1), but the effect is identical).

validity:[74] here, therefore, the raising of a defence can trigger the application of the Article. It seems to follow that the infringement proceedings have to be stayed pending the other court's ruling on validity unless it is argued that the question of validity is in fact the principal issue in the proceedings, with the consequence that Article 27 justifies the court with exclusive jurisdiction over the validity proceedings taking jurisdiction over the rest of the action as though it was ancillary to the principal issue.

Article 24(5) gives exclusive jurisdiction to the Member State in which a judgment from a[75] Member State is being enforced if the proceedings are concerned with its enforcement. There must have been a judgment: proceedings which seek to pave the way for enforcing a prospective judgment, such as by obtaining a freezing injunction, are outside the Article.[76] On the other hand, a court which makes orders by way of enforcing its own judgment should not need to rely on Article 24(5), as its original jurisdiction continues seamlessly to allow it to make post-judgment orders.

2. JURISDICTION BY APPEARANCE: ARTICLE 26

Unless Article 24 applies, the court before which the defendant enters an appearance has jurisdiction by virtue of that appearance, according to Article 26.[77] If there was a prior agreement on jurisdiction for a different court, it will be considered to have been tacitly varied.[78] However, if the appearance was entered to contest the jurisdiction of the court, the appearance will not confer jurisdiction under this rule. One of the bedrock principles of the Regulation is that a defendant must be allowed to appear, without prejudice, to argue for its correct application to his case, and that this must be done *in limine litis* rather than by objecting to recognition of the judgment after the event. So long as he does what is called for to contest the jurisdiction at the first opportunity allowed by the procedural law of the court, he will not surrender this jurisdictional protection if he is required in practice to file his defence to the merits of the claim at the same time.[79] By contrast, if he takes a clear

---

[74] Case C–4/03 *Gesellschaft für Antriebstechnik mbH & Co KG v Lamellen- und Kupplungsbau Beteiligungs KG* [2006] ECR I–6509.
[75] Not 'another'.
[76] Case C–261/90 *Reichert v Dresdner Bank (No 2)* [1992] ECR I–2149.
[77] Section 7 of Chapter II.
[78] Case C–150/80 *Elefanten Schuh GmbH v Jacqmain* [1981] ECR 1671.
[79] Case C–433/16 *BMW AG v Acacia srl* EU:C:2017:550.

step towards defending the claim on the merits, which was not in this sense required of him, he will have stepped out from beneath the cloak of jurisdictional invisibility which Article 26 offered him.[80] Of course, if the defendant ignores the proceedings, Article 26 cannot apply, even if the procedural law of the national court would consider this to be silent or tacit acceptance of its jurisdiction. Article 26 requires an appearance.[81]

3. PROTECTIVE JURISDICTION: ARTICLES 10–23

Where disputes arise from insurance contracts,[82] certain consumer contracts,[83] or individual contracts of employment,[84] there is such a risk of there being inequality between the parties that the insured or policyholder, consumer, and employee need jurisdictional advantages[85] if their contractual rights are in practice going to be enforceable. The three specific Sections of Chapter II conform to a template according to which the policyholder,[86] consumer, or employee has the option of suing the insurer, professional, or employer where the latter is domiciled, but also of suing in his 'own' Member State: for insureds and consumers, that is where he is domiciled; for employees it is where the work is habitually done.[87] Proceedings against the insured/policyholder, consumer, or employee must, however,[88] be brought in the courts of their domicile. To prevent the emasculation of this jurisdictional advantage, jurisdiction agreements are mutually binding only entered

---

[80]   cf (in a case not governed by the Regulation) *Marc Rich & Co AG v Soc Italiana Impianti PA* [1992] 2 Lloyd's Rep 624 (CA).

[81]   Case C–464/18 *ZX v Ryanair DAC* EU:C:2019:311 [2019] 1 WLR 4202.

[82]   Articles 10–16; Section 3 of Chapter II.

[83]   Articles 17–19; Section 4 of Chapter II.

[84]   Articles 20–23; Section 5 of Chapter II.

[85]   In many respects it would make sense to refer to these as privileges, but as they may not be renounced by the weaker party if sued in the court which is given such jurisdiction, the terminology of 'jurisdictional privilege' is not quite right. And see *Merinson v Yukos International BV* [2019] EWCA Civ 830 [39]. The provisions which give jurisdictional advantage to English consumers and employees have been copied and pasted into the Civil Jurisdiction and Judgments Act 1982, to take effect as primary rules of English jurisdiction after the United Kingdom leaves the European Union: SI 2019/479, reg 26 inserting ss 15A–E into the 1982 Act.

[86]   In addition to those general rules described in the text there is specific provision for co-insurance (Art 11(1)(c)), liability insurance or insurance of immovables (Art 12), direct actions by an injured party against an insurer (Art 13), joinder of parties (Art 13), and counterclaims (Art 14). Jurisdiction agreements are regulated by Arts 15 and 16.

[87]   As one might picture it, where the employment (rather than the employee) is at home. See Case C–168/16 *Nogueira v Crewlink Ireland Ltd* EU:C:2017:688, [2018] ICR 344.

[88]   Whether they like it or not: *Merinson v Yukos International BV* [2019] EWCA Civ 830 [39].

into after the dispute arose;[89] if entered before then, they are effective only if they are non-exclusive, widening the choice of courts open to the insured/ policyholder,[90] consumer,[91] or employee.[92] The original position was that where the insurer, supplier, or employer neither had, nor was deemed by reason of his having a branch or agency to have had, a domicile in a Member State, the residual Regulation jurisdiction provided for by Article 6 would apply to claims against it;[93] but the recast Regulation provides that a consumer or employee who is domiciled in a Member State may sue the professional or the employer in that Member State regardless of the domicile of the professional or employer. And to reinforce the scheme, a judgment which violates these rules will on application be denied recognition.

The general view is that these rules do not depend for their availability on proof of a relationship of actual inequality: this may have contributed to the view that they are to be construed restrictively.[94] However, if it is inherent in being an employee that one is subordinate to the employer, very mighty 'employees', whose workplace autonomy is pretty much untrammelled, will not count as employees for the purpose of these provisions.[95] Whether a similarly powerful 'consumer' loses the advantage which she does not need if she is to protect her rights has yet to be finally decided.[96]

More particularly, the *insurance* provisions do not apply to reinsurance, which is not a relationship of inherent inequality,[97] but they do apply to direct actions by the injured party against the insurer.[98] The restrictions on jurisdiction agreements are relaxed in the cases of marine insurance and in the case of large risks.[99]

A *consumer* contract is one in which an individual concludes the contract for a purpose which is for all practical purposes wholly[100] outside her

---

[89] For the difficulty in pinpointing when, precisely, that is, see *Merinson v Yukos International BV* [2019] EWCA Civ 830.

[90] Article 15.

[91] Article 19.

[92] Article 23; Case C–154/11 *Mahamdia v Algeria* EU:C:2012:491, [2013] ICR 1.

[93] Case C–412/98 *Universal General Insurance Co v Groupe Josi Reinsurance Co SA* [2000] ECR I–5925.

[94] Case C–464/01 *Gruber v BayWa AG* [2005] ECR I–439.

[95] Case C–603/17 *Bosworth v Arcadia Petroleum Ltd* EU:C:2019:310.

[96] *Ang v Reliantco Investments Ltd* [2019] EWHC 879 (Comm), [2019] 3 WLR 161.

[97] Case C–412/98 *Universal General Insurance Co v Groupe Josi Reinsurance Co SA* [2000] ECR I–5925.

[98] Article 13(2). In England this will most commonly arise under the Third Parties (Rights Against Insurers) Act 2010.

[99] Articles 13(5) and 14.

[100] Case C–464/01 *Gruber v BayWa AG* [2005] ECR I–439.

trade or profession and is one which in general secures the individual's needs in terms of private consumption:[101] this appears to make contracts to buy clothes, computers, cars, mobile telephones, and so on, for work and non-work purposes, difficult to fit in. So far, at least, there is no automatic exclusion of investment or other middle-class contracts so long as they otherwise satisfy the definition;[102] a jurisdictional rule which aimed to differentiate between vulnerable consumers and self-reliant consumers would be tricky, even if justifiable by reference to the purpose of the rule.[103] Within that general definition, the types of consumer contracts actually covered by Section 4 of Chapter II are more restrictive than might be expected: Article 17(1) applies only to (a) a contract for the sale of goods on instalment credit terms, or (b) a contract for a loan repayable by instalments, or other credit, made to finance the sale of goods, or (c) a contract concluded with a person who pursues commercial or professional activities in the Member State of the consumer's domicile or, by any means, directs such activities to that Member State or to several states including that Member State, the contract falling within the scope of such activities. Point (c) will be the most significant. It replaced an earlier version which was focused on targeted invitations or advertising, but which was probably too narrow in scope. The current rule is liable to apply to purchases made by computer or smart phone, though whether it does actually apply in a given case will depend on its being shown that the trader was evidently minded to contract with consumers hailing from the Member State in question. This tricky issue is assessed by looking at the language used on the website, indications such as the domain name, telephone numbers given with or without an international dialling code, the currency of dealing, points of departure (where the contract is a holiday contract, for example) and itinerary, and so forth: in short, the question may be whether a reasonable man, looking at the external appearance of the website, would conclude that the trader was open to dealing with, inter alia, consumers in the

---

[101] Case C–269/95 *Benincasa v Dentalkit Srl* [1997] ECR I–3767; and see also Case C–99/96 *Mietz v Intership Yachting Sneek BV* [1999] ECR I–2277.

[102] Case C–498/16 *Schrems v Facebook Ireland Ltd* EU:C:2018:37, [2018] 1 WLR 4343. If the consumer has assigned his rights to a professional, the jurisdictional protection is lost for there is nothing to protect: Case C–89/91 *Shearson Lehmann Hutton v TVB* [1993] ECR I–139; Case C–498/16 *Schrems v Facebook Ireland Ltd* EU:C:2018:37, [2018] 1 WLR 4343; likewise in insurance: Case C–106/17 *Hofsoe v Landwirtschaftlicher Versicherungsverein Münster AG* EU:C:2018:50.

[103] Though something along these lines is done in the case of 'employees': Case C–603/17 *Bosworth v Arcadia Petroleum Ltd* EU:C:2019:310.

Member State in question. The question will be very fact specific. The bare fact that a website is accessible by the consumer may not be enough to satisfy the rule.[104] It is not, however, a requirement that the contract actually be concluded at a distance, so long as the steps leading up to it satisfy the requirements of Article 17(1)(c).[105]

The *employment* contract provisions now found in Section 5 developed more slowly than the others, but they now protect workers from some of the inevitable inequalities arising from relationships governed by contracts which are rarely the result of free and equal negotiation. If the relationship between them is sufficiently hierarchical, which means that the individual is sufficiently subordinate to count as an employee,[106] then where the proceedings relate to the employment contract the employee may sue where her employer is domiciled or in the Member State in which the worker habitually carries out her work, so as to secure the benefits of local employment law; but the employer must sue in the employee's domiciliary court. Attempts by the employer[107] to formulate the claim as alleging an ordinary civil wrong, which just happens to be brought against a wrongdoer who happens to be an employee, should be repelled, as Section 5 is intended to be exhaustive;[108] and if an employer could annul the employee's jurisdictional protections by the simple expedient of accusing her of being a common thief, the potential for abuse is obvious. Where the employment involves duties in more Member States than one, jurisdiction is sorted out on a common sense, centre-of-gravity, basis, which works well enough in most cases.[109]

4. JURISDICTION AGREEMENTS: ARTICLE 25

Apart from the cases mentioned above in which their effect is excluded or restricted, agreements for jurisdiction for the courts of a Member State are

---

[104] Joined Cases C–585/08 *Pammer v Reederei Karl Schluter GmbH & Co KG* and C–144/09 *Hotel Alpenhof GmbH v Heller* [2010] ECR I–12527.

[105] Case C–190/11 *Mühlleitner v Yusufi* EU:C:2012:542; Case C–218/12 *Emrek v Sabranovic* EU:C:2013:666.

[106] Case C–603/17 *Bosworth v Arcadia Petroleum Ltd* EU:C:2019:310.

[107] For the complications which arise when the employer's side comprises a group of companies, see *Cunico Resources NV v Daskalakis* [2019] EWHC 57 (Comm).

[108] Case C–47/14 *Holterman Ferho Exploitatie BV v Spies von Büllesheim* EU:C:2015:574, [2016] ICR 90.

[109] Case C–47/14 *Holterman Ferho Exploitatie BV v Spies von Büllesheim* EU:C:2015:574, [2016] ICR 90.

given effect by Article 25.[110] The domicile of the parties to the agreement is no longer relevant at all.[111] A compliant agreement must be respected: by the court designated and by the courts whose jurisdiction is excluded, for the agreement serves to prorogate and derogate. By contrast with the approach taken by the common law, there is no discretion to override a valid jurisdiction agreement, say on grounds of overall trial convenience.[112] An agreement to confer jurisdiction on the courts of the United Kingdom is effective so far as the Regulation is concerned, but raises some practical difficulties: it probably gives jurisdiction to the courts in any part of the United Kingdom unless it can be construed as being more particular than first appears.[113] An agreement nominating the courts of two Member States should be effective;[114] one which is construed as giving non-exclusive jurisdiction to a court will do exactly what it says.[115] But an agreement for the courts of a non-Member State is outside Article 25, not least because the Regulation cannot bind such a court to accept jurisdiction. For them, the relevant question is whether a court with jurisdiction under some other provision of the Regulation may decline it in favour of an agreed-to court of a non-Member State. The issue is considered below.[116]

The effect of the agreement, when made, is to accept as exclusive[117] the jurisdiction of a court which would not otherwise have such jurisdiction, and to relinquish access to the jurisdiction which otherwise would be applicable. Given its significance, therefore, this agreement must be in writing or evidenced in writing, which now includes electronic means which provide a durable record in writing.[118] It will not be enough to point to a printed term in standard conditions of business unless the party to be bound has written his agreement to it, because it is to the agreement, not the term which is being

---

[110] Section 7 of Chapter II.

[111] By contrast with the corresponding provisions of the Brussels Convention, Lugano Convention, and original Brussels I Regulation, which required one of the parties to be domiciled in a Member State.

[112] *Hough v P&O Containers Ltd* [1999] QB 834.

[113] cf *The Komninos S* [1991] 1 Lloyd's Rep 370 (CA).

[114] Case 23/78 *Meeth v Glacetal Sàrl* [1978] ECR 2133 (but each court had exclusive jurisdiction over particular actions; there was no overlapping of competences).

[115] Article 25(1).

[116] At p91.

[117] Unless the agreement is expressed to be non-exclusive, in which case it takes effect differently but still according to its terms.

[118] This will include a printed or printable message by e-mail. For agreement by clicking an electronic button (generally compliant with Article 25), see Case C–322/14 *El Majdoub v CarsOnTheWeb.Deutschland GmbH* EU:C:2015:334, [2015] 1 WLR 3986.

agreed to, to which the requirement of writing is directed.[119] Alternatively, it may be in a form which accords with the parties' established practice, or in a form which is well known to accord with international trade usage of which the parties were or should have been aware; a settled course of dealing or a trade usage will establish a binding form.

There is an inevitable tension between the desire to prevent sharp practice by unbending application of the rules on form, and awareness that this may be inappropriate where both parties knew perfectly well that they were dealing on terms which were intended to include a jurisdiction agreement. Though the Court has generally insisted on strict application of these formalities,[120] it has also endorsed a more flexible approach where a party pleading the formal invalidity would seem to be doing so in bad faith.[121] More radically, a shareholder was held to be bound by a jurisdiction agreement contained in the company's constitution on the ground that he knew or had the means of knowledge of it, and had assented to be bound by his becoming a shareholder:[122] how far this principle may extend remains to be seen, but it probably does not apply to ordinary bilateral contracts with small print on the back page, even if the customer has a copy of the document in his possession.

If it meets the requirements of Article 25, an agreement *derogating* from the jurisdiction of a court may not be objected to on the ground that it fails to comply with some provision, whether as to form[123] or substance,[124] of national law which would otherwise prevent its being given effect. A contention that the substantive contract of which the agreement on jurisdiction may be a term is ineffective or void is irrelevant to the validity of the jurisdiction agreement, not least because the latter is considered to be distinct from the substantive contract to which it relates.[125] Likewise, an agreement *prorogating* the jurisdiction of a court which meets the requirements of Article 25 should

---

[119] Case 24/76 *Estasis Salotti v RÜWA Polstereimaschinen GmbH* [1976] ECR 1831; Case C–366/13 *Profit Investment Sim SpA v Ossi* EU:C:2016:282, [2016] 1 WLR 3832.

[120] Case 24/76 *Estasis Salotti v RÜWA* [1976] ECR 1831, reiterated in Case C–105/95 *MSG v Les Gravières Rhénanes Sàrl* [1997] ECR I–911.

[121] Case 221/84 *Berghofer v ASA SA* [1985] ECR 2699; Case 313/85 *Iveco Fiat v Van Hool* [1986] ECR 3337 (previous course of dealing).

[122] Case C–214/89 *Powell Duffryn plc v Petereit* [1992] ECR I–1745.

[123] Case 150/80 *Elefanten Schuh GmbH v Jacqmain* [1981] ECR 1671 (wrong language).

[124] Case 25/79 *Sanicentral GmbH v Collin* [1979] ECR 3423 (ousting the jurisdiction of the local employment tribunal). The point is of general importance and application and is not just confined to Article 25 cases: Case C–9/12 *Corman-Collins SA v La Maison du Whisky SA* EU:C:2013:860, [2014] QB 431.

[125] Case C–269/95 *Benincasa v Dentalkit Srl* [1997] ECR I–3767.

not be open to objection that it fails to comply with some provision of the law of the court chosen (say, the language of the agreement, or the prominence of the typeface), either. But the recast Regulation now says that if the agreement is 'null and void' under the law[126] of the court prorogated the agreement cannot have effect; the meaning of this unhelpful condition is not clear. It will presumably mean, for example, that an agreement for a specialist national court may be treated as void if that court has no power under its own law to entertain the dispute; but if it is intended to allow a challenge to be made on the ground that there was fraud or misrepresentation[127] in procuring the agreement of the party to be bound, as a result of which the agreement is voidable at his option, it would open the door to all manner of chicanery.

Where written consent was furnished by original contracting parties, but the proceedings now involve another who has been inserted into the legal relationship, it is necessary to distinguish two cases. If the third party has succeeded as a matter of law to the contractual position of one of the parties, as under a bill of lading[128] which is designed to be negotiable and to be taken over by third parties,[129] or as an insurer subrogated to the position of his insured,[130] he may be held, by operation of law, to the existing agreement on jurisdiction, even though the written and effective consent was not his own.[131] By contrast, where a third party acquires rights or obligations under a contract otherwise than by means of succession to the position of another under a document designed to have that effect, he can be bound to a prior agreement on jurisdiction only by making his own act of agreement.[132] That tells us something important about what 'agreement', in this context, is and is not. It suggests that we should interpret Article 25 as applying where one party tells another, who consents to it, that he accepts the jurisdiction of a court which would not otherwise have it, and gives up the privilege of being sued only in another court. If that is right, it means that jurisdiction agreements in the context of the Regulation operate quite differently from the way they function within the framework of the common law. On this view, and

---

[126] Including private international law.

[127] Neither of which makes an agreement void (as very distinct from voidable) as a matter or English law.

[128] Case 71/83 *The Tilly Russ* [1984] ECR 2417.

[129] Case C–366/13 *Profit Investment Sim SpA v Ossi* EU:C:2016:282, [2016] 1 WLR 3832.

[130] *Airbus SAS v Generali Italia SpA* [2019] EWCA Civ 805.

[131] Case C–387/98 *Coreck Maritime GmbH v Handelsveem BV* [2000] ECR I–9337; Case C–366/13 *Profit Investment Sim SpA v Ossi* EU:C:2016:282, [2016] 1 WLR 3832.

[132] Case C–112/03 *Soc Financière & Industrielle de Peloux v Soc AXA Belgium* [2005] ECR I–3707.

as a matter of common sense, there is no particular need for an agreement to waive or renounce the general jurisdictional rule of Article 4 to be contained in a contract; there is no need to assess that party's agreement to the jurisdiction of another court in contractual terms. It just requires a sufficiently formal, serious, communication. The end result is that Article 25 deals with agreements (created by writing) about jurisdiction made before proceedings are commenced, and Article 26 with jurisdictional agreements (created by conduct) after the writ is served; and that both belong, as they are found, in a Section of the Regulation headed 'Prorogation of Jurisdiction'. None of this calls for, still less is helped by, forcing the analysis into a contractual framework.

This may be the reason why the European Court had insisted, long before the clarification now appearing in Article 25, that the validity or invalidity of the substantive contract is irrelevant to the application of Article 25. It may also be why compliance with the formality rules set out in Article 25 is all the validation, or confirmation, which a defendant's agreement to accept the jurisdiction of a court requires. Of course, if a defendant claims that his writing was procured by improper means, or that the writing is not his, a forgery, a court must be allowed to find that he did not agree in writing to jurisdiction of the named court. An autonomous conception of what amounts to a party's agreement will be sufficient for the task.

The jurisdiction given by Article 25 is exclusive unless the agreement says otherwise, but this 'exclusivity' is less potent than that conferred by Article 24. For example, a judgment which violates Article 25 may not be refused recognition.[133] For many years English courts struggled with that idea, and sought instead to treat jurisdiction agreements as contractual obligations which somehow overrode the rest of the Convention or Regulation, were liable to be reinforced with injunctions and the threat of being in contempt of court, and so on. All this has now ceased. Part of the motivation for this well-intentioned, but tragically misguided, approach was that a party who sought to undermine an agreement on jurisdiction, which they knew jolly well they had made, might start proceedings—referred to as 'torpedo' proceedings—before the courts of another Member State[134] and, by ensuring that these subversive proceedings made as slow progress as possible, delay[135] for years the

---

[133] Article 45 makes no reference to Section 7 of Chapter II.

[134] Italy was favoured as the legal land that time forgot. The nomenclature of the 'Italian torpedo' was devised by an Italian lawyer, though 'Italian torpor' would perhaps have been more apt.

[135] By reason of the *lis pendens* rule now in Art 29.

bringing of proceedings before the prorogated court. This abuse[136] was dealt with when the recast Regulation made a specific adjustment to the first-seised rule of priority in favour of the apparently-prorogated court;[137] and the result is that jurisdictional decisions in the area of Article 25 are now more likely to be taken by the designated court. All in all it is a fairly satisfactory outcome; but the distraction caused by false analogies with the common law approach to contractual terms providing for the jurisdiction of courts took longer to resolve than perhaps it should have.

5. GENERAL JURISDICTION: ARTICLE 4

If none of the provisions examined so far establishes or denies the jurisdiction of the court, the rule in Article 4,[138] that general jurisdiction exists where or wherever the defendant has a domicile, will apply. 'General jurisdiction' is not limited by reference to its subject matter, or by the form of the action. The definition of domicile in the United Kingdom, and in England, has been mentioned in Section (B) above. It is striking that although this is always said to be the fundamental rule on which the rest of the Regulation is constructed,[139] its place in the hierarchy of rules is relatively low.

6. SPECIAL JURISDICTION: ARTICLES 7–9

If none of the provisions examined so far gives the court jurisdiction, the defendant will have a domicile somewhere other than the United Kingdom. Articles 7 to 9[140] confer special jurisdiction over defendants who are domiciled in another Member State. Article 7 responds at some level to a sense of *forum conveniens*, though if jurisdiction is justified by the wording of Article 7 it is not open to challenge by showing that the court is, in the particular case, not a *forum conveniens*: the relevance of *forum conveniens* was spent when the Article was drafted. Article 8 deals with some forms of multipartite litigation, including a limited rule about jurisdiction by joinder; and

---

[136] Case C–116/02 *Erich Gasser GmbH v Misat srl* [2003] ECR I–14693 is the exemplary case.
[137] Article 31(2)–(4).
[138] Section 1 of Chapter II.
[139] See, for example, Case C–9/12 *Corman-Collins SA v La Maison du Whisky SA* EU:C:2013:860, [2014] QB 431.
[140] Section 2 of Chapter II.

Article 9 with proceedings to limit liability in maritime claims. Article 7 gives special jurisdiction to the courts for a place, as distinct from the courts of a Member State: it determines local as well as international jurisdiction, and when it has done that, no more remains to be done. In other words, if it gives jurisdiction to the English courts, there is no power to stay on the ground that the Scottish courts are *forum conveniens*.

By far the most important provisions are Articles 7(1) and 7(2), which provide respectively for special jurisdiction over defendants domiciled in another Member State in matters relating to a contract and in matters relating to tort. The European Court has clearly established that these two categories of special jurisdiction are comprehensive (in that they cover all cases of liability), mutually exclusive (in that they do not overlap), and autonomous in their operation (in that the nature of the civil liability arising must be evaluated independently of the way it is analysed in national law). Given the enormous number of types of claim which may come within the scope of these two provisions, one sees that the Court has set itself a truly challenging task. Its doing so is, however, justified by reference to the principle of legal certainty.

(a) Matters relating to a contract: Article 7(1)

In matters relating to a contract, Article 7(1)(a) gives special jurisdiction to the courts for the place of performance[141] of the obligation in question.

A matter does not relate to a contract for the purpose of this jurisdictional rule unless it involves an obligation freely entered into with regard to another,[142] but if it does so it is irrelevant that the matter might not be regarded as substantively contractual by a court applying its national law. The contract does not need to be express: Article 7(1) will apply even though the contract is implied in nature, or tacit in origin.[143] Most cases are obvious, of course; but contract is a large idea, with a substantial periphery. A claim to enforce the rules of a club against a member,[144] or the relationship between shareholder and company,[145] or between a flat-owner and the management association,[146] is contractual even if a national law may consider its law of

---

[141] The French text renders this as the place where the obligation was or should have been performed, and this is the sense in which it must be understood.

[142] Case C–26/91 *Soc Jakob Handte GmbH v Soc Traitements Mécano-chimiques des Surfaces* [1992] ECR I–3967; Case C–25/18 *Kerr v Postnov* EU:C:2019:376.

[143] Case C–196/15 *Granarolo SpA v Ambrosi Emmi France SA* EU:C:2016:559.

[144] Case 34/82 *Martin Peters Bauunternehmung GmbH v Zuid Nederlandse AV* [1983] ECR 987.

[145] Case C–214/89 *Powell Duffryn plc v Petereit* [1992] ECR I–1745.

[146] Case C–25/18 *Kerr v Postnov* EU:C:2019:376.

associations or of companies to be distinct from its law of contract. A claim by a sub-buyer against a manufacturer is on the face of it not contractual, even if it is regarded as contractual under national law,[147] though if the sub-buyer—or anyone else—has taken an express assignment of the benefit of the contract of sale, or if the contract expressly contemplates that a third party will have direct rights under it,[148] it will surely be otherwise. It remains to be decided whether it covers a claim by someone who obtained negligent advice from another who had voluntarily assumed responsibility for that advice and whose liability in English law is regarded as non-contractual only because of the absence of consideration.[149]

Less obviously, perhaps, it applies also to a claim for contribution or re-imbursement made by a joint debtor, who has discharged their liability to a third party, against the other debtor who has benefited from it.[150] Least obviously, perhaps, if a claimant, party to a contract, brings proceedings against a third party who has received assets from the other contracting party, trans-ferred in potential fraud of the claimant,[151] it has been held that the matter is still one which relates to the original contract, even though the defendant was not privy to it. Taken by themselves, these decisions may suggest that 'relating to a contract' should be understood as 'relating to or indissociably linked to a contract'.[152] That may be sensible and may not be wholly wrong:[153] it may reflect the interlaced nature of modern commercial arrangements. Indeed, something similar has been foreshadowed in consumer[154] and

---

[147] Case C–26/91 *Soc Jakob Handte GmbH v Soc Traîtements Mécano-chimiques des Surfaces* [1992] ECR I–3967.

[148] By the Contracts (Rights of Third Parties) Act 1999 or foreign law mechanism analogous to it.

[149] Under the principle in *Hedley Byrne & Co v Heller & Partners* [1964] AC 465.

[150] Case C–249/16 *Kareda v Benkö* EU:C:2017:472, [2018] QB 445. This, as well as Case C–366/13 *Profit Investment Sim SpA v Ossi* EU:C:2016:282, [2016] 1 WLR 3832 and Case C–337/17 *Feniks sp zoo v Azteca Products and Services SL* EU:C:2018:805, may be taken to show that 'tidying-up' claims closely associated with contracts will be liable to fall within Art 7(1), even if the precise claim, considered out of its context, does not so clearly do so.

[151] Described in many systems as the *actio Pauliana*. See Case C–337/17 *Feniks sp zoo v Azteca Products and Services SL* EU:C:2018:805. The decision is controversial, especially when viewed from the perspective of the defendant to the proceedings.

[152] See also C–274/16 *flightright GmbH v Air Nostrum Lineas Aéreas de Mediterráneo SA* EU:C:2018:160, [2018] QB 1268 (claims arising from connecting flight with third company ar-ranged by contracted airline within Art 7(1)).

[153] In Case 189/87 *Kalfelis v Bankhaus Schröder, Münchmeyer, Hengst & Co* [1988] ECR 5565, the Advocate-General Darmon proposed that where there was a contract, associated matters should be 'channelled' into its special jurisdiction. His suggestion was not taken up, but its time may now have come.

[154] Case C–478/12 *Maletic v lastminute.com GmbH* EU:C:2013:735, [2014] QB 424.

employment[155] contexts. But it is bound to cause doubt. A claim against a defendant who has induced a party to break his contract with the claimant does not relate to a contract but falls within Article 7(2).[156] Neither does it when A makes a contract with B, and C makes a derivative contract with B in reliance on statements published by A: C's claim against A is not a matter relating to a contract, even though the contract between A and B will be an essential part of the narrative.[157] The edges of the law are evidently still being mapped.

The fact that the validity of the contract is disputed does not prevent the application of the Article,[158] even if it is the claimant who is asserting, contrary to the submission of the defendant, that an alleged contract is ineffective or has been rescinded for misrepresentation, non-disclosure, or duress:[159] the Article does not say 'in proceedings to enforce a contract', or anything like that. However, once the issue of special jurisdiction has been settled, the national court may apply its own substantive law, including its conflicts rules, to determine the merits of the claim, and these need not be part of its law of contract.[160]

The place of performance of the obligation in question, which pinpoints the court with special jurisdiction, is selected from a menu of four items. The first three are stated in Article 7(1)(b), which had no predecessor in the Brussels Convention. In a contract for the sale of goods it is where under the contract the goods were or should have been delivered. In a contract for the provision of services it is where under the contract the services were or should have been provided. And in either case, it will instead be the place which the parties otherwise agreed upon if that is what they did.[161] If the contract is worded clearly enough, the application of these rules is reasonably straightforward; the case where the contract is not so well drafted is examined below.

---

[155] *Samengo-Turner v J&H Marsh & McLennan (Services) Ltd* [2007] EWCA Civ 723, [2008] ICR 18.

[156] *AMT Futures Ltd v Marzillier* [2017] UKSC 13, [2018] AC 439.

[157] Case C–375/13 *Kolassa v Barclays Bank plc* EU:C:2015:37, [2016] 1 All ER (Comm) 753.

[158] Case 38/81 *Effer SpA v Kantner* [1982] ECR 825; Case C–366/13 *Profit Investment Sim SpA v Ossi* EU:C:2016:282, [2016] 1 WLR 3832.

[159] Case C–366/13 *Profit Investment Sim SpA v Ossi* EU:C:2016:282, [2016] 1 WLR 3832, which therefore casts doubt on *Kleinwort Benson Ltd v Glasgow City Council* [1999] 1 AC 153.

[160] Case C–26/91 *Soc Jakob Handte GmbH v Soc Traitements Mécano-chimiques des Surfaces* [1992] ECR I–3967, 3984.

[161] A wholly artificial stipulation of the place of performance will be ineffective for this purpose: Case C–106/95 *MSG v Les Gravières Rhénanes Sàrl* [1997] ECR I–911: such a thing will be re-characterised as a jurisdiction agreement and required to comply with Article 25.

If these do not apply, the fourth, default, rule is given by Article 7(1)(c): the court for the place of performance of the primary[162] obligation on the basis of which the claimant founds the claim.[163] It used to be the only rule for this head of special jurisdiction. Despite its now marginal role, its story is an illuminating one. If the contract specifies the place for performance of the obligation which founds the claim in this sense, the application of Article 7(1)(c) will be straightforward, but if it does not, the court has to apply its conflicts rules to ascertain the law which governs the contract, and then use that law to locate the place of performance.[164] It could be a laborious exercise: a court had to decide what law governed the contract in order to decide whether it had special jurisdiction to decide what law governed the contract, and so on. And there was more. Where the claimant was an unpaid seller the obligation in question would be the payment of the price, which was not always due somewhere with a close connection to the facts giving rise to the dispute.[165] Even worse, an unpaid seller under a contract governed by English law would be able to sue for the price in his own court, for English law generally provides that a debt is payable where the creditor resides:[166] an outcome which challenged the principle that it was generally defendants, not claimants, who were intended to have home advantage. That went down very badly in some quarters.

The legislative response to all this was to provide a uniform identification of the place of the obligation in question for the contracts falling within Article 7(1)(b), as we have just considered. However, if the place of performance of the matters stated in Article 7(1)(b) had to be located by applying rules of the conflict of laws, simply in order to determine whether the court had special jurisdiction to determine a claim which might involve asking that same conflicts question, little would have been gained. The judicial response was radical. The Court ruled that in a contract for the sale of goods, the place of delivery will be taken as the place where the contract provided for the physical transfer of the goods to the purchaser who thereby obtains actual power of disposal at the final destination of the transaction of sale, which is to be identified directly from the provisions of the contract, or by observation,

---

[162] That is to say, a performance obligation as distinct from a secondary obligation to compensate for breach of a primary obligation.

[163] Case 14/76 *De Bloos Sprl v Bouyer SA* [1976] ECR 1497.

[164] Case 12/76 *Industrie Tessili Italiana Como v Dunlop AG* [1976] ECR 1473.

[165] Case C–288/92 *Custom Made Commercial Ltd v Stawa Metallbau GmbH* [1994] ECR I–2913.

[166] *The Eider* [1893] P 119.

and not by recourse to the *lex contractus*.[167] In a contract for the provision of services, it will be where the contract provides for the services (or the greater part of the services[168]) to be delivered. The aim is clearly to allow a court to decide whether it has special jurisdiction without the need to first conduct an exercise in the conflict of laws, and this has much to recommend it.

Of course there will be tricky cases: consider the sale of goods by transfer of documents of title, which may be effected by transferring the documents to the purchaser, as the contract allows, in state A, while the goods themselves are in state B. Yet the question in principle is to ask where, in reality or according to the contract, the buyer was to be placed in a position to dispose of the goods at the end point of the sale, or was to receive the end product of the service provided. That is an answerable question.

Article 7(1)(b) requires contracts to be classified, and this is done by identifying the 'characteristic obligation' of the contract.[169] Contracts for the sale of goods will usually be easy to identify as such. Contracts for the provision of services will include contracts for the supply of goods on hire or hire purchase, and contracts for goods which the seller first has to make,[170] as well as the supply of goods and services, as in a contract for work and materials. It will include the agreement under which the management company maintains the common parts of a block of flats;[171] and commercial agency,[172] and exclusive distribution contracts.[173] But it will not include a licensing agreement,[174] or barter; and many arrangements made within the realm of what is referred to as 'financial services' may fit only awkwardly, if they fit at all, within Article 7(1)(b). Some difficulty will be encountered as the law is hammered out. But no rational mind could deny that the law has been significantly improved.

Whichever provision of Article 7(1) is applicable, the decisive obligation may involve performance at several places in the one Member State,[175] or

---

[167] Case C–381/08 *Car Trim GmbH v KeySafety Systems srl* [2010] ECR I–1255.

[168] Case C–47/14 *Holterman Ferho Exploitatie BV v Spies von Büllesheim* EU:C:2015:574, [2016] ICR 90.

[169] Case C–47/14 *Holterman Ferho Exploitatie BV v Spies von Büllesheim* EU:C:2015:574, [2016] ICR 90.

[170] Case C–381/08 *Car Trim GmbH v KeySafety Systems srl* [2010] ECR I–1255.

[171] Case C–25/18 *Kerr v Postnov* EU:C:2019:376.

[172] Case C–19/09 *Wood Floor Solutions Andreas Domberger GmbH v Silva Trade SA* [2010] ECR I–2121.

[173] Even though goods are also sold: Case C–9/12 *Corman-Collins SA v La Maison du Whisky SA* EU:C:2013:860, [2014] QB 431.

[174] Case C–533/07 *Falco Privatstiftung v Weller-Lindhorst* [2009] ECR I–3327 (on the basis that as Art 7(1)(b) was an exception to the general rule preserved in Art 7(1)(c), it should be construed in a restrictive manner. The result is right, the reasoning wrong).

[175] Case C–386/05 *Color Drack GmbH v Lexx International Vertriebs GmbH* [2007] ECR I–3699.

in more Member States than one, such as delivery to sites in Belgium and the Netherlands, sales representation[176] in the United Kingdom and Ireland, and so on. In such cases one asks where this obligation was principally to be performed, and locates special jurisdiction at the courts for that place:[177] this will often yield a workable and predictable answer. Similarly, in a case falling within Article 7(1)(c), if two obligations are relied on, the obligation which is principal will be the decisive one.[178] Where it is not possible to marshal the place or places of performance in this way, it is unclear what the outcome should be. The proposition that there may be special jurisdiction over only so much of the obligation as was located within the jurisdiction of the court is possible[179] but unattractive. It has also been held that the claimant may elect as he chooses between the various places in which substantial performance of the obligation in question was due, which may be a preferable outcome for cases which are awkward, and probably rare, by nature.[180]

(b) Matters relating to tort, delict, or quasi-delict: Article 7(2)

Article 7(2) gives special jurisdiction in matters relating to tort to the courts for the place where the harmful event occurred or may occur: the difference is only one of timing.

A 'matter relating to tort' means any action which seeks to establish the liability of a defendant and which is not a matter relating to a contract within Article 7(1):[181] this judicial definition is the foundation for the rule that Articles 7(1) and 7(2) are all-embracing and mutually exclusive. It follows that Article 7(2) will naturally apply where there is no relationship of or equivalent to contractual privity with the defendant.[182] So for example, a claim for wrongfully inducing a breach of contract will fall within Article 7(2), because the relationship which founds the claim is not contractual, even though a broken contract lies at the heart of the complaint.[183] When

---

[176] But if this were seen as a contract of employment, it would have fallen under Arts 20–23.
[177] Case C–125/92 *Mulox IBC v Geels* [1993] ECR I–4075; Case C–383/95 *Rutten v Cross Medical Ltd* [1997] ECR I–57; Case C–19/09 *Wood Floor Solutions Andreas Domberger GmbH v Silva Trade SA* [2010] ECR I–2121; Case C–47/14 *Holterman Ferho Exploitatie BV v Spies von Büllesheim* EU:C:2015:574, [2016] ICR 90; Case C–64/17 *Saey Home & Garden NV/SA v Lusavouga-Máquinas e Accessórios Industriais SA* EU:C:2018:173.
[178] Case 266/85 *Shenavai v Kreischer* [1987] ECR 239.
[179] Case C–420/97 *Leathertex Divisione Sintetici SpA v Bodetex BVBA* [1999] ECR I–6747.
[180] Case C–386/05 *Color Drack GmbH v Lexx International Vertriebs GmbH* [2007] ECR I–3699; Case C–204/08 *Rehder v Air Baltic Corp* [2009] ECR I–6073 (but cf Case C–19/09 *Wood Floor Solutions Andreas Domberger GmbH v Silva Trade SA* [2010] ECR I–2121).
[181] Case 189/87 *Kalfelis v Bankhaus Schröder, Münchmeyer, Hengst & Co* [1988] ECR 5565.
[182] Subject to the possible exceptional cases mentioned in the text to n 151.
[183] *AMT Futures Ltd v Marzillier* [2017] UKSC 13, [2018] AC 439.

proceedings are brought against a trader for using unfair contract terms in dealings with consumers, the relationship between the enforcing body and the trader is not contractual, even though the broader context is all about contracts; Article 7(2) will apply.[184] When an investor, who contracted with an investment company as a result of his relying on false information provided by a bond issuer, sues the issuer, there was certainly a contract, but the claim against the issuer is not based on it,[185] and the claim against the issuer is not dependent on the terms of the contract, so Article 7(2) will apply. Article 7(2) will cover the statutory liability (where it exists) of a corporate officer to a third party for the debts of a company.[186] It will extend to wrongs which English law defines as equitable, such as dishonest assistance of a breach of trust, or breach of confidence, as well as to statutory wrongs such as infringement of intellectual property, or occupiers' liability.[187]

Yet despite the width of this formulation, and despite the fact that there is no clear line which ring-fences restitutionary claims,[188] it has been contended that Article 7(2) is confined to cases where the claim is based on some semblance of wrongdoing and does not extend to claims for restitution which are founded on the injustice of retaining a gain at the expense of another. According to this view, in support of which the Court[189] has never said a single word, a claim for the repayment of money paid to another on the basis of mistaken identity, for example, would not be within Article 7(2).[190] If this is correct, which must surely be doubtful, it proceeds not from a doctrinaire view about the nature of unjust enrichment in English domestic law, but from the fact that other language versions of what in English is rendered as 'liability' connote more clearly the sense of liability for doing wrong or inflicting loss.[191] Guidance from the Rome II Regulation[192] is fatally ambivalent, for that Regulation treats torts and unjust enrichment for the purposes

---

[184] Case C-167/00 *VfK v Henkel* [2002] ECR I–8111.

[185] Case C-375/13 *Kolassa v Barclays Bank plc* EU:C:2015:37, [2016] 1 All ER (Comm) 753.

[186] Case C-147/12 *ÖFAB v Koot* EU:C:2013:490, [2013] 2 All ER (Comm) 969.

[187] *Mecklermedia Corp v DC Congress GmbH* [1998] Ch 40.

[188] Indeed, the Advocate General in Case C–89/91 *Shearson Lehmann Hutton Inc v TVB* [1993] ECR I–139 was clear (at 178) that the effect of *Kalfelis* was to bring claims alleging unjust enrichment within Art 7(2).

[189] Though various Advocates-General have invited it to reconsider the principle of binary division, the Court has refused to reconsider.

[190] *Kleinwort Benson Ltd v Glasgow City Council* [1999] 1 AC 153. Even so, it is challenging to understand how refusing to return money which you should not have received is neither wrongful nor wrong: such depravity is the kind of thing which gets lawyers a bad name.

[191] In *Kalfelis*, the language of which case was German, the term is 'Schadenshaftung', where the sense of loss caused by wrong is said to be more palpable.

[192] Regulation (EC) 864/2007 [2007] OJ L199/40.

of applicable law as non-contractual obligations, but it places unjust enrichment, and cases of pre-contractual fault, outside the provisions which deal with choice of law for tort and delict. Only the European Court can give a decisive answer to a question squarely put: this has not happened yet.

If there is a contract between the parties, and if the essence of the complaint could have been framed as a breach of that contract, it falls for the purpose of special jurisdiction under Article 7(1), and not Article 7(2), even though the claimant seeks to advance it as a claim (such as for tort or for breach of fiduciary duty) which may well, in national law, be legally and conceptually independent of any contract.[193] This vitally important principle helps secure the uniform application of Article 7, and protects it from the divergent views of national laws to the concurrency, cumulation, or non-cumulation of causes of action.

Claims founded on pre-contractual misrepresentation require a little care, as they often arise within a relationship of contractual privity. Insofar as they seek the rescission of the contract, and consequential relief, they obviously fall within Article 7(1), as they seek to establish the (in)validity of a real contract, even if they also include a claim for consequential relief.[194] Where the claim is for compensation for tortious wrongdoing, the loss being established by entering into the contract, it is more likely that the matter is within Article 7(2), as the validity of the contract as such is not put in issue. Even so, the measure of damages in the latter case is designed to place the parties in the same financial position as if the contract had not been made, and it may therefore be seen as the cash equivalent of rescission: on that basis, the Court[195] may yet consider Article 7(1) to be its more natural jurisdictional home. A claim based on the proposition that the failure to conclude a contract was actionable as a wrong is not within Article 7(1), and was therefore within Article 7(2).[196] In the final analysis, the strict separation of Articles 7(1) and 7(2) is harder to accomplish whenever the gist of the complaint is that a tort induced the victim to enter into, or to not enter into, a contract.

---

[193] Case C–548/12 *Brogsitter v Fabrication de Montres Normandes EURL* EU:C:2014:148, [2014] QB 753; Case C–47/14 *Holterman Ferho Exploitatie BV v Spies von Büllesheim* EU:C:2015:574, [2016] ICR 90.

[194] Case C–366/13 *Profit Investment Sim SpA v Ossi* EU:C:2016:282, [2016] 1 WLR 3832.

[195] No English decision offers any support for this argument, though. *Aspen Underwriting Ltd v Credit Europe Bank NV* [2018] EWCA Civ 2590, [2019] 1 Lloyd's Rep 221 is particularly hostile to the idea.

[196] Case C–334/00 *Fonderie Officine Meccaniche Tacconi SpA v Heinrich Wagner Sinto Maschinenfabrik GmbH* [2002] ECR I–7357.

The place where the harmful event occurred means the place where the damage occurred, or the place of the event giving rise to it: the claimant[197] may elect between the two of them where they diverge.[198] For example, when river water was polluted and used by a downstream horticultural enterprise, with disastrous consequences, the damage occurred where the crop was ruined; the event giving rise to the damage was the discharge of poison into the river; and the claimant was entitled to elect between them.[199]

Starting with the place where the damage occurs, its location is sometimes easy, sometimes not. In principle, the decisive damage is that which occurs where the physical damage, or financial loss, as the case may be, first materializes and not, if it is different, where it or its consequence may later be felt.[200] The cases offer some guidance. If property is wrongfully taken, the damage occurs at the place of the taking, rather than where the claimant's financial records of the loss are kept.[201] Where a road accident causes a loss of earnings, the damage occurs where the bodily injury took place, rather than where the earnings would have been made. Where a road accident causes traumatic shock to relatives of the victim, the damage occurs where the accident took place, rather than where the secondary victims first experience their trauma.[202] Where a conspiracy or other wrongful act injures a trader, the loss occurs in the market where sales would have been made, rather than where the losses are recorded in the accounts.[203] Where a malign ingredient was supplied and was incorporated into a manufactured product, the damage occurs at the place of manufacture, rather than where legal liability was incurred as a result of selling that corrupted product.[204] Where a defendant induces a contracting party to bring legal proceedings where it had promised not to, the loss occurs in the place of the wrongful proceedings which require

[197] 'Claimant' does not necessarily mean the victim, for the rule applies equally to declarations of non-liability: Case C–133/11 *Folien Fischer AG v Ritrama SpA* EU:C:2012:664, [2013] QB 523.

[198] Case 21/76 *Handelskwekerij GJ Bier BV v Mines de Potasse d'Alsace* [1976] ECR 1875; Case C–364/93 *Marinari v Lloyds Bank plc* [1995] ECR I–2719; Case C–68/93 *Shevill v Presse Alliance SA* [1995] ECR I–415.

[199] Case 21/76 *Handelskwekerij GJ Bier BV v Mines de Potasse d'Alsace* [1976] ECR 1875.

[200] Case C–220/88 *Dumez France SA v Hessische Landesbank* [1990] ECR I–49.

[201] Case C–364/93 *Marinari v Lloyds Bank plc* [1995] ECR I–2719. It is probable that this also excludes the jurisdiction of the place where the claimant's shares are traded.

[202] Case C–350/14 *Lazar v Allianz SpA* EU:C:2015:802, [2016] 1 WLR 835 (a case on the Rome II Regulation).

[203] Case C–27/17 *AB flyLAL-Lithuanian Airlines v Starptautiskā lidosta Rīga VAS* EU:C:2018:533, [2019] 1 WLR 669; Case C–451/18 *Tibor-Trans Fuvarozó és Kereskedelmi Kft. v DAF TRUCKS N.V.* EU:C:2019:635.

[204] Case C–189/08 *Zuid-Chemie BV v Philippo's Mineralenfabriek NV/SA* [2009] ECR I–6917.

fees to be incurred.[205] In defamation cases, the damage occurs where people read defamatory material in the press and lower their opinion of the victim, rather than in the place where the victim lives,[206] though by way of pragmatic exception, where insolent or insulting material is published on the internet, the damage may be taken to occur, in its entirety and if the victim wishes, at the place which represents the centre of the victim's interests, for the ubiquity of the internet makes it, in some respects, a law unto itself.[207]

Financial loss caused by poor investment has proved to be more difficult to deal with, and the Court has not succeeded in finding a settled line. Where an investor acts on negligent legal information published by a third party, where does her financial loss occur? It does not appear to be in the place where the worthless investment is located. The Court seemed to suggest that it was where the investor's bank account was depleted, as the place from which the investor's funds departed.[208] But the objection that this was liable to be opaque (the defendant would often have no way of knowing where the money was going to depart from) then led the Court to say that the damage occurs where the victim makes the legal commitment which means that loss is inevitable.[209] However, not all contracts are made face-to-face across a desk, and if this view would require an analysis of where a contract was made, it comes with difficulties of its own. Most recently, the Court appears to have reverted to the place of the depleted bank account, at least if there are other, objective, connections with that place.[210] The last word on this issue has not yet been written.

Even in personal injury cases there will be challenges in locating the immediate damage. In asbestosis cases, for example, is the place where the damage occurs where the malevolent fibre is ingested, assuming that this place can be identified, which it may not be,[211] or where the outward symptoms of asbestosis first manifest themselves, or where these symptoms first reveal their cancerous nature? For all that, the difficulties which the law of tort may pose

---

[205] *AMT Futures Ltd v Marzillier* [2017] UKSC 13, [2018] AC 439. Even so, if one were to focus on the place where the client committed itself to retain the services of a lawyer, this may not always be in the place of the wrongful litigation, as instructions may be given from home.

[206] Case C–68/93 *Shevill v Presse Alliance SA* [1995] ECR I–415.

[207] Joined Cases C–509/09 *eDate Advertising GmbH v X* and C–161/10 *Martinez v MGN Ltd* [2011] ECR I–10269; Case C–194/96 *Bolagsupplysningen OÜ v Svensk Handel AB* EU:C:2017:766, [2018] QB 963.

[208] Case C–375/13 *Kolassa v Barclays Bank plc* EU:C:2015:37, [2016] 1 All ER (Comm) 753.

[209] Case C–12/15 *Universal Music International Holding BV v Schilling* EU:C:2016:449, [2016] QB 967.

[210] Case C–304/17 *Löber v Barclays Bank plc* EU:C:2018:701.

[211] *Fairchild v Glenhaven Funeral Services Ltd* [2002] UKHL 22, [2003] 1 AC 32.

do not call into question the general principle by which the Court has been guiding the development of the law.

In identifying and locating the damage, the template used is that of an autonomous view of the nature of the complaint, rather than one constrained by the particular cause of action as pleaded in accordance with national law: the technique, in this respect, diverges from the approach the Court takes to Article 1 of the Regulation.[212] A similar principle applies to identify the event giving rise to the damage, which has tended to be seen as the causative event at the beginning of the story. For example, the event giving rise to the damage caused by defamation in the press is the production of the newspaper and not (as it might be seen in English domestic law) the sale of the newspaper to its readership;[213] the printing of misinformation and not (as it would be seen in English domestic law) its reception by the person who acts on it;[214] the manufacture of the thing which, when sold by another, causes damage and not (as it would be seen in English domestic law) the marketing of the thing without warning as to the potential for harm;[215] the place where the conspiracy to injure was hatched and not (as it might otherwise have been) the implementation of the plot.[216] The event must be one brought about by a party to the proceedings, rather than an act by a non-party which is attributable, in some way, to the defendant.[217] It will take a while for the notional book of causes of action in tort and delict to be compiled from the judgments of the Court, but we are getting there.

(c) Other cases of special jurisdiction under Article 7

For *civil claims in criminal proceedings*, Article 7(3) allows a court hearing a criminal claim to order damages or restitution to a claimant who, in accordance with the procedure of the court, has intervened as a 'civil party'. This has little practical relevance in England where this is not a common form of procedure. Article 7(4) allows an owner to sue for the *return of a 'cultural object'* in the courts for the place where the object is when the court is first seised.

Article 7(5) deals with *liability arising out of the operation of a branch, agency, or other establishment*: such claims may be brought in the place where

---

[212] See p 52.
[213] Case C–68/93 *Shevill v Presse Alliance SA* [1995] ECR I–415.
[214] *AMT Futures Ltd v Marzillier* [2017] UKSC 13, [2018] AC 439.
[215] Case C–45/13 *Kainz v Pantherwerke AG* EU:C:2014:7, [2015] QB 34.
[216] *JSC BTA Bank v Ablyazov* [2018] UKSC 19, [2018] 2 WLR 1125.
[217] Case C–228/11 *Melzer v MF Global UK Ltd* EU:C:2013:305, [2013] QB 1112; Case C–360/12 *Coty Germany GmbH v First Note Perfumes NV* EU:C:2014:1318. How this would apply in asbestos cases is very hard to say.

it is situated. The concept of a branch, agency, or establishment occupies a slippery patch of territory between being too dependent to count as anything at all, and too independent to be a branch or agency of another.[218] A useful test is probably to ask whether it has power on its own account to make contracts which will bind the defendant: if it does, it will probably be a branch.[219] It is important to note that this rule applies only to the extent that the claim arises out of the operations of the branch,[220] though it is not implicit that the acts of the defendant must have been performed in that place.[221] The equivalent provision in common law jurisdiction would ask whether the defendant was present within the jurisdiction; and, if so, permit the bringing of any claim against him, whether or not connected to activities undertaken in that place. There is much to be said for the more focused rule contained in Article 7(5).

In relation to *trusts*, Article 7(6) gives special jurisdiction over a settlor, trustee, or beneficiary, who is sued as such,[222] to the courts of the Member State where the trust is domiciled. For this provision to apply, the trust must be created by the operation of a statute, or by a written instrument, or created orally but evidenced in writing. In relation to claims for payment in respect of *salvage of cargo or freight*, Article 7(7) gives special jurisdiction to the place of the court under the authority of which the freight was arrested to secure payment or could have been arrested but for the fact that bail or other security was given.

(d) Joinder litigation and consolidated claims: Articles 8 and 9

Where a claimant has *several claims against the one defendant*, the Regulation does not give special[223] jurisdiction over a claim on the simple basis that it is related or accessory to another claim over which the court does have special jurisdiction. If a claimant wishes to join several claims against a single defendant in a single proceeding, this must be done in the courts of the defendant's domicile, which have general jurisdiction under Article 4.

Otherwise, Articles 8 and 9[224] go some way towards allowing the consolidation of separate claims in the interest of coordinating the judicial function

---

[218] Case 218/86 *SAR Schotte GmbH v Parfums Rothschild Sàrl* [1987] ECR 4905.
[219] Opinion of the AG in Case C–89/91 *Shearson Lehmann Hutton Inc v TVB* [1993] ECR I–139, 169.
[220] Case C–464/18 *ZX v Ryanair DAC* EU:C:2019:311 [2019] 1 WLR 4202.
[221] Case C–439/93 *Lloyds Register of Shipping v Soc Campenon Bernard* [1995] ECR I–961.
[222] *Gomez v Gomez-Monche Vives* [2008] EWCA Civ 1065, [2009] Ch 245.
[223] Case 189/87 *Kalfelis v Bankhaus Schröder, Münchmeyer, Hengst & Co* [1988] ECR 5565.
[224] Section 2 of Chapter II.

and avoiding inconsistent judgments, but the limits on their operation are surprisingly strict, and at this point the Regulation operates less than optimally. There are several cases to consider.

Where claims are brought against *several defendants*, Article 8(1) allows them to be joined in the one action if the proceedings are brought where one of them is domiciled, and if it is necessary to join the claims so as to avoid the risk of irreconcilable[225] judgments which might result from separate trials: both requirements must be satisfied. It is not necessary that the defendant who is sued where he is domiciled, the 'anchor' defendant, be the principal target of the claim, for if there were such a requirement there would be no end to the argument. On occasion, though, a court may suspect that there is no real intention to pursue the local defendant once he has served the claimant's purpose of providing a jurisdictional hook to catch the other co-defendants. The Court has rather wavered on the question whether a distinct and additional jurisdictional objection is available by satisfying the court that the proceedings are brought, or prolonged,[226] against the local defendant principally or solely to remove the non-local defendant from the court which would otherwise have jurisdiction over him.[227] The drafting of Article 8(1), especially when read alongside Article 8(2), would not suggest that this is an admissible argument, though the most recent decisions of the Court may suggest otherwise. In any event, the argument that Article 8(1) may not be used abusively, which is to say, for the *sole* purpose of undermining Article 4, appears to be one which may be raised.[228]

As for the degree of connection between the claims, an exercise in judgment is called for. The predominant need to avoid irreconcilable judgments should surely incline a court to err on the side of joinder and against taking a restrictive view.[229] As said above, there is, however, no analogous right to join co-defendants into proceedings in a court having only special jurisdiction under Article 7, or having jurisdiction by prorogation under Articles 25 or 26;

---

[225] Case C–366/13 *Profit Investment Sim SpA v Ossi* EU:C:2016:282, [2016] 1 WLR 3832.

[226] Case C–352/13 *Cartel Damage Claims Hydrogen Peroxide SA v Akzo Nobel NV* EU:C:2015:335, [2015] QB 906.

[227] Case C–51/97 *Réunion Européenne SA v Spliethoff's Bevrachtingskantoor BV* [1998] ECR I–6511; Case C–103/05 *Reisch Montage AG v Kiesel Baumaschinen Handels GmbH* [2006] ECR I–6827; C–98/06 *Freeport plc v Arnoldson* [2007] ECR I–839; Case C–616/10 *Solvay SA v Honeywell Fluorine Products Europe BV* EU:C:2012:445; Case C–352/13 *Cartel Damage Claims Hydrogen Peroxide SA v Akzo Nobel NV* EU:C:2015:335, [2015] QB 906.

[228] *Vedanta Resources plc v Lungowe* [2019] UKSC 20, [2019] 2 WLR 1051.

[229] Case C–98/06 *Freeport plc v Arnoldsson* [2007] ECR I–839; Case C–616/10 *Solvay SA v Honeywell Fluorine Products Europe BV* EU:C:2012:445; Case C–366/13 *Profit Investment Sim SpA v Ossi* EU:C:2016:282, [2016] 1 WLR 3832.

it is hard to see a really convincing reason why these cases were not brought within the framework of Article 8(1). It goes without saying that there is no access to Article 8(1) where jurisdiction is founded on Article 6.[230]

Article 8(2) allows a claim against a *third party* for a warranty, guarantee, contribution, or indemnity, or brought in some other third-party proceeding, to be brought in the court hearing the original action unless the original action[231] was instituted with the sole object of allowing the defendant to ensnare the third party:[232] this is, presumably, a rare event. It seems probable that the original action must still be live[233] but, by contrast with Article 8(1), the jurisdictional basis of the original action has no bearing on the availability of Article 8(2). The court may refuse joinder of the third party so long as its reasons do not, in effect, contradict the general scheme of the Regulation: for example, if the third-party claim is raised very late, so that its admission would cause the trial date to be lost.[234] But if there is an Article 25 jurisdiction agreement between defendant and third party, this will bar access to Article 8(2), no matter how inconvenient the overall result may be, for, by contrast with the modestly flexible view taken by the common law, there is no judicial discretion to overlook Article 25 when it applies.[235]

Article 8(3) allows a *counterclaim* to be brought in the court in which the original action is pending. The Article is limited to claims which arise out of the same relationship or other essential facts as the original claim,[236] but a pleaded set-off which will not overtop the claim is a defence, not a counterclaim, and need not be justified by reference to this rule.[237] It is not clear whether Article 8(3) extends to a counterclaim against a party other than the original claimant, but in the context of insurance, at least, it has been held that it does not where to allow it would deprive an insured or policyholder of his special jurisdictional protections.[238]

---

[230] Case C–51/97 *Réunion Européenne SA v Spliethoff's Bevrachtingskantoor BV* [1998] ECR I–6511.

[231] According to Jenard. But according to Case C–77/04 *GIE Réunion Européenne v Zurich España* [2005] ECR I–4509, the third party claim (instead? as well?) must not have this bad motivation.

[232] Case C–521/14 *SOVAG v If Vahinkovakuutusyhtiö Oy* EU:C:2016:41, [2016] QB 780.

[233] *Waterford Wedgwood plc v David Nagli Ltd* [1999] 3 All ER 185; cf *The Ikarian Reefer* [2000] 1 WLR 603 (CA).

[234] Case C–365/88 *Kongress Agentur Hagen GmbH v Zeehaghe BV* [1990] ECR I–1845.

[235] *Hough v P&O Containers Ltd* [1999] QB 834.

[236] Case C–306/17 *Nothartová v Boldizsár* EU:C:2018:360.

[237] Case C–431/93 *Danvaern Productions A/S v Schuhfabriken Otterbeck GmbH & Co* [1995] ECR I–2053.

[238] *Jordan Grand Prix Ltd v Baltic Insurance Group* [1999] 2 AC 127.

Article 8(4), which deals with contract actions joined with actions against the same defendant in *matters relating to rights in rem in immovable property*, has already been mentioned. It is obviously sensible that an action against a mortgagor should be able to enforce the security right as well as the borrower's personal covenant to repay and this is, in effect, what Article 8(4) allows.

Article 8 still falls short of the ideal of securing the efficient disposal of related claims, and if its provisions are given a restrictive interpretation, it will be even less successful. To be effective, jurisdictional rules of this kind depend on the judge having a certain discretion. If it is now expected that courts will trust each other to interpret the Regulation properly, it may be time to allow judges more general flexibility in this area, and the provisions for the coordination and consolidation of claims be made a little more accessible.[239]

7. RESIDUAL REGULATION JURISDICTION: ARTICLE 6

If none of the rest of the Regulation has applied, the defendant is someone who does not have a domicile in a Member State. At this point, the Regulation gives up the attempt to lay down primary jurisdictional rules for a claim against a defendant who has no material connection to a Member State.[240] Article 6 authorizes the claimant to use the jurisdictional rules which are native to the court in which he wishes to sue. These rules, which we will encounter in more detail below, are co-opted into the Regulation, and may be referred to as rules of 'residual Regulation jurisdiction', which is to say, rules which apply to the residue of cases falling within the scope of the Regulation but not dealt with by its primary rules. So for example, Article 6 will allow a claimant to serve process on an Australian defendant present in England, or to apply for permission under CPR Part 6 to serve process on an American defendant out of the jurisdiction, and so on: in short, to invoke the traditional jurisdiction of an English court.

---

[239] Article 9 allows a court which has jurisdiction 'by virtue of this Regulation' in an action relating to liability from the use or operation of a ship to entertain a claim for the limitation of such liability. No more needs to be said here.

[240] A proposal to replace this Article with a rule which would, loosely, have extended something resembling Art 7 to cases in which the defendant had no domicile in a Member State was not found acceptable, which was perhaps a pity. But its time will come.

But the Regulation has not washed its hands of the dispute. Article 6 is an integral part of Chapter II, and in case it was not already clear, it spells out that Articles 18(1),[241] 21(2),[242] 24[243] and 25[244] prevail over it. Moreover, as Article 6 will result in a judgment enforceable under Chapter III of the Regulation, its operation is also subject to the rules on *lis pendens* in another Member State. So a claimant may not rely on Article 6 if proceedings between the same parties and involving the same cause of action were instituted in a court which was seised earlier in time, not even if that court has also based its jurisdiction on Article 6.[245] It is therefore wrong to picture Article 6 as opening a door back into the world outside the Regulation. It is properly understood as incorporating by reference traditional jurisdictional rules; and the effect of their being taken up into the Regulation means that they have to be tailored to fit their new surroundings. Even so, there is room for unease at the resulting combination of residual jurisdictional rules, many of which will appear to defendants against whom they are asserted as being outrageously wide in their sweep, and the automatic recognition under Chapter III of judgments based on such provisions. The point will be examined when we look at the recognition of foreign judgments, but the sense of gross unfairness does not go away.

8. *LIS ALIBI PENDENS*: ARTICLES 29–34

The original aim of the Regulation, that judgments should be enforceable in other Member States without impediment, would be jeopardized if there were to be concurrent litigation of identical or similar disputes in the courts of Member States. Articles 29 to 34[246] provide the means of control for situations of *lis alibi pendens* and related situations. It is necessary to deal separately with *lis pendens* involving the courts of two Member States, and then with the involvement of non-Member States.

---

[241] Claims by consumers against professionals not domiciled in a Member state.
[242] Claims by employees against employers not domiciled in a Member state.
[243] Exclusive jurisdiction regardless of domicile.
[244] Jurisdiction agreements for the courts of a Member State.
[245] Case C–351/89 *Overseas Union Insurance Ltd v New Hampshire Insurance Co* [1991] ECR I–3317.
[246] Section 9 of Chapter II.

(a) *Lis pendens* in the courts of two Member States

Where the *same action, between the same parties*, is brought before the courts of two Member States, Article 29 requires the court which was seised second to dismiss the proceedings before it. Its only alternative is to stay the proceedings while any challenge to the jurisdiction of the first court is dealt with, but to dismiss proceedings if the first court confirms its jurisdiction. It is implicit that the duty of the court first seised is to adjudicate.

The basic rule is simple and clear and is entirely dependent on which action was first to get started. It takes no account of considerations of comparative appropriateness, for all courts with jurisdiction under the Regulation are in this sense equally appropriate and their jurisdiction may be invoked with equal propriety. The court seised second is absolutely forbidden to inquire whether, still less decide that, the court first seised erred in concluding that it had jurisdiction. All courts are equally competent to apply the Regulation, and where the competences are equal, the first in time prevails.[247] This abrupt solution to the problem of *lis pendens* may provoke a rush to be the first to commence litigation: so be it. It will be self-defeating to threaten the opposite party that proceedings will be commenced without further notice after a period of so many days.[248] *Celui qui hésite est perdu*, as is said in Europe; *carpe curiam!* as others might prefer. The rule is to start proceedings as quickly as possible in the court which is preferred, and to draft a writ which is broad and comprehensive and leaves no gaps which might allow a defendant to formulate and sneak through with a distinct claim of his own, claiming to have been the first to seise a court with it. 'Speak softly and hurry a big writ', as the great Theodore Roosevelt nearly said. 'Negotiation is for losers', as another, who shall be nameless, might have tweeted.

So far as the Regulation is concerned, two exceptions to the basic rule have been developed. The first is judicial: where the court seised second is satisfied that it has exclusive jurisdiction under Article 24. The logic of this is clear: there is no point in ceding priority to a court seised first, for if that court adjudicates in violation of Article 24 its judgment is liable to be refused recognition,[249] so that there is nothing to wait for. Whether a similar argument may be made about the protective jurisdiction rules for insurance, consumer,

---

[247] Case C–351/89 *Overseas Union Insurance Ltd v New Hampshire Insurance Co* [1991 ECR I–3317.
[248] *Messier Dowty Ltd v Sabena SA* [2000] 1 WLR 2040 (CA).
[249] Article 45(1).

and employment contracts is yet to be decided, but the logic of doing so may not be enough to justify the stretching of the exception.

The second exception is legislative, in Article 31(2)–(4) of the recast Regulation. It applies where the court seised second has been, or appears to have been, prorogated with exclusive jurisdiction in accordance with Article 25: in such a case the court seised first will be required, if its jurisdiction is challenged, to give way and allow the second seised[250] court to rule on the Article 25 question, in an inversion of the usual rule. This provision of the recast Regulation addresses the problem of 'torpedo' proceedings, which we mentioned above.[251] If the court first seised declines to stay its proceedings, perhaps because it has reached its own conclusion that there is no relevant agreement on jurisdiction, it is not yet clear whether the designated court loses the power to proceed, but it seems likely that it does.[252]

Back to the basic rule. For its operation, Article 29 requires three identities: of parties (but procedural differences between the formulation of the claimants and defendants are not decisive); of object (the two actions must have the same end in view); and of cause (they must be founded on the same facts and rules of law).[253] In relation to the identity of parties, an action brought *in rem* against a vessel may still be found to be between the same parties as one *in personam* against those having an interest in the vessel; a useful test may be whether the interests of the parties are identical and indissociable.[254] As regards identity of object and cause, an action for damages for breach of contract shares identity with one for a declaration that the contract had been rescinded for fraud,[255] for the one could be raised as a complete, mirror-image, defence to the other; an action by a cargo-owner in respect of damage to cargo shares identity with one against the cargo-owner for a declaration of non-liability,[256] whereas an action for damages for breach of warranty of quality is not the mirror image of an action for the price of goods delivered, and Article 29 will not apply to it.[257] An action in a foreign court for damages for tortious wrongdoing does not share identity with (is not the

---

[250] Proceedings must actually have been commenced in the second, and allegedly prorogated, court.

[251] See p 69, above.

[252] But the judgment of the court first seised will, when given, be required to be recognised: cf Case C–386/17 *Liberato v Grigorescu* EU:C:2019:24.

[253] Case C–406/92 *The Tatry* [1994] ECR I–5439.

[254] Case C–351/96 *Drouot Assurances SA v CMI* [1998] ECR I–3075.

[255] Case 144/86 *Gubisch Maschinenfabrik KG v Palumbo* [1987] ECR 4861.

[256] *The Tatry.*

[257] Article 30 may apply, though.

mirror image of) proceedings for a declaration that the foreign proceedings have been brought in breach of contract; it would be otherwise if the local proceedings were to be for a declaration of non-liability.[258]

As to the date of seisin, the original, rather chaotic, approach was that it was defined and determined by each system of national law for its own courts. This caused real difficulty, for it asked a question which national laws had not previously been required to address; and it was soon clear that it was quicker and easier to seise a court in some states than in some others. The solution provided by the Regulation is now found in Article 32, which deals with two kinds of system: (a) in countries where the claimant lodges a document at court before serving it, the court is seised on the date of lodging, provided the claimant has not failed to take the subsequent steps, such as payment of fees or provision of a translated copy, he needs to take for service to be effected; (b) in countries where the document has to be served before being lodged with the court, the court is seised at the time when it is received by the authority responsible for service, provided the claimant has not failed to take the subsequent steps he needs to take for lodging to take place, such as the payment of fees.[259] England is a category (a) country, and the date stamped on the claim form by the court will in principle identify the date of seisin. There may be cases and circumstances which do not fit quite so easily into this framework at all, such as where proceedings are amended to add a fresh claim or a new cause of action, or an additional defendant is added into proceedings which are already pending *inter alios*. The concept of seisin also requires some modification to cater for systems in which national law requires a would-be claimant to go through mediation before being permitted to open real hostilities with a writ.[260] But all this is detail, and it would be ungrateful to cavil. The confusion which preceded this reform was ghastly, and if problems emerge with Article 30, they can be tidied up in due course.

If Article 29 is inapplicable, Article 30 may apply if there are *related actions* in the two courts: that is, actions which are so closely connected that it would be expedient to hear them together to avoid the risk of irreconcilable judgments resulting from separate proceedings. If the actions are related, the

---

[258] *The Alexandros T* [2013] UKSC 70.

[259] See Case C–173/16 *MH v MH* EU:C:2016:542; cf *MB v TB* [2018] EWHC 2035 (Fam).

[260] Case C–467/16 *Schlömp v Landratsamt Schwäbisch Hall* EU:C:2017:993: it may well be that the correct answer is to regard the whole of the (foreign) process as a single procedural unit; cf Case C–296/10 *Purrucker v Vallés Pérez* EU:C:2010:665, [2011] Fam 312. So also where foreign law requires proceedings for judicial separation to precede filing for a divorce: *Giusti v Ferrageno* [2019] EWCA Civ 691.

second court—Article 30 extends only to the court seised second; the duty of the first court being, as always, to adjudicate—may dismiss the action before it if this may be consolidated with the proceedings pending in the first court, or it may stay its proceedings to await the outcome in the first court, or it may do neither.[261] Where Article 30 applies, the English preference appears to be dismissal for consolidation of actions in the first court.[262] This will be appropriate if the two actions involve different parties but have essentially the same cause of action: to bind all concerned into the one hearing and one judgment is sensible, and if the cause of action is substantially the same, the joinder of parties should not lengthen the trial in the first court. But if the same parties are litigating different causes of action in the two Member States, it may be more efficient to stay the second action to await the outcome of the first, and apply Chapter III of the Regulation to the recognition of the first judgment so as to curtail the second action; by contrast, if the second action is dismissed for consolidation with the first, the effect will be to lengthen the first trial by the length of the second; a stay may mean that the second trial never needs to take place.

Where two courts have exclusive jurisdiction regardless of domicile, Article 31(1) provides that the court seised second must decline jurisdiction in favour of the first court. Although a court with jurisdiction under a jurisdiction agreement is said by Article 25 to have exclusive jurisdiction, Article 31(1) does not apply to it. The solution provided for such cases is now found in Article 31(2)–(4), as was mentioned above.

(b) *Lis pendens* in the courts of a non-Member State

If there are proceedings pending before the courts of a non-Member State when proceedings are instituted in a Member State, it would be odd if no account was taken of this fact. Yet until the recast Regulation, the legislative text was completely silent on this point and commentators were not all of one mind. Now, where the jurisdiction of the court is based on Articles 4, 7, 8, or 9, and when proceedings were started there were in the courts of a non-Member State proceedings pending in respect of the same cause of action between the same parties (Article 33), or related proceedings (Article 34), the court is permitted to stay its proceedings where it is in the interests of justice to do so. Where the proceedings in the non-Member State are well on the way towards a judgment which appears to be liable to be recognized under the

---

[261] *The Alexandros T* [2013] UKSC 70, [2014] 1 All ER 590.
[262] *Sarrio SA v Kuwait Investment Authority* [1999] 1 AC 32.

law of the court seised, it may well be appropriate to order a stay; at all events, the court has a broad, and entirely rational, discretion which allows it to take account of facts and matters concerning the proceedings in the foreign court which it is expedient not to spell out in detail.

(c) *Lis non pendens* in the courts of a non-Member States

Articles 33 and 34 deal with two situations in which there exists a significant connection to the courts of a non-Member State. But what of other cases, such as where the proceedings concern title to land in a non-Member State, or the validity of a patent granted under the law of a non-Member State? What if the parties appear to have made a jurisdiction agreement for the courts of a non-Member State, but no proceedings have been brought there, perhaps because the other party does not wish to make an assertive claim? Does the court have any power to decline to adjudicate, and if it does, where does it come from? Or is it obliged to ignore a matter for which the Regulation makes no explicit provision, and if it is, what is the sense in that?

That this is a vivid question has been well known for a long time. A question on this point was referred to the Court in *Owusu v Jackson*, but it went unanswered. A very superficial reading of the judgment in that case might suggest that such connections to a non-Member State, not being mentioned in the Regulation, are irrelevant and furnish no basis for jurisdictional relief, but to any rational mind this is plainly wrong. The Court had made it clear only a few years earlier that a jurisdiction agreement for a non-Member State took whatever effect it had according to the national law of the court seised.[263] There is no reason to suppose that the Court changed its mind, and no reason to suggest that legal certainty is best served by pretending that agreements for courts in places like New York do not exist. Nor would legal certainty be much advanced by insisting that a court with general jurisdiction under Article 4, for example, rule on the validity of a non-Member State patent or on title to land in a non-Member State.

A possible doctrinal justification for this general conclusion would be that a court seised with Regulation jurisdiction may give 'reflexive effect' to Articles 24 and 25 of the recast Regulation;[264] a more English idiom would be to apply these Articles by analogy. This, however, is not quite how the Court

---

[263] Case C–387/98 *Coreck Maritime GmbH v Handelsveem BV* [2000] ECR I–9337.
[264] The argument was first advanced by Mr Droz, which absolutely guarantees its credentials. See [1990] Rev Crit 1, at 14. The fact that it was spurned in *Gulf International Bank BSC v Sheikh Badr Fahad Ibrahim Aldwood* [2019] EWHC 1666 (QB) does nothing to cast doubt upon it.

dealt with jurisdiction agreements for a non-Member State,[265] and it would not be ideal for 'reflexive effect' to operate in as unbending a way as these Articles do when they are dealing with the familiar courts of a Member State.

A plausible reason why there is no mention in the Regulation of these particular connections to non-Member States is that the Regulation cannot, any more than the Convention could, direct a non-Member State court to hear or not hear a case: lacking the authority to harmonize the laws of non-Member States, it left these issues untouched.[266] It may also be that the legislators cannot yet quite agree whether there should be a uniform statement of the powers of the court, as now with Articles 33 and 34, or a simple remission of the power to grant relief, or not, to national laws. But for now, there should be no serious doubt about it: a court seised with general or special jurisdiction should apply its own law to give effect to a choice of court for a non-Member State; it should not be not obliged to adjudicate title to land in New York, or the validity of patents granted under the law of Japan, simply because the defendant to the claim is domiciled in its territory. If this is the only sane result, the better way of reaching it, for the time being, is by remission to the more flexible approaches of national laws. This, after all, would better reflect the fact that legal systems beyond the borders of the European Union are somewhat variable.

9. PROVISIONAL OR PROTECTIVE MEASURES: ARTICLE 35

Provisional or protective measures obtained before the trial may critically affect the way the dispute is resolved: measures freezing assets and (especially) ordering disclosure of their whereabouts, orders for an interim payment, and so on, will affect the balance of power prior to the trial. Yet the jurisdictional control of these measures is touched only lightly by Article 35 of the recast Regulation,[267] which has been interpreted to mean that the Regulation places no jurisdictional restriction on where or when they may be obtained.[268]

In fact, the law is a little more complex than that. Where the substantive claim to which the measures are ancillary falls within the scope of the

---

[265] Case C–387/98 *Coreck Maritime GmbH v Handelsveem BV* [2000] ECR I–9337.
[266] Opinion C–1/03 *Lugano* [2006] ECR I–1145.
[267] Section 10 of Chapter II.
[268] Not even where jurisdiction over the substance is governed by Art 24: Case C–616/10 *Solvay SA v Honeywell Fluorine Products Europe BV* EU:C:2012:445.

Regulation it is necessary to distinguish two types of case in which provisional, including protective, measures may be applied for. First, if the court applied to has jurisdiction over the merits of the substantive dispute, there is no external limit upon the relief it may order, provisional or otherwise, before or after the judgment.[269] Second, if it does not have substantive jurisdiction over the merits of the dispute, an application for relief may still be made by reference to Article 35 of the Regulation; the only jurisdictional requirements to be satisfied are those which national law places upon the applicant. In England, therefore, all that is needed is to serve the respondent with the claim form by which the measure is sought: within the jurisdiction as of right, or out of it with the prior permission of the court (though in deciding whether to grant permission the court may take account of the fact that the trial will not be taking place in England and may ask whether this makes it inexpedient to grant the relief applied for).[270] However, where Article 35 is relied on, two further limitations, not exactly jurisdictional in nature, apply.[271] First, the measure must be one which is truly provisional, in that it is guaranteed to be reversible if it turns out, once the merits have been tried, not to have been warranted. An English freezing order, which will require an undertaking in damages often fortified by a bank guarantee, is a good example of what is meant by this. Secondly, the relief may not extend to assets within the territorial jurisdiction of another Member State. This is more problematic, for although this limitation makes complete sense if the order is expressed to take effect directly against assets,[272] an English freezing order does not do that, as it works by ordering an individual who is subject to the personal jurisdiction of the court not to dissipate his assets. It remains unclear whether the presence or residence of the respondent within England immunizes such an order from this limitation,[273] or whether the order must instead be taken as one which, in substance and notwithstanding its form,[274]

---

[269] Case C–391/95 *Van Uden Maritime BV v Deco Line* [1998] ECR I–7091 (where the court did not have merits jurisdiction, an agreement to arbitrate having denied every court merits jurisdiction).

[270] Civil Jurisdiction and Judgments Act 1982, s 25(3): *Credit Suisse Fides Trust SA v Cuoghi* [1998] QB 818. The proposition, advanced in that case and elsewhere, that an English court may properly 'assist' a foreign court in this way is remarkably unconvincing if the foreign court has not requested any assistance. But the objective value of English 'assistance' is now a matter of dogma.

[271] Case C–391/95 *Van Uden Maritime BV v Deco Line* [1998] ECR I–7091.

[272] Which is understood to be the way in which a French order of *saisie conservatoire* operates.

[273] This appears to have been the view in *Crédit Suisse Fides Trust SA v Cuoghi*.

[274] For an analogous refusal by the Court to accept that the precise form of an English admiralty action *in rem* renders it different from an action *in personam* in the context of Art 29 see Case C–406/92 *The Tatry* [1994] ECR I–5439.

does affect assets in another Member State so that, to that extent, it may not be sought under cover of Article 35.

10. PROCEDURAL RULES AND OTHER POWERS

It is necessary to conclude with an examination of the circumstances in which an English court may supplement or modify the jurisdictional scheme of the Regulation by recourse to its procedural and similar laws.

(a) Disputes about jurisdiction

A defendant who disputes jurisdiction *in limine* may deny that the court has the jurisdiction asserted by the claimant: he does this by using the procedural mechanism of CPR Part 11. In general, factual doubt on any material jurisdictional point is resolved by asking who has the better of the argument on the jurisdictional question: the court will be well aware that its knowledge of the facts is incomplete, but it is hard to see how one can do otherwise than to ask who has made the better showing on the point.[275] As the decision for the court that it has jurisdiction entails the consequence that the courts in every other Member State will not have jurisdiction, it is rational, and consistent with the Regulation, to frame the test as asking who has the better of the argument on the jurisdictional point. In this respect, the test applied is functionally and rationally different from that which applies when dealing with non-Regulation jurisdiction.

(b) Forum *non conveniens* apart from Article 6 jurisdiction

When the claimant invokes a jurisdictional rule other than the residual Regulation jurisdiction provided by Article 6, a court obviously has no discretion to stay its proceedings to leave the claimant to proceed instead in another Member State on the ground that it would be the natural forum;[276] it is irrelevant whether the claimant is domiciled in a Member State.[277]

Where the natural forum is in a non-Member State, the original view[278] of the English courts was that the Regulation did not prevent a defendant applying for, and the court ordering, a stay of proceedings on the ground of

[275] *Canada Trust Co v Stolzenberg (No 2)* [2002] 1 AC 1.
[276] Schlosser Report [1979] OJ C59/71 at para 78.
[277] For the Regulation draws no distinction: Case C–412/98 *Universal General Insurance Co v Groupe Josi Reinsurance Co SA* [2000] ECR I–5925.
[278] *Re Harrods (Buenos Aires) Ltd* [1992] Ch 72 (CA).

forum non conveniens. This followed from the perception that the Regulation had no application to a question, or a 'jurisdictional contest', which arose as between a Member State and a non-Member State. This view, however, was firmly repudiated by the European Court,[279] which may have been startled by the thought that whether a judge had jurisdiction, and a duty to adjudicate, involved a 'contest' between courts. A claim had been brought in England by a claimant who sustained grievous personal injury while on holiday in Jamaica. Only one of the six defendants was domiciled in England;[280] the natural forum was undoubtedly in Jamaica. The Court's conclusion was that as Article 4 gave the English court jurisdiction, and as the Regulation made no provision for a stay of Article 4 jurisdiction on the ground of *forum non conveniens*, the exercise of such a power was inconsistent with the Regulation. True, the Court seemed to be under the misapprehension that English procedural law allowed an English court to order a stay even though the defendant had not applied for it, but this howler cannot nullify the rest of the judgment. And from the perspective of the European Court, it must have been almost beyond belief that, eight years after he had been rendered quadriplegic by what he claimed was the defendants' fault, a claimant could be ordered by an English court to take his wheelchair and team of carers and start from scratch in the courts of a third world country, several thousand miles away. The Court of Appeal must have been out of its mind even to have entertained the thought that it could properly stay the proceedings; making a reference to the European Court was utterly unnecessary. If the judgment of the European Court is a wound to the body of the common law, one can only say that the Court of Appeal sat up and begged for it.

(c) *Forum non conveniens* and Article 6 jurisdiction

Where residual Regulation jurisdiction under Article 6 is concerned, a court must take into account issues of *forum conveniens* in determining whether to grant or to set aside permission to serve out of the jurisdiction, for, as a matter of English jurisdictional law, service out may only be made, and jurisdiction will only therefore exist, if England is the proper place to bring the proceedings.[281] It has also been held that a stay of proceedings commenced as of right under Article 6 may be granted on the basis of *forum non conveniens*.[282]

---

[279] Case C–281/02 *Owusu v Jackson* [2005] ECR I–1383.
[280] The other five in Jamaica.
[281] CPR 6.37(3).
[282] Including the effect of any *lis alibi pendens*, which is why Art 6 is not mentioned in Arts 33 and 34.

Where the natural forum is a non-Member State, this makes sense as the doctrine of *forum non conveniens* is an integral part of the jurisdictional rules which Article 6 absorbs into the Regulation. It has also been held to apply where the natural forum is another Member State, which is a little more controversial,[283] given that an English court which grants a stay of proceedings remains seised of them,[284] and may at a later stage be asked to lift the stay.

(d) Anti-suit injunctions

As a court seised second has no right to assess the jurisdiction of a court seised first,[285] a court has no right to order a respondent who is claimant in proceedings before another Member State to discontinue his action, for, whatever the theory of the matter, the practical effect of such an order would appear to be that the court would be ruling on the foreign court's jurisdiction and granting relief on the basis that it was lacking, or would be interfering with the foreign judge's control of proceedings in her own court. Whatever might be said in support of the anti-suit injunction as a means of securing respect for jurisdictional agreements in particular, these objections are overwhelming. As soon as it was given the opportunity to do so, the Court declared that anti-suit injunctions, targeted at proceedings before the courts of another Member State, were inconsistent with the scheme of the Regulation.[286] To the submission that an anti-suit injunction did not depend on a finding that the foreign court lacked jurisdiction, but simply sought to enforce the parties' personal rights and obligations to each other, the Court responded, fairly enough, that the effect of the order was to interfere with proceedings before a judge in another Member State: the ends evidently condemned the means. In this respect the Court may have departed from an earlier approach to equitable rights and duties, which were understood as operating *in personam* only,[287] but judicial antipathy to anti-suit injunctions had long been a part of the civil law; and it is undeniable that a judge in a Member State, doing her duty according to her judicial oath, is unlikely to take time to appreciate the subtlety of the distinction between direct

---

[283] *Haji-Ioannou v Frangos* [1999] 2 Lloyd's Rep 337 (CA).
[284] *Rofa Sport Management AG v DHL International (UK) Ltd* [1989] 1 WLR 902 (CA); *The Alexandros T* [2013] UKSC 70, [2014] 1 All ER 590.
[285] Case C–351/89 *Overseas Union Insurance Ltd v New Hampshire Insurance Co* [1991] ECR I–3317.
[286] Case C–159/02 *Turner v Grovit* [2004] ECR I–3565 (a case on the Brussels Convention).
[287] Case C–294/92 *Webb v Webb* [1994] ECR I–1717.

and indirect interference with the proceedings before her court, it making little difference whether interfering instructions from a foreign judge are sent directly or via one of the parties at the bar.

Luxembourg locuta, causa finita. Even so, it is worth reflecting on what caused the misunderstanding in the first place. When an English judge says 'on the application before me I am not asked to decide whether the foreign court has jurisdiction, which I cannot and will not; I am asked to decide whether the parties concluded an obligation, a tie of law, so that the respondent is in breach of his agreement, which I will' he is performing the 'judge as umpire' role which English civil procedure ascribes to him. It is misleading to accuse the judge of doing indirectly that which he may not do directly; he is doing what the parties ask, and the law requires, him to do, by acting as umpire in relation to a particular dispute, giving his decision, decreeing the legal consequences of it, and leaving it to the parties to work out what happens next. It is perverse to assert that, even so, a judge in such circumstances is deciding whether a foreign court has jurisdiction. He is not: he is simply drawing the legal conclusions which flow from his decision as umpire of the issue brought before him for his decision. This may still offend the scheme of the Brussels Regulation, but the real basis of the objection, as it is submitted, lies in the failure to appreciate the relativity of judicial adjudication in the common law. It is far from clear that this has ever been explained; it is unclear whether it would have, or should have, led to any different outcome if it had been; and it is now all water under the bridge. Even so, the course of the modern law has been charted in something of a fog for which no one and everyone is to blame.

(e) Damages for breach of a contractual promise not to sue

Nothing has yet been shown to stand in the way of an action brought to obtain damages for breach of contract; and if the contract contains a term according to which a defendant promises not to sue in a particular court, a claim for damages for its breach, while not as immediately effective as the injunction in holding parties to their obligations, may be better than nothing. Such claims are increasingly seen outside the scope of the Regulation;[288] the English courts, at least, consider that they can be accommodated within it.[289] After all, the incentives to forum shop and to prevent forum shopping

---

[288] *Union Discount Co v Zoller* [2001] EWCA Civ 1755, [2002] 1 WLR 1517.
[289] *The Alexandros T* [2013] UKSC 70, [2014] 1 All ER 590.

never die, but simply move to higher ground: *plus ça change, plus c'est la même chose.*

D. COMMON LAW JURISDICTION

We turn to examine the rules of jurisdiction which apply in an English court when the Regulation does not. These are in fact established by a mixture of common law, statute, judicial decision, and rules of court, but it is convenient to refer to them all as 'common law jurisdiction'.

1. DOMAIN OF COMMON LAW JURISDICTION

If the dispute is not a civil or commercial matter, or is otherwise excluded from the scope of the Regulation, the traditional rules of English law, made up as just described, determine the jurisdiction of the court. *Ex hypothesi,* the Regulation has no bearing on the existence or the exercise of jurisdiction, even in the event of a *lis alibi pendens* before the courts of a Member State; and the judgment will not qualify for recognition in other Member States under Chapter III of the Regulation.

As was said before, if the dispute is in a civil or commercial matter in relation to which Article 6 of the Regulation provides that the jurisdictional rules of English law are to be applied, it is wrong to suppose that the Regulation is inapplicable. The jurisdiction in such a case functions as residual Regulation jurisdiction. The control of *lis alibi pendens* in the courts of Member States, and the recognition of judgments, will still be governed by the Regulation, as will an application for provisional or protective measures. As was also said above, rules which serve as residual Regulation jurisdiction 'receive shape from the subject matter and wording of the [Regulation] itself'.[290] We dealt with this above and need say no more about it now. We proceed from this point to examine the traditional approach to the jurisdiction of an English court, that is, the common law rules of jurisdiction.

---

[290] Mance LJ in *Raiffeisen Zentralbank Österreich AG v Five Star Trading LLC* [2001] EWCA Civ 68, [2001] QB 825 [33]. The case concerned the impact of the then Rome Convention on common law rules on assignment of intangibles, but the point is important and general.

2. JURISDICTION OVER DEFENDANT IN ENGLAND

(a) Establishing jurisdiction by service as of right

Common law jurisdiction draws a fundamental distinction between cases where the defendant is and is not within the territorial jurisdiction of the court when the proceedings are commenced by service of process. The jurisdiction of a court is established by the service of process, and the law on service depends fundamentally on where the person to be served actually is. A claimant is entitled to serve process on any person who is present in England: jurisdiction may in that case be established 'as of right'. The common law takes the view that any person present in England is, or has chosen[291] to put himself in the position of being, liable to be summoned to court by anyone else. The time, manner, and place of service within the jurisdiction is prescribed by procedural rules, but, in principle, service may be made personally, or by post, or by certain electronic means.[292] The significant consequences of an action having been commenced mean that a modest degree of formality, and therefore of technicality, is appropriate.

Primary legislation allows an English company to be served at its registered office[293] (if in liquidation, on its liquidator, and then only with permission of the court[294]). An overseas company may be served within the jurisdiction by making service on the person authorized to accept service on its behalf, but if this is not possible, process may be served by leaving it at or posting it to any place of business within the jurisdiction.[295] In this context, a place of business denotes a fixed and definite place from which the business of the company is carried out.[296] A place at which contracts are made which bind the company will probably count as a place of business of the company.[297] But the procedures for service on corporations set out in Part 6 of the Civil Procedural Rules are additional to statutory service; they widen the methods for service on a company.[298]

---

[291] Cases of kidnap and detention make for slightly silly examination questions; they are of no adult interest. For the marginal case of good service being made within the jurisdiction 'on' a person who is temporarily overseas, see *SSL International plc v TTK LIG Ltd* [2011] EWCA Civ 1170, [2012] Bus LR 858, [54].

[292] CPR 6.3. For service by WhatsApp [*sic*], *Gray v Hurley* [2019] EWHC 1636 (QB).

[293] Companies Act 2006, s 1139(1).

[294] Insolvency Act 1986, s 130(2).

[295] Companies Act 2006, s 1139(2).

[296] *South India Shipping Corp Ltd v Export-Import Bank of Korea* [1985] 1 WLR 585 (CA).

[297] cf *Adams v Cape Industries plc* [1990] Ch 433 (CA), a case on the recognition of foreign judgments.

[298] *Saab v Saudi American Bank* [1999] 1 WLR 1861 (CA).

Jurisdiction for the purpose of an action *in rem*, something which is really confined to admiralty law, is established by effecting service on the vessel while it is within territorial waters.

(b) Disputing jurisdiction after service

A defendant who considers that as a matter of law the court has no jurisdiction over him or over the subject matter of the claim, or who contends that service was irregular or on some other ground seeks to have service set aside, must first acknowledge the service which was made on him. This is a purely formal step, but it is what entitles him, within a defined period, to make an application under CPR Part 11[299] for a declaration that the court has no jurisdiction, and for consequential relief such as the setting aside of service. Where he has been served within the jurisdiction, the most common ground for objection is that the case is one of Regulation jurisdiction and the Brussels I Regulation provides that he is not liable to be sued in the English courts. He may also plead a personal immunity from the jurisdiction of the courts or that the subject matter of the claim is something over which the court has no common law jurisdiction: in any such case if the objection is sustained service should be set aside and the action dismissed; he may also complain that the service purportedly made on him did not comply with the rules governing service.[300] But if the application to dispute the jurisdiction is made, everything apart from the question of any provisional or protective measures is then put on hold, pending the final determination of the challenge to the jurisdiction. Proceedings on the merits only start after that. The process, including appeals, can take a considerable length of time.

If the defendant acknowledges service but makes no application under CPR Part 11, or if he takes a step in the action which is not relevant to a challenge to the jurisdiction, he will, at least if the step taken is sufficiently unequivocal,[301] be taken to have submitted to the jurisdiction. In these circumstances either the original service, or this apparent submission, or both, will mean that there is no objection to the jurisdiction of the court, no matter that a challenge might have been made or pursued successfully.[302]

---

[299] This procedure for contesting the jurisdiction is applicable whether the case is one to which Regulation jurisdiction applies, one based on common law jurisdiction by service within the jurisdiction, or one based on common law jurisdiction by service out of the jurisdiction.

[300] The court has a power to cure or overlook 'irregularities', and that power may be deployed where the setting aside of service would be followed, inevitably, by re-service.

[301] *Zumax Nigeria v First City Monument Bank plc* [2016] EWCA Civ 567.

[302] The exception to this proposition is that where there was no subject-matter jurisdiction, personal submission cannot remedy the deficiency, and jurisdiction remains non-existent.

(c) Admitting jurisdiction but seeking a stay of the proceedings:
    forum non conveniens

A defendant who cannot argue that the court lacks jurisdiction and that
he should not have been served and that service should now be set aside,
but who is unhappy about being sued in England rather than elsewhere, is
in a different position. He may apply to stay the proceedings on the ground
that, although the court has jurisdiction over him in relation to the claim,
the claimant should nevertheless bring the proceedings before the courts
of another country: in other words, that England is a *forum non conveniens*.
Confusingly, to be sure, the application for a stay is generally required to be
made within the framework of CPR Part 11, even though the defendant is at
this point not disputing the jurisdiction of the court properly so called.[303] If
his argument succeeds, the English action will not be dismissed[304] but will
remain stayed: that is, pending, but held in abeyance.[305] Although he certainly cannot be ordered to, the claimant may then conclude that he has no
real alternative to suing in a foreign court. In principle a stay may be lifted if
some problem arises, or if an undertaking given to the court by the defendant
is not observed: as the action will have remained pending throughout, there
is no problem of limitation if it resumes.

Where service was made within the jurisdiction, two main grounds
may justify a stay of proceedings. The first ground is universally referred
to as *forum non conveniens*. If the defendant can show that there is another
court to whose jurisdiction he is amenable[306] and which is available to the
claimant, and that it would be clearly more appropriate than England for the
trial of the action (that is, a *forum conveniens*), a stay will generally be ordered unless the claimant can then turn the tables by showing that it would
be unjust for him to have to take his chances before that foreign court. The
two limbs of the test are initially distinct, with separate burdens of proof, but,
in the end, a court will put all the information together to decide whether, in
the light of the answers to these questions, the interests of justice require a
stay of proceedings.

---

[303] However, a later application for a stay may be permitted if, for example, the grounds for it
were not apparent at the time of service, but only emerged later: *Texan Management Ltd v Pacific
Electric Wire & Cable Co Ltd* [2009] UKPC 46.

[304] Although for the proposition that it may be dismissed if a stay would leave the claimant
unable to sue in the foreign court, see *Haji-Ioannou v Frangos* [1999] 2 Lloyd's Rep 337 (CA).

[305] *The Alexandros T* [2013] UKSC 70, [2014] 1 All ER 590.

[306] Even if this arises only by virtue of his submission to its jurisdiction: *Vedanta Resources plc
v Lungowe* [2019] UKSC 20, [2019] 2 WLR 1051.

This radical and potent principle was entirely judge-made, principally by the House of Lords in half a dozen bold and brilliant cases.[307] It made a distinctive contribution to common law jurisdictional thinking which went around the common law world at the speed of light. What underpins it is the simple wisdom of the common law, that if the parties are content to have a trial in England no one, least of all a judge, will stand in their way;[308] but if they are not in agreement, there is no principled reason why the claimant alone should get to decide where the resolution of *their* dispute will take place. Once that is accepted, all that remains is to refine the test which will implement the principle. In England this is done by showing that there is a court, clearly more appropriate than England for the trial of the action, and asking whether there would be any injustice in having the trial take place there.

In Australia, the same broad principle is accepted but is applied rather differently: the immediate focus is not on the comparative appropriateness of the foreign court as against the local one, but on whether the Australian court is clearly inappropriate for the trial.[309] Even so, it should be observed that the leading Australian cases have tended to be personal injury cases, where the prospect of making the injured claimant, who is entitled to sue in Australia, drag himself several thousand miles to a foreign court, just because the defendant prefers it that way, is not immediately compelling. The English doctrine, by contrast, was developed in unemotional commercial disputes. But the Australian approach also reflects a doctrinal view that if a court is given jurisdiction it should require clear and convincing grounds for it to decline to exercise it; and this is therefore closer to a civilian view that if the legislator has vested the judge with jurisdiction, the judge has been told to adjudicate rather than to consider that he or she has power to set aside the law, whether on grounds of *forum conveniens* or otherwise.

This aspect of the inherent power of an English court to regulate its own proceedings is a natural counterpart to its inherent jurisdiction. It is a necessary counterpart to rules of jurisdiction which are really only rules

---

[307] The leading authorities are *Spiliada Maritime Corp v Cansulex Ltd* [1987] AC 460; *Connelly v RTZ Corp plc* [1998] AC 854; *Lubbe v Cape plc* [2000] 1 WLR 1545 (HL); *VTB Capital plc v Nutritek International Corp* [2013] UKSC 5, [2013] 2 AC 337; and *Vedanta Resources plc v Lungowe* [2019] UKSC 20, [2019] 2 WLR 1051. For the steps which led to *Spiliada*, see *The Atlantic Star* [1974] AC 436, *MacShannon v Rockware Glass Ltd* [1978] AC 705, and *The Abidin Daver* [1984] AC 398.

[308] Unless there is an absence of subject-matter jurisdiction.

[309] *Oceanic Sun Line Special Shipping Co v Fay* (1988) 165 CLR 197; *Voth v Manildra Flour Mills Pty Ltd* (1990) 171 CLR 538; *Henry v Henry* (1996) 185 CLR 571 (which says that it may well be inappropriate if the foreign action was started first); *Régie Nationale des Usines Renault v Zhang* (2003) 210 CLR 491.

about service and which are far too broad and insensitive to be sufficient as jurisdiction-defining rules; but it is a subtle counterpart, for it has avoided being trapped within rigid lines of operation. It has been confirmed, but not constrained, by statute.[310] It has been embraced by the profession;[311] and has been taken up throughout the common law world. Lord Goff of Chieveley, the principal architect of the developed law, described the doctrine as the 'most civilised of legal principles',[312] and he was right. It allows a judge in England to accept the contention, from a defendant, that the courts of another country, which are available, would be better placed to give the parties the adjudication they deserve and for which they will pay. It reflects judicial comity in acknowledging that where sovereignties collide, a sensitive solution is preferable to a mechanical one.

Courts occasionally scold parties for spending their time and money on a stay application when they would do better, in the opinion of the judge, to get on with trying the merits of the claim instead. 'Litigating about where to litigate' is, from this perspective, a Bad Thing. But this does not convince everybody. A brisk preliminary skirmish on jurisdiction may well allow each side to gauge the strength of the other's case and the stomach each has for the fight. After the issue has been decided, the case may well settle and, if it does, on better informed terms than would otherwise have been the case. If this be accepted, the doctrine of *forum conveniens* contributes to efficient dispute resolution, and the occasional judicial rebuke may just be a price which has to be paid.

Turning now to the detail of the test, the first limb requires that the foreign court be shown to be available to the claimant, and to be clearly or distinctly more appropriate than England. So far as concerns being 'available', the fact that the claimant lacks the resources to sue in the foreign court does not make that court unavailable, although it may well be relevant under the second limb.[313] As to appropriateness, attention will focus on the location of the events and of the witnesses to them, on the law which will be applied to determine the case, on general issues of trial convenience, on the relative strength of connection with England and with the alternative forum, on whether the foreign court will be able to gather in and tie up all the loose ends

---

[310] Civil Jurisdiction and Judgments Act 1982, s 49.

[311] Perhaps too enthusiastically? See *VTB Capital plc v Nutritek International Corp* [2013] UKSC 5, [2013] 2 AC 337; *Vedanta Resources plc v Lungowe* [2019] UKSC 20, [2019] 2 WLR 1051.

[312] *Airbus Industrie GIE v Patel* [1999] 1 AC 119.

[313] *Lubbe v Cape plc* [2000] 1 WLR 1545 (HL).

better than the English court, and so on.[314] Evaluation of these factors is a matter for the judge who hears the application, and appeals are supposed to be discouraged.[315]

Once the defendant has shown the more appropriate (and in this sense, natural) forum to be a court overseas, the claimant may still resist a stay by showing that it is unjust to confine her to whatever her rights and remedies will be before the foreign court. Arguments that damages will be lower or civil procedure less helpful to her will not usually be good enough,[316] for as long as the foreign court has a developed system of law it is inappropriate for the English courts to pass judgment on it, and still less on individual rules self-servingly highlighted and then moaned about. But if funding the action in the foreign court is beyond the practical means and resources of the claimant, whereas financial support would be available to her in England, it may well be unjust to stay, at least in a case which requires substantial labour to prepare the evidence and conduct the trial. Though this may make an inroad on the principle that critical comparison with the foreign court's procedure will not be invited,[317] the interests of justice demand that it be permitted. So also if there is cogent[318] evidence that the claimant will not receive a fair trial, especially on racial or religious grounds: a stay of English proceedings in such a case would surely be unthinkable.

Until very recently, attempts by a claimant to show a court that the foreign court favoured by the defendant was objectively unsatisfactory as a tribunal were treated by the English courts with chilly disapproval. But, perhaps under unacknowledged pressure from the European Convention on Human Rights, courts have now accepted that it is permissible and proper to point to and demonstrate serious fault with the alternative court, and to allow the English proceedings to continue despite the fact that the natural forum lies

---

[314] For example, see *VTB Capital plc v Nutritek International Corp* [2013] UKSC 5, [2013] 2 AC 337.

[315] A point made by Lord Templeman in *Spiliada Maritime Corp v Cansulex Ltd* [1987] AC 460 (HL), and reiterated periodically since: see *VTB Capital plc v Nutritek International Corp* [2013] UKSC 5, [2013] 2 AC 337; *Vedanta Resources plc v Lungowe* [2019] UKSC 20, [2019] 2 WLR 1051. For light relief, a peerless evaluation of the view from the courthouse in Galveston, Texas is found in *Smith v Colonial Penn Insurance Co* 943 F Supp 782 (1997) (US Dist Ct).

[316] *Spiliada* at 482.

[317] *Lubbe v Cape plc* [2000] 1 WLR 1545 (HL), explaining *Connelly v RTZ Corp Ltd* [1998] AC 854; *Vedanta Resources plc v Lungowe* [2019] UKSC 20, [2019] 2 WLR 1051. Were the common law otherwise, it probably would have fallen foul of Art 6 of the European Convention on Human Rights.

[318] *The Abidin Daver* [1984] AC 398: attack by innuendo is disreputable.

elsewhere.[319] It will require cogent evidence, but if this shows that there is a real risk that the court will not deliver justice according to the law, it cannot really be proper to stay English proceedings which have been commenced as of right. If that involves passing judgment on the quality of a foreign legal system, too bad. Passing judgment is what judges are in office to do.

The argument that the claimant will lose in the foreign court, because the claim she makes in England will not be available to her in the foreign court or because the defendant will have a good defence to the action, should be an irrelevance: after all, strict impartiality should be the watchword, and in every case, in every court, someone has to lose. But there is occasional support for the view that in such a case it would be unjust to order a stay, on the seductive, but surely wrong-headed, basis that a claim should not go unheard. Yet to favour claimant over defendant in this way is hard to justify: the idea that the rules are different in a case where the claimant has only one court in which she can expect to win is as wrong as it would be if a defendant were to say that the foreign forum is the only court in which his defence can be successfully advanced. Save for undefined exceptional cases, no account should be taken of this fact.

If relief is granted, the case is stayed, and remains pending. The stay may well be ordered on terms which reflect undertakings given to the court by the defendant, so that if these turn out to be ineffective the stay can be lifted and the action allowed to proceed. If, by contrast, the action were to have been dismissed, it is difficult to see how these undertakings could then be enforced, or the action revived.

(d) Admitting jurisdiction but seeking a stay of the proceedings: breach of contract

The second, distinct, basis for the defendant to seek a stay of proceedings is by pointing to a contract by which the claimant promised the defendant not to sue in England but only in a foreign court.[320] Here matters stand very differently. Rather than the defendant having to carry the burden of persuading the court to order a stay, a stay will be ordered on the defendant's application unless the claimant, who is breaking his contract, can establish jolly good reasons for the court not to order a stay.[321] There are two parts to the analysis.

---

[319] *Altimo Holdings & Investment Ltd v Kyrgyz Mobil Tel Ltd* [2011] UKPC 11, [2012] 1 WLR 1804 is probably the leading decision. cf, however, *Mengiste v Endowment Fund for the Rehabilitation of Tigre* [2017] EWCA Civ 1326.

[320] If the argument is that there is a valid and binding arbitration agreement, the Arbitration Act 1996, s 9 makes a stay mandatory, and no element of discretion arises.

[321] *Donohue v Armco Inc* [2001] UKHL 64, [2002] 1 All ER 749.

First, the agreement must be examined. It will have to be shown (if it is disputed) that the agreement was made and is binding on the parties; that on its true construction it applies to the particular action brought by the claimant; and that on its true construction it means that the bringing of English proceedings is a breach of contract. If so, a stay will usually be the most appropriate remedy, and will usually be ordered.[322]

If they arise, questions of construction and validity are undertaken by reference to the law which governs the jurisdiction agreement, which will often be the law governing the contract of which it is a term, and any overriding provision of the *lex fori*.[323] So far as concerns its material scope, the defendant will need to show that the words were wide enough to encompass the action brought by the claimant: a term which says it applies to 'all disputes arising from this contract', may, for example, be said not to extend to a claim alleging pre-contractual misrepresentation or claims in respect of equitable obligations. But where the law governing the contract term is English, such old-school nit-picking will be very strongly disfavoured: there is a very strong judicial instinct to construe the clause and the intentions of the parties widely and inclusively, so that the untidiness, or worse, of two courts having competence over parts of a single matter will not arise;[324] if the parties have entered into a relationship comprising several contracts, each with its own jurisdiction clause, a different, and obviously tricky, question of construction arises.[325]

So far as concerns the personal scope of the agreement, if on its true construction A had promised B not to bring proceedings in a particular court against C, C may not be entitled to enforce the contract term in his own right,[326] but B, as promisee, should be able to. As regards the exclusivity of jurisdiction, the contract is not broken unless the parties obliged themselves

---

[322] *Donohue v Armco Inc* [2001] UKHL 64, [2002] 1 All ER 749.

[323] Invalidity may be brought about, for example, by the Consumer Rights Act 2015. In the case of a consumer contract or employment contract to which Civil Jurisdiction and Judgments Act 1982 ss 15A–15E apply (inserted by SI 2019/479, reg 26), ss 15B(6) and 15C(6) restrict the validity of choice of court agreements in the same way as the Brussels Regulation; cf above, p 62.

[324] *Premium Nafta Products Ltd v Fili Shipping Co Ltd* [2007] UKHL 40, [2007] Bus LR 1719. The authorities are mainly on arbitration agreements, but the principles are general.

[325] See, for example, *Bank Paribas SA v Trattamento Rifiati Metropolitani SpA* [2019] EWCA Civ 768.

[326] Though he may point to the promise of A in aid of his own application for a stay on the general ground of *forum non conveniens: Global Partners Fund Ltd v Babcock & Brown Ltd* [2010] NSWCA 196, (2010) 79 ACSR 383; cf *VTB Capital plc v Nutritek International* [2013] UKSC 5, [2013] 2 AC 337.

and each other not to sue in the English court.[327] They do not need to have used the word 'exclusive', but it certainly helps if they did: less adroit wording, as where 'the parties submit to the jurisdiction of the courts of X' or 'the courts of Y are to have jurisdiction over all disputes', is harder to construe with confidence,[328] which rather defeats the whole object of making jurisdiction a matter of certainty rather than chance.

If the clause is interpreted in such a way as to make it a breach of contract for the English proceedings to have been brought, a stay is highly probable, though not inevitable.[329] If England is the natural forum, and if there are additional powerful reasons why the claimant should nevertheless not be held to his jurisdictional promise,[330] the action may be allowed to continue. A possible reason for not staying the proceedings will appear if persons who are not party to the agreement are involved in the dispute: if they are not privy to, hence bound by, the particular agreement, it would be very inconvenient for the litigation to be fragmented.[331] After all, a court has a distinct public duty to secure the proper administration of justice, and this may mean that a private bilateral agreement on jurisdiction has to be subordinated to the broader interest. But otherwise, the claimant should not be heard to complain about particular aspects of the legal system which he agreed to.

If the action is nevertheless allowed to proceed in England despite the agreement on exclusive jurisdiction, it is unclear what, if anything, prevents the defendant counterclaiming for damages for any demonstrable loss flowing from the breach of contract. To permit an action to continue despite a perfectly (bilaterally) valid choice of court agreement is only to refuse relief by way of specific enforcement; a remedy for damages for breach of contract is a common law right which, in principle, the defendant may assert, and by counterclaim if necessary. It may be difficult to prove and quantify loss, and it may feel awkward to allow such a claim to proceed in a court which has refused to prevent the breach. But damages for breach of contract remains a common law right; they have been allowed for breach of jurisdiction agreements by suing overseas;[332] and if the agreement on jurisdiction was bought

---

[327] If they did not, and the clause is non-exclusive, see below.

[328] Although it may still be a breach of a non-exclusive agreement on jurisdiction to sue or to continue outside the nominated court: *Sabah Shipyard (Pakistan) Ltd v Pakistan* [2002] EWCA Civ 1643, [2003] 2 Lloyd's Rep 571.

[329] *The El Amria* [1981] 2 Lloyd's Rep 119 (CA); *The Pioneer Container* [1994] 2 AC 324 (PC).

[330] But for a damages claim, see below.

[331] *Bouygues Offshore SA v Caspian Shipping Co (Nos 1, 3, 4, 5)* [1998] 2 Lloyd's Rep 461 (CA); *Donohue v Armco Inc* [2001] UKHL 64, [2002] 1 All ER 749.

[332] *Union Discount Co Ltd v Zoller* [2001] EWCA Civ 1755, [2002] 1 WLR 1517.

and paid for, it would denature it to withhold the rightful common law remedy for its breach.

A word is called for in connection with agreements said to be for the non-exclusive jurisdiction of a court. Where on its true construction this is what the parties have chosen, the court will generally respect their agreement. That will mean that it will be unlikely to entertain jurisdictional objections to the chosen court, whether it is English or foreign, though it will not consider it to be a breach of contract to sue in a different court. It may, however, interpret the clause as giving either party an option to invoke the jurisdiction of the named court, and the exercise of that option as obliging the other to litigate only in that court.[333] An arbitration clause, after all, works in pretty much the same way, and that 'optional to begin with, but mandatory as soon as invoked by one of the parties' character has never been seen as problematic. Only if the language of 'non-exclusive' is taken to mean that no restriction is placed, at any time or in any circumstances, on the right to bring proceedings elsewhere, whether in place of or in parallel with the chosen court, will such a clause be seen as imposing no limitations at all on the parties who agreed to it; and in that case one may fairly wonder what the point of it really was. In any event, it cannot prevent a court taking control to prevent what appear to be needlessly parallel proceedings.

3. JURISDICTION OVER DEFENDANT NOT IN ENGLAND

(a) Jurisdiction by service overseas with the permission of the court

If the defendant is not in England he cannot be served with process as of right. Process must therefore be served on him overseas—out of the jurisdiction, or *ex juris* as it is sometimes said—in order to establish the jurisdiction of the court; and this generally[334] requires the prior permission of the court. The procedure is set out in CPR Part 6, but the authorities on the interpretation of predecessor texts are, inevitably, still pertinent. The claimant will first apply, without notice to his opponent, for permission to serve out. The

---

[333] *Sabah Shipyard (Pakistan) Ltd v Pakistan* [2002] EWCA Civ 1643, [2003] 2 Lloyd's Rep 571.

[334] Permission is not required for service out if a statute provides, in effect, that there is a right to bring the proceedings in England even though the defendant is not in England or the facts did not arise within the jurisdiction: CPR 6.33(3). These cases are rare, but this procedure will be applicable, for particular example, in relation to claims made by consumers and employees in the context of Civil Jurisdiction and Judgments Act 1982, ss 15A–E (as inserted by SI 2019/479).

application must state the grounds on which it is made, and must identify the specific grounds relied on.[335] As the application is made in the absence of the defendant, the application must, as is said, be 'full and frank' in alerting the court to arguments which would be made by the defendant in opposition to the application. Once permission has been granted and service has been made, a defendant who objects to defending the claim in England is required to first acknowledge service but may then apply, under CPR Part 11, for an order declaring that the court has no jurisdiction, and for consequential relief such as setting aside of the permission, and of the service made pursuant to that permission. On the hearing of this application, it will be the claimant who bears the burden of proof on all those issues which determine whether permission should have been given in the first place: it is only a procedural quirk that the application is made by the defendant; it cannot and does not mean that the burden has somehow now shifted to him. Access to this species of jurisdiction is not a right. Jurisdiction based on service out is an exorbitant jurisdiction,[336] and the onus of persuasion lies on the claimant seeking to invoke it.

The claimant must show three things. The first is that each pleaded claim falls within one or more of the sub-paragraphs of paragraph 3.1 of Practice Direction 6B to CPR Part 6. These are sometimes referred to as 'grounds', or 'gateways' to jurisdiction; but the rules call them 'paragraphs', and so shall we. It used to be said, almost as an article of faith, that each claim must fall within the 'letter and spirit' of the rule,[337] lest an exorbitant jurisdiction be widened still further by lax construction of its language; but this has rather gone out of fashion in recent days. The second requirement is that England is the proper place in which to bring the claim;[338] and the third is that the claimant believes that his claim has a reasonable prospect of success on its merits.[339] Though these three elements are distinct and must be individually satisfied, so that a clear success in one cannot condone failure in another,[340] the broader issue of the relationship between them is still subject to debate.

---

[335] CPR 6.37(1)(a).
[336] So said Lord Diplock in *Amin Rasheed Shipping Corp v Kuwait Insurance Co* [1984] AC 50, 65.
[337] *The Hagen* [1908] P 189 (CA); *Johnson v Taylor Bros* [1920] AC 144, 153; *Mercedes-Benz AG v Leiduck* [1996] 1 AC 284, 289 (PC).
[338] CPR 6.37(3).
[339] CPR 6.37(1)(b).
[340] *Seaconsar Far East Ltd v Bank Markazi Jomhouri Islami Iran* [1994] 1 AC 438.

(b) The paragraphs which define when a court may authorize service out

The paragraphs, now set out in the Practice Direction,[341] number twenty or so. These define the claims in respect of which the court is authorized to grant permission to serve out. At first sight it may make sense for the law to have categories of case into which the claims must fit before permission can be given, but second sight leads one to think again. Permission will not in any event be granted unless England is the proper place to bring, or natural forum for, the claim. If this condition, which emerged as a specific and discrete requirement only relatively recently,[342] is satisfied, it is harder to see what useful function is served, or value added, by these earlier, more primitive, pigeonhole criteria.[343] The overall structure of the law, which evolved without an overall plan, now needs to be re-thought. The vivid question is whether, if the central role of *forum conveniens* had been appreciated from the outset, the law would have devised these pigeonholes, insisting on compliance with their letter (and their spirit) before permission to sue in the natural forum was granted. One may ask: if England is clearly the proper place to bring the claim, should it really matter, for example, where the contract was made, or broken? Nevertheless, the paragraphs of the Practice Direction are, if in a rather bargain-basement sense,[344] the law.

If there is any uncertainty about any fact which is required to bring the claim within the paragraph relied on, the claimant is required to make out a good arguable case for its satisfaction. This is a laxer requirement than having to satisfy a balance of probability as to it[345] and, notwithstanding some recent, rather painful, analysis in the Supreme Court,[346] it should not be taken to require the claimant to have the better of the argument on the point. After all, the load-bearing element of the test is whether England is the proper place to bring the claim; this fact also explains why the test is not the same as

---

[341] CPR PD 6B 3.1.

[342] In *Spiliada Maritime Corp v Cansulex Ltd* [1987] AC 460, although there had been occasional trailers for it in earlier cases.

[343] Compare *Abela v Baadarani* [2013] UKSC 44, [2013] 1 WLR 2403 with *Four Seasons Holdings Inc v Brownlie* [2017] UKSC 80, [2018] 1 WLR 192.

[344] Because they can be changed by the Civil Procedure Rule Committee, very easily indeed.

[345] *Seaconsar Far East Ltd v Bank Markazi Jomhouri Islami Iran* [1994] 1 AC 438. But *Altimo Holdings & Investment Ltd v Kyrgyz Mobil Tel Ltd* [2011] UKPC 7, [2012] 1 WLR 1804 reinterpreted this as a requirement to have much the better of the argument on the point, which is a great leap backwards if England has been distinctly shown to be the proper place to sue.

[346] *Four Seasons Holdings Inc v Brownlie* [2017] UKSC 80, [2018] 1 WLR 192; *Goldman Sachs International v Novo Banco SA* [2018] UKSC 34, [2018] 1 WLR 3683; see also *Kaefer Aislamientos SA de CV v AMS Drilling Mexico SA de CV* [2019] EWCA Civ 10, [2019] 1 WLR 3398.

that which applies in relation to Regulation jurisdiction, where this question simply does not arise.

If, therefore, the claimant applies for permission to serve on the basis that the claim arises from a contract made within the jurisdiction but the defendant, whilst admitting that there is a contract, denies that it was made in England, the claimant must show a good arguable case that England is where it was made. These geographical points are located, if any law is needed, by reference to English domestic law; the broad legal concepts are defined by English law, including its conflicts rules. So in the case just mentioned, if the defendant were to accept that there was a contract as a matter of English domestic law, but to deny that it was a valid contract by reference to the law which actually governs it, the question will be referred to the law which governs the contract. But if he contests the proposition that it was made in England, this will be tested by reference to English domestic law.

Each claim advanced must be distinctly referable to one or more of the paragraphs of the Practice Direction.[347] Any which are not will be deleted, though the recent addition of paragraph (4A) makes that less likely than it used to be. A claimant is not necessarily precluded from adding further claims after service has been made, but the court should exercise its discretion to disallow amendment to prevent a claimant seeking permission to serve process on a narrow basis, only to seek to amend it, and reveal the whole of the iceberg, once the defendant has accepted jurisdiction.

In the account which follows we will focus on the paragraphs which are of greatest practical importance. Those which are applicable to commercial matters are mentioned first; then those less frequent in commercial litigation; and then the remainder.

So far as concerns claims related to contracts, three paragraphs are provided. Under paragraph (6), service may be permitted where a claim is made in respect of a contract where the contract was made within the jurisdiction, or was made through an agent trading or residing within the jurisdiction, or is governed by English law, or contains a term to the effect that the court shall have jurisdiction to determine any claim in respect of the contract. In principle, the contract must be one by which the parties are bound, but as assignees and third parties may enforce contracts which they did not make, it is not necessary that the claimant and defendant be the original parties. Under paragraph (7), service may be ordered when a claim is made in respect

---

[347] For otherwise the scope of the rule would be extended: *Metall und Rohstoff AG v Donaldson, Lufkin & Jenrette Inc* [1990] 1 QB 391 (CA).

of a breach of contract committed within the jurisdiction. Paragraph (8) provides for service where a claim is made for a declaration that no contract exists where, if the contract were found to exist, it would have fallen within paragraph (6).

As said above, if it is not conceded, there must be a good arguable case that there is a contract,[348] valid according to rules of English law including its conflicts rules;[349] the place of its making is determined by English domestic law.[350] Though these provisions are drawn widely, the contract must be one by which the claimant and defendant are said to be bound: it should not suffice that a contract *inter alios* forms the background to the claim.[351] For the purposes of paragraph (7), it is generally considered that breach by a repudiatory act occurs where the act was done; breach by non-performance where the required act was to have been performed, though the line between these is neither clear nor stable. Paragraph (8) is designed to make it straightforward to bring a claim for a declaration of non-liability in relation to a contract or an alleged contract. It probably applies generally to claims which deny that a contractual duty is owed to the defendant, but which the defendant alleges is owed, rather than being limited to cases in which it is claimed that no contract ever existed.[352] It is also to be expected that a claim for relief which is consequential upon holding that there is no contract is also covered by this ground: convenience and common sense suggests that it should be; if that is not enough, paragraph (4A) will do the job.

As to torts, under paragraph (9), if a claim is made in tort, service out may be authorized if damage was sustained within the jurisdiction, or if the damage sustained resulted from an act committed within the jurisdiction.[353] A predecessor rule, which required that the claim be 'founded on *a* tort', had been interpreted to require that there be an actual tort, ascertained, if it was not conceded, by reference to rules of English law including its conflicts rules.[354] The omission of the indefinite article from the corresponding

---

[348] *Ex hypothesi*, if the claim for *quantum meruit* is on the footing that services were rendered and accepted, but there was no contract, it cannot fall within this paragraph: *Sharab v Al-Waleed* [2012] EWHC 1798 (Ch).

[349] *Amin Rasheed Shipping Corp v Kuwait Insurance Co* [1984] AC 50; *Bank of Baroda v Vysya Bank Ltd* [1994] 2 Lloyd's Rep 87.

[350] *Chevron International Oil Co v A/S Sea Team (The TS Havprins)* [1983] 2 Lloyd's Rep 356.

[351] *Global 5000 Ltd v Wadhawan* [2012] EWCA Civ 13, [2012] 1 Lloyd's Rep 239.

[352] A court will grant permission to serve a claim for a negative declaration if it is an appropriate case for the seeking of such relief: *Messier Dowty Ltd v Sabena SA* [2000] 1 WLR 2040 (CA).

[353] *VTB Capital plc v Nutritek International Corp* [2013] UKSC 5, [2013] 2 AC 337.

[354] RSC Ord 11, r 1(1)(f) as interpreted in *Metall und Rohstoff AG v Donaldson, Lufkin & Jenrette Inc* [1990] QB 391 (CA).

wording in paragraph (9) makes it uncertain whether it is still necessary to show, to the standard of a good arguable case, that there was *a* tort. If the rule now requires only that the pleaded claim be properly formulated as one in tort, or be characterized as tortious, there will be no need to show a good arguable case upon actual liability before service out is authorized.[355] It does seem odd that, because the term 'contract' does not describe a cause of action, whereas 'tort' does, a jurisdictional requirement of liability might be imposed by the tort paragraph which is absent from the contractual counterparts. No obvious policy requires this and, as a result, it may therefore be better to read paragraph (9) as referring to the characterization of the claim rather than to the existence of liability, and to pass over what it used to require.

Damage is sustained in England if some significant damage is sustained in England: it need not be all, nor even most, of it.[356] There is no earthly reason why 'sustained' in paragraph (9) should reflect or reproduce the interpretation of where 'immediate' damage 'occurred' within Article 7(2) of the Brussels I Regulation, and every reason why it should not, as the functions of the two rules are very different.[357] And as a matter of plain English, damage (say loss of earnings) can be sustained in England even though the initial blow was inflicted overseas.[358] An act is committed within the jurisdiction if substantial and efficacious acts were committed within the jurisdiction, even if other substantial acts were committed elsewhere.[359]

The new paragraph (21) applies when a claim is made for breach of confidence or misuse of private information where detriment was suffered, or will be suffered, within the jurisdiction; or detriment which has been, or will be, suffered results from an act committed, or likely to be committed, within the jurisdiction. It is no longer necessary to debate whether these examples of wrongful conduct count as torts for the purpose of paragraph (9).[360]

So far as concerns constructive trusteeship and restitution, paragraph (15) allows service out to be authorized where a claim is made against the defendant as constructive trustee or resulting trustee and his alleged liability

---

[355] Although the requirement of CPR 6.37(1)(b) will still need to be satisfied, and the claim shown to raise a serious issue on the merits.

[356] *Metall und Rohstoff AG v Donaldson, Lufkin & Jenrette Inc* [1990] 1 QB 391 (CA).

[357] The European rule is not augmented, or qualified by a *forum conveniens* discretion, and is in any event an exceptional rule, given a construction no wider than is necessary to achieve its purposes. It therefore operates in a very different way from the common law rule.

[358] *Four Seasons Holdings Inc v Brownlie* [2017] UKSC 80, [2018] 1 WLR 192: the judgments on this point, however, are expressions of *obiter dicta*.

[359] *Metall und Rohstoff AG v Donaldson, Lufkin & Jenrette Inc* [1990] 1 QB 391 (CA).

[360] Thus making redundant the sterile debate in *Vidal-Hall v Google Inc* [2015] EWCA Civ 311, [2016] QB 1003.

arises out of acts committed, or events occurring, or property located, within the jurisdiction. The former rule was explicit that the acts committed within the jurisdiction were not required to be those of the defendant; it is unlikely that the omission of these words from the current version of the rule reflects a desire to narrow the scope of the paragraph. The acts must still have something to do with the defendant. Only some of the acts, not necessarily the receipt of assets, need take place within the jurisdiction.[361] So as long as a participant in fraud takes part in a scheme where one of the wrongdoers did acts in the jurisdiction, service out may probably be authorized for all of them.[362] Paragraph (16), which has been considerably widened, now allows service where a claim is made for restitution and either the defendant's alleged liability arises out of acts committed within the jurisdiction, or the enrichment is obtained within the jurisdiction, or the claim is governed by English law.

So far as other types of claim are concerned, paragraph (1) is available if the defendant is domiciled within the jurisdiction,[363] but unless the matter is not a civil or commercial one, the Regulation will apply and the case will not be one of common law jurisdiction at all. Paragraph (2) applies if the claim is made for an injunction ordering the defendant to do or to not do an act within the jurisdiction. The injunction must comprise a substantial element of the relief sought,[364] and it must be an injunction in respect of substantive rights: an application for a freezing order, or other relief not predicated on the existence of substantive rights, is not within this provision[365] but is specifically provided for by paragraph (5) instead. Paragraph (3) is available if the defendant proposed to be served is a necessary or proper party to a claim against another defendant who has been or will be served;[366] the paragraph is a broad one which encourages the efficient disposal of claims; the disjunctive wording should not be misinterpreted, for many defendants who are not necessary parties may still be proper parties to the claim.[367] In this

---

[361] *ISC Technologies Ltd v Guerin* [1992] 2 Lloyd's Rep 430.

[362] If one can be served otherwise, it will also be possible to apply for permission under paragraph (4) to serve a co-defendant as a necessary or proper party to the claim against the defendant served otherwise.

[363] Within the meaning of the Civil Jurisdiction and Judgments Act 1982: CPR 6.31(1)(i). However, as CPR 6.31(1) is to be repealed on Exit Day (SI 2019/521, reg 16(a)), it may be that the meaning of 'domiciled' in this context will revert to its common law meaning, which would be rather unsatisfactory.

[364] *Rosler v Hilbery* [1925] 1 Ch 250 (CA).

[365] *Mercedes-Benz AG v Leiduck* [1996] 1 AC 284 (PC).

[366] Paragraph (4) makes corresponding provision for third parties to be brought in by defendants.

[367] See *Altimo Holdings & Investment Ltd v Kyrgyz Mobil Tel Ltd* [2011] UKPC 7, [2012] 1 WLR 1804.

particular case the court has a more pressing responsibility to ensure that the rule is not abused,[368] for it does allow a claimant to serve the defendant on the basis of what one may call 'jurisdictional liability by association' with another. The court should therefore be satisfied that the claim against the 'anchor' defendant really is one which it is reasonable for the court to try:[369] a spurious or contrived claim should not be enough. And where the anchor defendant is liable to be sued in England because Article 4 of the Regulation means he cannot contest the jurisdiction on *forum* grounds, a court should look carefully to ensure that this European point does not distort what is, after all, an independent, common law, jurisdictional rule.[370] Paragraph (4A) is new: it is available if a claim is made against the defendant in reliance on one or more of paragraphs (2), (6) to (16), (19), or (21) and a further claim is made against the same defendant which arises out of the same or closely connected facts.[371]

Paragraph (10) applies if the proceedings seek the enforcement in England of any judgment or arbitral award.[372] Claims relating wholly or principally to property in England fall under paragraph (11); given the broad nature of 'property', this provision appears to be of substantial, but largely untested, width.[373] Claims made in respect of English law trusts come under paragraph (12); claims made in respect of trusts which provide for English jurisdiction are covered by the new paragraph (12A). Claims in the administration of the estate of an English domiciliary, or of a deceased who left assets within the jurisdiction, fall under paragraph (13). Probate actions, or proceedings to rectify a will, are covered by paragraph (14). Ground (18) applies when a party seeks an order that costs be awarded to or against someone who was not a party to the proceedings.[374] Grounds (17), (19), and (20) complete a list of other causes of action, almost all statutory and where the substantive statutory duty is (often implicitly) reinforced by giving the claimant the right to seek permission to serve out.[375]

---

[368] *Altimo Holdings & Investment Ltd v Kyrgyz Mobil Tel Ltd* [2011] UKPC 7, [2012] 1 WLR 1804.

[369] *Erste Group Bank AG (London) v JSC 'VMZ Red October'* [2015] EWCA Civ 379; *Vedanta Resources plc v Lungowe* [2019] UKSC 20, [2019] 2 WLR 1051.

[370] *Vedanta Resources plc v Lungowe* [2019] UKSC 20, [2019] 2 WLR 1051.

[371] *Eurasia Sports Ltd v Aguad* [2018] EWCA Civ 1742, [2018] 1 WLR 6089.

[372] The judgment or award must have been given by the time permission is sought: *Mercedes-Benz AG v Leiduck* [1996] 1 AC 284 (PC).

[373] *Re Banco Nacional de Cuba* [2001] 1 WLR 2039.

[374] Senior Courts Act 1981, s 51.

[375] For illustration, *Orexim Trading Ltd v Mahavir Port and Terminal Pvt Ltd* [2018] EWCA Civ 1660, [2018] 1 WLR 4847.

(c) England is the proper place to bring the claim

The second requirement placed on the claimant is in rule 6.37(3): to satisfy the court that England is the proper place to bring the claim. This is intended to reproduce the earlier rule[376] that England must be shown, clearly or distinctly, to be the most appropriate forum, or the natural forum; the change in language has not altered the substance of the law.[377] The factors which are relevant when a stay is sought of proceedings commenced by service within the jurisdiction apply, *mutatis mutandis*, here as well. However, there will be cases in which England may be considered to be the proper place to bring a claim even though England is not, at least in a geographical sense, the natural forum. For example, if the only alternative[378] forum is some war-torn, depraved, or hopeless corner of the globe, England may be the only possible place in which a trial can take place: that seems likely to satisfy a 'proper place' requirement.[379] It is increasingly accepted that in technically complex cases in which financial support for the claimants is available only in England but not in the alternative forum, so that there is, in practice, no substantial 'access to justice' overseas, England may also be the proper place to bring the claim.[380] At one level this is disconcerting: it makes the jurisdiction question turn on the apparent preparedness of an English solicitor to underwrite the possible costs of the case.[381] On the other hand, if a plausible claim could be heard in England, and cannot in practice be heard where it really belongs, is the court really supposed to say that the defendant is safe from litigation, no matter what the merits may be? That might be even more alarming.

(d) The claimant has a reasonable prospect of success

Service out will not be authorized unless the claimant states his belief that the claim has a reasonable prospect of success. If the defendant considers that the claim falls below this standard, he may challenge the grant of permission

---

[376] *Spiliada Maritime Corp v Cansulex Ltd* [1987] AC 460 distilled this as a discrete component of RSC Ord 11, r 4(2), which required that the case be shown to be a proper one for service out.

[377] *Vedanta Resources plc v Lungowe* [2019] UKSC 20, [2019] 2 WLR 1051.

[378] In this context this will probably be where the defendant is resident and can, in principle at least, otherwise be sued.

[379] *Cherney v Deripaska* [2009] EWCA Civ 849, [2010] 2 All ER (Comm) 456.

[380] *Vedanta Resources plc v Lungowe* [2019] UKSC 20, [2019] 2 WLR 1051.

[381] It might once have made it turn on the availability of English legal aid, but that requires a long memory of a gentler and more civilised time.

on the ground that the claimant could not properly have held and stated this belief; and if he succeeds on this point the court will declare that it has no jurisdiction, and set aside the permission and the service of process.[382] It was formerly required of a claimant that he show a good arguable case on the merits of his claim, which seemed to require a higher standard of probability of winning; but this was deliberately relaxed in 1994.[383] It appears to be entirely justified: if England is the proper place to bring the claim, why should a claimant who needs to start the ball rolling by serving out be called upon, at this early stage, to demonstrate a higher apparent chance of success than the claimant who can, perhaps only by chance, effect service within the jurisdiction? Even so, if a defendant rises to the challenge, the material placed before the court can appear to the judge as though it is just a dress rehearsal for the forthcoming trial. From time to time the courts complain about this,[384] but until the rules are changed it is hard to see how complaint is really justifiable.

4. HAGUE CONVENTION ON CHOICE OF COURT AGREEMENTS

The European Union subscribed to the 2005 Hague Convention on Choice of Court Agreements which brought it into force for the Member States on 1 October 2015. If or when the United Kingdom departs from the EU, it is promised that the Convention will again enter into force for the United Kingdom in relation to the remainder of the EU as well as the small number of other countries to which it applies.[385] In broad terms, the effect of the Convention is to bind the states party to it to give effect to exclusive jurisdiction agreements for the courts of states bound by the Convention, and to provide for the recognition and enforcement of judgments given in accordance with the Convention. In practice the effect of the Convention on the jurisdiction of an English court will be small, for the common law already

---

[382] cf *Seaconsar Far East Ltd v Bank Markazi Jomhouri Islami Iran* [1994] 1 AC 438.

[383] *Seaconsar Far East Ltd v Bank Markazi Jomhouri Islami Iran* [1994] 1 AC 438.

[384] *Vedanta Resources plc v Lungowe* [2019] UKSC 20, [2019] 2 WLR 1051.

[385] Technical problems may arise if there is a gap between these two points, or if it is argued that a choice of court agreement which took effect in English law by reference to European law may (or may not) be given effect after the United Kingdom has ceased to benefit from this element of European law. They are beyond the scope of this book.

treated agreements of the kind comprehended by the Convention with due seriousness; it is, however, beneficial that an English judgment, given by a court which had jurisdiction in accordance with the Convention, will be recognized and enforced in other states bound by the Convention more effectively than would otherwise be the case.

5. JURISDICTION TO OBTAIN INTERIM RELIEF

For completeness we should revert to the issue of interim relief, which includes provisional and protective measures. This may be ordered in support of actions in the English courts, or of civil or commercial claims in the courts in another Member State (Article 35 cases), or in support of other actions in those courts or elsewhere.[386] If the respondent is present within the jurisdiction of the court he may be served with process as of right: it is irrelevant that he may be domiciled in another Member State and not subject to the jurisdiction of the English courts over the merits of the claim. If he is outside the territorial jurisdiction, an application for permission to serve the claim form out of the jurisdiction must be made under paragraph (5) of the Practice Direction: this is so even in relation to applications falling within Article 35 of the Regulation. But in all cases, the fact that the court may lack jurisdiction to try the case on the merits is a material factor in determining whether it is expedient to grant the relief;[387] and it will also be relevant in deciding whether the court should grant permission to serve out, as rule 6.37(3) also applies to applications under paragraph (5). As to when it may be inexpedient to grant the relief, it has been suggested that where the court seised of the merits could have granted relief but decided not to, an English court should be slow to appear to contradict it; but where it had no power to grant relief, an English court should be inclined to make an order to assist the foreign court. Not everyone will instantly see that it is right to speak of 'assisting' a court whose legislator has, one supposes deliberately, withheld certain powers from it for a good and proper purpose.[388] But there it is.

---

[386] Civil Jurisdiction and Judgments Act 1982, s 25.
[387] ibid, s 25(2).
[388] *Crédit Suisse Fides Trust SA v Cuoghi* [1998] QB 818 (CA); *Motorola Credit Corp v Uzan (No 2)* [2003] EWCA Civ 752, [2004] 1 WLR 113.

6. RESPONDING TO LITIGATION OVERSEAS

The rules of common law jurisdiction which we have examined curtail the extent to which a claimant may forum shop in (which is to say, to take advantage in a self-serving way of the open jurisdiction of) the English courts, principally by using the principle of *forum (non) conveniens* to control inappropriate dragging of defendants to the English courts. But there are at least three ways in which the common law responds to the practice of forum shopping to a *foreign* court. These are now examined.

(a) Anti-suit injunctions

To start by taking a step back from the common law, one should recall the observation of Lord Goff of Chieveley,[389] to the effect that whereas the jurisdictional scheme put in place by the Regulation is common to the Member States, and has the European Court sitting above it to supervise the proper interpretation of its rules, the common law world is organized differently. Order and fairness between states is achieved, in general, by judicial comity, and in particular by the doctrine of *forum non conveniens*, by which a court directly limits its own jurisdiction, and by the anti-suit injunction, by which a court indirectly places limits on the effective jurisdiction of other courts. It is the last of these with which we are now concerned.

A court with personal jurisdiction over a respondent may order him not to bring, or to discontinue, proceedings in a foreign court, by issuing an appropriately-worded injunction against him. The order is, obviously, not addressed to the foreign judge, who is neither subject to the personal jurisdiction of the English court nor referred to in the order which the court makes; and in any event, the question whether she has been given jurisdiction by her sovereign to adjudicate in his courts (and what it means if she has) is probably not even justiciable in an English court. But the order is addressed to the respondent, who is directed to exercise self-restraint or suffer the consequences prescribed by English law for those in contempt of the order of a court. That said, a foreign judge may not appreciate the subtlety of the distinction;[390] and for this reason, a concern for

---

[389] *Airbus Industrie GIE v Patel* [1999] 1 AC 119.

[390] For a telling German refusal to see the point see *Re the Enforcement of an English Anti-suit Injunction (Case 3 VA 11/95)* [1997] ILPr 320 (Düsseldorf CA). For an even more telling English refusal to see the very same point when the boot was on the other foot, see *Tonicstar Ltd v American Home Insurance Co* [2004] EWHC 1234 (Comm), [2005] Lloyd's Rep IR 32.

comity constrains the court in the exercise of its equitable power to restrain wrongdoers.[391]

This potent remedy gives the English court an international reach by which to prevent what it finds to be wrongful recourse to a foreign court. Though the remedy is also found in other common law systems, it is less well known (though it does occasionally pop up) in civilian systems. It has no place within the scheme of the Brussels I Regulation,[392] but all this actually means that it may not be sought or ordered against respondents who are bringing civil or commercial proceedings in the courts of another Member State. It is necessary to deal separately with two points: the existence of personal jurisdiction over the respondent; and the right which forms the basis for the injunction to be asked for and ordered as a remedy.

First, the respondent must be served with process to be made subject to the personal jurisdiction of the court in respect of the claim for an injunction. An anti-suit injunction is an application for final[393] relief in respect of legal or equitable rights not to be sued, and process by which the relief is claimed must be lawfully served on the respondent. Where personal jurisdiction is to be established by reference to common law jurisdictional rules, as just described, it may therefore be necessary to obtain permission to serve the respondent out of the jurisdiction in the first place. None of the grounds set out in the Practice Direction is specifically dedicated to applications for an anti-suit injunction, but there is nothing to prevent the cause of action which founds the claim to relief being brought under any ground which will accommodate it. So if the claim for an injunction is based on the fact that there is a contract falling within paragraph (6), which gives a legal right not to be sued overseas, this may be relied on in the application for permission. (Of course, where the injunction is sought in relation to a civil or commercial matter within the domain of the Brussels I Regulation, say to prevent an Irish domiciliary bringing proceedings in New York, the jurisdiction of the court over him is determined by the Regulation; the defendant or respondent will plead the Regulation as a reason why he is not liable to be brought before

---

[391] *Airbus Industrie GIE v Patel* [1999] 1 AC 119. By contrast, an injunction to restrain a wrongful *arbitration* does not invade the sovereignty of a foreign *court*, and the need for restraint is rather less: *Sabbagh v Khoury* [2019] EWCA Civ 1219.

[392] Case C–159/02 *Turner v Grovit* [2004] ECR I–3565; Case C–185/07 *Allianz SpA v West Tankers Inc* [2009] ECR I–663.

[393] Although it is also possible to apply for an interim anti-suit injunction to preserve the status quo until the application for a final injunction can be heard.

an English court. In such a case, the court is actually called upon to exercise Regulation jurisdiction, not common law jurisdiction.)

Second, if jurisdiction is established, there must be a cause of action, or similar substantive basis or right, for the grant of relief. An applicant may seek to show that he has been wronged by his opponent, on the ground that he has a legal right not to be sued in the foreign court, or an equitable right not to be sued in the foreign court: in short, his complaint is that the respondent is committing a legal or equitable wrong against him, and that this justifies him in asking for a remedy. The example of a legal right not to be sued in the foreign court is easy to comprehend. An exclusive jurisdiction clause will exemplify it, but so also will a settlement agreement, an arbitration agreement,[394] the right to enforce an arbitration award,[395] and perhaps even the right to enforce an English judgment;[396] and if there is a legal right not be sued in the foreign court, an injunction will usually be ordered to enforce or reinforce it.[397]

The more challenging task has been to elucidate what it means to have an equitable right not to be sued overseas. The point of departure, in this latter case, is a general requirement that England must be shown to be the natural forum for the litigation of the substantive dispute.[398] This is because, if England is where the trial of the dispute should have its natural home, it is no departure from the principles of judicial comity for the English court to make an order in relation to it. Subject to satisfying this pre-condition, the applicant may show that the respondent is acting vexatiously or oppressively in bringing the foreign action.[399] The meaning of these terms retains an element of necessary flexibility, so as to be able to respond to newly-invented forms of deviousness, but if the foreign action is brought in bad faith or to harass, or if it is bound to fail if defended but its defence is certain to cause trouble and expense, or if its consequences may be unjustifiably involved or convoluted,[400] the party bringing it may be ordered to listen to his conscience and restrain himself. The absence of a real link between the acts complained

---

[394] *C v D* [2007] EWCA Civ 1282, [2008] Bus LR 843.
[395] ibid.
[396] *Masri v Consolidated Contractors International Co SAL (No 3)* [2008] EWCA Civ 625, [2009] QB 503.
[397] *Donohue v Armco Inc* [2001] UKHL 64, [2002] 1 All ER 749.
[398] *Société Nationale Industrielle Aérospatiale v Lee Kui Jak* [1987] AC 871 (PC); *Airbus Industrie GIE v Patel* [1999] 1 AC 119.
[399] *Société Nationale Industrielle Aérospatiale v Lee Kui Jak* [1987] AC 871 (PC).
[400] ibid (consequential contribution proceedings would be unacceptably complex).

of and the foreign court may help to indicate that there is oppression;[401] if it is otherwise unconscionable to bring the action it may be restrained.

Australian equity apparently considers that foreign proceedings are unobjectionable if the party bringing them seeks relief which would not be available from an Australian court,[402] but this seems perverse,[403] for it seems to mean that the further from its own standards of justice the foreign action is, the less it will be possible to order restraint. That does not seem right. According to Canadian equity,[404] before applying for the injunction, the applicant must generally make a jurisdictional application to the foreign court: that done, an injunction will not be granted unless the foreign court fails to respect principles of *forum conveniens* but then, having refused to observe comity, it can expect no comity in return.[405] Although this has occasionally been said to be the general rule in England,[406] it is actually a thoroughly bad idea. First, the clear requirement that England be shown to be the natural forum makes it unnecessary to seek relief elsewhere. Second, there is something rather distasteful in allowing or encouraging an English court to sit as if on an appeal from a foreign court which has refused to grant relief;[407] and if the application is delayed until the issue has been fought in the foreign court, it may mean that the time for an injunction has come and long gone.

To revert to the case of a legal right not to be sued in the foreign court, where the claim to an injunction is founded on an allegation of breach of an agreement on jurisdiction, it is debatable whether England must also be the natural forum for the action.[408] If England is the chosen court, there will be no difficulty, but otherwise the answer is less clear. On one view the existence of a legal right not to be sued is enough by itself, but it may also be said that if neither the nominated court nor the action to be restrained is in England, it is none of the English court's business to lay down the law on where the trial

---

[401] *Midland Bank plc v Laker Airways Ltd* [1986] QB 689 (CA).

[402] *CSR Ltd v Cigna Insurance Australia Ltd* (1997) 189 CLR 345.

[403] It is also contrary to *Midland Bank plc v Laker Airways Ltd* [1986] QB 689 (CA).

[404] *Amchem Products Inc v British Columbia (Workers' Compensation Board)* [1993] 1 SCR 897, (1993) 102 DLR (4th) 96.

[405] This may be thought of as the 'Be-Done-By-As-You-Did' version of comity, in respectful homage to Charles Kingsley, *The Water-Babies*.

[406] *Barclays Bank plc v Homan* [1993] BCLC 680. It gained no support from *Airbus Industrie GIE v Patel* [1999] 1 AC 119.

[407] cf The Angelic Grace [1995] 1 Lloyd's Rep 87, 95 (CA); *Ecobank Transnational Inc v Tanoh* [2015] EWCA Civ 1309, [2016] 1 WLR 2231; *Sabbagh v Khoury* [2019] EWCA Civ 1219.

[408] The point was left open in *Airbus Industrie GIE v Patel* [1999] 1 AC 119.

should take place, however much the respondent may appear to be open to judicial criticism.[409] But where it is appropriate for the court to exercise its discretion, there is no need to demonstrate vexation or oppression: an injunction in support of a legal right not to be sued in the foreign court will be granted unless there is good reason not to do so.[410]

In addition to the cases in which the applicant complains that he is the victim of a wrong, an injunction may also be applied for, justified, and ordered, on the basis that the respondent is bringing proceedings in a foreign court which undermine the established or exclusive jurisdiction of the English court. In such a case, the basis for the order is not so much the commission of a wrong against the applicant, but that the administration of justice in England is being interfered with. For example, for a creditor to bring proceedings which are designed to secure a benefit which would not be available to him in a pending English insolvency would be for him to interfere with, or undermine, the integrity and effectiveness of the English collective proceedings. An injunction is plainly appropriate in such a case; the principle that an injunction is necessary to prevent the undermining of the English court's jurisdiction is obviously open to adaptation and to extension and (dare one say) abuse.[411]

A party who is bringing, or who intends to bring, proceedings before a foreign court may have an apprehension that an anti-suit injunction will be sought against him. If the foreign court is one which may grant such relief, he may therefore consider applying to the foreign court for an anti-anti-suit injunction, the point of which speaks for itself. There are even cases in which this thinking has led to an application for an anti-anti-anti-suit injunction.[412] In cases in which the venue for litigation can be of such surpassing significance, litigation can get very exciting indeed.

(b) Proceedings for (negative) declaratory relief

The development of the doctrine of *forum conveniens* was the first substantial means by which a defendant could challenge the jurisdictional power of the claimant; and an anti-suit injunction may be seen as the second. The

---

[409] The Bermuda Court of Appeal displayed no hesitation about it in *IPOC International Growth Fund Ltd v OAO 'CT Mobile'* [2007] Bermuda LR 43.

[410] *Donohue v Armco Inc* [2001] UKHL 64, [2002] 1 All ER 749.

[411] *Stichting Shell Pensioenfonds v Krys* [2014] UKPC 41, [2015] AC 616; but cf *UBS AG New York v Fairfield Sentry (in liq)* [2019] UKPC 20, where the argument failed pretty spectacularly.

[412] See *Shell (UK) Exploration & Production Ltd v Innes* [1995] SLT 807.

next possibility is the bringing of proceedings on the merits of the claim by a party, the 'natural defendant', for a declaration that he owes no liability to the opponent. This, if successful, will either prevent the opponent bringing proceedings of her own or may mean that, if she does, the principles of *res judicata* may forestall the enforcement of a foreign judgment.

The early history of such actions showed deep judicial hostility to the very idea.[413] Courts would be slow to exercise jurisdictional discretion in support of them;[414] they ran a serious risk of being struck out as premature or abusive, or otherwise impeded. The suspicion that they were open to abuse by forum shoppers was widely held, not least because their potential to harass an opponent, who may not have decided whether to sue and who may not yet be ready for the fight, was considerable. But the sea changed, and there is now much less judicial disapproval of such actions. Three principal reasons may be given. First, it became the practice of the Commercial Court to entertain such actions and to decide on the merits of the individual case whether they were justifiable: insurers, suppliers, and others will often need to know whether they have legal obligations to an insured (so they can step in and take over the defence if they do) or a distributor (so they can terminate supplies and retain another if they do not). Secondly, in the adjacent context of the Brussels I Regulation, it is well settled that an action for a declaration of non-liability brought in a court which has jurisdiction over the defendant thereto, cannot be objected to on jurisdictional grounds: there is no jurisdictional wrong in suing in a court with jurisdiction under the Regulation.[415] Thirdly, the Court of Appeal has given its seal of approval to this new approach,[416] seeing the merit in such claims as a good and useful means of resolving disputes. It is hard to disagree: the legal certainty which can be brought about by a prompt application for a declaration of legal relations may be far preferable to the paralysing limbo of waiting to see whether proceedings are commenced by the other party. Abusive use of the procedure can still be prevented, but there will now be no presumption of abuse; and as this new wisdom beds down in the law, the need for separate mention of proceedings for negative declaratory relief should become a thing of the past.

---

[413] *Guaranty Trust Co of New York v Hannay* [1915] 2 KB 536 (CA); *The Volvox Hollandia* [1988] 2 Lloyd's Rep 361 (CA).
[414] By refusing permission to serve out of the jurisdiction.
[415] Case C–406/92 The Tatry [1994] ECR I–5439.
[416] *Messier Dowty Ltd v Sabena SA* [2000] 1 WLR 2040 (CA).

(c) Suing for damages for breach of a jurisdiction clause

If parties concluded a contract which provided that proceedings would not be brought by either of them before the courts of a foreign country, and then one party, in breach of this promise, brings such proceedings, he breaks his contract.[417] It is the bringing of proceedings which constitutes the breach. No one forced him to do that; and a party to a contract who breaks his promise is liable in damages which are, at least when English law governs the contractual promise, a common law right. It took the courts a long time to acknowledge what now seems blindingly obvious,[418] but there is no principled basis for complaining about such civil proceedings.[419] In particular, it is irrelevant that the foreign court found that it had jurisdiction to hear the matter brought before it, for the complaint of wrong lies in the bringing of the proceedings, whether or not the court considers itself to have jurisdiction to entertain them, full stop. It is probably irrelevant that the foreign court ruled specifically on the effect of the jurisdiction agreement, for unless the defendant to those proceedings (claimant in the current action) submitted to the jurisdiction of the foreign court, its judgment cannot be used as *res judicata* against him.[420] And it is for the same reason irrelevant that the foreign court has given final judgment: this fact may be very relevant in the assessment of damages for loss resulting from the breach, but that is all.[421] The loss for which damages will be recoverable will be measured by the difference between the defendant (claimant in the foreign proceedings) not having brought proceedings, and the position the claimant in the English proceedings (defendant in the foreign proceedings) finds himself in as a result of those proceedings having been brought. The assessment of damages does not suppose that if the party in breach had not broken his contract, he would have sued in the designated court, but if that is his contention, he is, in accordance with principle, entitled to put it to the court and to show that the measure of loss just described is not the correct measure.

---

[417] A more adventurous argument, that an analogous complaint may be based on an express agreement as to the law to govern a contract, has yet to be accepted. Its time will come.

[418] *Union Discount Co Ltd v Zoller* [2001] EWCA Civ 1755, [2002] 1 WLR 1517 appears to be the first such decision; see also dicta in *Donohue v Armco Inc* [2001] UKHL 64, [2002] 1 All ER 749.

[419] The decision of the Supreme Court in *The Alexandros T* [2013] UKSC 70, [2014] 1 All ER 590 is decisive.

[420] Civil Jurisdiction and Judgments Act 1982, s 32.

[421] *Ellerman Lines Ltd v Read* [1928] 2 KB 144.

3

Foreign Judgments

In this Chapter, and prior to Exit Day, the private international law of foreign judgments was covered in part by a number of European Regulations and other instruments. These were the Brussels I Regulation 44/2001 and the recast Brussels I Regulation 1215/2012; the 1988 Lugano Convention and the 2007 Lugano II Convention; the 1968 Brussels Convention as amended from time to time; and a number of minor Regulations such as the European Enforcement Order Regulation 805/2004. According to the Civil Jurisdiction and Judgments (Amendment) (EU Exit) Regulations 2019, SI 2019 No 479, these instruments are revoked or, in the case of the Conventions given effect by the Civil Jurisdiction and Judgments Act 1982, as amended, repealed. Until Exit Day they are in full force and effect, but unless further legislative arrangements are made they will not apply to judgments obtained in proceedings instituted after that date. In principle, the gap will be filled by the existing rules of the common law, or by the provisions of a bilateral Convention made under the Foreign Judgements (Reciprocal Enforcement) Act 1933 (or in the case of Cyprus and Malta, presumably by registration under the Administration of Justice Act 1920).

However, in the context of recognition and enforcement in England of judgments from other Member and Contracting States, given in civil and commercial proceedings which were instituted prior to Exit Day, Part 6 of SI 2019 No 479 provides that these otherwise-revoked European instruments will continue to apply. It follows that there will be a period of indeterminate length during which judgments from the courts of Member States and Contracting States may take their effect in English law according to these otherwise-revoked and otherwise-repealed instruments.

The Conflict of Laws. Fourth Edition. Adrian Briggs, Oxford University Press (2019). © Adrian Briggs
DOI: 10.1093/oso/9780198838500.003.0003

A. RECOGNITION AND ENFORCEMENT

The first and most important thing to understand about foreign judgments is that judgments of foreign courts have no direct effect in England, for foreign judges have no authority in England. Unless legislation has provided otherwise, foreign judgments cannot be enforced by execution, and no person is in contempt of court, or otherwise in peril, if he fails to do what he has been ordered to do by a foreign judge. If adjudication is thought of as an exercise of state sovereignty,[1] this will come as no surprise: state sovereignty ends at the border of the state, and while international comity requires respect be given to exercises of that power within the sovereign's own territory, that is where the obligations of comity end. But it has long been accepted that there is a general public interest which requires that those who have had a hearing and received judgment from a court should generally abide by its terms, and that the law should discourage or prevent the reopening of disputes which have been heard and determined. A related idea would encourage or require litigants to put forward all their issues for adjudication at once, rather than holding some back for a subsequent dispute. This broad principle is not limited to cases where the first judgment was obtained in England but, subject to conditions, applies just as much to foreign judgments.

Accordingly, foreign judgments may have effect in England according to the rules of the common law as well as the legislative schemes also examined in this chapter. But there is more than one way of giving effect to a foreign judgment; and it is important to remember the differences. Where statutory registration is provided for, the legislation will normally provide that, when registered, the foreign judgment itself may be enforced as though it were a local one. But where there is no registration scheme, and the common law is relied on, then although the foreign judgment may be recognized as *res judicata*, it cannot be enforced as a judgment. Instead, the judgment creditor uses the foreign judgment to obtain an original, albeit derivative, English judgment; and it will be this English judgment that may then be enforced and executed upon. The English court does not rubber stamp or authorize enforcement of the foreign judgment: it does not grant '*exequatur*', or leave, to enforce the foreign judgment in the manner in which the civilian tradition has it. It gives a judgment of its own.

---

[1] Which it is. The fact that a foreign court's adjudication is not a non-justiciable Act of State (so confirmed in *Yukos Capital Sarl v OJC Rosneft Oil Co (No 2)* [2012] EWCA Civ 8555, [2014] QB 458) does not entail the conclusion that adjudication is not an act of sovereign power.

So far as statutory registration of foreign judgments is concerned, the picture has become rather complex. There are two main schemes to notice. One applies to judgments from a number of states and territories which are party to a bilateral treaty with the United Kingdom, or to a larger number of States or territories of the Commonwealth. For these, legislation sets out the conditions for registration, as the route to enforcement, these conditions reflecting the common law as it was understood at the time. Enforcement is direct, as the legislation provides that the foreign judgment may, when registered, be enforced and executed upon in the same way as if it were an English judgment. An even simpler scheme covers judgments from other parts of the United Kingdom.

The other registration scheme was or is multilateral, and far more ambitious, covering judgments from the Member States of the European Union given in civil and commercial matters.[2] For such judgments, the legislation until recently provided for enforcement upon registration. However, in the most recent iteration—under the 'recast' Brussels I Regulation—the requirement of registration before enforcement was deleted, and judgments to which these newest rules apply may be enforced in the United Kingdom without prior registration.[3] The EU model, tried and tested as it has been, inspired international negotiations for a worldwide framework for the enforcement of judgments. It will therefore be described, with an eye to the future rather than the past, in outline form.

It bears repetition: where the foreign judgment is not subject to a statutory registration or post-registration scheme, the common law alone supplies both the rules for recognition and enforcement, as well as the procedure for enforcement. For these cases, the foreign judgment may be recognized, but if anything is to be enforced, it will be an English judgment derived, by one means or another, from the foreign judgment. It is sometimes said that at common law one enforces a foreign judgment by bringing an action on it. The common law may be represented this way, but as it is written the proposition is liable to mislead. The foreign judgment provides the cause of action for proceedings to obtain an English judgment, which is what the judgment creditor may then enforce.

---

[2] Or states parties to the Lugano Convention, for which the rules were substantially the same.
[3] Because this later registration system was also used for judgments from the rest of the United Kingdom and Gibraltar, and for judgments to which the 2005 Hague Convention on Choice of Court Agreements applies. It thereforeremains important but operating in reduced circumstances.

Another important distinction must be noted at the outset: between the recognition of a judgment and its enforcement; and between these and the other effects which can be derived from a foreign judgment. *Recognition* of a judgment means treating the claim which was adjudicated as having been determined conclusively, once and for all. It does not matter whether it was determined in favour of the claimant or the defendant, though judgments *in personam* are only ever recognized as effective against particular parties, and the material question will be whether that person is bound to accept and abide by the judgment given. By contrast, judgments *in rem*[4] are recognized generally or universally, and not just against particular parties to the litigation. When a judgment is recognized, the matter comprehended by it is *res judicata*, and the party bound by it is liable to be estopped from contradicting it in proceedings in an English court.[5] For the foreign judgment to achieve recognition, qualifying conditions have to be met. These specify the connection between the foreign court and the parties, accommodate and limit the scope of objections to the judgment, and so define the judgments to which this status of *res judicata* will be accorded. The common law principles of *res judicata* can operate in relation to entire causes of action ('cause of action estoppel') as well as on discrete issues which arose and were determined in the course of the trial of a cause of action ('issue estoppel').[6] Given a *res judicata*, a party bound by the judgment who brings proceedings in England to try and obtain a ruling which contradicts it may be met with the plea of estoppel by *res judicata*, and stopped in his tracks.

Recognition therefore serves various purposes. A judgment given in favour of the defendant, dismissing the claim, allows the defendant who has defeated the claimant in a foreign court to rely on this if the claimant makes a second attempt. Here, recognition is generally all that the successful defendant requires. A foreign judgment in favour of the claimant is more complex. If the claimant[7] obtained judgment in respect of the whole of the claim, he may wish to go beyond mere recognition, to bring proceedings for the *enforcement* of the judgment, say by demanding the sum which the foreign court ordered to be paid and which remains unpaid. Not every judgment entitled to recognition as *res judicata* may be enforced in England, but, to be enforced, a foreign judgment must first be recognized.[8] If it is to be enforced

---

[4] For example, on the status of a person, or the ownership of a thing.
[5] See, generally, Spencer Bower and Handley, *Res Judicata* (4th edn, LexisNexis, 2009).
[6] *Carl Zeiss Stiftung v Rayner & Keeler Ltd (No 2)* [1967] 1 AC 853.
[7] Which expression includes counterclaimant or party, not excluding a defendant, in whose favour an order was made.
[8] *Clarke v Fennoscandia Ltd* [2007] UKHL 56, 2008 SLT 33, [18].

at the behest of the successful party, the foreign judgment must meet further conditions; but if these are met, the English court will give its own judgment which the claimant may enforce precisely because it is an English judgment.

If, however, the claimant was partially successful, say he succeeded on his claim but recovered a smaller sum in damages than he had hoped for, he may seek to improve on the first result by suing once more on the underlying cause of action. In this case, recognition of the earlier judgment in his favour[9] will not stand in his way, but the manifest unfairness of his trying to have a second bite at the cherry induced Parliament to legislate to remove the right to sue again.[10]

It makes sense today to start with the recognition and enforcement of judgments at common law, where the rules are restricted neither by geography, nor by subject matter, nor by type of court: they are universal in their scope. This will also provide some of the background detail for the registration-for-enforcement schemes contained in the 1920 and 1933 Acts. We will then examine the mechanism which applied to judgments taking effect under the EU scheme and which will be likely to inspire any future international agreement. In this chapter the main focus of attention will be on judgments *in personam*; the recognition of judgments in family law, the administration of estates, and insolvency are dealt with within the chapters which examine this subject matter.

Finally, though only for the sake of comparison, we will consider the recognition and enforcement of arbitral awards.

B. THE COMMON LAW RULES FOR FOREIGN JUDGMENTS

Save where it has been overwritten by statute, the common law determines the effects in England of judgments from the courts of the whole of the world: from Afghanistan to Yemen;[11] from China to Peru. Although the common law will certainly recognize foreign judgments as *res judicata* it does not enforce foreign judgments, even though courts and commentators say that it does, for English judgments are the only ones enforced in England

---

[9] For there will be no discrete issue on which the defendant won (though if there is, such as a refusal to award a particular head of damages, issue estoppel in the defendant's favour on this issue will be available).

[10] Civil Jurisdiction and Judgments Act 1982, s 34.

[11] Zambia and Zimbabwe are included within the 1920 Act.

unless Parliament has provided otherwise. The fact that the common law does not enforce foreign judgments, the reason why it does not, and a correct understanding of what the common law does do when it comes to enforcement, teaches something important about the common law of private international law.

The basic scheme of common law recognition is that if the foreign court is adjudged to have been competent, as a matter of *English* law, to give a judgment by which the losing party must accept that he is bound, the judgment may, and if there is no other defence to recognition will, be recognized as making the cause of action or the issue *res judicata*. If all that a litigant requires is for the foreign judgment to be recognized, it suffices for him to plead it as *res judicata*, but if the judgment creditor wishes to enforce the judgment, using it as a sword rather than a shield, as one may say, he will need to bring an action on it at common law, by original proceedings in the High Court. The foreign judgment, if it satisfies the requirements of the common law, is understood to create an obligation, a tie of law,[12] by which the parties are bound and which may be enforced. The foreign judgment provides the cause of action; but an action, and an English judgment, is needed because the common law only enforces English judgments in England.[13]

1. RECOGNITION

The common law will recognize a foreign judgment if it is the final and conclusive decision[14] of a court which, as a matter of English private international law, had 'international jurisdiction', and as long as there is no sustainable defence to its recognition. There is no requirement that the judgment be that of a superior court: any judicial body[15] will suffice for the common law. This therefore excludes the award of an arbitral tribunal,[16] as well as the decision

---

[12] Institutes of Justinian, 3.13pr.

[13] *Godard v Gray* (1870–71) LR 6 QB 139; Briggs (2013) 129 LQR 87.

[14] For a decision which tests the limits of the definition, see *Midtown Acquisitions LP v Essar Global Fund Ltd* [2017] EWHC 519, [2017] 1 WLR 3083 (New York judgment by confession without an actual action).

[15] For a marginal case: *Teece v Kuwait Finance House (Bahrain) BSC* [2018] 2 NZLR 257.

[16] These do not give rise to issues of recognition in this sense; and their enforcement is regulated by specialist Convention and statute. Even so, parties to an arbitration may be estopped from contradicting its findings, for estoppels can arise from contracts as well as from judgments.

of an administrative body. The judgment of a court, but only of a court, will do.[17]

In principle, at least, only those orders which are 'final and conclusive' may be recognized. The familiar terminology may trip off the tongue, but it is not quite so easy to define. A judgment is 'final' if it cannot be reopened or reconsidered in the court which made it, even though it may be subject to appeal to a higher court; it is 'conclusive' if it represents the court's settled answer on the substance of the point adjudicated.[18] For this reason, a typical freezing order will not be recognized as *res judicata*, assuming that it is neither predicated upon a final determination of the validity of the claim nor immune from reconsideration and revision by the court which ordered it. Likewise, recognition will not be accorded to a decision that there is, for example, a good arguable case on a disputed point, jurisdictional or otherwise: the decision may be final, in that the court will not itself reconsider the question, but is not conclusive if it would not tie the hands of the same court when, later, the merits are tried. By contrast, an order made on an interlocutory matter *may* be conclusive if it represents the last word of the court on the point in issue. Take an order dismissing an action on the ground that it was covered by a jurisdiction agreement for a specific court: if this really is the court's final decision on the issue of whether there was a jurisdiction agreement, it is in principle entitled to recognition.[19] A small but irritating problem is posed by default judgments. These are often susceptible to being reopened in or by the court in which they were entered, perhaps on conditions, but not usually only within an inflexible time limit. It would appear to follow that these are not final judgments, with the counter-intuitive consequence that if the defendant's position is so hopeless that he allows judgment to be entered in default of appearance, the claimant may be left with a judgment of reduced effectiveness. This argument may be countered by contending that a default judgment is not, in the material sense, a provisional one which the court

---

[17] For the curious case in which a recognizable first instance judgment is annulled by an appellate judgment which is liable to be refused recognition, and the question whether the obligation created by the original judgment still survives for recognition and enforcement, see *Merchant International Co Ltd v NAK Naftogaz* [2012] EWCA Civ 196, [2012] 1 WLR 3036. As the common law enforces personal bilateral obligations, rather than judgments as such, it should not matter that the original judgment has been adversely affected by an unrecognised judicial act which, *ex hypothesi*, cannot affect the obligation resulting from the original judgment. It might be different if the common law enforced foreign judgments as such, for if no judgment, there can be nothing to enforce. But this is not how the common law works.

[18] Which may be the whole dispute or a single point: *The Sennar (No 2)* [1985] 1 WLR 490 (HL).

[19] ibid; cf *Desert Sun Loan Corp v Hill* [1996] 2 All ER 847 (CA).

expects to reconsider: it represents the court's firm and settled conclusion unless and until something happens which is not expected and which may never happen.[20] On the other hand, the claimant may be wise to hurry a little more slowly, and to ask instead for summary judgment on the merits of the claim, even though the defendant is not there to contest them. Most courts will see the point, and should cooperate.

2. 'INTERNATIONAL JURISDICTION'

A foreign judgment is liable to recognized if, to use the traditional terminology, the foreign court is regarded as having had 'international jurisdiction' as this is defined by English private international law. The terminology is decidedly unhelpful; the concept has nothing whatever to do with whether the judge had jurisdiction according to the laws of the foreign court, and the relevant rules of law are English, not 'international'; it would be much better to use different language. The substance of the point is clear, though: it is necessary that the party against whom the judgment was given *either* accepted or consented or submitted to the jurisdiction of the foreign court, *or* was present within the jurisdiction of that court when the proceedings were instituted:[21] nothing more is needed, but nothing else will do. The occasional suggestion that the nationality of the defendant is sufficient[22] is not credible today. We proceed to the details.

(a) Presence

We start with the traditional principle. If the defendant was present within the territorial jurisdiction of the foreign court on the date on which the proceedings were commenced, he is in principle bound to accept and abide by the judgment if it goes against him.[23] If justification is required, several may be given. The fundamental principles of comity between states require the English court to respect the exercise of sovereign power over a person (or, indeed, property) within the territory of the sovereign. If that seems too arcane, one may argue that a person who chooses to locate herself in a certain place makes, by her conduct or body language, an open offer to anyone with a claim

---

[20] *Ainslie v Ainslie* (1927) 39 CLR 318.
[21] Which probably means when process was served: *Adams v Cape Industries plc* [1990] Ch 433 (CA) 518.
[22] *Emanuel v Symon* [1908] 1 KB 302 (CA).
[23] *Adams v Cape Industries plc* [1990] Ch 433 (CA).

to come and sue her there, and that she therefore agrees to the jurisdiction of the local court when this is invoked by service on her; but whatever the justification, this is clearly the law. It is sometimes suggested that the rule should be framed, solely or in the alternative, in terms of residence rather than presence, on the supposed basis that it describes a more durable connection with the court,[24] but this would be a very bad idea indeed. A defendant served with a foreign writ who is advised that the judgment will be recognized if he was resident in the country of service may be very unsure whether his connection with that state counts as (or will in due course be seen as having been) residence: the proposition is easily tested by asking any graduate student in the lecture class who hails from overseas and whose plans to return there are contingent or hazy. Residence lacks sharp edges; adding 'habitual' to it does not make it any better. A test of judgment recognition based on residence would make the common law worse and much less convenient.[25] If legislation were to provide for the registration of judgments from a state in which the judgment debtor was resident one would have to bear it. But the common law knows better than to invent a rule which will simply generate doubt.

If the defendant did not satisfy this condition on the day in question, but did in due course enter an appearance in response to the summons, this later act will count as a submission to the jurisdiction of the court and the issue of presence or not will be moot. As to precisely where the presence must be to be effective, it has been held[26] that the relevant territorial jurisdiction is defined by reference to the court seized. This means that a defendant sued in a state court must be present within the territorial jurisdiction of the state; if sued in a federal court all that is required is that he be within the federation. Insofar as this ascribes an international relevance to rules of local jurisdiction it is debatable whether it is or should be held to be correct.

From one point of view this rule appears to acknowledge in a foreign court a jurisdiction effectively wider than English law would assert for itself, it being irrelevant to the issue of presence that the foreign court was a *forum non conveniens* and that, if the roles were reversed, an English court might have stayed its proceedings and declined to adjudicate. But there is no reason why rules for the taking of jurisdiction should reflect those for the recognition of judgments: the slippery use of the word 'jurisdiction' creates a

---

[24] *State Bank of India v Murjani Marketing Group Ltd*, 27 March 1991 (CA).
[25] ibid.
[26] *Adams v Cape Industries plc* [1990] Ch 433 (CA); *Estate of Heiser v Islamic Republic of Iran* [2019] EWHC 2074 (QB).

mirage. The common law has never doubted that a court has, and is entitled to assert, jurisdiction over a person present within its territory, whether this means adjudication before the English court or recognition of the judgment of a foreign court. Indeed, it goes further, in recognizing a judgment *in rem* given by a court at the place where the thing in question was. That an English court might be persuaded to not exercise its jurisdiction in a particular case is entirely a matter for it; but it is quite wrong to deduce, from that simple and discretionary fact, that a foreign court has exceeded what international comity permits and requires simply because its law does not make the same choice: 'we are not so provincial as to say that every solution of a problem is wrong because we deal with it otherwise at home'.[27] And if the very act of being present is read as an invitation to come and sue, presence may even be subsumed in the broader submission principle, to which we will soon come.

As to the detail, the (actual) presence of a natural person is not generally difficult to ascertain, but the same rule applies also to corporate defendants, and the idea of a company's presence is a rather artificial one. Trading[28] companies do their business through others: by individuals, through other companies, which may or may not be in common ownership, through representatives and agents of various kinds, and by means of websites and other intangible manifestations. The presence rule is adapted to the extent necessary, but English law does not regard a company as being present in a place just because it can be said to have done, or to be still doing, business in that place or environment. The 'presence' of a company entails a reasonably fixed and definite place of business, maintained by the corporation and from which its business is done.[29] Neither the mere presence of the chief executive officer on the golf course, nor that of a peripatetic sales representative in a hotel room, nor a display at a trade fair will count as the presence of the company, even if a foreign court may regard such or similar facts as satisfying its own jurisdictional rules. The same is true of a local representative who merely acts as a conduit for customers wishing to transact business with the company which is otherwise not present within the jurisdiction.[30] But if the local entity or representation has been given power to make contracts which bind

---

[27] Cardozo J, *Loucks v Standard Oil Co of New York* 224 NY 99, 120 NE 98 (1918).
[28] There is a good question to ask about how a holding or parent company fits into this framework. On one view it does no business, but on another its business is to hold or own, which it presumably does where the entity held or owned has a place of business. The questions may be very hard to answer; it may be better to avoid them.
[29] *Adams v Cape plc* [1990] Ch 433 (CA).
[30] cf *Littauer Glove Corp v Millington (FW) (1920) Ltd* (1928) 44 TLR 746.

the defendant without further ado, it is probable that the test of corporate presence is satisfied, provided always that this is done from a fixed place of business.[31] It has yet to be held that a company has a place of business 'where its website is located', whatever that would mean. And there is no broader English doctrine which allows all the members of an economic or corporate group to be dealt with on the basis that if one is present all are present there,[32] or that one member of the group is the *alter ego* of the others: only if the corporate veil can be lifted can the formal position be departed from, and for English law this is a rather rare event.[33]

The recognition rule reflects one aspect of the general jurisdictional rule of English law: that if a company is present, in the sense of having a place of business, within the jurisdiction it can be sued there.[34] Nothing turns on whether the claim arises out of the conduct of the company in that place, or arose only after the company started doing business in that place. A finding of presence means that the company is, as far as English law is concerned, subject to the unlimited jurisdiction of the court or not at all; there is no middle way. This may explain why the common law's requirements are fairly stringent, not satisfied by a casual or delocalized 'doing a spot of business in' connection. Were it otherwise, London might become a very risky place for parent companies to incorporate and keep their assets.

(b) Submission, consent, or agreement to the jurisdiction of the foreign court

No injustice is done to a party who submits to the jurisdiction of a court if its adverse judgment is taken as binding him. A defendant who has voluntarily submitted to the jurisdiction of a foreign court is, in principle, bound to abide by its judgment if the decision goes against him. A claimant, or counterclaiming defendant, also clearly submits to the jurisdiction for the purposes of a decision against him; though whether a claimant is taken to submit to any and every counterclaim raised against him will depend on whether the counterclaim arises out of the same facts or transaction as his claim or out of facts which are reasonably connected: a test of broad common sense applies.[35] A party who agreed by contract to the jurisdiction of a foreign court

---

[31] *Adams v Cape Industries plc* [1990] Ch 433 531.
[32] *Adams v Cape Industries plc* [1990] Ch 433 (CA) 532–39.
[33] *Prest v Petrodel Resources Ltd* [2013] UKSC 34, [2013] 2 AC 415.
[34] By being served there: Companies Act 2006, s 1139.
[35] *Murthy v Sivasjothi* [1999] 1 WLR 467 (CA).

clearly submits to its jurisdiction and will be bound to accept its judgment, at least if the matter falls within the material scope of the clause.

The law is usually expressed in terms of submission: there is nothing wrong with that. However, the rational principle, which underpins this basis for recognition, is that an English court may find that there was, and may give effect to, a personal, bilateral, agreement made by the parties by which they agreed, either in advance of proceedings or after the service of the writ, to accept the adjudication of the foreign court and abide by its judgment.[36] If this is right, what the English court actually gives effect to, and enforces, is the obligation arising from this agreement: not the judgment as such, but the bilateral agreement to accept it. In this respect, the law reflects the principle first ascertained in *Penn v Baltimore*,[37] namely that a court may enforce a personal agreement made in respect of subject matter the adjudication of which might otherwise lie beyond the competence of the court. And this also explains why, and how, the common law says that the foreign judgment creates an obligation which the court can enforce.[38]

Submission may obviously be made by contractual agreement. If this is the basis proposed, the dispute and the particular court in which proceedings are brought will need to be aligned with the term; it may raise a question of construction, the principles of which have been seen earlier.[39] But the agreement need not be contractually binding so long as sufficient consent to the jurisdiction of the foreign court in respect of the claim is shown. In a proper case it may be sufficient to agree or consent in advance to the jurisdiction of a court without the need for this to be contractually binding.[40] In principle, at least, an agreement to submit may be implied, but caution is needed.[41] It will not normally be immanent or found to be implicit in a term which merely expresses the parties' choice of law and which makes no mention of jurisdiction: indeed, it is arguable that its absence from a dispute-resolution clause is as good as express. In truth, it is not easy to say when such an agreement will be implied, but a common lawyer never says never.

---

[36] It was explained above how this notion of agreement may also explain the recognition of judgments based on the presence of the defendant within the jurisdiction of the court who says, in effect 'come and sue me . . .'.

[37] See Ch 7.

[38] The utility of this explanation was doubted in *Rubin v Eurofinance SA* [2012] UKSC 46, [2013] 1 AC 236. It should not have been: see Briggs (2013) 129 LQR 87.

[39] Chapter 2, p 106.

[40] *Vizcaya Partners Ltd v Picard* [2016] UKPC 5.

[41] *Vizcaya Partners Ltd v Picard* [2016] UKPC 5.

If a defendant appears in the proceedings for the single purpose of contesting the jurisdiction of the court, or to seek a stay in favour of another court or for arbitration, or to protect property threatened with seizure in the proceedings, the Civil Jurisdiction and Judgments Act 1982, section 33(1), provides that the appearance will not on that account be a submission. This reverses a decision[42] which had held that to appear before a court simply to ask for jurisdictional relief was to submit to that jurisdiction:[43] one may respect the logic while weeping at the absurdity of it. Analysis is more tricky if local law and procedure requires the defendant, strictly or as a matter of good practice or to give weight to the genuineness of the jurisdictional defence, to plead to the merits at the same time as making his jurisdictional challenge, or if the defendant finds that he cannot avoid being drawn into other interlocutory procedures before the court has ruled on and disposed of the jurisdictional challenge, but in all such cases the protection of the statute should not be lost.[44] What, then, if the regular practice of the foreign court is (unlike the English) not to make a preliminary ruling on jurisdiction, but to hear the case on its merits and to deliver a single judgment, starting with the issue of jurisdiction, only at the very end? If he participates throughout, it is hard to say that the defendant appeared only for the purpose of contesting the jurisdiction, for surely he has two purposes, one contingent on the failure of the other. A generous view of section 33 would suggest that the defendant sued before such a court does, in effect, win if the court rules in his favour, but does not have to accept defeat if it rules against him on jurisdiction and then on the merits. 'Heads I win, tails you lose' is not usually a compelling plea, but in this context the reason it should probably succeed is because all the alternatives are worse.[45]

---

[42] *Henry v Geoprosco International* [1976] QB 726 (CA).

[43] The reasoning being that if relief is applied for, the very making of the application involves accepting that the court has jurisdiction to grant it; and there is therefore a submission. A more sophisticated analysis would have been that to submit to the power of a court to rule on its jurisdiction is not the same thing as to submit to its power to rule on the merits: *Williams & Glyn's Bank v Astro Dinamico* [1984] 1 WLR 438 (HL).

[44] *AES Ust-Kamenogorsk Hydropower Plant LLP v Ust-Kamenogorsk Hydropower Plant JSC* [2011] EWCA Civ 647, [2012] 1 WLR 920 (the point was not dealt with on the appeal to the Supreme Court); *Marc Rich & Co AG v Soc Italiana Impianti PA (No 2)* [1992] 1 Lloyd's Rep 624 (CA). If the foreign court does not see the defendant's participation as amounting to submission or appearance, an English court should not do so either: *Adams v Cape Industries plc* [1990] Ch 433 (CA) 461, but cf *Rubin v Eurofinance SA* [2012] UKSC 46, [2013] 1 AC 236.

[45] But see the judgment of the Supreme Court of Canada in *Barer v Knight Bros LLC* [2019] SCC 13 (applying the statute law of Québec, which is materially different from English law), which rejects the analysis preferred here, and treats an appearance before the foreign court for mixed purposes as a submission to its jurisdiction. Québec does not have legislation corresponding to the Civil Jurisdiction and Judgments Act 1982, s 33.

A troublesome argument, which has proved more attractive than it should have, proposes that if a party has made an application to a court for a particular form of relief, issue estoppel will in principle arise from the decision of the court on that specific point if it is adverse to the applicant, with such consequences as her opponent may derive from it.[46] It follows, so the argument runs, that if a party applies to a foreign court for a stay or dismissal on the ground that the court has no jurisdiction, the decision of the foreign court that it does, and any factual finding made in support of this decision, may give rise to an estoppel and be utilized by the opposite party in an attempt to secure recognition of the consequent judgment. Though this may appear sound—a party who has made an application ought surely to be bound by the court's decision on it—it plainly is not. A litigant is not bound to accept a foreign judgment as binding her unless she agreed or submitted to the jurisdiction of the foreign court in the first place. If the appearance was for the purpose of contesting the jurisdiction, section 33(1) provides a complete answer to the contention that making it was in any material sense a submission: before any question of recognition as *res judicata* can arise by reason of a party's submission, there must actually be something which the English court is entitled to see as a submission. If section 33(1) rules that out, that is the end of the argument.

(c) Judgments *in rem*

The principles derived from presence and submission, as these apply to judgments *in personam*, are reflected in the rules for the recognition of judgments *in rem*. A foreign judgment which purports to decide *in rem* upon, for example, the ownership of property will be recognized if the property in question was within the territorial jurisdiction of the court, and if not, not:[47] this accords with the principle that title to property is governed by the law of the place where the property was when something happened to it;[48] an adjudication of title counts as a something. But if the property was not within the territorial jurisdiction of the court, the judgment may still be given *in personam* effect between the parties as creating a personal obligation in relation to that property, binding on each by virtue of their bilateral agreement to submit to the jurisdiction of the foreign court and

---

[46] *Desert Sun Loan Corp v Hill* [1996] 2 All ER 847 (CA).
[47] *United States v Abacha* [2014] EWCA Civ 1291, [2015] 1 WLR 1917 (in any event unenforceable as based on a foreign penal law).
[48] See Ch 7.

abide by its judgment, if the principles applicable to judgments *in personam* are satisfied.[49]

(d) The difficulty of judicial reform

The grounds stated above are exhaustive. It follows that English law does not recognize a foreign judgment just because the foreign court had jurisdiction under its own law, or exercised a jurisdiction which mirrors that which English law would exercise itself,[50] or was the natural forum for the trial of the action: neither comity between states (as the common law understands it), nor any sensible bilateral or mutually accepted obligation to abide by the judgment, can be discerned from such facts. But not all common law systems see matters this way. The Supreme Court of Canada has embarked on a programme of reform, in which it aims to weave together the exercise of jurisdiction, the grant of anti-suit injunctions,[51] and the recognition of foreign judgments into a single tapestry. It now recognizes judgments from courts having 'a real and substantial' connection to the dispute, just so long as the foreign proceedings accorded with fairness and natural justice, on the basis that this treats a foreign court, and its judgment, as being in principle equivalent to its own.[52] If the foreign court is, in Canadian eyes, an appropriate place for the claimant to start proceedings, and if the foreign court has acted in a way which corresponds to Canadian standards of order and fairness, what reason is there to deny its judgment recognition? The pragmatic answer would be that it makes life very difficult for a defendant (or his lawyer) who, when served with nothing more than the writ, will have to predict whether, at some later date, the foreign court will be seen to have had a sufficient connection to the dispute to make its judgment enforceable in Canada, in which case he had better appear and defend the claim, or will not, in which case it may make sense to not appear and allow the proceedings to go by default. That, one may think, poses its own challenge to idea of order and fairness.[53]

As a matter of English law, so shocking a development would require legislation.[54] And it is important to appreciate how radical this departure is. For as

---

[49] *Pattni v Ali* [2006] UKPC 51, [2007] 2 AC 85.

[50] Traditionally this proposition is supported by *Schibsby v Westenholz* (1870) LR 6 QB 155. The analogy is inexact, for it took no account of the fact that an English court would not have exercised the jurisdiction invoked unless it was also the natural forum for the claim.

[51] See, in particular, *Amchem Products Inc v British Columbia (Workers' Compensation Board)* [1993] 1 SCR 897, (1993) 102 DLR (4th) 96.

[52] *Morguard Investments Ltd v De Savoye* [1990] 3 SCR 1077, (1991) 76 DLR (4th) 256.

[53] See *Beals v Saldanha* [2003] 3 SCR 416, (2003) 234 DLR (4th) 1.

[54] cf *Owens Bank plc v Bracco* [1992] 2 AC 443; *Rubin v Eurofinance SA* [2012] UKSC 46, [2013] 1 AC 236.

has been shown, the English common law asks whether the party to be bound to the judgment has assumed, in relation to the other, a personal, mutual, obligation to abide by the judgment, which may then be recognized and enforced. The new Canadian law, however, does not focus on whether the party to be bound has assumed such an obligation, but on whether the Canadian court should order recognition for reasons—which may place respect for foreign courts at the top of the list—of its own. There may be things to be said in favour of such a law (though none come to mind), but far from being a modernization of the details, it would in fact demolish the common law of foreign judgments and erect something quite different where it had stood.

3. DEFENCES TO RECOGNITION UNDER THE COMMON LAW RULES

A judgment will be denied recognition as *res judicata*, and there can therefore be no question of its enforcement, if any of the admissible defences to recognition, examined below, is made out. All obligations are liable to be untied and undone if a defence applies to them, and the obligation created by a foreign judgment is no different.

It needs to be said at the outset that it is no defence that the foreign court got the law or the facts, or both, wrong or that it tried to apply English law and made a real mess of it,[55] or that it determined the issue by the application of a conflicts rule different from that which the English court would have applied.[56] The merits of the judgment cannot be re-examined, so the allegation that the foreign court erred in its fact-finding or reasoning is irrelevant and inadmissible, no matter how patent its truth. Were it otherwise, every judgment would be re-examinable, and the advantage of the rule would be utterly lost. To put it another way, an obligation to abide by a judgment only if it is 'right' would be no obligation at all.

By contrast, when parties are considered to have agreed and bound themselves to abide by the judgment of a foreign court, it is inconceivable that their agreement extends to judgments procured by fraud, or to judgments obtained by fundamental disregard of the rules of natural justice or procedural fairness: their agreement is presumably to a judgment arrived at by a reasonable judicial procedure, even if it is very different from the procedure one

---

[55] *Godard v Gray* (1870) LR 6 QB 288.
[56] *First Laser Ltd v Fujian Enterprises (Holdings) Co Ltd* [2013] 2 HKC 459.

would find in an English court. But it bears repeating: parties to litigation in a foreign court do not, in English eyes, agree to abide by the judgment only if it is correct in fact or law. This is why simple error by the foreign court does not carry the judgment outside the terms of their agreement.

It should follow from this that a judgment obtained in breach of a choice of court or arbitration agreement should not be recognized at common law, as the proceedings, and the judgment, would fall outside the four corners of the parties' agreement. The common law never quite decided this question;[57] the issue is now covered by a bespoke statutory defence to recognition. In looking at the defences which will undo the obligation created by a foreign judgment, it is convenient to start with this one.

(a) Violation of arbitration or choice of court agreement

If the foreign court was called upon to exercise jurisdiction in breach of what English law would find to be a valid choice of court or arbitration agreement, its judgment will not be recognized at common law, even if the foreign court addressed the very issue and concluded, entirely and correctly and in accordance with its own laws, that there was no such breach. English law now has a clear statutory policy which reinforces such agreements by refusing to give effect to judgments which it considers to violate them. In accordance with principle and the statute, it is otherwise if the complaining party had acquiesced in and waived the breach, say by defending the case on its merits;[58] if more justification is needed, this will be a tacit agreement on new terms. Once again, there is a potentially tricky problem for a defendant who has done his level best to persuade the foreign court to give effect to the agreement, but who also has no real or practical choice but to defend himself in the substantive proceedings which continue while the court makes up its mind on his challenge. In principle he should have the benefit of the doubt, and should not be held to have waived the defence which the Act would give him.[59] But there will certainly be cases which fall close to the line, and on either side of it.

It is obvious that if the court rules against the claimant, it does not lie in his mouth to complain about the disregard of the agreement of which he was

---

[57] It may have come close, in *Ellerman Lines Ltd v Read* [1928] 2 KB 144.

[58] Civil Jurisdiction & Judgments Act 1982, s 32; *Marc Rich & Co AG v Soc Italiana Impianti PA* [1992] 2 Lloyd's Rep 624 (CA).

[59] See *AES Ust-Kamenogorsk Hydropower Plant LLP v Ust-Kamenogorsk Hydropower Plant JSC* [2011] EWCA Civ 647, [2012] 1 WLR 920. The point was not dealt with on the further appeal.

the instigator.[60] It is much less obvious whether the statutory defence to recognition can extend—and it certainly would be an extension—to a judgment obtained from a court which failed to give effect to an express choice of law not accompanied by a jurisdiction agreement. It would certainly seem unlikely, for no account is usually taken of the conflicts rules which are applied by the foreign court. But where the claimant has brought proceedings before a court which decides otherwise than in accordance with the parties' express agreement, it is not obvious that an English court should just shrug and rec ognize the offending judgment as inoffensive.[61]

(b) Fraud

Fraud, it is said, is a thing apart.[62] Fraud unravels everything: if it negates obligations it can certainly negate the obligation to abide by a foreign judgment. Where this defence is raised, the really contentious issue is what may be said, and in particular whether it is permitted to repeat what was said to the foreign court or to say what could have been said to the foreign court but was not. The principles are now less tangled than they were. Although, as said above, the merits of a foreign judgment may not be re-examined by an English court, a different approach prevails if there is a credible allegation that it was procured by fraud.[63] The investigation of an allegation of fraud is bound to revisit at least some the merits, not least to check whether the facts and matters complained of had any effect on the judgment which resulted: an alleged or attempted fraud which had no effect will be ignored.[64]

The definition of fraud has been held to encompass any misleading or duping of the foreign court. It may include advancing a claim known to be false, fabricating evidence, intimidating witnesses, and so on: fraud will generally lie in the use of improper means to defeat, or pervert, the course of justice to prevail over the defendant.[65] Whether it covers the case where a

---

[60] *The Sennar (No 2)* [1985] 1 WLR 490 (HL).

[61] *JSC BTA Bank v Türkiye Vakıflar Bankası TAO* [2018] EWHC 835 (Comm) is unhelpful but distinguishable.

[62] *HIH Casualty and General Insurance Ltd v Chase Manhattan Bank* [2003] UKHL 6, [2003] 2 Lloyd's Rep 61 [15].

[63] *Abouloff v Oppenheimer* (1882) 10 QBD 295 (CA); *Vadala v Lawes* (1890) 25 QBD 310 (CA); *Syal v Heyward* [1948] 2 KB 443 (CA); *Jet Holdings Inc v Patel* [1990] 1 QB 335 (CA); *Owens Bank Ltd v Bracco* [1992] 2 AC 443; *Altimo Holdings & Investment Ltd v Kyrgyz Mobil Tel Ltd* [2011] UKPC 7, [2012] 1 WLR 1804.

[64] *Gelley v Shepherd* [2013] EWCA Civ 1172.

[65] Although the defendant may also use fraud to support a defence which defeats the claim and, if this happens, the claimant may seek to impeach the judgment which the defendant seeks to have recognized in his favour; cf *Merchant International Co Ltd v NAK Naftogaz* [2012] EWCA Civ 196, [2012] 1 WLR 3036.

claimant pleads a claim to which he knows the defendant may have a good answer is unclear, but it cannot realistically be expected that in an adversary *inter partes* procedure the claimant has a duty to make his opponent's case for him. It may, in the end, be a question of degree, with all the difficulty that sometimes brings.

The facts and matters which support the allegation of fraud may be put forward to oppose an application for summary judgment in the enforcement action, and if credible will be investigated by trial of an issue.[66] The common law never required a defendant who alleged that a foreign judgment was obtained by fraud to base his application on a fresh discovery of evidence which could not reasonably have been put forward at trial. Now that the view that such a fresh discovery, untainted by negligence, was required to impeach a *local* judgment for fraud has been shown to be wrong,[67] the rules for local and foreign judgments, said to have been procured by fraud, are more closely aligned, and the law on foreign judgments stands out rather less than it did. However, where foreign judgments are concerned, the defendant may recycle the evidence which failed to persuade the foreign court; where local judgments are concerned, that aspect of the law may not be the same.

The law is, and has always been, on a sure footing. To begin with, in order to have the allegation of fraud investigated, the defendant will have to make a credible case that the foreign court in question was the victim of, or party to, fraud. The evidence required to reach this threshold of credibility will vary from case to case. It is reasonable to suppose that an English court will take much more persuading that an Australian or American court judgment was obtained by fraud than where the judgment came from a court with little international reputation for fearless judicial excellence. The standard required to trigger a fraud review is, on this view of the matter, contextual; it could not be otherwise.[68] Next, if it is objected that all this should be left to the foreign court, whose judgment should be regarded as conclusive, it would be unprincipled for the law to require a defendant to make his allegations in a court which may—who knows?—have been selected by the claimant in his own self-interest. The proposition that the defendant is entitled to a hearing of a serious allegation in a court over which no suspicion or taint may float is hardly shocking; and in any event, a finding of fraud in relation to a foreign

---

[66] *Jet Holdings Inc v Patel* [1990] 1 QB 335 (CA).

[67] *Takhar v Gracefield Developments Ltd* [2019] UKSC 13, [2019] 2 WLR 984.

[68] See the analysis in *Altimo Holdings & Investment Ltd v Kyrgyz Mobil Tel Ltd* [2011] UKPC 7, [2012] 1 WLR 1804.

judgment means only that the judgment may not be recognized in England, just as a finding that an arbitral award was contrary to English public policy means only that the award cannot be enforced in England. That is something which an English court can properly investigate for itself. A finding of fraud does not purport to impeach or annul the foreign judgment so as to prevent its recognition and enforcement outside England.

If the allegation of fraud has already had an independent hearing in, and been rejected by, a court of the *defendant's* own free choosing, this fact should prevent its being raised once more in England. Either the ordinary principles of *res judicata* will mean that the second judgment ties the hands of the defendant who picked the court for those proceedings, or it may be an abuse of the process of the English court for it to be advanced (yet) again.[69] Even so, too vigorous a use of the 'abuse of process' doctrine has the potential to overwhelm much of the fraud defence;[70] there is need for caution. For even if the defendant has chosen to make the allegation of fraud in fresh proceedings before the courts of the country of the original judgment, he may only have 'chosen' that court because he faced the prospect of imminent execution against assets which he had in that country. Against this background, to find that there is no right to raise the defence anew will require some care.[71]

(c) Failure to observe standards of procedural fairness

If the proceedings in the foreign court fell short of the standards set by the rules of natural justice such as the right to be sufficiently notified, properly represented, and fairly heard,[72] or if the foreign court violated the principle of finality by reopening a decision for no proper reason,[73] it may be possible to deny recognition to the judgment. The common law provided rather little supporting authority, but it was never doubted that the defence, usually framed in terms of natural or substantial justice, was available to prevent recognition.

---

[69] *House of Spring Gardens Ltd v Waite* [1991] 1 QB 241 (CA). There is no reason in principle why the findings against the judgment debtor in the second action should not give rise to an estoppel, but cf the Civil Jurisdiction and Judgments Act 1982, s 33(1)(c).

[70] *Owens Bank Ltd v Etoile Commerciale SA* [1995] 1 WLR 44 (PC); *Desert Sun Loan Corp v Hill* [1996] 2 All ER 847 (CA).

[71] *Takhar v Gracefield Developments Ltd* [2019] UKSC 13, [2019] 2 WLR 984.

[72] cf, from the context of judgments falling within the Regulation, Case C–7/98 *Krombach v Bamberski* [2000] ECR I–1935.

[73] *JSC Aeroflot-Russian Airlines v Berezovsky* [2012] EWHC 3017 (Ch); *Merchant International Co Ltd v NAK Naftogaz* [2012] EWCA Civ 196, [2012] 1 WLR 3036; *Pravednaya v Russia* [2004] ECHR 641.

The Human Rights Act 1998 has raised the profile of this objection and put it on a new foundation. The Act, as a Parliamentary direction to the judges, is separate and distinct from the common law defences whose territory it has largely taken over. If the English court is called on to make an order which will give domestic effect to a foreign judgment which resulted from an unfair judicial procedure, Article 6 of the European Convention on Human Rights is directly engaged. It does not matter where the foreign judgment comes from, for the obligation created by Article 6 binds the English court, never mind the foreign court.[74] An unconvincing strand of English authority suggests that Article 6 will not be engaged in this context unless the procedural shortcomings on the part of the foreign court, which deprived the defendant of what Article 6 aims to secure, can be described as 'flagrant'.[75] This cannot be correct: the proposition that a defendant's right to a fair trial can be trashed but not flagrantly trashed is as insupportable in law as it is painful to write.

By contrast with the defence of fraud, where the common law clearly allows the recycling of old material, it is less certain whether the argument that the foreign judgment involved a breach of the rules of procedural fairness may be advanced on the basis of material which was put, or could reasonably have been put, to the foreign court in the original proceedings. It has been judicially suggested that, as with fraud, the view of the foreign court does not preclude the English court from making its own assessment,[76] and that the court may therefore consider or reconsider material rejected by the foreign court; but a more subtle view might be that it depends on the precise nature of the shortcoming complained of:[77] a complaint that the foreign judge should have recused himself on grounds of interest or bias should be something which may be raised again;[78] a complaint that there was no opportunity to cross-examine a witness may not be allowed to be raised again, on the ground that it is just the reflection of a difference in reasonable procedural laws. But even if the analogy with fraud is the right one, one supposes that the court will not allow an argument to be advanced past the point where it becomes an abuse of process.

---

[74] *Pellegrini v Italy* (2002) 35 EHRR 2 (ECtHR); *Laserpoint Ltd v Prime Minister of Malta* [2016] EWHC 1820 (QB).

[75] *Barnette v United States* [2004] UKHL 37, [2004] 1 WLR 2241.

[76] *Jet Holdings Inc v Patel* [1990] 1 QB 335 (CA).

[77] *Adams v Cape Industries plc* [1990] Ch 433 (CA) 564–67.

[78] Denied in *Mengiste v Endowment Fund for the Rehabilitation of Tigray* [2017] EWCA Civ 1326, though perhaps because the argument, based (only) on apparent bias, was factually weak.

(d) Public policy

Recognition of the judgment must be refused where this would offend English public policy. Judgments based on laws which are objectively disgraceful, or on laws which produce an outcome which is equally repellent, for example, will be denied recognition. The usual suspects are Nazi laws, or the laws by which Iraq purported to dissolve Kuwait and steal everything its thieving officials could lay hold of;[79] but public policy may also be offended by judgments based on foreign laws which are incompatible with English notions of freedom, equality, and respect. Some legal systems consider that a judgment delivered without reasons offends their public policy, but a jury verdict would run into trouble with such a rule. English law has not so far had to consider such an issue, but a judgment devoid of reasons might give rise to some concerns on this point.

(e) Lack of local jurisdiction

It is debatable whether the fact that the court lacked jurisdiction under its internal law may furnish a defence, for the authorities are old and inconclusive.[80] If under the foreign law the judgment is a complete nullity, and not just voidable—presumably a rare state of affairs, but never mind—it would be odd for it to be recognized as giving rise to an obligation to accept it. If the judgment is, however, voidable it is, *ex hypothesi*, valid unless and until proceedings are taken to set it aside, which may never happen; an English court must surely recognize the judgment as giving rise to an obligation, notwithstanding the fragility of local jurisdiction.

(f) Prior English judgment

If the foreign judgment is inconsistent with an English judgment, or with a foreign judgment handed down earlier in time and which is already entitled to recognition in England as *res judicata*, the judgment cannot be recognized.[81]

4. THE EFFECT OF RECOGNITION AT COMMON LAW

The most usual reason to seek the recognition of a foreign judgment will be to pave the way for the judgment creditor to bring a claim against the

---

[79] The case of Russia and the Ukrainian territory of Crimea cannot be any different. There are others *in pari delicto* with these, but it is expedient to leave the reader to fill in the blanks.

[80] *Vanquelin v Bouard* (1863) 15 CBNS 341; *Pemberton v Hughes* [1899] 1 Ch 781.

[81] *Showlag v Mansour* [1995] 1 AC 431 (PC).

judgment debtor. If the party in whose favour the foreign judgment was given wishes to collect on it, he may sue on the obligation, the cause of action, created by the judgment, subject to the further limitations examined below. However, before we do that, there are two further consequences of recognition which may be of importance and which should be noted now. First, if the party against whom the judgment was given was subject to the international jurisdiction of the foreign court—the claimant will necessarily[82] have been, the defendant may have been—and no relevant defence is applicable, the cause of action or the issue, as the case may be, will be regarded as against him[83] as *res judicata*. This means that he may not contradict it in or by later English proceedings unless some exception to the application of the doctrine of *res judicata* applies.[84] But secondly, if the party in whose favour the judgment was given, and *against whom* there is therefore no *res judicata*,[85] had been hoping for a better outcome, or seeks to raise a claim which was not put forward the first time around, she may fail: Civil Jurisdiction and Judgments Act 1982, section 34, now generally prevents a claimant from suing for a second time on the same underlying cause of action in the hope of improving on the result obtained first time around:[86] a statute was required because, as a matter of theory, a cause of action does not merge and disappear into a foreign judgment. In the interpretation of the 'same cause of action' it has been held that any claim which arises out of a single contract constitutes the same cause of action as any other, so that a failure to deliver part of a consignment of goods has the same cause of action as the failure to deliver the balance of the cargo. Even so, a claimant who manages to steer a careful course around section 34 may still find that his claim or claiming is considered to abuse the process of the court if it raises a matter which could and should—which does not mean could—have been advanced in the first action.[87]

---

[82]   Except in his capacity as defendant to a counterclaim which was not sufficiently within the penumbra of the claim he advanced.

[83]   And against his privies: those with the same interest or title in the matter, especially if they have stood by, hoping to be regarded as strangers, while one with the same interest as them fights the case: *House of Spring Gardens Ltd v Waite* [1991] 1 QB 241 (CA).

[84]   *Carl Zeiss Stiftung v Rayner & Keeler Ltd (No 2)* [1967] 1 AC 853.

[85]   *JSC Ingosstrakh-Investments v BNP Paribas SA* [2012] EWCA Civ 644, [2012] 1 Lloyd's Rep 649.

[86]   *Republic of India v India Steamship Co Ltd (The Indian Grace)* [1993] AC 410; *Republic of India v India Steamship Co Ltd (The Indian Grace) (No 2)* [1998] AC 878.

[87]   *Henderson v Henderson* (1843) 3 Hare 100; *Virgin Atlantic Airways Ltd v Zodiac Seats UK Ltd* [2013] UKSC 46, [2014] AC 160.

5. ENFORCEMENT BY ACTION AT COMMON LAW

A foreign judgment which satisfies the criteria for its recognition against the losing party creates an obligation—it is the obligation, rather than the judgment, which is enforced by action in England—upon which the judgment creditor may sue the judgment debtor.[88] The action is brought as one for debt, which means that only final and conclusive judgments for fixed sums of money can be enforced this way. As for its being final and conclusive, a judgment which may be reviewed or revised by the court which gave it is not final,[89] but its being subject to appeal to a higher court is irrelevant. This is for all practical purposes the same requirement as will already have applied to its recognition, and although it is always stated as a condition for enforcement, this reflects only the habit of seeing the law on foreign judgments as focused on enforcement rather than on recognition. As a debt claim must be based on a judgment for the payment of a fixed sum in money, if the sum is open to variation by the court which awarded it, it is not final and cannot be enforced.[90] It is irrelevant, however, that the foreign court would have allowed the judgment debtor to discharge his overall liability by instalments: if the judgment sum has been finally fixed, it may be enforced as a debt immediately. Foreign procedural rules, such as those about the time and manner of payment, are ignored by an English court.

It follows that if the judgment was not final and for a fixed sum in money it cannot be enforced by proceedings of this kind; and if that were all there was to say, it would make the effect of foreign judgments rather unsatisfactory. But it is not all there is to say. If the foreign judgment was final on the issue of liability but did not order payment of a fixed sum—say the quantum could be reassessed, or that the order was for delivery up, or was in the nature of specific performance or an injunction—the claimant, unable to sue on the obligation created by the judgment, will have to sue on the original cause of action. But the foreign court's finding of liability may be recognized, making the substance of the claim *res judicata*, and meaning that all the court will

---

[88] If the defendant is out of the jurisdiction, permission to serve out will be required; CPR PD 6B 3.1(10) is the relevant gateway. There is no need to show assets currently within the jurisdiction: *Tasarruf Mevduatı Sigorta Fonu v Demirel* [2007] EWCA Civ 799, [2007] 1 WLR 2508: it would be absurd if the law were otherwise.

[89] *Nouvion v Freeman* (1889) 15 App Cas 1.

[90] In personal injury cases, in which a court may have a power to review and adjust the damages awarded, this will cause real trouble.

need to do is find a suitable remedy to go with it. When it is further recalled that a foreign money judgment cannot be enforced as such, but requires an original English judgment on the debt to give the judgment creditor an order on which execution is possible, the line between the 'enforcement' of money and non-money judgments becomes noticeably faint, and the proposition that the former may be, the latter may not be, 'enforced' is seen to be misleading.

However, English proceedings may not be brought to enforce a foreign penal, revenue, or analogous public law; and if the action on the judgment would have this effect it will be dismissed. So if a foreign tax authority has obtained a foreign judgment in its favour, enforcement of the judgment by action in England will necessarily fail.[91] Nor, by reason of the Protection of Trading Interests Act 1980, section 5, may an action be brought to recover any sums ordered to be paid by a foreign judgment for multiple damages, even—perhaps unexpectedly—for the basic, un-multiplied, compensatory element for the cause of action in question: the statute is as clear as the policy is indefensible. By curious contrast, it appears that judgments for exemplary damages, unless truly extreme and on that account contrary to public policy, are not covered by the Act and prevented from enforcement by the rule, just so long as the judgment debt has not been calculated by 'doubling, trebling or otherwise multiplying' the sum fixed as compensation.[92] The logic of this is also elusive: not only because the difference between multiplication and addition has not generally been thought of as legally, as opposed to mathematically, significant, but also because the award of multiplied damages is often in partial amelioration of the fact that costs may not be recoverable.[93]

C. REGISTRATION OF FOREIGN JUDGMENTS FOR ENFORCEMENT

As explained earlier, there are some countries from which certain kinds of judgment may be registered for enforcement, pursuant to two, long-established, statutory schemes. It makes sense to look at these immediately

---

[91] *United States of America v Harden* (1963) 41 DLR (2d) 721 (Can SC).
[92] Protection of Trading Interests Act 1980, s 5.
[93] And see, for the same proposition in the European context, *SA Consortium General Textiles SA v Sun & Sand Agencies Ltd* [1978] QB 279 (CA).

after the common law, for the substantive terms of the statutes which spell out the conditions for registration of the judgment are very close to the common law as it was understood at the date of enactment. But if registration under the Acts of 1920 and 1933 were to be no more than a footnote to the rules of the common law, it would obscure the important fact that under these Acts, it is the foreign judgment which is registered and which may itself be enforced and executed upon; and that this makes the scheme very different indeed from the mechanism, but also from the understanding, of the common law.

As to the entitlement to register, the conditions are close to those of the common law. Instead of its being necessary to commence original proceedings by service of a claim form, proceeding in short order to make an application for summary judgment, the statutes allow the judgment creditor to register the judgment for enforcement. Once registered, the foreign judgment is of the same force and effect, for the purpose of enforcement, as if it had been an English judgment. The respondent may then, if so advised, make an application to set aside the registration and the order for registration; and it is on the hearing of this application, if made, that the principal issues will emerge.

In addition to judgments registrable under the 1920 and 1933 Acts, judgments from other parts of the United Kingdom and from Gibraltar, and judgments from the courts of states which are party to or bound by the 2005 Hague Convention on Choice of Court Agreements, and which fall within the terms of that Convention, may be registered for enforcement under various provisions of the Civil Jurisdiction and Judgments Act 1982.

1. ADMINISTRATION OF JUSTICE ACT 1920

Part II of the Administration of Justice Act 1920 applies to many Commonwealth and similar territories; it no longer applies to Australia or Canada, but of the larger countries it still extends to Malaysia, Nigeria, New Zealand, and Singapore.[94] It does not depend on any treaty with the foreign state; it applies to judgments from 'superior courts', which may be registered under the Act within 12 months of their being delivered.[95] Upon

---

[94] Reciprocal Enforcement of Judgments (Administration of Justice Act 1920, Part II) (Consolidation) Order 1984 (SI 1984/129), as amended by SI 1985/1994, SI 1994/1901, and SI 1997/2601. It no longer applies to Hong Kong. The Act has never applied to South Africa.
[95] Section 9.

an application to set aside the registration, the grounds which satisfy the requirement of jurisdiction under the Act, and the defences to registration allowed by the Act, differ from those of the common law only in minor detail; although if the judgment is still subject to appeal it may not be registered.[96]

2. FOREIGN JUDGMENTS (RECIPROCAL ENFORCEMENT) ACT 1933

The Foreign Judgments (Reciprocal Enforcement) Act 1933 allows the enforcement by registration of judgments in civil and commercial matters from designated courts in countries with which a bilateral treaty has been concluded. Some of the countries to which the Act was extended are Member States of the European Union,[97] or party to the Lugano Convention.[98] While the United Kingdom was also a Member State these bilateral treaties were superseded, but they were never repealed, and after a long lay-off, they may now be returning to work. The Act also applies to judgments from Australia[99] and Canada,[100] as well as India, Israel, Pakistan, Guernsey, Jersey, and the Isle of Man. It applies only to courts identified by name in the Order which implements the bilateral treaty: judgments from other courts in these countries may still be enforced by action at common law. The grounds which satisfy the requirement of jurisdiction and the defences to registration[101] differ from those of the common law only in minor detail; if the judgment is subject to appeal the application for registration may be stayed.[102]

3. CIVIL JURISDICTION AND JUDGMENTS ACT 1982

The 1982 Act provides that the effect of registration under it is that the judgment is treated, for the purposes of enforcement, as though it were an original judgment of the High Court. Its original purpose was to provide the

---

[96] Section 9(2)(e).
[97] Austria, Belgium, France, Germany, Italy, and the Netherlands.
[98] Norway.
[99] SI 1994/1901.
[100] SI 1987/468, 2211; SI 1988/1304, 1853; SI 1989/987; SI 1991/1724; SI 1992/1731; SI 1995/2708. Québec is not included.
[101] Section 4.
[102] Section 5.

supporting apparatus for the enforcement by registration of judgments from the courts of member states of the EU given in civil and commercial matters, under the Brussels Convention, original Brussels I Regulation, and Lugano Convention, but the opportunity was taken to use it for a few other cases. Its original purpose may now be coming to an end: even before the departure of the United Kingdom from the EU, judgments covered by the recast version of the Brussels I Regulation, Regulation (EU) 1215/2012, could be enforced in the United Kingdom without any need for prior registration. The 1982 Act therefore now applies to a slightly odd assortment: judgments from other parts of the United Kingdom, whether for money or otherwise, which may be registered for enforcement subject to only minor restrictions;[103] judgments from Gibraltar, which are recognized and enforced on the basis of provisions derived from and modelled on the rules of the Brussels Convention;[104] and judgments which may be enforced in England pursuant to the 2005 Hague Convention on Choice of Court Agreements, which requires a little more attention.

The Hague Convention came into force in the United Kingdom when the EU acceded to the Convention.[105] On its withdrawal from the EU the United Kingdom was free to adopt the Convention in its own right, which was done with transitional provisions which are complicated but designed to work seamlessly.[106] Judgments from states to which the Convention applies, and which fall within its scope, may be enforced by registration.[107] The states to which the Convention applies are the Member States of the EU, Mexico, Montenegro, and Singapore, and the list will, no doubt, grow; the judgments to which it applies are those given by a court designated by an exclusive choice of court agreement for that court. When the application is made, registration should be ordered without any consideration of (still less debate about) whether any of the admissible defences to registration may be available to the judgment debtor;[108] but the judgment debtor may apply to have registration set aside by reference to a number of grounds set out in the

---

[103] Civil Jurisdiction and Judgments Act 1982, s 18; Schs 6, 7.

[104] Civil Jurisdiction and Judgments Act 1982, s 39; Civil Jurisdiction and Judgments Act 1982 (Gibraltar) Order 1997 (SI 1997/2602). At least, it was supposed to. In fact it is not clear that the Act made any provision at all for the registration of judgments from Gibraltar; a little tidying up of the law is still needed.

[105] The Civil Jurisdiction and Judgments (Hague Convention on Choice of Court Agreements 2005) Regulations 2015, SI 2015/1644.

[106] The Civil Jurisdiction and Judgments (Hague Convention on Choice of Court Agreements 2005) (EU Exit) Regulations 2018, SI 2018/1124.

[107] Civil Jurisdiction and Judgments Act 1982, s 4B.

[108] Article 8.

Convention.[109] In seeking to limit the grounds of permissible objection to enforcement, the drafters of the convention had to find a balance between (on the one hand) holding parties to the full consequences of their voluntary jurisdictional agreement, and (on the other) allowing a court called upon to enforce the judgment to be sufficiently assured that the judgment fell within the scope of the Convention and had been regularly arrived at.[110] The resulting text is predictable and rational, though so far as it provides for enforcement of judgments in England it provides little (save for registration) that the common law rules had not already secured or that the recast Brussels I Regulation had not already done, and done better. A particular novelty is the provision which allows non-enforcement of a judgment for damages which extends beyond compensation for loss of harm suffered.[111]

It is worth remembering that the Convention provides for the recognition and enforcement of judgments which fall within its scope. It does not provide for the non-recognition of judgments which were given by a court which had failed to respect an exclusive jurisdiction agreement.[112] If that is to be done, as it certainly should be done, it is left to national law, which means to the Civil Jurisdiction and Judgments Act 1982, section 32, to do it.

D. FOREIGN JUDGMENTS ENFORCEABLE WITHOUT REGISTRATION: BRUSSELS I REGULATION (RECAST)

The evolution of the scheme for the recognition and enforcement of judgments within the EU is, even if the United Kingdom is turning its back on it, fascinating and instructive. The original 1968 Brussels Convention was made to secure the straightforward free circulation of judgments in civil and commercial matters across the community.[113] Its genius lay in the realization that if the contracting states had uniform rules of jurisdiction, which they could be trusted to operate properly, the recognition and enforcement of judgments could proceed on the assumption that there should be little to object

---

[109]   Article 9.
[110]   Articles 8, 9.
[111]   Article 11.
[112]   It does not provide, either, for the granting of an injunction to restrain a breach of contract committed by bringing proceedings contrary to the terms of an exclusive jurisdiction agreement, which was considered in Chapter 2.
[113]   Article 220 of the Treaty of Rome.

to. A limited number of defences, mostly procedural in nature, would be admissible, as would—inevitably—be an objection on grounds of public policy. Objections to the exercise of jurisdiction by the original court would by severely restricted, on the basis that if there were such an objection to be made, it could and should have been made to the original court; but for those few jurisdictional rules which were of overriding importance, or which served to protect the weaker party in certain kinds of contractual relationship, the recognizing court was permitted or required to check for itself. But any and all review of the merits of the judgment was strictly prohibited.

The Brussels Convention, as implemented in the United Kingdom,[114] required the judgment creditor to register the judgment for enforcement under the 1982 Act. That done, the judgment debtor would be notified of the registration, and would have a very short period within which to make an application for the registration to be set aside, on the grounds exhaustively set out in the Convention. The basic mechanism remained the same when the Convention was re-made as Regulation 44/2001,[115] though the admissible defences to recognition, and hence to registration, were trimmed back.

However, by the time the Regulation was recast as Regulation 1215/2012,[116] it had come to be understood that a requirement that the judgment creditor must invariably make and pay for an application to register the judgment, which the defendant could then apply to have set aside, was unjustified. Analysis showed that the number of challenges to registration actually made by judgment debtors was very small; the number of successful ones smaller still. The idea that the judgment creditor should always have to make and pay for such application for a registration which was rarely challenged was seen to be a barrier to the free movement of judgments and, perhaps more importantly, a waste of time and money. Accordingly, the recast Regulation provided for the original court to issue a procedural certificate to accompany the judgment, and for this to be served on the judgment debtor together with the judgment. Measures of enforcement could then be taken unless the judgment debtor made a prompt application for a refusal of enforcement or recognition. If she did that, the investigation of admissible defences would take place; if she did not, enforcement could proceed.

The provisions of the provisions now found in Regulation 1215/2012 represent the most significant development in the private international law of foreign

---

[114] By the Civil Jurisdiction and Judgments Act 1982.
[115] [2001] OJ L12/1.
[116] [2012] OJ L351/1.

judgments for at least a century. The Regulation is a legislative instruction to the laws and courts of Member States, requiring them to treat judgments from courts of other Member States as legally effective and directly enforceable, almost as though they were not foreign judgments at all. Where the Regulation prescribes the recognition and enforcement of the judgment, what is enforced, and what may be executed upon, is the foreign judgment itself.

1. RECOGNITION

For a judgment to be recognized under Chapter III of the Regulation, it must be an adjudication from a court in a Member State, given in a civil or commercial matter. If an application for refusal of recognition or enforcement is made, the judgment must be found to be safe from impeachment for jurisdictional error or for procedural or substantive reasons as set out, and narrowly defined, in Chapter III. It is often said that if it fails to meet these criteria, so that recognition is refused, there is nothing to prevent an attempt to secure recognition and enforcement of a judgment under the rules of the common law, on the footing that Chapter III of the Regulation is a permissive, not an exclusive, regime. That may be so, though it remains to be confirmed that the effect of an order refusing recognition or enforcement, as the case may be, is confined to recognition or enforcement under the Regulation and has no relevance to an attempt to enforce at common law. Be that as it may, according to Article 36 it is not necessary to bring any form of action or procedure to obtain recognition of a judgment under the Regulation, beyond pleading it, so if a successful defendant wishes to rely on a judgment to which the Regulation applies, all he need do is plead it as satisfying the criteria for recognition. There is no objection to his bringing proceedings for a declaration that there are no grounds for a refusal of recognition, but it will rarely be necessary.

2. JUDGMENT IN A CIVIL OR COMMERCIAL MATTER

A judgment is an adjudication by a court of a Member State, including an order as to costs.[117] This obviously excludes judgments from a non-Member State, but it equally excludes orders made by a judge in a Member State declaring such a judgment to be enforceable:[118] this is sometimes

---

[117] Article 2(a).
[118] Case C–129/92 *Owens Bank Ltd v Bracco* [1994] ECR I–117.

summarized by saying that *exequatur sur exequatur ne vaut*. The Regulation applies to adjudications by a judge in a Member State, but not to instances where a judge validates or approves, or allows to be enforced, a decision taken by someone who is not. Member States have their own rules for dealing with judgments from non-Member States, but the effect of satisfying these cannot be to admit such a judgment, via the doorway of one Member State's private international law, into the privileged domain of Chapter III of the Regulation. Similar considerations explain why a judicial decision to enforce an arbitration award is not a judgment within Chapter III of the Regulation either.[119] 'Judgment' does include a provisional or interlocutory judgment unless it was one designed to be obtained without notice to the respondent;[120] there is no requirement that the judgment be *res judicata* in the court which pronounced it. An order dismissing a case on jurisdictional grounds, say by reference to a choice of court agreement for another Member State, is a judgment.[121] A judgment by consent is included, for it is still made on the authority of a judge,[122] as is judgment entered in default of defence such as when a defendant is debarred for contempt (although recognition may give rise to issues of public policy).[123] A judgment which orders a periodical payment imposed as a penalty for disobedience to a court order is included,[124] although it may be enforced only if the sum due has been finally quantified by the court which ordered it.[125] Settlements approved by courts in the course of proceedings[126] and authentic instruments[127] (unknown to English domestic law: documents authenticated by a public authority or a notary, and which are enforceable under some laws without the need for legal action) are not judgments, but are enforceable under similar, but not identical, conditions.[128]

---

[119] In addition to this, the 1958 New York Convention deals with the enforcement of arbitral awards, and it would be wrong in principle to trespass on the domain of that Convention.

[120] Article 2(a).

[121] Case C–456/11 *Gothaer Allgemeine Versicherung AG v Samskip GmbH* EU:C:2012:719, [2013] QB 548. The case concerned the Lugano Convention as the jurisdiction clause was for Iceland, but the principle is general.

[122] It does not include a settlement; and if it is desired to make binding the terms on which a claim is compromised, a judgment is much to be preferred to a contractual disposal: Case C–414/92 *Solo Kleinmotoren GmbH v Boch* [1994] ECR I–2237.

[123] Case C–394/07 *Gambazzi v DaimlerChrysler Canada Inc* [2009] ECR I–2563.

[124] Article 55, or other fine imposed to encourage compliance with a court order: Case C–406/09 *Realchemie Nederland BV v Bayer Crop Science AG* [2011] ECR I–9773.

[125] Article 49.

[126] Article 59; see *Yukos International UK BV v Merinson* [2019] EWCA Civ 830.

[127] Article 58.

[128] For the points of difference, see Case C–414/92 *Solo Kleinmotoren GmbH v Boch* [1994] ECR I–2237.

The judgment must be in a civil or commercial matter, the meaning of which was examined in Chapter 2. If the point is raised on an application to refuse enforcement, one might suppose that the recognizing court must decide for itself whether the judgment was given in a civil or commercial matter: it would not be logical for it to be bound simply to accept the view of the adjudicating court, for it is only bound to recognize the judgment if it was given in a civil or commercial matter, and recognition cannot pull itself up by its own bootstraps. However, when the adjudicating court issues the certificate provided for by Article 53, which is, in effect, the judgment's passport to recognition and enforcement across the Member States, its conclusion is probably conclusive, as it is best placed to make the necessary assessment.[129]

A judgment in respect of subject matter excluded by Chapter I of the Regulation from its domain will not be recognized under Chapter III. A judgment which simply declares that the parties are not bound to arbitrate a dispute will, therefore, not be recognized.[130] Where the judgment was obtained despite an agreement to arbitrate, it might appear, from what has just been said, that recognition is not required and should on application be refused, for otherwise a court would have to contradict its own law on arbitration, which lies outside the domain of the Regulation.[131] But if Article 1(2)(d) merely means that no court has adjudicatory jurisdiction over the merits of what is still a civil or commercial claim,[132] and as jurisdictional error is not generally a basis on which recognition may be refused,[133] it would follow that recognition of the offending judgment is required unless the collision with the national public policy of enforcing agreements to arbitrate to the extent possible is just too great. There is some working out of the precise effect of Article 1(2)(d) still to be done.

Where a single judgment deals with included and excluded matter it may be possible to sever it: this may happen when a criminal court imposes a criminal penalty and orders compensation to a civil party. Where severance is not possible, the substantial presence of excluded matter in an indivisible judgment may preclude recognition under the Regulation of the whole of the judgment.[134]

---

[129] Case C–579/17 *BUAK v Gradbeništvo Korana d.o.o.* EU:C:2019:162; Case C–361/18 *Weil v Gulácsi* EU:C:2019:473.

[130] See Recital 12 to Regulation 1215/2012; see also Case C–536/13 *Gazprom OAO* EU:C:2015:316, [2015] 1 WLR 4937.

[131] cf Case 145/86 *Hoffmann v Krieg* [1988] ECR 645.

[132] Case C–391/95 *Van Uden Maritime BV v Deco-Line* [1998] ECR I–7091.

[133] See Art 45(3).

[134] Case C–220/95 *Van den Boogaard v Laumen* [1997] ECR I–1147.

3. GROUNDS FOR REFUSAL OF RECOGNITION OR ENFORCEMENT

The grounds on which a court may, on the application of the judgment debtor, make an order refusing enforcement or recognition are of two kinds: jurisdictional and non-jurisdictional.

(a) Jurisdictional grounds for a refusal order

The adjudicating court may have erred in its application of the Regulation by accepting jurisdiction when it should have held that it did not have it. In most cases this is irrelevant to the recognition of the judgment under Chapter III.[135] This is because every Member State court is to be trusted to apply the Regulation properly, and the defendant will have been at liberty to make the relevant argument to the adjudicating court. That being so, there is no reason to allow a collateral attack on the jurisdiction of the original court to be made at the point of enforcement of the judgment. Indeed, there is every reason not to, for it would impede the free circulation of judgments if it were otherwise.

While this may be reasonable for defendants domiciled in a Member State, whose jurisdictional exposure to the courts of other Member States is defined and limited by Chapter II of the Regulation, it is a different story for those not so domiciled and who may be sued on the basis of the residual jurisdictions referred to by Article 6. They have no opportunity to object to the width or arm-length of the jurisdictional rules used to hale them into court: neither at trial, because Article 6(2) makes them expressly subject to these unreconstructed rules, nor by applying for an order for refusal of enforcement, because jurisdictional points may not generally be entertained on that application.[136] One would think that something must have gone wrong with the drafting, for such institutionalized discrimination is hardly the writing of a civilized hand. But it was conscious and deliberate,[137] and *res ipsa loquitur*.

Exceptions apply only where the lack of jurisdictional complaint is that the provisions on protective jurisdiction applicable to insureds, consumers, and employees, and those which ascribe exclusive jurisdiction regardless of domicile,[138] meant that the court did not have jurisdiction to adjudicate. These particular jurisdictional rules enshrine policies of such importance that the recognizing court

---

[135] Article 45(3).
[136] Article 45(3), which also forbids the conclusion that the jurisdictional rules of the court are contrary to public policy.
[137] Jenard [1979] OJ C59/20.
[138] Article 45(1)(e). Breach of a jurisdiction agreement is not included.

should be permitted or required take a second look; but this power does not extend to a complaint that the adjudicating court has failed to give effect to a jurisdiction agreement which should have been regarded as valid by reason of Article 25. This places Article 25 in a relatively low position in the hierarchy of jurisdictional rules.[139] It was in partial response to this that the jurisdiction rules in Chapter II of the Regulation were recast to make it more likely that the court designated or allegedly designated would take the effective (and correct) decision on jurisdiction, so reducing the likelihood of such errors. In any event, the rule of national law which would allow the court to refuse to recognize a judgment which conflicted with a jurisdiction agreement was excluded from application to the scheme of the Regulation.[140] The possibility that breach of an agreement on jurisdiction by one of the parties to it might found a claim for damages has never been conclusively dealt with. The English courts seem inclined to allow it, but the view of the European Court has never been spelled out.

Those limited cases apart, a plea that the adjudicating court should have realized that it had no jurisdiction is inadmissible.

(b) Non-jurisdictional grounds for a refusal order

Four non-jurisdictional objections may be relied on for an order refusing recognition or enforcement of the judgment; they are exhaustively listed in Article 45.[141] Over time, these objections have been cut back and narrowed, in order to make the circulation of judgments from and within the Member States even more free.

First, if recognition of the judgment would be manifestly contrary to public policy, Article 45(1)(a) provides that recognition shall be refused.[142] The content of English public policy is, of course, a matter for English law, although as 'public policy' is a definitional term of the Regulation, the European Court is entitled to define its outer boundaries. It has done this in a way designed to emphasize how limited this objection is allowed to be. Where recognition of the judgment would infringe a law which is regarded as fundamental in the recognizing state, such as where the adjudicating court had failed to comply with the standards of the European Convention on Human Rights

---

[139] Although jurisdictional protection of the weak may justly be seen as enjoying a higher priority than reinforcing agreements made between equals who ought to be able to look after themselves.

[140] Civil Jurisdiction and Judgments Act 1982, s 32(4).

[141] For the additional points covered by Articles 71 and 72, see p 164.

[142] Article 45(1)(a).

by denying one party the right to be heard,[143] recognition may be found to be manifestly contrary to public policy. By contrast, to recognize a judgment which contained a botched application of European competition law could not be considered to be contrary to public policy, not least because the dissatisfied party would have had the opportunity of bringing an appeal from the adjudicating court which could have put things right at the source.[144] For similar reasons, a contention that recognition should be refused because the judgment was obtained by fraud will almost certainly fail unless the foreign system has no provision for allowing such a plea to be raised and investigated, which is most improbable.

It has been held, surely wrongly, that a court may refuse on grounds of public policy to recognize an English default judgment if it finds that the absence of reasons in the judgment, and the unmeritorious contention that this may make it impossible to bring an appropriate and effective appeal against it, means that there has been a manifest breach of the right to a fair trial.[145] It is hard to understand how a defendant who chooses not to participate in the trial, or whose defence has been struck out for contempt,[146] can properly complain that the resultant judgment was insufficiently reasoned, but rather than debate this small piece of judicial silliness, the solution is for the claimant to ask for a (reasoned) summary judgment.

The use of the word 'manifestly' signifies that the defence is meant to be narrow. The Commission had proposed to remove the (national) public policy defence altogether, but the Member States wisely refused to agree. From an English perspective, it ought to be possible to argue, though it has yet to be held, that if a foreign court has refused to give effect to a commercial arbitration agreement, recognition of the offending judgment would be considered to be contrary to English public policy. Section 32 of the Civil Jurisdiction and Judgments Act 1982 mostly supports the argument that respect for arbitration agreements is a matter of fundamental importance in English law, though some may argue that if arbitration is a merely private activity, it does not rise to this level of importance in the English system. It does not seem likely that a judgment for a disproportionately large sum could be

---

[143] Case C–7/98 *Krombach v Bamberski* [2000] ECR I–1935; *Laserpoint Ltd v Prime Minister of Malta* [2016] EWHC 1820 (QB).

[144] Case C–38/98 *Régie Nationale des Usines Renault SA v Maxicar* [2000] ECR I–2973; Case C–681/13 *Diageo Brands BV v Simiramida-04 EOOD* EU:C:2015:471, [2016] Ch 147.

[145] Case C–619/10 *Trade Agency Ltd v Seramico Investments Ltd* EU:C:2012:531.

[146] Case C–394/07 *Gambazzi v Daimler Chrysler Canada Inc* [2009] ECR I–2563.

refused enforcement on grounds of public policy,[147] though were a court in a Member State ever to hand one down, recognition of a judgment for multiple damages, to which the Protection of Trading Interests Act 1980 applies, would certainly conflict with English public policy.

Second, recognition or enforcement may be refused in accordance with Article 45(1)(b) if the judgment was in default of appearance,[148] and the document instituting the proceedings was not served, according to the assessment of the judge in the recognizing state, in sufficient time to allow the defendant to arrange for his defence.[149] This provision aims to reinforce the legal protection of the defendant, by giving him the right to be sufficiently and timeously summoned, even though 'in time' means only time enough to allow him to forestall judgment in default of appearance. As to that, whether the time was sufficient may depend on the way in which service was made. Where service was on the defendant personally, a relatively short period is probably all one needs to prevent judgment being given in default; where service was made otherwise, say be sending the papers to the local consulate for onward transmission to the defendant, or by leaving it at a post office or the last known address, the time period may properly be rather longer.

If the judgment was in default of appearance the defendant will forfeit the ground for refusal of recognition if he makes an application to have the judgment set aside but which is heard and dismissed,[150] or if he could have challenged the judgment when he was notified of it but failed to do so.[151] In each case the court should assess whether the defendant, in challenging the original default judgment, was or would have been at a material disadvantage, such as facing a burden of proof which he would not have faced first time around.[152] But each of these rather severe limitations on the right to object to recognition aims to prod or steer the defendant into the original court, which is, within the European context, the best place, in terms of legal coherence, for matters to be sorted out.

---

[147] Though cf Case C–302/13 *flyLAL-Lithuanian Airlines AS v Starptautiskā līdosta Riga VAS* EU:C:2014:2319, [2105] ILPr 28.

[148] There is an autonomous definition of the term: it essentially covers the case where the defendant was denied a proper right to be heard or represented: Case C–78/95 *Hendrickman v Magenta Druck & Verlag GmbH* [1996] ECR I–4943.

[149] Case 228/81 *Pendy Plastic Products v Pluspunkt* [1982] ECR 2723; Case 49/84 *Debaecker and Plouvier v Bouwman* [1985] ECR 1779.

[150] Case C–420/07 *Apostilides v Orams* [2009] ECR I–4207.

[151] Case C–70/15 *Lebek v Domino* EU:C:2016:524, [2016] 1 WLR 4221.

[152] cf Case C–474/93 *Hengst Import BV v Campese* [1995] ECR I–2113.

Orders obtained without notice to the respondent will be denied recognition; indeed, at their very beginning they do not count as judgments at all.[153] But once the defendant has challenged, or has been notified and has had the opportunity to challenge, the order, it will count as a judgment; and if Article 2(a) is taken at face value, all that is actually required is that the order made without notice is served on the defendant prior to any measures of enforcement. That all being so, such orders will almost always turn out to be enforceable as judgments.

Third, if recognition of the foreign judgment produces consequences which are irreconcilable with an English judgment in a dispute between the same parties, whether this was handed down earlier or later than the foreign one, recognition will be refused by Article 45(1)(c).[154] In principle, parallel proceedings which might give rise to this unhappy clash of judgments should have been forestalled by the provisions on *lis alibi pendens* when the second action was commenced; if not, the rules of *res judicata* should have applied to avoid the problem as soon as the first judgment was handed down. If all goes according to the plan of the Regulation, there will be little work for this point to cover. But when this does not happen, an English court is bound to prefer its own judgment. Irreconcilability involves a measure of evaluation. A judgment that a contract was lawfully rescinded is certainly irreconcilable with an order that damages be paid for its breach,[155] for the one might be a simple defence to the other. But a decision that A is liable to B for breach of warranty of quality is not obviously irreconcilable with a judgment that B was liable to pay the price of goods sold and delivered by A: a set-off is not, in this sense, a defence. Again, a decision that C is liable to D for damage to D's cargo is irreconcilable with one that C owes no liability for damage to the cargo, but is not irreconcilable with a claim for damages for late delivery.

Fourth, if a judgment from a non-Member State was given in proceedings between the same parties and involving the same cause of action, and if it satisfies the criteria for its own recognition in England, and was the first to be handed down, and is irreconcilable with a later Member State judgment, Article 45(1)(d) provides that the later, Member State, judgment will not be recognized. The text does not say that proceedings to secure or declare enforcement of the non-Member State judgment must have been instituted: indeed, as that judgment may well be entitled to recognition without any such proceedings, there would be no reason to infer such a limitation. Where

---

[153] Art 2(a).
[154] Case 145/86 *Hoffmann v Krieg* [1988] ECR 645.
[155] Case 144/86 *Gubisch Maschinenfabrik KG v Palumbo* [1987] ECR 4861.

there is irreconcilability between two different and foreign Member State judgments, the first one is recognized, and the second one, if irreconcilable with it, is not. This is consistent with the view taken in English common law as well;[156] the answer is derived from pragmatism and common sense.

The fifth point is that there are certain treaties which may mean that a judgment falling within Chapter III is not to be recognized. For example, when they were in force, the Brussels and Lugano Conventions permitted Contracting States to conclude bilateral treaties with a non-Contracting State to provide for the non-recognition of a judgment from another Contracting State which had been founded on the residual jurisdictional rules now in Article 6 of the Regulation, and which had been given against a national or a domiciliary of the particular non-Contracting State. The United Kingdom concluded treaties with Australia[157] and Canada,[158] and Article 72 preserves them in force. But there will be no new bilateral treaties, as competence in external relations in the field of the Regulation was claimed by the European Union from the Member States.[159]

Likewise, other treaties, particularly in the context of international transport and carriage of goods, have their own provisions for jurisdiction and its exercise, and for the recognition of judgments. If the particular convention provides for the recognition of judgments, its provisions will continue to apply; but unless the convention also specifies, clearly and precisely, that a judgment shall not be recognized, it appears to be possible to secure its recognition under the Regulation even though this would not have been provided for by the particular convention.

It seems likely that the points which may be taken under Articles 71 and 72 have to be raised within the same procedural framework as applies to the objections in Article 45, despite the fact that they are not objections 'internal to' the Regulation. Any other solution would be terribly untidy.

(c) Absence of other grounds for non-recognition

There is no other basis for an application for refusal of recognition or enforcement. Article 45(3) precludes any further review of the jurisdiction of

---

[156] *Showlag v Mansour* [1995] 1 AC 431 (PC).

[157] Reciprocal Enforcement of Foreign Judgments (Australia) Order 1994 (SI 1994/1901), Sch, Art 3.

[158] Reciprocal Enforcement of Foreign Judgments (Canada) Order 1987 (SI 1987/468), Sch, Art IX.

[159] Opinion C–1/03 *Lugano Convention* [2006] ECR I–1145; cf Case C–230/15 *Brite Strike Technologies Inc v Brite Strike Technologies SA* EU:C:2016:560, [2016] ILPr 759.

the foreign court; it also provides that public policy may not be invoked to launch a collateral attack on the jurisdiction of the adjudicating court. This is obviously aimed at judgments based on Article 6;[160] but it need not prevent the refusal of recognition of judgments which disregard a valid and binding arbitration agreement if, in such a case, it is not the jurisdiction, but the rejection of the arbitration defence (an excluded matter), which is the basis for objection. And Article 53 forbids any review of the merits of the judgment, although this must give way to the extent which is required to apply the provisions of Article 45.[161]

The appearance of an exception arises when a court is called upon to recognize a provisional or protective measure which was granted on the basis of Article 35, that is, by a court which does not consider itself to have jurisdiction over the merits of the claim. The extent of the permitted review is to ascertain that the order really is, as a matter of substance, a provisional or protective one, for if it is not it will be denied recognition. This limitation appears to be necessary to counter the inherent weakness of Article 35, which simply abnegates any jurisdictional control over such measures. Accordingly, if a foreign court has made an order for an interim payment, but does not have jurisdiction over the merits of the claim (perhaps because the parties have agreed to arbitrate, with the result that no court has jurisdiction to try the merits), an English court, called on to recognize and enforce the order, must, if the defendant objects, check that it really is provisional or protective: that is to say, limited to assets within the territory of the court which made the order so as to show a real connecting link to the dispute,[162] and guaranteed to be fully reversible in the event that the applicant does not succeed on the substantive claim.[163]

4. MECHANISM

By contrast with its predecessor instruments, and perhaps uniquely, the recast Regulation allows the judgment creditor to enforce the judgment

---

[160] But also what is now Art 7(4): Case C–7/98 *Krombach v Bamberski* [2000] ECR I–1935.

[161] Case C–78/95 *Hendrickman v Magenta Druck & Verlag GmbH* [1996] ECR I–4943.

[162] If that requirement is taken seriously, it may be very rare for such an order ever to be presented for recognition in another country. But in the case of an English freezing order, not made in relation to assets as distinct from being ordered against a defendant personally, this limitation may be an irrelevance, and the order more likely to be presented for recognition in another country.

[163] Case C–391/95 *Van Uden Maritime BV v Deco-Line* [1998] ECR I–7091; Case C–99/96 *Mietz v Intership Yachting Sneek BV* [1999] ECR I–2277.

without the need for registration, *exequatur*, permission, application, approval, or any such thing. If this were not obvious from Articles 39 and 41 of the Regulation, it is underlined by the English legislation, which provides that 'a judgment to be enforced under the Regulation shall for the purposes of its enforcement be of the same force and effect, the enforcing court shall have in relation to its enforcement the same powers, and proceedings for or with respect to its enforcement may be taken, as if the judgment had been originally given by the enforcing court'.[164]

What is required, according to Article 42, is a copy of the judgment, together with the certificate provided for by Article 53 and set out in Annex I to the Regulation, by which the original court certifies the essential details and the enforceability of the judgment together with certain procedural information; this serves as the judgment's passport to recognition and enforcement. As long as this has been served on the judgment debtor, the enforcement measures which English law provides may be taken. If the judgment debtor wishes to prevent this he will need to make his application for an order refusing enforcement: there is neither time allowance nor time limit for his doing so, but if the application is made the court may suspend the enforcement. The court to which the application is made is required to rule on it without delay;[165] the order made by the court may be appealed once,[166] and that decision may, in limited circumstances, be appealed once more.[167]

During the procedure in which an application for a refusal order is being dealt with, the court has a variety of managerial powers to limit enforcement to provisional or protective measures, or to allow enforcement on conditions as to security, or to stay the proceedings.[168] It may also stay the proceedings if the judgment is subject to appeal in the state of origin.[169] An important and innovative power is conferred by Article 54: if the judgment contains an order which is not known in the law of the enforcing court, it is to be 'adapted' to a measure which is known, so long as this does not give the judgment creditor more rights than the original order did. This is likely to be useful in relation to non-money judgments.

---

[164] Civil Jurisdiction and Judgments Order 2001, SI 2001/3929, Sch 2 para 2(2), as substituted by SI 2014/2947, Sch 2.

[165] Article 48.

[166] Article 49.

[167] Article 50.

[168] Article 44.

[169] Article 51.

As the provisions of Chapter III of Regulation 1215/2012 only apply to judgments in proceedings which were instituted after that Regulation came into effect in 2015, there have been few cases to test its working. It is not hard to imagine that enforcement in this fashion will be easier and more comfortable in the case of judgments from parts of Europe which are closer to home than those which are not, and that a judgment from a court in a provincial town in eastern Europe, which no one could find on the map, will give rise to more unease. To some extent the translation requirements applicable to judgment and certificate prior to enforcement mean that a judgment debtor will not be taken completely aback, but one cannot help but be struck by the fact that as the European Union extends itself further and further from its heartland, into states whose legal systems are, frankly, in need of special measures, the idea that judgments may be enforced without any real judicial supervision is not intuitive.

5. RECOGNITION AND TERMINOLOGY

It will have become apparent that the context in which a judgment debtor may make his application will most usually be an application for the refusal of enforcement. This is what it is called in Articles 46 and 47, and it reflects the fact that the application will not normally be made unless and until the judgment creditor moves to enforce the judgment: what the judgment debtor seeks to do is to stop the enforcement. However, the grounds on which this can be sustained, set out in Article 45 as discussed above, are described in that provision as grounds on which recognition of the judgment may be refused. If the judgment is refused recognition, it must be refused enforcement; and in the end the correct nomenclature is less important than the substance of the law. In the foregoing account of Chapter III and the application which a judgment debtor may make, it is sometimes natural to use the one, and sometimes the other. It is not intended to have any wider significance.

Recognition of a judgment to which Chapter III applies does not require any special procedure, though a party who wishes to establish that there are no grounds for the refusal of recognition may use the procedure described above to obtain a declaratory judgment to this effect.[170] The main consequence of recognition will usually be to provide the basis for the enforcement of the

---

[170] Article 36.

judgment, the procedure for which has been examined above. But this is not the only effect the recognition of the judgment may bring about. To recognize a judgment means, in principle at least, to give it the effect it has under the law of the state in which it was given.[171] So if the judgment is in the nature of a provisional order, which would not be taken as binding or conclusive in subsequent proceedings in the adjudicating court, it should be given neither more nor less an effect in England. In certain cases a judgment may be regarded by the adjudicating court as impinging upon non-parties,[172] such as sureties for the defendant, or an insurer; but whether this must be respected and given effect by an English court is unclear. The problems arise at a number of levels. First, it may be argued that, so far as the non-party was concerned, the judgment was necessarily given in default of his appearance, and so must be denied recognition against him by reason of Article 45(1)(b). Secondly, it may be contrary to public policy for a person to be bound by the effect of a judgment *in personam* in proceedings in which he had no right to be heard.[173] Thirdly, it may be that once the judgment has been shown to qualify for recognition as between the parties to it, it is thereafter for English private international law, not for the Regulation, to determine what further effects it may have.

6. JUDGMENTS IN UNCONTESTED PROCEEDINGS

In the case of judgments to which the recast Regulation does not apply, because the proceedings were instituted before it came into effect, the procedure for enforcement of a judgment from another Member State was less easy. In partial response to that, and to give effect to the idea that a defendant who had no defence to the claim should not be able to delay the enforcement, a Regulation was made to provide for judgments on 'uncontested' claims to be certified by the issuing court with a 'European Enforcement Order'. This allowed them to be registered in other Member States, with only minimal rights of opposition before the registering court.[174] It was permitted only for

---

[171] Case C–145/86 *Hoffmann v Krieg* [1988] ECR 645. This was not precisely the approach in *Calyon v Michailides* [2009] UKPC 34, where the court asked what would be the effect of a local judgment of the kind which the foreign court had given.

[172] cf Schlosser [1979] OJ C59/71, 127–28.

[173] But if he does have a right to be heard, these two objections dissolve: Case C–559/14 *Meroni v Recoletos Ltd* EU:C:2016:349, [2017] QB 85.

[174] Regulation (EC) 805/2004, [2004] L143/15. However, for the possible view that the certificate issued by the original court might not be required to be accepted as conclusive, see Case C–619/10 *Trade Agency Ltd v Seramico Investments Ltd* EU:C:2012:531.

judgments in proceedings which the defendant did not contest. However, the methods of enforcement under the recast Regulation are so brisk and easy that it is only to be expected that the EEO procedure, with its own rather tricky limitations, is destined to be sidelined and forgotten.

Despite the occasional wrinkle, the sum and substance of the law set out in Regulation 1215/2012 is that once judgment has been obtained in the courts of a Member State, its non-recognition or non-enforcement will be, and should be, exceptional; and the burden of bringing proceedings to secure an order to that effect lies on the judgment debtor. If the United Kingdom were to have remained a Member State, it would have absorbed the new scheme for the enforcement of judgments, and the new scheme for the enforcement of judgments would have absorbed the United Kingdom. It is not inconceivable that a mirror, or shadow, or parallel scheme will be developed to replicate these effects when the United Kingdom faces the consequences of being a non-Member State. Whatever else may be true—and much else is—the fact that judgments from the courts of the United Kingdom will lose their European passport, which had just become more powerful than ever before, does not look like a shining example of what it means to take back control.

E. FOREIGN ARBITRAL AWARDS

Though properly the subject of a chapter by themselves, arbitral awards offer a useful point of contrast with the law on foreign judgments, and so it makes sense to mention them here.

By contrast with the law on foreign judgments, the law on foreign arbitral awards exhibits an astonishingly high degree of international consensus. The awards of arbitral tribunals, at least in civil and commercial arbitrations, are liable to be given effect in countries outside that of the seat of the arbitration (which will have its own provision for awards made within its jurisdiction) under the provisions of the 1958 New York Convention, to which 160 states have signed up.[175] The rules of the Convention, directly or as transposed into national law, provide for the recognition and enforcement of awards, and are extremely effective. Although every system has its quirks, the scheme of the New York Convention can seem almost magisterial by comparison with the fractured and tortured laws on foreign judgments.

---

[175] Those which have not are not great players in international trade and commerce.

Why is this so? It is simple, really. In commercial arbitration the point of departure is that the parties agreed to resolve their disputes before the tribunal of their choosing, and the initial agreement is easily and naturally extended to an agreement to abide by and perform the award made. It follows that there will not usually be any post-award objection that the tribunal lacked jurisdiction to decide; and one of the principal issues which arises with foreign judgments is sidelined. Where there is an objection to the jurisdiction of the tribunal, it arises from the very contractual nature of that jurisdiction. Arbitration makes perfect sense, and a court should refer the parties to arbitration if called on to do so, if there is no doubt that the parties did make the agreement and it remained valid and binding on them. But as we shall see in relation to the rules applicable to contractual obligations, there are curiously slippery problems if there is disagreement at the outset about whether the parties came to the effective arbitration agreement which one asserts but the other denies. All solutions to the conundrum are susceptible to allegations of bootstrapping, or of unfairness by assuming that one party is more likely to be right than the other, which is what appears to happen when the court decides to let the arbitral tribunal decide whether the parties agreed to it. Contract law theory can at times generate more heat than light; and it does here. Insofar as there are post-award jurisdictional points to be taken, they concern the agreement on which the arbitration is based.

The New York Convention sets out in Article V the grounds upon which the recognition and enforcement of the award may be refused, but these are sensibly narrow. In effect they allow refusal if the agreement to arbitrate was legally a nullity, whether by reason of incapacity on the part of a party or because the matter was not capable of arbitration, or if the tribunal went beyond the terms of the reference and purported to deal with a matter which the parties had not agreed to settle by arbitration. If there are grounds for complaint about the conduct of an arbitrator, or if the procedure of the tribunal went awry, or if recognition of the award would be contrary to public policy, recognition and enforcement may be refused. But because the setting within which the analysis takes place is that arbitration is consensual, the initial presence of that consensus reduces very substantially the number of ways in which objection may be taken to the recognition and enforcement of its end product.

A particular difficulty arises when a court—usually this will be the court at the seat of the arbitration—sets aside the award. The immediate reaction of an English lawyer will be that the award has been dissolved or disappeared, and that as a result there is nothing left to enforce; but this is not obviously right. For an award is not the same as a judgment. When a court annuls or sets aside a judgment, the legal system is dealing with its own product, and when a system sets its own judgment aside, there really does appear to be nothing left to enforce.[176] But when a court sets aside an arbitral award, it is setting aside something which was not created by it and does not belong to it, and it does not follow that just because the parties arbitrated in London or Geneva, an English court or a Swiss court has, uniquely, the power of life and death over the award.[177] Why should they? It is not their property; they did not make it; it is not their thing. A more thoughtful approach would treat the judgment of a court setting aside an award (or purporting to set it aside) as though it were a judgment of a court setting aside a contract: its effect depends on the usual common law[178] rules which govern the recognition of foreign judgments, and which start by asking whether the party against whom the judgment is sought to be enforced agreed to or submitted to the jurisdiction of the foreign court. If he took part in the set-aside proceedings, the answer will probably be that he did;[179] but if he did not, the fact that he agreed to arbitrate at a place within the territorial jurisdiction of that court plainly cannot be seen as a submission to the civil jurisdiction of that court. The proposition that in agreeing to arbitrate in Paris one has already submitted to the French legal system is not credible: the whole point of arbitration is to keep the dispute and its resolution as far away from the courts—all courts—as possible. If this reasoning is sound, as it is submitted that it is, it follows that a court may still enforce an award which a court at the place of the seat of the arbitration has purported to set aside, unless the party to whom the judgment was adverse agreed to accept as conclusive the decision of the court on the matter.

---

[176] In *Merchant International Co Ltd v NAK Naftogaz* [2012] EWCA Civ 196, [2012] 1 WLR 3036 it appears to have been held that if a foreign appellate court sets aside a judgment from a lower court, and the appellate judgment is refused recognition (on grounds of procedural unfairness), the lower court judgment remains intact: it may appear odd, but it is correct, as was explained above, at n 17.

[177] Article V(1)(e) of the New York Convention allows an award to be refused recognition and enforcement if it has been set aside, but it does not require that conclusion to be reached. The view proposed in the text is consistent with this, and also with what is understood to be French law: *Soc Hilmarton Ltd v Soc Omnium de traitement et de valorisation* (Cass civ I, 23 March 1994); *Putrabali v Rena Holding* (Case civ I, 29 June 2007).

[178] Statutory registration schemes often (though not invariably) exclude arbitration from their scope: partly because awards are not judgments, and partly because the New York Convention lays down the law.

[179] Even so, if the judgment from the courts of the seat is liable to be denied recognition on grounds, say, of fraud or public policy, it will be refused recognition, and the award will remain enforceable: *Yukos Capital sarl v Rosneft Oil Co (No 2)* [2012] EWCA Civ 855, [2014] QB 458.

4

THE *LEX FORI*

The subject matter of this chapter means that a specific Brexit warning is not necessary. That is not to say, of course, that the material discussed here will be exactly the same after Exit Day as it was before, but that it is better and more convenient to refer to the fuller notices which appear as the introduction to the other chapters.

The impact and role of the *lex fori* in English private international law has a significance which may be missed if it is examined only in pieces. It is convenient to undertake an examination of the role of the *lex fori* before proceeding to examine the rules of the conflict of laws applicable in an English court.

The conflicts rules which are examined in the following chapters will sometimes point to the *lex fori* as the law applicable to the issue in question. For example, English law is applied to the grounds for the dissolution (as distinct from nullity) of marriage, even if the marriage has little or nothing to do with England.[1] English law is applied to settle the distribution of assets in an insolvency, even though there may be significant overseas elements.[2] And until recently (and it has not been completely eliminated, even today) English law played a substantial part in determining liability in tort.[3] These are issues for which the rules of the conflict of laws select the *lex fori* as the law to be applied.

Where the rules of the conflict of laws select a foreign law, its application, even though it is proved to the satisfaction of the court, may be disrupted or derailed by a provision of the *lex fori* instead. The principal context in which this happens is where the relevant issue before the court is characterized as

[1] See Ch 8.
[2] See Ch 9.
[3] See Ch 6.

The Conflict of Laws. Fourth Edition. Adrian Briggs, Oxford University Press (2019). © Adrian Briggs
DOI: 10.1093/oso/9780198838500.003.0004

procedural: the substantive issues may be referred to a foreign law, but issues which are procedural will not be. Then there are instances in which a domestic rule of the *lex fori* is held to override the answer which the principles of the conflict of laws would otherwise have given: this is illustrated when a statute, forming part of the *lex fori*, is worded in such a way that the court is required to apply it in spite of the rules of the conflict of laws. These examples show how the *lex fori* imposes itself on a matter in which the issues are otherwise to be referred to a foreign law; it is examined in the first part of this chapter.

The second context is very different: it is where the conflicts rules of the *lex fori* tell the court to not apply a rule of foreign law which would otherwise have been applicable, and to decide the case without it. These rules may direct the court to not enforce, or sometimes to not even recognize the existence of, a rule of foreign law. This can be represented as the *lex fori dis*connecting a rule of foreign law which would otherwise be applied by the court; it is examined in the second part of this chapter.

A. APPLYING THE *LEX FORI* AND NOT THE *LEX CAUSAE*

1. APPLICATION TO PROCEDURAL ISSUES

The common law took the view that issues which it characterized as procedural rather than substantive were governed by English law, and a rule of the *lex causae* which conflicted with it would not be applied: the *lex causae* applies to issues of substance but not to matters of procedure. When applying the common law principles of private international law, the first point of characterization in any case may be to ask whether an issue upon which the court has to decide is one of substance or of procedure.[4] But where the substantive conflicts rules are provided, directly or by retention, by European legislation, the technique is different, for it starts and ends with the interpretation of the statutory text. However, most European legislation which makes rules of the conflict of laws excludes 'evidence and procedure' from the rules which it enacts, leaving a national court free to follow the approach of its own law. One may therefore say, with reasonable accuracy, that the *lex fori*

---

[4] Dicey, Morris, and Collins, *The Conflict of Laws* (15th edn, Sweet & Maxwell, 2012), Ch 8.

governs issues which are procedural, with the only reservation being that the legislative definition of 'procedure' in European legislation may be different, and perhaps narrower, than the counterpart definition in the common law of private international law.

It is therefore sensible to examine procedural issues as understood by the common law of private international law, and then briefly to note the places in which a European understanding of this expression might be different. We shall examine those issues which were and still are understood to be procedural in nature, and then those which were but are no longer matters of procedure.

(a) Matters which are procedural

Issues which are procedural, and on which an English court will apply its own laws rather than those of a foreign system, are mostly, though not exclusively, concerned with the process of adjudication in an English court.

Starting at the beginning, the question whether an intending litigant, with legal personality, is competent to sue or be sued in an English court is a matter of procedure and governed by English law: English law has to be able to accommodate the particular litigant within its system of civil litigation. That said, however, English law will be applied with a measure of flexibility. It certainly does not follow that juristic persons of a kind unfamiliar to English law may not litigate before an English court. Though it was once held that the curator, properly appointed by a Lebanese court, of a disappeared person had no *locus standi* to sue,[5] this was not an obviously compelling decision. By contrast, a Hindu temple, which enjoyed legal personality under Indian law, was recognized as competent to sue.[6] It seems probable that entities such as the Whanganui river, with legal personality under the law of New Zealand,[7] could be a litigant before an English court: why not? In the end, the court will have to decide whether the legal personality arising under a foreign law is compatible with the pre-trial and trial process in an English court; if any apparent problems are manageable, it should be.

The nature and process of trial in an English court will be as provided by English law. The availability of interim and interlocutory relief is a procedural

---

[5] *Kamouh v Associated Electrical Industries International Ltd* [1980] QB 199: the court was (excessively) concerned about who procedural orders could be made against, enforced against, and so forth.

[6] *Bumper Development Corp v Commissioner of Police of the Metropolis* [1991] 1 WLR 1362 (CA).

[7] Whanganui River Claims Settlement Act 2017.

matter: save where legislation compels a different specific conclusion,[8] orders are made or not made by reference to English law alone. Indeed, some even say that access to interim procedures represents one of the main prizes at stake when issues of jurisdiction are fought. An English court has no power to make orders unknown to English civil procedural law; but on the other hand, it will not withhold relief simply because the only connection to England is that the trial is taking place there. Although the granting or withholding of relief is entirely a matter for the *lex fori*, the powers of the court may be curtailed by legislation or by the exercise of the court's overall discretion. As to the former, it was held that the Brussels I Regulation prevented an English court from making an order, otherwise certainly open to it, to freeze a defendant's assets which were located on the territory of a Member State of the European Union unless the English court were seised of the substantive proceedings.[9] As to the latter, a court will normally order disclosure of documents in accordance with English law, but if, for example, the disclosure would expose the respondent to a disproportionate risk of criminal prosecution under foreign law, it may be proper to modify the order which would otherwise have been made.[10] But in all cases the relief, and the grounds upon which it may be ordered, is entirely a matter for English law.

So far as evidence is concerned, we have already seen that the manner in which an English court receives and deals with foreign law is a procedural issue, governed in large part by the rules for expert evidence. More generally on the law of evidence, the question whether or upon what matters witnesses may or may not be compelled to give evidence is a matter for English law to say. It has been held that where English law requires evidence to be in writing, this applies just as much in cases where the *lex causae* would not have imposed a similar requirement; but this may need to be reconsidered. For if the law which governs the substance sees no need for writing, it is not obvious why English law should still insist that it is needed: after all, the rule of English law will not have been designed with foreign cases in mind.[11] More flexibility may apply to the acquisition of evidence for use at trial. It may be counter-intuitive, but no rule of English law prevents the acquisition of

---

[8] *OJSC TNK-BP v Lazurenko* [2012] EWHC 2781 (Ch), which decides that where the substance of the claim falls within the Rome II Regulation, the law which governs the substance of the dispute may limit the availability of relief which would otherwise have been available from the English court: *sed quaere.*

[9] Case C-391/95 *Van Uden Maritime BV v Deco-Line* [1998] ECR I-7091.

[10] *Bank Mellat v HM Treasury* [2019] EWCA Civ 449.

[11] *Leroux v Brown* (1852) 12 CB 801.

evidence by means which are lawful[12] but unknown to English law. English law also allows its use in England, so the record of depositions taken under US federal pre-trial procedure is admissible at trial in England,[13] as will be documents obtained by disclosure or discovery under foreign rules which are more liberal than those of English law. If it is objected that this distorts the balance which each system of civil procedure establishes to hold the balance between the parties to litigation, the proper response is that in an extreme case the court may use its inherent powers to regulate the trial to prevent it.

It might be thought to follow from what has been said about evidence that the question of who bears the burden of proof should be viewed in a similar way; and that if this is so, the operation of presumptions must also be included within the category of procedure. But even if this is right it is barely supported by authority.[14] And if this point is pressed too hard, there is a risk that the substantive right to which it relates will be bent out of shape. For example, if the *lex causae* provides that a particular loss will be held to have been caused by the defendant unless he proves that it was not, it will appreciably alter the rights of the parties if an English court applies its contrary rule on the burden of proof in preference to the foreign presumption. The present state of the law is uncertain,[15] but in principle one would expect the category of procedure to contract rather than expand, in order to enhance the effect of the *lex causae*, always assuming it can be accomplished without impairing the process of the trial, which surely it can. As to whether this can be done by judicial means or requires legislation, the point is examined below.

This brings us to the distinction between rights and remedies, and the proposition of the common law that while legal rights are defined by the *lex causae* as identified by the rules of the conflict of laws, remedies in respect of those rights are defined by and available in accordance with the *lex fori*. There was certainly a view that this distinction was unnecessary and had outlived its usefulness. But when the opportunity arose, the House of Lords[16] declined to take the point, insisting that the assessment (quantification, calculation) of a head of damages which the *lex delicti* made recoverable was a procedural issue, on which English law applied and anything the *lex delicti* might say was

---

[12] The case of evidence obtained by torture which is lawful where it is applied will be covered by rules of public policy (considered in Section (B)) if not otherwise dealt with.

[13] *South Carolina Insurance Co v Assurantie Maatschappij De Zeven Provincien NV* [1987] 1 AC 24.

[14] *Re Fuld's Estate (No 3)* [1968] P 675.

[15] But for contracts, see now the Rome I Regulation, Art 18; for torts, the Rome II Regulation, Art 22.

[16] *Harding v Wealands* [2006] UKHL 32, [2007] 2 AC 1.

irrelevant. It was wrong. The judgment purported to find this answer in legislation, but it was not there:[17] all the Act said was that matters which were procedural before it was passed were unaffected by the enactment. This should have resulted in the court being free to consider as a matter of common law principle whether the procedural characterization should be retained. Be that as it may, the effect of the Rome II Regulation is to replace a bad rule with a much better one,[18] at least for the law of non-contractual obligations.

The common law rule that a court may grant only the remedies provided for by its own law covers more than the assessment of damages. It meant that an English court would award its remedies only where these dovetailed with the rights under the *lex causae* for which they were claimed. So for example, an English court would probably not order specific performance of a foreign contract in circumstances where English law would not decree it for an English one (say because damages would be a sufficient remedy), even though no such objection was to be found in the *lex causae*. In one exotic case it dismissed a claim brought by a daughter seeking an order that her father constitute her dowry, as no English remedy even remotely corresponded to the right arising under Greek law.[19] However, the more constructive approach taken by the Court of Appeal to litigation by entities unfamiliar to English law[20] suggests that the common law rule that remedies were governed by the *lex fori* even though rights were not, may today not be quite as rigid as authority might have led some to suppose.

(b) Matters which are no longer procedural

The lesson to be taken from the material just discussed might suggest that the common law rules of private international law were constrained by authority and were not likely to be reconsidered by an English court. However, on one notable occasion the House of Lords simply overturned an element of the rule that remedies were governed by the *lex fori*, when it rejected the argument that an English court could only ever give judgment in sterling. Until 1976 an English court invariably awarded damages in sterling and not in the currency of the *lex causae*: the rule of English procedural law was that the claim was quantified in sterling as at the date of the claim and judgment,

---

[17] Private International Law (Miscellaneous Provisions) Act 1995, s 14(3).
[18] *Cox v Ergo Versicherung AG* [2014] UKSC 22, [2014] AC 1379, [23].
[19] *Phrantzes v Argenti* [1960] 2 QB 19 (CA).
[20] *Bumper Development Corpn v Commissioner of Police of the Metropolis* [1991] 1 WLR 1362 (CA).

years afterwards, would be given for that sterling sum.[21] The more the pound depreciated, the more this profited a defendant whom the court had adjudged to be liable to a claimant. This had no rational defence and, worse, it was also liable to endanger London as a centre for commercial litigation. The court therefore held that if, in effect, the loss was sustained in a foreign currency, an English court could give judgment in that foreign currency or in its sterling equivalent as at the date of judgment.[22] This did not mean that a claimant may ask a court to assess and give judgment in a foreign currency of his fancy, but if the recoverable loss can be seen to have been sustained in a foreign currency, a court may give judgment for a sum in, or as if in, that foreign currency. This comes as close as makes no real difference to deciding that damages may be awarded in the currency of the law which governs the substance of the claim. This confirms that there is nothing apart from the principles of *stare decisis* to prevent a court taking a fresh look at other rules currently treated as procedural and getting rid of them where justice would be better done without them.

Another ancient procedural rule which had long since gone rotten, but where the reform which was called for was bound to be more complex than could be achieved by judicial decision, was dealt with by Parliament. Prior to the enactment of the Foreign Limitation Periods Act 1984, the approach to time bars and their impact on litigation was complicated. A legal rule which extinguished the right or the claim, by 'prescribing' it, was regarded as substantive, with the result that if there was such a provision in the *lex causae*, it was applicable in an English court. By contrast, a legal rule which did its job by preventing the bringing of proceedings, or by 'limiting' the period within which proceedings might be commenced in court, was regarded as procedural: such a provision forming part of the *lex fori* would be applied by an English court while such a provision in the *lex causae* would not be. As it happens, English time-bar provisions are made in the form of limitation of actions, not prescription of rights. The result was that English limitation periods *and* foreign rules of prescription (which most were) applied cumulatively, with the shorter of the two being decisive. Except as the arid product of logic, the sense of this was impossible to see.

---

[21] Although the judgment would carry interest, and interest rates will bear some relationship to local currency values.

[22] *Miliangos v George Frank (Textiles) Ltd* [1976] AC 443; *Services Europe Atlantique Sud v Stockholms Rederaktiebolag Svea of Stockholm (The Despina R)* [1979] AC 685.

The Foreign Limitation Periods Act 1984[23] provided, in effect, that whether there is an applicable time bar is an issue governed by the *lex causae* and not by English law unless English law happens to be the *lex causae*. This imposes a statutory rule which pays no attention to the distinction between substance and procedure. However, English law still defines the point at which proceedings are begun and the clock stops running, even where the time period will be measured by a foreign law.[24] English law also applies its own time period in cases where the application of the new statutory rule would yield a result contrary to public policy.[25] Public policy, as defined by the Act, includes cases where the operation of the 1984 Act would do undue hardship to a party, actual or potential. So for example, a period which is too short, or which does not allow for postponement while the claimant is incapacitated and unable to make the decision to litigate, may be contrary to English public policy; conversely, a period which is decades long, bearing in mind that a defendant may not have kept his papers and that an English trial relies on oral testimony, may also be one whose application is inconsistent with English public policy; and where any of this happens, the English time period applies without further ado.[26] Section 1(5), which provides that there is no *renvoi* on questions of limitation,[27] is unfortunate. One may suppose that its purpose was to ensure that once the relevant conflicts rules, including any *renvoi* which this may involve, have identified a domestic law for application to the merits, the time-bar provisions of that law will also apply. But if that is what was meant, it is regrettable that the draftsman could not find better words to say it.

(c) 'Procedure' in European legislation

In assessing the effect of European law on procedure, it is necessary to consider the manner in which the rule that 'procedure is governed by the *lex fori*' operates when the conflicts rules applicable to the substance were made in European legislation, whether in force as such or retained after the United Kingdom leaves the European Union.

In cases in which the conflicts rules are provided by the common law rules of private international law, the distinction between substance and procedure is defined by the rules and illustrated by the cases described above.

---

[23] Foreign Limitation Periods Act 1984, s 1.
[24] ibid, s 4.
[25] ibid, s 2.
[26] *Arab Monetary Fund v Hashim* [1996] 1 Lloyd's Rep 589 (CA) 599–600.
[27] Foreign Limitation Periods Act 1984, s 1(5).

But where the conflicts rules are contained in European legislation, however, the distinction does not work in quite the same way. The Rome I and Rome II Regulations, which contain the conflicts rules for obligations in civil and commercial matters, provide that they 'shall not apply to evidence and procedure';[28] and the European Court has on several occasions confirmed that the (former) Brussels I Regulation had no effect on rules of procedure of national law, save only that these may not be applied to the extent that they would jeopardize the practical effect of the Regulation. Where an issue is to be regarded as procedural, all these Regulations, whether by words or the absence of words, leave the national court to apply its procedural law.

But what counts as a procedural matter in this sense is, *ex hypothesi*, a matter of legislative definition. The Rome I and II Regulations do not define their scope so as to exclude themselves from issues which *national* law would regard as procedural, but from those matters which the *Regulation* treats, or leaves to be treated, as procedural, which is a rather different thing.[29] For example, the burden of proof and the impact of presumptions is, in a matter within the scope of the Rome Regulations, governed by the applicable law and not by the *lex fori*, no matter what the common law might otherwise have said, for this legislation, like all legislation, displaces the common law.[30] So is the assessment of damages, most clearly when the Rome II Regulation has identified the applicable law, with the result that the contrary rule of the common law no longer applies.[31] The question whether it would be open to an English court to order specific performance where the *lex contractus* would not provide for such an order to be made, or withhold it on grounds which are sufficient in English law but which would be disregarded by the *lex contractus*, is unclear for, as we shall see, the wording of the material rule in the Rome I Regulation[32] is debatable, but whatever the answer proves to be, it will come from elaboration of the Regulation, and not from the common law.

The European Court stated that the (former) Brussels I Regulation did not apply, or seek to harmonize, rules of procedure, for which the national court should look to its own law. Its view was that national rules on the admissibility of proceedings—in that case, whether a proposed joinder of a third party could be refused on the ground that it was sought to be made too close

---

[28] Rome I Regulation, Art 1(3); Rome II Regulation, Art 1(3).
[29] The expression 'same same but different', otherwise heard in the markets of the East, makes the point surprisingly effectively.
[30] Rome I Regulation, Art 18; Rome II Regulation, Art 22.
[31] Rome I Regulation, Art 12(1)(c); Rome II Regulation, Art 15(c).
[32] Rome I Regulation, Art 12(1)(c).

to the trial—were liable to be applied, as the issue was procedural, not jurisdictional, and the only restriction was that its application might not jeopardize the practical effect of the Regulation.[33] The meaning of this may be illustrated in the English context in several ways. It means that an English court may not grant an anti-suit injunction, even on an interlocutory basis and even though it might be thought of as a procedural order, which would have the effect of interfering with a judge in a civil or commercial matter in another Member State whose judicial duty is to apply the Regulation.[34] It means that an English court may not grant a procedural stay of proceedings in favour of a court in a non-Member State where the order would mean that it will not exercise the jurisdiction which the Regulation confers upon it.[35] On the other hand, a national court is at liberty to make or to not make orders for interim or protective relief according to its procedural law: even though the Regulation authorizes an applicant to apply for such relief it does not require the court to grant it.[36] All these instances go to make the general point, which is that where the relevant conflicts rules are made in or derived from European legislation, the meaning of 'procedural', and the extent to which national rules of procedural law may be applied by a court, is defined by the Regulation and not by national or common law.

2. APPLICATION OF STATUTES OF THE FORUM

Parliament has the power to enact legislation which it intends judges to apply to cases coming before them if, but not unless, the issue before them is governed by English law. It also has power to enact legislation which judges are to apply to cases coming before them and which fall within its terms even though English law is not otherwise applicable to the matter. For example, the Occupiers Liability Act 1957 applies when a claim in tort is governed by English law: no one would ever suggest it applied if a claim brought before an English court concerned access to land in France, which was otherwise to be governed by French law. On the other hand, employment legislation giving a worker certain rights in the workplace, or protections against wrongful dismissal, may well be intended and made to apply even though the contract of

---

[33] Case C-365/88 *Kongress Agentur Hagen GmbH v Zeehaghe BV* [1990] ECR I-1845.
[34] Case C-185/07 *Allianz SpA v West Tankers Inc* [2009] ECR I-663.
[35] Case C-281/02 *Owusu v Jackson* [2005] ECR I-1383.
[36] This follows from Case C-391/95 *Van Uden BV v Deco-Line* [1998] ECR I-6511, though cf Case 119/84 *Capelloni v Pelkmans* [1985] ECR 3147.

employment is governed by a foreign law. A judge may read the instruction given by Parliament as one which tells him to apply the legislation to (say) all employees whose place of work is England, or whose working relationship is rooted in England, even though their contract is not governed by English law. In this second case, a rule of the *lex fori* may be imposed on the determination of an issue to which English law does not otherwise apply. The question is how one is to tell one kind of statute from the other. The answer is that it is not easy to say, because Parliament tends not to address the point but leaves the issue to the courts, whose task is, in principle, to discern the unvoiced intention of Parliament.

The treatment of statutes is not something which private international law does well, but, as usual, it helps to frame the questions appropriately. In the first, the question is whether an English statute applies when English law is the *lex causae* but the facts have little connection to England: for example, when a contract of employment is governed by English law but the parties, and the place of work, are foreign;[37] when a court which has given judgment is asked to order that a transaction which the defendant had entered into be set aside, even though the property, the parties, and the whole of the story had no significant connection to England.[38] In such cases the issue before the court is governed by English law, but the question is whether the matter before the court falls within the grasp of the English statute. Predicting the answer which will be given is not always easy.

In the second, the question is whether an English statute applies even though the applicable law is not English law. As we shall see in relation to contractual obligations, this can be a serious issue when the parties have chosen a law which, if applied exclusively—as they probably intended—would prevent the application of an English statute. Sometimes this may not matter, but at other times it will: it cannot be the case that parties can, by the simple expedient of choosing foreign law to govern their relationship, automatically and utterly prevent an English court applying English laws on financial regulation, investor or consumer protection, fair dealing, and so on. In these cases the English statute may well override, or be of mandatory effect, on the basis that this is the instruction which Parliament has given to the judges. It will

---

[37] Or some other untidy combination: see for example *Lawson v Serco Ltd* [2006] UKHL 3, [2006] ICR 250; *Duncombe v Secretary of State for Children, Schools and Families (No 2)* [2011] UKSC 36, [2011] ICR 1312; *Ravat v Halliburton Manufacturing & Services Ltd* [2012] UKSC 1, [2012] ICR 389; *British Council v Jeffery* [2018] EWCA Civ 2253.

[38] *Re Paramount Airways Ltd* [1993] Ch 223; see also *Bilta (UK) Ltd v Nazir* [2015] UKSC 23, [2016] AC 1.

come as no surprise that the science by which instructions of this kind are decoded is not well developed. But it is a very important example of the way in which the law of the forum, because it is the law of the forum, can divert the court from the path otherwise indicated by its rules of the conflict of laws. Where Parliament has exercised its sovereignty in this way, there is no more to be said.

B. DISAPPLYING A RULE OF THE APPLICABLE LAW

The first area in which the common law of private international law declines to give effect to a provision of the law, to which its conflicts rules would otherwise point, is that of foreign penal, revenue, and other public laws: an English court will not enforce a foreign penal law, a foreign revenue law, or a foreign 'other public law'. It is sometimes said that the court 'has no jurisdiction' to enforce such laws, though the reference to jurisdiction tends to obscure the way the law really works. The identification of a foreign law as penal or revenue is usually straightforward; the meaning of 'other public law' is less so. The greatest difficulty is distinguishing between the enforcing of such laws, which is prohibited, and recognition, which is not. In particular, 'indirect enforcement' and recognition may not be easy to tell apart.

1. FOREIGN PENAL, REVENUE, AND (OTHER) PUBLIC LAWS

The core elements of a penal law are that it imposes a fine or forfeit or other obligation upon a lawbreaker, and that this is ordered to be performed to or in favour of the state. The identification of a foreign law as penal is a matter for English law, as the exclusionary rule is a rule of English private international law. The fact that the foreign system regards the law as compensatory, or generously compensatory, is not irrelevant but it is certainly not decisive.[39]

It is unlikely (though no case has had to decide) that a law which imposes a duty to make payment to a private individual is in this sense a penal law, even if one of the avowed purposes of the law is to deter wrongdoing by ordering a payment which is calculated as a multiple of any loss suffered. If this

---

[39] *Huntington v Attrill* [1893] AC 150.

is correct, a modern version of the classic Roman law *actio furti*, which allowed the victim to sue the thief for twice or four times the value of the thing stolen, would not be a foreign penal law, and the common law would not refuse to enforce it.[40] Likewise, laws under which a defendant may be ordered to pay damages assessed by trebling the loss caused to the victim, of which US anti-trust laws are the best-known example, would not be considered as penal laws whose enforcement is prohibited by the common law. This conclusion might be debatable, but if one state legislates to enforce standards of behaviour by imposing remedies for civil wrongs at a generous, or deterrent, level of payment to a victim,[41] while another pursues the same aim by imposing fines, payable to the state, there is no reason why the penal nature of the latter should cast doubt on the non-penal nature of the former.[42]

It is tolerably clear that where a regulatory body brings a civil action on behalf of a class of persons who have sustained losses at the hands of a criminal wrongdoer, this will not involve the enforcement of a penal law, at least where the sums recovered will be gathered in and paid to the individuals.[43] But it is irrelevant that the defendant has agreed to make the payment which was liable to be imposed on him in respect of a crime. The forfeit of a voluntary bail bond involves enforcement of a penal law;[44] and the payment of an agreed sum to prevent criminal prosecution will be treated in the same way.

It may not be very illuminating to define a revenue law as a tax law, but it is hard to improve on it; and this aspect of the rule is sometimes referred to as the 'revenue rule'. Foreign laws which impose income and capital taxes or sales and service taxes will be revenue laws, and claims founded on them cannot be brought in the English courts: a foreign tax collector may not use the right of action created by foreign tax law as the basis for a claim against a defendant. More marginal cases may arise from the collection of state medical insurance payments from employees, for it may be thought that if the state provides a benefit in return for the payment, the liability which is enforced is not so much a tax as a charge for services; the same analysis may be

---

[40] But see Protection of Trading Interests Act 1980, s 5.

[41] In states in which the court has no power to order the winning party to recover his costs, an enhanced level of compensation may, in its own way, serve as compensation for the financial loss of litigating. From this point of view, one can see the danger of leaping from 'penal' to 'incapable of enforcement in England'.

[42] But in the case of multiple damages, statute precludes enforcement: Protection of Trading Interests Act 1980, s 5; *Lewis v Eliades* [2003] EWCA Civ 1758, [2004] 1 WLR 692. It is unclear whether the fact that there is a statute reflects the view that such laws are not penal laws and could not otherwise be excluded under this rule.

[43] *Robb Evans v European Bank Ltd* (2004) 61 NSWLR 75.

[44] *United States of America v Inkley* [1989] QB 255 (CA).

applied to payments made to a state monopoly utility, or even to the BBC. But an argument formulated in this way is unhelpful, not least because it is capable of being applied, more or less directly, to practically all income taxes. Every taxpayer is said to get something—national defence, social security, the motorway system, that sort of thing—in return for his payment. The more incisive question is whether the payment is voluntary in the sense that the law which creates and imposes the charge on a person who meets the criterion for payment allows her to avoid her liability to pay by disclaiming the associated benefit. Whatever the practicalities may otherwise be, if a person has no power in law *to disclaim* the right to take advantage of the hospitals, national defence, etc, which are paid for and provided to her from her income taxes and national health insurance, *and thereby* be released from liability to make payment, the laws in question will be revenue laws. Likewise, if she is not entitled to disclaim or hand back whatever it is[45] which is said to be provided to the public in return for value added tax *and by so doing* be released from liability to pay VAT, the liability can be seen as imposed in the manner of a revenue law. This analysis can also be applied to a state provider of utility services: if a homeowner is legally entitled to tell the water utility that he does not want its services, *and by so doing* be released from liability to pay a charge, the payment is not made under a revenue law, no matter how unlikely it is that the person could take advantage of his technical freedom of contracting and non-contracting. But if the owner of a television remains liable in law to pay the licence fee even though he forswears any reception of the state broadcasting service, the payment is demanded and made under a revenue law.

It is nothing to the point that a householder can avoid liability for payment by having no television, or that an employee can avoid income tax by giving up his job, or that a customer can avoid VAT by not buying trousers, for on that basis the only true revenue laws would be death duties. The real question is whether a person who satisfies the condition which renders him liable to tax *may renounce* the benefit which is attributable to the payment, *and by so doing* be released in law from liability to pay. If he is not permitted to do that, the law is a tax law and is not a contractual liability. Or if there is a better test of what makes a foreign law a revenue law, no one has yet identified it.

The third category of foreign laws which an English court will not enforce is usually referred to as 'other public laws'.[46] One should not worry too much

[45] Does anybody actually know?
[46] *AG (UK) v Heinemann Publishers Australia Pty Ltd* (1988) 165 CLR 30; *AG of New Zealand v Ortiz* [1984] AC 1 (CA).

about the nomenclature. The existence of such a category makes sense, at least when a court is called upon to enforce a foreign law which is analogous to penal and revenue laws, such as those confiscating or nationalizing local[47] property, exchange control laws, laws regulating the duties of those employed in the security services, and so forth, and which should be dealt with similarly. For example, if a householder is obliged by law to pay water and electricity charges, whether he wishes to take the service or not, to a private or privatized company, it would be odd if the identity of the payee meant that as the payment was not under a revenue law it could be enforced. If it is treated as quasi-revenue, as an 'other public law', the difficulty mostly goes away.

Whether it is beneficial to call these 'other public laws' is debatable: indeed, whether they have any conceptual unity is unclear. In some cases, the courts have found it helpful to ask whether the relationship relied on, or the interest to be vindicated, is governmental, or sovereign, in nature. It is hard to see how else one may explain why a foreign state may not sue one of its former spies who, in breach of what certainly looks like a contract, has spilled the beans to make a profit, or why a repressive government may not sue the liberation army or terrorist organization which has blown up the post office, relying on the ordinary law of tort to do so. There is a wholly proper reluctance to allow courts to be used in this way by a foreign secret service,[48] or to allow a state to sue those who seek to overthrow it or eject it from occupied territory.[49] The fact that the claim may be got up as a private law action of the kind any master could bring against a disloyal servant, or any property owner against a trespasser who did damage, gives rise to a problem for which a robust answer must be found elsewhere. The High Court of Australia[50] saw this first, declining to adjudicate on claims which it described as being brought to vindicate a friendly foreign 'governmental interest' when a former spy went blabbermouth, for fear of what would happen when a rather different kind of state invoked the precedent. The English courts have, in substance if not quite in form, adopted this approach, holding that a claim to enforce a right which is uniquely governmental is not one which it can be asked to enforce. So for example, a state may bring proceedings to recover its property by relying on the kind of title—possessory, derivative, finder's—that any other owner may. But where its right to obtain possession is based on its legal right to divest a

---

[47] If the property is not local to the confiscating state, its law will not apply at all, and it will not matter what it is or isn't.

[48] *AG (UK) v Heinemann Publishers Australia Pty Ltd* (1988) 165 CLR 30.

[49] *Mbasogo v Logo Ltd* [2006] EWCA Civ 1370, [2007] QB 846.

[50] *AG (UK) v Heinemann Publishers Australia Pty Ltd* (1988) 165 CLR 30.

prior owner who still has possession, its claim will be based on a right which is uniquely governmental, and the court will not enforce its claim.[51]

2. ENFORCEMENT DISTINGUISHED FROM RECOGNITION

It is the enforcement[52] of foreign penal, revenue, and other public laws which is forbidden; there is no objection to their recognition[53] as foreign law, which may be taken into account and given effect in proceedings before the court, unless they are so repellent that even to notice that they have been enacted would shock the conscience of the court.[54] But the distinction between enforcement and recognition is not always easy to see. Take the case mentioned at the end of the last section: it was assumed that the foreign state, seeking to obtain the thing in question, is asking the English court to enforce its law, rather than to recognize the law or the effect it had. In seeking to show how the answer is to be found, it is necessary to start with easier cases.

The court is asked to enforce a foreign penal law when, for example, a foreign attorney general seeks to obtain an order for payment on dishonoured bail bond, or when a foreign collector sues for unpaid taxes.[55] The exclusionary rule also applies to indirect enforcement, so if the foreign attorney general, or collector of taxes obtains judgment, in ordinary civil form, from the foreign court, and seeks to enforce it by pointing (as common law theory has it) to the fresh obligation arising from the judgment, the English court will see that it is, in effect, being asked to enforce a foreign penal or revenue law, albeit indirectly.[56]

The recognition of a penal or revenue law is not prohibited. For example, if performance of a contract is seriously illegal under the law of the place where performance is due, that should render the contract unenforceable

---

[51] *Equatorial Guinea v Bank of Scotland International Ltd* [2006] UKPC 7; *Iran v Barakat Galleries Ltd* [2007] EWCA Civ 1374, [2009] QB 22.

[52] Save where legislation (which can make country-by-country provision) gives an answer which the common law could not give. In fact, much of the law on the effect in the United Kingdom of foreign tax laws will be legislated as the consequence of bilateral and multilateral treaties.

[53] *Re Emery's Investment Trusts* [1959] Ch 410.

[54] cf *Kuwait Airways Corpn v Iraqi Airways Co (Nos 4 and 5)* [2002] UKHL 19, [2002] 2 AC 883, where the court refused to recognize Iraqi legislation purporting to dissolve Kuwait and to seize the assets of the Kuwaiti state airline, in flagrant breach of international law.

[55] *Government of India v Taylor* [1955] AC 491.

[56] *United States of America v Harden* (1963) 41 DLR (2d) 721 (Can SC).

in the English courts. That result would be out of reach if the foreign penal law were to be denied recognition.[57] Even so, the separation of recognition from indirect enforcement is not always easy to explain. The point may be considered in relation to foreign revenue laws. Some rather loosely reasoned authorities have stated that if judgment in the action 'would increase the likelihood' that a tax would be paid, the action is prohibited by this rule.[58] This has been used to justify the dismissal of a claim brought by a company against a director who stripped its assets, on the utterly spurious ground that sums recovered by the company would be used to discharge its corporation tax liability.[59] What nonsense. For a supposed rule of the common law to license theft from a company is anarchic, the very antithesis of law.[60] A more sensible approach has allowed a foreign tax authority to obtain an order for the taking of evidence in England, even though the entire purpose of the application was to assist the foreign state in collecting taxes.[61] The explanation may be that a right to obtain evidence was legally and conceptually distinct from any purpose to which that evidence might be put, but also that the state intended to collect taxes on its own territory.

Consider a claim brought by a seller or provider of services upon an unpaid invoice which included a sum for value added tax. It makes no sense to see an action on the invoice as involving the indirect (because the proceedings are brought by a person obliged by law to levy the charge and collect the dues on behalf of the state, to which an account must be made) enforcement (because it seeks an order that the defendant hand over his own money) of a revenue law. If this is seen as the indirect enforcement of a foreign revenue law, and if the court were to deduct the tax element from the sums claimed, the claimant would presumably still have to account to the state for the proper fraction of this reduced sum, which would then have to be further reduced, which would be absurd; moreover, it would make it impossible for an employee to sue for unpaid but taxable wages. The solution is simply to ask whether the right upon which the claim is founded, the *jus actionis*, is a revenue law, or something else, such as a contractual promise to pay money, or the liability of a thief to compensate for loss wrongfully caused. If the claim

---

[57] *Ralli Bros v Compania Naviera Sota y Aznar* [1920] 2 KB 287; *Regazzoni v KC Sethia (1944) Ltd* [1958] AC 301.

[58] *Rossano v Manufacturers' Life Insurance Co Ltd* [1963] 2 QB 352; *QRS 1 ApS v Fransden* [1999] 1 WLR 2169 (CA).

[59] ibid.

[60] *Williams & Humbert Ltd v W & H Trade Marks (Jersey) Ltd* [1986] AC 368.

[61] *Re Norway's Application (Nos 1 and 2)* [1990] 1 AC 723.

may be established without mention of any tax law it does not involve the enforcement by the English court of a revenue law, even if it is clear that the claimant will use the money recovered to pay his taxes. If a foreign revenue law is pleaded as mere datum, the answer should probably be the same.

Similar care, and a similar approach, will be required in relation to governmental seizure of property, where close attention needs to be paid to whether law which provided for the seizure is being pleaded as due for enforcement[62] or is merely part of the history of an accomplished fact, with the claim being based on a property right which has been obtained.[63] If, therefore, the claimant can plead that it had possession and was then unlawfully dispossessed, it can make good its claim without the need to refer to the law under which it obtained possession in the first place: its recovery of the property in question does not involve the enforcement of foreign revenue or other public law. If, by contrast, it needs to plead that it has a right to possession, and it needs to plead a rule of foreign law to make good its claim, it will be asking the court to enforce the foreign law, and it may therefore fail.

The traditional analysis is that, in these cases, the *lex fori* supervenes to defeat a claim which was otherwise well founded under a foreign *lex causae*. There may be another way of looking at it, though. It may be better to say that penal and revenue claims are governed by the *lex fori*: if the claim being advanced is of that nature, it must be founded on the domestic law of the court in which it is brought. Liability for a crime may be enforceable under the English law of extradition, or under those rare English laws which criminalize conduct taking place overseas or which allow effect to be given in England to a specific criminal law of another state. A revenue claim may be enforceable in accordance with a treaty with the foreign state implemented in England by domestic legislation. Seen in these terms the *lex fori* is applied because it is the applicable law. These cases would be integrated into the mainstream of the common law conflict of laws, and would no longer need to be explained as some sort of overriding exception to the general scheme of the conflict of laws.

Where the applicable conflicts rules are those made in European legislation, the status of the common law rules just described will depend on the terms of the legislation. In practice there will rarely be difficulty. Where Regulations are defined so as to apply only to civil and commercial matters,

---

[62] *Banco de Vizcaya v Don Alfonso de Borbon y Austria* [1935] 1 KB 140.
[63] *Williams & Humbert Ltd v W & H Trade Marks (Jersey) Ltd* [1986] AC 368; *Islamic Republic of Iran v Barakat Galleries Ltd* [2007] EWCA Civ 1374, [2009] QB 22.

they will not apply where the claim is a penal or a revenue one, or one of public law, or one which arises *jure imperii*. A claim to recover taxes would fall outside the jurisdictional provisions of the former Brussels I Regulation, as would an attempt to enforce a judgment from another Member State ordering the payment of a tax liability. A claim for compensation for property damage arising from enemy action in time of war will be outside the domain of the Regulation, for the right to wage war, and the duty to reparate, is all a matter of public law, unique to governments and states.[64] But a claim for payment of sums to reimburse for the discharge of another's customs liability, which the defendant had contracted to make, is within the domain of the Regulation, for the claim is founded on an ordinary contractual promise to pay for services rendered;[65] and a claim brought by a company against a thieving former director will be within the domain of the Brussels I Regulation, even if the company is acting by a liquidator appointed at the behest of a taxing authority.[66] Likewise, if a claim is, according to the Rome I Regulation, considered to be a civil or commercial matter and governed by a particular foreign law, it would be surprising if the court could nevertheless decline to apply that law on the ground that it was, as it saw it, a foreign penal or revenue law. However, the right of a court under the Regulation to not apply foreign laws where the application would contradict public policy might be pressed into service if any such case—which could only be rare— were to arise.

3. FOREIGN LAWS OFFENSIVE TO PUBLIC POLICY

At various points we will encounter the proposition that a particular result otherwise provided by our conflicts rules may be departed from on grounds of public policy. It is helpful to set out some lines of demarcation. The public policy engaged is only ever that of English law, but where, and to the extent that, it is engaged it prevents the application of a rule of foreign law which would otherwise have been applicable. If an English court is called upon to recognize a foreign law which is so repellent to English standards that even to acknowledge that it was made is unbearable, it will be completely ignored. So for example, if a defendant resists a claim for the return of property by

---

[64] Case C-292/05 *Lechouritou v Germany* [2007] ECR I-1519.
[65] Case C-266/01 *Préservatrice foncière TIARD SA v Netherlands* [2003] ECR I-4867.
[66] cf *QRS 1 ApS v Frandsen* [1999] 1 WLR 2169.

relying on a law which divested the claimant on grounds of race or religion, the defence will be struck out on the basis that the relevant rule of foreign law is too corrupt even to be recognized as datum.[67] If a defendant denies liability for personal injury on the basis that he, as a torturer, owed no duty of care to his victim under the foreign law, the rule of foreign law in question will be wholly ignored. With that introduction, we may examine how and when English public policy overrides an otherwise-applicable foreign rule. We will look separately at public policy within the domain of European private international law, as this applies in English courts, at the end of this section.

Where foreign rules are picked out for application by the conflicts rules of English law, a provision of the *lex causae* will not be applied if its content is repugnant to English public policy, or if the result of its application in the given context would be contrary to English public policy. So for example, a law depriving a racial group of its property,[68] or one invalidating marriage across racial or religious lines will, or should, be regarded as so offensive to English public policy that it will be treated as if it had never been enacted, no matter the factual context in which it arises; alternatively, a court will refuse to receive evidence of such foreign law and will therefore not be put in a position to apply it. Iraqi laws purporting to seize Kuwaiti assets in time of war and in defiance of United Nations sanctions with mandatory effect have also been denied recognition.[69] Extreme cases like this are easy. There are less obvious examples, which may be less persuasive. For example, it has been held that although a contract containing a covenant restricting the freedom of a party to take employment elsewhere may be valid and enforceable according to the *lex causae*, it may still conflict with the English doctrine that such agreements are illegal restraints on trade;[70] and the English rule of freedom may prevail.[71] We are still waiting for a court to hold that a foreign 'religious' law, by which a husband may repudiate his marriage and his wife without allowing her a right to be heard, or by which he invokes religion to refuse his wife the freedom of a divorce, should be refused recognition. Discrimination of this kind is peculiarly rancid when 'justified' by religion; judicial assertion of the primacy of secular reason over such obscurantist nonsense is long overdue.

---

[67] *Oppenheimer v Cattermole* [1976] AC 249; *Kuwait Airways Corpn v Iraq Airways Co (Nos 4 and 5)* [2002] UKHL 19, [2002] 2 AC 883.
[68] *Oppenheimer v Cattermole* [1976] AC 249.
[69] *Kuwait Airways Corpn v Iraq Airways Co (Nos 4 and 5)* [2002] UKHL 19, [2002] 2 AC 883.
[70] *Rousillon v Rousillon* (1880) 14 Ch D 351.
[71] The issue will be reconsidered in the context of the Rome I Regulation in Ch 5.

'Public policy' in this sense refers to the fundamental values of English law; it is clear that these may change with time. It was not so long ago that English law took little or no notice of discrimination on grounds of sex, race, or sexual orientation, but foreign laws which have resisted evolution will now be liable to offend the public policy of English law, which has adopted the values of the new enlightenment with the zeal of the convert. So for example, if an employee under a contract governed by a particular foreign law is dismissed because of his sexual orientation or because she is living with a man to whom she is not married, the fact that the dismissal would be lawful under the foreign law will be disregarded by an English court, dealing with a claim for breach of contract by the employer, on grounds of public policy. Or so one would hope. Sixty, or even 16, years ago, one imagines, it would have been different.

Public policy usually refuses to recognize a provision of foreign law in the sense that the objectionable element will be excised and the remainder of law applied without it.[72] It is not confined to a refusal to accept something (confiscation, divorce) as a fait accompli; it can, it is submitted, be deployed to create rights. For example, if two men who wish to marry are domiciled in a country which refuses to allow same-sex marriage, if they celebrate marriage in a country which is not so backward, the impediment in their personal laws is liable (if not certain) to be disregarded.[73]

It has been said that public policy should have a restrictive meaning. As the great Cardozo J put it: 'we are not so provincial as to say that every solution of a problem is wrong because we deal with it otherwise at home';[74] various English judges have likened it to an 'unruly horse', which is liable to go out of control. Even so, the Human Rights Act 1998 may now provide a more transparent basis for the law to deal with many of the concerns which arise in this context;[75] and as the 1998 Act is a specific direction to the judges, it may well be that its impact on this aspect of the conflict of laws will now be more interventionist than the doctrine of public policy was allowed to be.

By contrast with indisputably wicked or evil laws, other laws may need to be evaluated in their context, and the facts shown to have a sufficient

---

[72] *Kuwait Airways Corpn v Iraq Airways Co (Nos 4 and 5)* [2002] UKHL 19, [2002] 2 AC 883.
[73] The result may also be derived from the Marriage (Same Sex Couples) Act 2013; see further below, p 316.
[74] *Loucks v Standard Oil Co* 120 NE 198 (1918).
[75] Although it may be more correct to understand the Human Rights Act 1998 as applying part of the *lex fori*, by virtue of a direct instruction from legislature to judge, rather than as something which relies on the common law doctrine of public policy.

connection to England before any similar conclusion can be drawn about them. For instance, though a law giving a husband, but not a wife, a unilateral right to divorce should certainly be considered to be contrary to public policy when applied to a wife who is resident in England,[76] it may, just possibly, be regarded differently, and not immediately disqualified from recognition, when applied to parties who have no material connection with England.[77] Likewise, a foreign law which allows an uncle to marry his niece will not be regarded as so objectionable that it will be overridden by English public policy when a court is called on to assess the validity of a marriage which has nothing to do with England.[78] Clarity may result from separating the two ways—the first being absolute, the second contextual—in which public policy may work; and it may be that the restraint of trade example considered above would be better seen as falling into the contextual category.

Another way to express this idea might be that the first category of public policy applies whatever the *lex causae* or connection to England, whereas the second applies only if the issue before the court has a real and substantial connection with England. This could be seen either as a disguised choice of law rule, or as analogous to the 'sufficient connection' principle which must be satisfied before an English court will grant certain forms of equitable relief, such as an anti-suit injunction.[79] And if this were to be accepted, attention could be focused on the question which ought to lie at the heart of the analysis, namely what degree of connection with England ought to be required before this context-dependent form of public policy might be invoked.

The common law has no mechanism for applying or otherwise giving effect to the public policy of a country whose law is not identified as applicable by the rules of the conflict of laws: that is as it should be. Of course, where a provision of a foreign law which is applicable is described under that law as, or as enshrining, a rule of foreign public policy, there is no reason whatever for an English court to decline to give it effect, for it is still part of the *lex causae*, whatever else it may also be said to be. And there never was any such thing as 'European public policy': public policy is national.

Where the issue in question falls within the domain of European private international law as this applies in an English court, the initial question may be formulated a little differently, but the substance is the same: one may go

---

[76] cf *Chaudhary v Chaudhary* [1985] Fam 19 (CA).
[77] Lachaux v Lachaux [2019] EWCA Civ 735.
[78] *Cheni v Cheni* [1965] P 85.
[79] See p 121 above.

in through a different door, but they open into the same room. Recourse to English public policy will be dependent upon the legislation first authorizing it: in a civil or commercial matter, there is no possibility of departing from the answer given by the Regulation unless the Regulation says so itself. But for practical purposes, the legislation with which we will be concerned does permit a court to veer away from the answer to which the Regulation is otherwise steering it by reference to its own public policy. For example, a judgment from another European state may be denied recognition where recognition would be manifestly contrary to public policy;[80] the application of a law otherwise required by the Rome I and Rome II Regulations may be refused if the application would be manifestly contrary to public policy;[81] under the European Regulations which formerly governed the issues a divorce or annulment may be refused recognition if recognition would be manifestly contrary to public policy;[82] and even insolvency proceedings in another Member State were liable to be refused recognition on this ground.[83] Given the general restrictiveness of the doctrine of public policy in any event, it is unlikely that 'manifestly' adds much to the operation of the law. However, as the former Brussels I Regulation made no specific provision for the application of the European Convention on Human Rights, those cases in which a court considers that it is required to implement a provision of that Convention will need to be identified as those where recognition of the judgment would manifestly conflict with its public policy. The same may be true in the context of the Rome I and Rome II Regulations, for example, though in the case of these instruments, provision is also made for the application of a law of the forum as one which is of mandatory application, and the Human Rights Act may be given effect by this means instead. When looking at the various substantive issues which form the remaining chapters of this book, it will be necessary to look at the individual ways in which each piece of European legislation authorizes the application of laws of the forum as mandatory laws. But it does not call for any more by way of introductory treatment.

---

[80] Brussels I Regulation, Art 34(1).
[81] Rome I Regulation, Art 21; Rome II Regulation, Art 26.
[82] Regulation 2201/2003, Art 22(a).
[83] Regulation 1346/2000, Art 26.

5

CONTRACTUAL OBLIGATIONS

*On Exit Day, and unless any further legislative provision is made,
the provisions of EU law set out in the Rome I Regulation, Regulation
593/2008, will be retained as the law of the United Kingdom.
The adjustments necessary to allow the Rome I Regulation
to operate as English private international law are made by the
Law Applicable to Contractual Obligations and Non-Contractual
Obligations (Amendment etc) (EU Exit) Regulations 2019, SI
2019 No 834: these adjustments are of no substantial importance.
It follows that it is possible to refer in this chapter to the Rome
I Regulation without needing to draw attention to its status as EU
legislation (as it was prior to Exit Day) or as retained EU legislation
(as it is on and after Exit Day).*

A. INTRODUCTION

Until 1991, the conflicts rules for contractual obligations were those of
the common law. Most issues were referred to the 'proper law of the contract', which was to say: the law chosen, expressly or impliedly, by the parties, or if no law had been chosen, the law with which the contract had its
closest and most real connection. Marginal roles were given to the law of
the place of performance (illegality under which may affect whether performance of the contract would be ordered), the personal law of a contracting party (incapacity according to which may affect the validity of the
contract made), the law of the place where the contract was made (formal
requirements would be satisfied if that law said that they had been), and
the *lex fori* (for all issues of public policy, and for all issues which were procedural in nature). But in principle, the proper law of the contract, as the
common law defined it, governed almost all substantive issues characterized as contractual in nature; and the freedom of the parties to choose
the law of any country to govern their contract was, for all practical

The Conflict of Laws. Fourth Edition. Adrian Briggs, Oxford University Press (2019). © Adrian Briggs
DOI: 10.1093/oso/9780198838500.003.0005

purposes,[1] untrammelled. Although the common law rules were rather more problematic than common lawyers tended to admit, and their respect for party autonomy was in fact respect for the autonomy of the powerful at the expense of the weak, their hegemony was never seriously questioned.

The sun set on these common law rules when, by two distinct steps, legislation made in Europe provided uniform conflicts rules for contractual obligations arising in civil and commercial matters. The legislation defined the area within which it was to be applied, and provided the conflicts rule to operate within it; it was designed to harmonize across the EU the conflicts rules in relation to contractual obligations, and for this reason was liable to be interpreted independently of any national law or legal system.

For contractual obligations in civil and commercial matters arising from contracts made after 1 April 1991[2] the conflicts rules were made by the 1980 Rome Convention on the law applicable to contractual obligations, which was enacted into English law by the Contracts (Applicable Law) Act 1990. The Convention was a stepping stone towards a more ambitious project covering the entire law of obligations. In 2007 the Rome II Regulation governing non-contractual obligations was adopted:[3] it is examined in the following chapter. Parallel negotiations to convert the Rome Convention into a 'Rome I' Regulation, which should have been the easier task, made slower progress, but in 2008 the Rome I Regulation was finalized and adopted, to apply to contracts made after 17 December 2009.[4] The immediate result was that, subject to the date in relation to which the question has to be addressed, the conflicts rules for obligations in civil and commercial matters were to be found, in their entirety, in the Rome I and Rome II Regulations.

On the departure of the United Kingdom from the European Union, the two Rome[5] Regulations, in the form in which they stood, and as amended[6] on Exit Day, are to be retained as the conflicts rules which will apply in English courts. Of course, where a contract is not made in or as a civil or commercial

---

[1] A famous decision of the Privy Council on appeal from the courts of Nova Scotia, *Vita Food Products Inc v Unus Shipping Co Ltd* [1939] AC 277 said, without further explanation, that the choice of law had to be 'bona fide and legal'. No English case ever rejected a choice of law which had been made by the parties by reference to this statement; it appears to have no content.

[2] SI 1991/707, Art 17.

[3] Regulation (EC) 864/2007, [2007] OJ L199/40.

[4] Regulation (EC) 593/2008, [2008] OJ L177/6.

[5] One wishes that, as it all happened on the 500th anniversary of Martin Luther's great publication, these two instruments could have been retained as the Reformation I and Reformation II Regulations. But the opportunity to honour a monumental event in the history of Europe and of England went begging. It is such a shame.

[6] SI 2019/834.

matter it was never within the scheme of this legislation, and for such contracts the conflicts rules of the common law remain applicable. However, such cases do not form the mainstream of the law, and they are not examined in any detail in this chapter.

The Rome I Regulation applies to contracts concluded after 17 December 2009.[7] In the rare case in which the date of conclusion of the contract is in dispute (which may include cases in which an existing contract undergoes such substantial alteration that it could be said to be new)[8] it would make sense to apply English rules on offer and acceptance, that contracts are generally made upon communication of the acceptance, and to avoid the more complicated answers which could also be proposed. However, the European Court has suggested[9] that such a solution is opposed to the uniformity and legal certainty which the Regulation seeks to create, which may be true but does not help a court to answer a question which, perhaps, will not arise very often.

The version of the Rome I Regulation retained after Exit Day will not be very different from the original Rome Convention or from the real Rome I Regulation. This will generally mean that decisions on the interpretation of earlier versions will be at least helpful in the interpretation of the Regulation. In principle, European law favours consistency of interpretation as between the Rome I Regulation and the Rome Convention, and there is no reason for English courts to take a different view.[10]

This chapter is organized on the footing that the primary legislative text is the Rome I Regulation, that is to say, it concerns itself with choice of law for contracts made after 17 December 2009. At the end of the chapter it will be necessary to say a little about the conflicts rules applicable to contracts made before that date.

It is also necessary to say something preliminary about contracts and the autonomy of contracting parties. As will be seen, the general principle which underpins the conflicts rules for contracts is that so long as parties have contractual capacity, they have very substantial contractual autonomy.[11] If they can choose to make any contract they wish, it appears to follow that they can,

---

[7] Article 28.
[8] Case C–135/15 *Hellenic Republic v Nikiforidis* EU:C:2016:774, [2017] ICR 147.
[9] Case C–135/15 *Hellenic Republic v Nikiforidis* EU:C:2016:774, [2017] ICR 147.
[10] Point 7 of the Recitals; Case C–359/14 *ERGO Insurance SE v If P&C Insurance AS* EU:C:2016:40, [2016] ILPr 451 (though as the former Brussels I Regulation is not to be retained in English law, the point cannot be pressed too far).
[11] Nygh, *Autonomy in International Contracts* (Oxford University Press, 1999).

perhaps within defined limits, choose any law they wish to govern it: it is their contract to make as they wish. But this attractive proposition almost immediately leads into a logical thicket: we can at this stage mention a number of problems which we will try to deal with in this chapter. First, suppose it is not common ground that the parties made a choice of law which the court should now apply. The question whether parties made a choice of law which the court must respect has to be determined by reference to a law: but which law is to do it? Can it be right to refer this question to the law whose status, and relevance to the court, depends upon its having been chosen by the parties? Can the law which it is said that the parties chose be used to decide whether they chose it? It would seem strange if it could, for a choice of law can hardly pull itself up by its own bootstraps. Second, if the parties disagree on whether a binding contract was made, can the law which would govern the alleged contract it if it were found or assumed to be valid be used to answer the anterior question whether the contract *is* valid or whether an alleged choice of governing law is effective? Third, if it is argued that the parties have, or that one of them has, altered the law they had originally chosen to govern their contract, which law is to decide whether they were free to do so and did so? Should it be the first-chosen law, or the new-chosen law, or a combination of both, or something different from all of these? And fourth, where the identification of a governing law does not depend on express choice by the parties, but on the terms of the contract, if the identification of the terms of the contract itself depends on knowing the governing law, where should the analysis begin?

There is a common thread to these questions. The principle of party autonomy is a fine and proper thing, but the one thing it cannot justify is itself: when there is a dispute about it, an external point of reference[12] is needed to explain whether or when or how recourse to the idea of party autonomy is justified. Yet despite these questions, which are at one level rather fundamental and have in the past rather hypnotized writers, in practice the conflicts rules for contracts honour the principle of party autonomy and work well. This is especially so, but not only so, where it is common ground that the parties are contractually bound and the only issue concerns the interpretation and performance of their agreement. We will certainly need to deal with the cases which are not so easy at the appropriate point, but their existence

---

[12] This was a problem which the common law never solved, for there was no external point of reference. The statutory scheme for applicable law put in place by the Regulation provides the missing element.

does not call into question the basic tenet of the private international law of contract, which is to respect exercises, and apparent exercises, of party autonomy to the extent possible.

B. THE ROME I REGULATION

The Rome I Regulation applies to contractual obligations in civil and commercial matters where the contract was concluded after 17 December 2009, except for the matters specifically excluded from its material scope by Article 1; the retained Rome I Regulation is to apply to such contracts made on or after Exit Day. The Regulation defines its own domain or sphere of operation *as well as* providing the conflicts rules for issues falling within that domain, which is defined by Article 1. But even outside the material or temporal scope of the Regulation, and for most of which the common law must supply the relevant conflicts rule, there is nothing to stop the common law, on its own authority, referring issues to which the Regulation lays no claim to the law governing the contract which has been identified by the Regulation. For example, arbitration agreements are excluded from the material scope of the Rome I Regulation by Article 1(2)(e). The Regulation therefore makes no claim to impose its rules for determining the applicable law upon a court which has to consider the validity of an arbitration agreement and which needs a conflicts rule with which to do it. Nevertheless, an English court, applying common law conflicts principles to the issue, is free to decide for itself that the law which governs an arbitration agreement which is contained in a larger contract is the law which governs the contract, and this law is identified by the Regulation. The common law is free to incorporate and use the Regulation, and the answers it gives, for purposes which are, and remain, its own business. A dynamic equilibrium is at work.

The Rome I Regulation applies to cases involving a contractual obligation in civil and commercial matters before an English court which involve a conflict, or a choice (in the sense of a choice to be made by the court), between the laws of different countries.[13] Its scope and terms of art will be interpreted independently of national laws.[14] Until it is necessary to say otherwise, those established principles of interpretation remain part of English law.

---

[13] Article 1(1). For this purpose the separate parts of the United Kingdom are treated as separate countries: Art 2 (of the retained Regulation), which supersedes the original Art 22.

[14] Article 18, which is *not* deleted from the retained version of the Regulation.

The material scope of the Regulation is defined inclusively and exclusively: to determine whether an issue is regulated by the conflicts rules contained in the Regulation the issue must be within the general scope of the Regulation, and not specifically excluded from it. It is to this that we first turn.

1. DOMAIN OF THE REGULATION

The Regulation identifies the law applicable to 'contractual obligations'. The meaning of this term is neither taken from nor dependent on national law.[15] The definition is an autonomous one; or, in more graphic imagery, is of metric design rather than imperial measurements. In the analysis which follows, we will examine the meaning of 'contractual' and then 'obligations'.

(a) 'Contractual' as an obligation freely assumed

The definition of 'contractual' will, no doubt, encompass most obligations regarded as contractual in English law, and will exclude most which are not. The core definition of 'contractual' is the same as that which was developed under the Brussels I Regulation for cases of special jurisdiction in matters relating to a contract: it means an obligation that was freely entered into with regard to another (identified) person;[16] the obligation may be expressly entered into, or tacitly assumed.[17] If one looks to the decisions of the European Court interpreting the Brussels I Regulation for guidance, for example, the obligations of a member to his trade association or of a shareholder to her company, and vice versa, will be contractual, even if a particular national law might categorize the relationship differently, because the relationship between the parties is one in which the obligations were freely undertaken in relation to another;[18] if the obligations were freely entered into in relation to another, the relationship between those parties is contractual.[19] By this reasoning, a

---

[15] Case C–196/15 *Granarolo SpA v Ambrosi Emmi France SA* EU:C:2016:559, [2016] ILPr 667.

[16] Case C–26/91 *Soc Jakob Handte & Co GmbH v Soc Traitements Mécano-Chimiques des Surfaces* [1992] ECR I–3967; Case C–359/14 *ERGO Insurance SE v If P&C Insurance AS* EU:C:2016:40, [2016] ILPr 451.

[17] Case C–196/15 *Granarolo SpA v Ambrosi Emmi France SA* EU:C:2016:559, [2016] ILPr667. A relationship established by tacitly assumed obligations, sufficient to make the relationship contractual, must be established by evidence; it should not be presumed to exist.

[18] Case 34/82 *Martin Peters Bauunternehmung GmbH v Zuid Nederlandse AV* [1983] ECR 987.

[19] Case C–196/15 *Granarolo SpA v Ambrosi Emmi France SA* EU:C:2016:559, [2016] ILPr667 [25]: '. . . the national court therefore has the task of examining, first of all, whether . . . the long-standing business relationship which existed between the parties is characterised by the existence of obligations tacitly agreed between them, so that a relationship existed between them that can be classified as contractual'.

claim by a sub-buyer against a manufacturer, to enforce the warranties the manufacturer gave to the buyer of the goods, concerning their quality, will not be based on obligations agreed between them, even if national law would see the obligation at the root of the proceedings as arising because of a contract, and even though the manufacturer's obligations were undertaken by him—but not to the sub-buyer—freely and voluntarily.[20] It may well be different, though, if the manufacturer knows that the buyer is merely an intermediary acting on behalf of another, even if the identity of that other is not known. It seems probable that any obligation said to be contractual must be tested by reference to both components of this definition—the voluntariness of the assumption of obligation, and the ability to have foreseen or identified the counterparty—though the extent to which it must always satisfy them is less easy to say.

The proposition that the obligation be one which was freely and voluntarily assumed in relation to the other does not mean that it must have been expressly agreed to.[21] Indeed, most contracts made in everyday life are short of expressly agreed terms.[22] Were it otherwise, the obligations of a supplier in a consumer contract, which are often imposed by law and immune from exclusion by contractual term, would not be contractual, nor would some of the terms and conditions implied by law into a contract for the sale of goods. It appears that it is the bilateral[23] relationship voluntarily created, as distinct from the individual terms found within it, which must be voluntarily assumed; indeed, it has even been held that obligations imposed by law on someone who has provided performance on behalf of a contracting party are liable to be seen as contractual obligations:[24] this seems to go to the limit of the law. The conclusion is that the obligational relationship must be freely assumed in relation to the other; if it is, the relationship, and the obligations arising from it, will be contractual.

It is practically certain that the relationship or obligation is still contractual, with the applicable law being determined by the Rome I Regulation, even if it is argued by way of defence that the alleged agreement was vitiated from the outset,[25] or even that it was void *ab initio*.[26] It is common enough in

---

[20] Case C–26/91 *Soc Jakob Handte & Co GmbH v Soc Traîtements Mécano-Chimiques des Surfaces* [1992] ECR I–3967.

[21] Case C–196/15 *Granarolo SpA v Ambrosi Emmi France SA* EU:C:2016:559, [2016] ILPr667.

[22] See for example *Wells v Devani* [2019] UKSC 4, [2019] 2 WLR 617.

[23] Multilateral relationships may also qualify.

[24] Case C–274/16 *flightright GmbH v Air Nostrum Lineas Aeréas del Mediterráneo SA* EU:C:2018:160, [2018] QB 1268; *Committeri v Club Méditerranée SA* [2018] EWCA Civ 1889.

[25] cf *Agnew v Länsförsäkringsbolagens AB* [2001] 1 AC 223.

[26] But cf *Kleinwort Benson Ltd v Glasgow City Council* [1999] 1 AC 153.

domestic law to talk of a 'void contract', even if it is, from one point of view, something of a nonsense: if 'it' is void, it cannot be anything and certainly cannot be a contract. More to the point, the Rome I Regulation, as we shall see, specifies the conflicts rule to be applied when it is alleged that a party did not consent,[27] and when dealing with the consequences of nullity.[28] If the Regulation provides the conflicts rule for an issue, that issue is necessarily within the material scope of the Regulation. For voidable contracts, if a claim alleges that the claimant was entitled to rescind a contract for misrepresentation, or avoid it for non-disclosure, or to have it set aside by reason of the other's undue influence, the matter is one of contractual obligation, for the entire question is the validity or otherwise of a contractual obligation. By contrast, where the claim is for monetary compensation for loss brought about by being tricked or coerced into a contract, or for the failure of the counterparty to negotiate the conclusion of a contract in good faith,[29] the obligation which forms the basis for the claim or the dispute is non-contractual, a matter of pre-contractual fault. If this is not obvious,[30] then (echoing the reasoning just deployed) as the Rome II Regulation provides the applicable conflicts rule, the obligation falls within the scope of that Regulation. However, as we shall see,[31] the solution arrived at by the application of the Rome II Regulation will almost always be the same as that which the Rome I Regulation would have given, so even if there is any doubt about the line of demarcation just proposed, it is doubtful that it will make any difference.

A partial picture of the meaning of 'contractual' may be put together from a number of propositions which appear to be justified. (1) If it is common ground that there was a contract between the parties, the Rome I Regulation will in principle determine the law applicable to the issues which arise between the parties. (2) If the claimant frames a claim in tort, but the substance of the claim could have been advanced as a breach of contract, the obligation in question is a contractual one and the Rome I Regulation will determine the law applicable to it.[32] (3) If the claimant seeks to enforce a contract,

---

[27] Article 10.

[28] Article 12(1)(e).

[29] Cf Case C–334/00 *Fonderie Officine Mecchaniche Tacconi SpA v Heinrich Wagner Sinto Maschinenfabrik GmbH* [2002] ECR I–7357.

[30] It might be pointed out that the compensation which the court may order will often be the money equivalent of rescission, that is, to put the parties in the position they would have been in if the contract had not been made. That might suggest that the two kinds of claim should be seen to be two aspects of a single issue, which would then have to be contractual.

[31] Chapter 6.

[32] C–548/12 *Brogsitter v Fabrication de Montres Normandes EURL* EU:C:2014:148, [2014] QB 753; *Committeri v Club Méditerranée SA* [2018] EWCA Civ 1889.

but the defendant counters with an assertion that the alleged contract was not made, or was not legally valid, the obligation relied on as the basis of the claim, and sought to be enforced, is contractual, and the Rome I Regulation will in principle apply. (4) If the roles are reversed, and the claimant seeks to rescind a contract for pre-contractual fault, or seeks relief predicated on the basis that he has rescinded the contract, the defendant contending by way of answer that the contract is valid, the obligation in dispute between the parties is contractual, and the Rome I Regulation will in principle apply.[33] (5) If the claimant seeks to enforce a contract but the defendant asserts that whether or not the contract is valid, he is not party to it, the obligation in question is still a contractual one, and the Rome I Regulation will in principle apply. (6) If it is now common ground that a supposed contract was a nullity, and the claim is for relief which is consequential upon this state of affairs, the dispute concerns the consequences of nullity of a contractual obligation, and the Rome I Regulation, which deals specifically with it, will in principle apply.[34] (7) If the claimant seeks monetary compensation for being tricked or deceived or pressured into a contract, but which he now cannot or does not seek to escape from, the obligation is founded on an allegation of pre-contractual fault, which does not call into question the validity of the contract, which is simply part of the data which show the extent of the loss. The Rome II Regulation deals specifically with the obligation, so that it, rather than the Rome I Regulation, will apply to it. (8) If the claimant seeks monetary compensation for the counterparty's wrongful failure to negotiate in good faith towards the conclusion of a contract, the obligation in question is one to which the Rome II Regulation specifically applies; it is therefore a non-contractual obligation and the Rome I Regulation will not apply to it.

Civil or commercial obligations can be freely assumed outside what English domestic law would regard as contract, and, for an English lawyer, locating these within the framework of the Rome I and Rome II Regulations requires some care. Liability for statements negligently made to someone who was expected to rely on them can be explained, as a matter of domestic law, as resting on a voluntary assumption of responsibility to another,[35] which comes very close to the definition of a contractual obligation. Moreover, if liability under this principle of domestic law is said to arise from a relationship 'equivalent to contract', which is not contractual only because of the lack

---

[33] Case C–366/13 *Profit Investment Sim SpA v Ossi* EU:C:2016:282, [2016] 1 WLR 3832.
[34] Article 12(1)(e).
[35] *Henderson v Merrett Syndicates Ltd* [1995] 2 AC 145.

of consideration,[36] it is plausible that these may be tacitly assumed contractual obligations for the purpose of the Rome I Regulation. It might even be argued, for example, that the question whether A, who has agreed to provide a confidential reference to B on behalf of C, owes liability to B[37] or to C,[38] or to each, if he is said to have been careless in what he writes, would be a matter for the Rome I Regulation, as the obligations which A assumed to B and to C were assumed to each of them freely and voluntarily. In a similar way, the liability of someone who volunteers to assume fiduciary duties in relation to another may be seen as resting on an obligation freely and voluntarily entered into in relation to that other. That would mean that the existence of these duties, their extent, and their consequences will be subject to the conflicts rules of the Rome I Regulation.[39] Yet again, the same may be said of a former employee said to owe continuing obligations of confidentiality to his former employer. After all, the fact that such obligations may be seen as equitable obligations in the context of domestic laws is an historical and doctrinal accident which is irrelevant to the proper interpretation of the Rome I Regulation; and in any case, the obligations on which the claim is based would not have arisen to bind the employee had it not been for the contract of employment.[40]

The eventual answer in relation to the 'contractual' part of the autonomous definition will be to ask whether the relationship out of which the liability is said to arise can be described as one in which the defendant freely assumed obligations in relation to another and, if he did, the law which governs the relationship will be likely to be that specified by the Rome I Regulation. If in the end this all seems rather more difficult than it needs to be, there are two things to remember which put it all in context. First, even when the law was simpler than it is today, the finer points of the division of the law of obligations into contract and delict was difficult for Gaius and Justinian,[41] so the problem is neither new nor one which is particularly hard on common lawyers. Second, and most importantly, in many of the cases which one may feel inclined to locate within the Rome II Regulation but where the Rome I Regulation remains

---

[36] *Hedley Byrne & Co Ltd v Heller & Partners Ltd* [1964] AC 465.
[37] *Spring v Guardian Assurance plc* [1995] 2 AC 296.
[38] *Hedley Byrne & Co Ltd v Heller & Partners Ltd* [1964] AC 465.
[39] Case C–548/12 *Brogsitter v Fabrication de Montres Normandes EURL* EU:C:2014:148, [2014] QB 753.
[40] Case C–548/12 *Brogsitter v Fabrication de Montres Normandes EURL* EU:C:2014:148, [2014] QB 753.
[41] All the more so as the Rome Regulations do not have, as Justinian did have, the benefit of quasi-contract and quasi-delict to accommodate some forms of liability.

within easy reach, the applicable law generated by the Rome II Regulation is liable to be the same as it would have been if the issue had been accepted as contractual and governed by the Rome I Regulation. Indeed, this approach to the issues in which the natural territory of the two Regulations might be thought to overlap is characteristic of the eminently practical, sensible, solutions which the Regulations work together to produce.

(b) 'Contractual' as an obligation undertaken to an identified other

The second aspect of the definition of 'contractual' appears to require, at least in principle, that the obligation be assumed in relation to another who can be identified, so that if the defendant has no idea who the other party is, the relationship is, on the face of it, not likely to be a contractual one. As has been explained, this is why the obligations owed by a manufacturer to a sub-buyer, who purchased the object from the original buyer, are not seen as contractual: they are not obligations freely and voluntarily assumed in relation to that other.[42]

Although this answer is indicative, it cannot be taken to be decisive. If it were decisive, for example, Mrs Carlill, whose purchase and use of the carbolic smoke ball failed to ward off influenza, and through whom every first year law student discovers the law of contract,[43] would not be party to a contractual obligation. The Carbolic Smoke Ball Company neither knew nor cared who it contracted with: its public offer, by advertisement in the Pall Mall Gazette, was to users of the smoke ball, not to purchasers, still less to purchasers who obtained it directly from them. It was, in this respect, in the same position as the person who advertises a reward to whomever finds a missing cat, dog, or ring[44] or, indeed, the shipper of goods who offers whichever unknown stevedore unloads them certain exemptions from liability for causing loss or damage.[45] Nor, perhaps, would an assignee[46] or other successor in title have a contractual claim to enforce against the original obliged party; and in those countries in which the doctrine of privity of contract has

---

[42] Case C–26/91 *Soc Jakob Handte v Soc Traitements Mécano-chimiques des Surfaces* [1992] ECR I–3967; Case C–543/10 *Refcomp SpA v Axa Corporate Solutions Assurance SA* EU:C:2013:62, [2013] 1 All ER (Comm) 1201.

[43] *Carlill v Carbolic Smoke Ball Co* [1893] 1 QB 256 (CA).

[44] *Gibbons v Proctor* (1891) 64 LT 594.

[45] *New Zealand Shipping Co Ltd v Satterthwaite & Co Ltd (The Eurymedon)* [1975] AC 154; *Port Jackson Stevedoring Pty Ltd v Salmond & Spraggon (Australia) Pty Ltd* [1981] 1 WLR 138.

[46] Assignment by operation of law was, evidently, the basis for the claim to enforce the manufacturer's obligations in Case C–26/91 *Soc Jakob Handte v Soc Traitements Mécano-chimiques des Surfaces* [1992] ECR I–3967.

been relaxed to allow non-parties to enforce contractual promises made to another, the claim of the third party against the promisor would not be contractual in nature. In none of these cases is the identity of the other party known to, or probably even discoverable by, the supplier, advertiser, shipper, or debtor; and that would appear to take the obligations of the relationship outside the scope of Rome I Regulation, which cannot be correct. These obligations, promissory in nature, must be contractual, for there is no other category into which it would make any sense to fit them. The existence of an identified or identifiable 'other' to whom the obligation is assumed, and who now seeks to enforce it may be typical, but is not essential. An obligation will therefore be contractual if one party freely assumes an obligation to another or to others, but if the promisor does not care or wish to know[47] the identity of the other, this will not affect the nature of the obligation which will still be within the scope of the Rome I Regulation. It may mean that the claim of the sub-buyer to enforce the original obligations of the manufacturer might yet be based on a contractual obligation, of which the sub-buyer is the assignee, for the purpose of the Rome I Regulation.[48] That would be a perfectly sensible outcome.

(c) The meaning of 'obligations'

English lawyers habitually think of contractual obligations as promissory. The Giuliano–Lagarde report on the Rome Convention stated that gifts were within its scope where they are seen as contractual: this will, no doubt, also be true for the Rome I Regulation. For an English lawyer this is a curious proposition.[49] The sense in which gifts give rise to obligations, still less promissory obligations, is obscure, especially as the Regulation does not apply to the constitution of trusts.[50] However, a challenge to the validity of a gift (referred to as a 'contract of gift') *inter vivos* was held to be contractual for the purposes of the Brussels I Regulation;[51] the assignment of a contractual right by way of gift will be within the scope of the Rome I Regulation, and at that point the inclusion of gifts makes sense.[52] There may be requirements of formal validity; if there is a right to revoke a gift on account of ingratitude or because of

---

[47] Such as where an offer is made to the world for acceptance without the need for communication, or where the offer is made to a single promisee, but without restraint on assignment.

[48] Not least in the case where the rights of the buyer are voluntarily assigned to the sub-buyer; cf Art 14.

[49] [1980] OJ C282/1, 10.

[50] Article 1(2)(h).

[51] Case C–417/15 *Schmidt v Schmidt* EU:C:2016:881, [2017] ILPr 127.

[52] *Gorjat v Gorjat* [2010] EWHC 1537 (Ch).

material mistake, this right of revocation is in the nature of a personal right or obligation and it will probably be contractual.

The creation, existence, validity, and effect of property rights as such, not being part of the law of obligations, are not within the scope of the Regulation. The creation, effect, and transfer of intellectual property is therefore outside the scope of the Regulation, although contracts to create, or licence the use of, or to transfer such property will be within the Rome I Regulation; in a similar way, the obligation not to infringe a right of intellectual property is within the Rome II Regulation. The obligations arising from contracts to transfer land and cars are within the scope of the Regulation, even though the rules for the determination of title to land and chattels are not.

A more troublesome question arises in connection with the assignment of intangible movable property in general, such as shares, policies of insurance, contractual debts, and so on. On the face of it, these things are all contractual in nature: rights and correlative obligations created by being assumed voluntarily in relation to another. However, there is also a respectable view that all these are property, albeit property created by a contract, and that, as property, they are separate and distinct from the contract which created them. To put the same point another way, a contract may be needed to create the right/obligation, but once this act of creation has taken place what results is (a right of) property which can be bought, sold, mis-sold, mortgaged, pledged, charged, assigned, alienated, bequeathed, confiscated, discharged, destroyed, interfered with, hijacked, and obtained by deception. From this it follows, so the argument runs, that the legal relationships thus arising, at least between donor and donee, or assignor and assignee, of the right against a debtor, are proprietary and are not contractual, and that the issue of what law governs dealings with these rights is therefore not governed by the Rome I Regulation. The immense importance of these issues in business finance and financial engineering mean that it is essential, at this point, that the law be as clear as possible.

It is true that the process conveniently[53] regarded as transfer or assignment of certain intangibles, such as shares and intellectual property rights, is proprietary in nature and effect. In English law there are many contexts—insolvency is one, but the financing of business by the sale of future receivables is another—in which it is natural and convenient for contractual rights/

---

[53] But not always accurately: in the case of some, such as registered shares, there is no transfer or assignment of the shares. As far as the technicalities go, there is a surrender to and re-grant by the company, but no actual assignment of shares from the former to the new shareholder.

debts to be regarded as property. However, the difference between owning a debt (a statement made in proprietary language) and being owed a debt (a statement in contractual language) may be more apparent than real. The question of who owns a debt is the same as asking to whom the debt is now owed, and there is no easy way in which the two can be separated so as to draw a distinction between them. That would suggest that the issues which arise here are within the scope of the Rome I Regulation because they are, at their base, aspects and consequences of the contractual obligation; but there is more. The Rome I Regulation contains the conflicts rule for issues arising in relation to these relationships: Article 14 contains the rule which determines the law applicable to the various aspects of the voluntary assignment of contractual obligations. It answers the question of which law governs the assignment (but by natural construction, also the multiple assignment) of such rights; and it answers the question of which law governs the relationship between assignee and debtor (but by natural construction, the priority of claims against a debtor if the debt has been assigned more than once). These two rules show that the Rome I Regulation has asserted its authority over the issue, and, as said before, if the Regulation provides a rule, it is pointless to contend that the Regulation does not apply to it. Unless or until there is amending legislation,[54] that is really the end of the debate.

(d) Concurrent obligations

In some contexts—take employment, and the provision of professional services,[55] for example—English domestic law allows a claimant to frame his claim, if the facts warrant it and if he wishes, concurrently in contract and in tort, or to elect between them. The common law rules of private international law were understood to allow this as well.[56] If one asks why, the answer is that (in domestic law) there may be different limitation periods and (in private international law) very different conflicts rules; and if one asks why it is allowed, one response is that a thief is no less a thief for being party to a contract with his victim. It is likely that the same permissive approach is taken by the common law when a claimant bases his claim on contractual and on fiduciary duties which he says were owed to him and have been broken.

---

[54] If it is made by the EU, any such legislation will not affect the retained Rome I Regulation.
[55] *Henderson v Merrett Syndicates Ltd* [1995] 2 AC 145.
[56] cf *Coupland v Arabian Gulf Oil Co* [1983] 1 WLR 1151 (CA); *Base Metal Trading Ltd v Shamurin* [2004] EWCA Civ 1316, [2005] 1 WLR 1157.

The question whether this claimant-favouring freedom is compatible with the Rome Regulations is concerned only with the issue of private international law: if the Regulation directs a court to apply English domestic law, the claimant may then formulate her claim in contract, and in tort, and in any other manner which may be available to her. As far as the conflicts issue is concerned, the better view is that the claimant does not have the freedom which the common law allowed: if the obligation which he seeks to enforce could be, or could have been, formulated as a breach of contract, the law applicable to it will be identified by the Rome I Regulation.

This is because the two Regulations are designed to not overlap.[57] The European Court has interpreted the Rome Regulations to be as consistent as possible with the (former) Brussels I Regulation. That Regulation made it clear that, for special jurisdictional purposes, where a matter was capable of being framed as a matter relating to a contract, it was not open to the claimant to present it as a matter relating to a tort, even if national law would have permitted him to do so. The claimant who has contracted with the defendant is not at liberty to pick and select from the content of that relationship the ingredients of an obligation which, if it had stood alone, would have fallen under the Rome II Regulation.

If this reasoning is sound, then for the purpose of finding the applicable law it is not open to her to say that the solicitor or investment adviser, or the surveyor or repairer, owed her the common duty of care which is, in English law, perfectly capable of arising between parties who have no contractual relationship, and to argue that this is enough to allow the claim to be brought under the conflicts rules of Rome II Regulation. The relationship which brought the parties into proximity was the contract, and the claim against the defendant could be framed as one for breach of contract. That makes it, for the purposes of the Rome Regulations, just as under the Brussels I Regulation, a matter of contractual obligation.[58] To put the same point yet another way, the fact that the defendant is said to have committed a tort (or a breach of fiduciary duty[59]) is not the point; the question is whether the wrong which he is said to have committed is one which could be formulated as a breach of contract.

---

[57] Case C–359/14 *ERGO Insurance SE v If P&C Insurance AS* EU:C:2016:40, [2016] ILPr 451.
[58] Case C–548/12 *Brogsitter v Fabrication de Montres Normandes EURL* EU:C:2014:148, [2014] QB 753; *Committeri v Club Méditerranée SA* [2018] EWCA Civ 1889.
[59] Case C–548/12 *Brogsitter v Fabrication de Montres Normandes EURL* EU:C:2014:148, [2014] QB 753.

That, at least, is the answer which follows most naturally from the jurisprudence of the European Court and from the general structure of the Regulations. However, if one were to ask the question which (on this view) should not arise, and ask what law would be applied to the obligation on the basis of its being non-contractual, the Rome II Regulation would, by means of Article 4(3), point very clearly to the law which governed the contract between the parties. Though there may be very unusual cases in which this would not be correct, the general result is clear. The issue is, therefore, of theoretical interest to some, but of small practical importance to anybody.

(e) Issues specifically excluded from the Regulation

The Regulation makes no claim to apply to obligations arising in revenue, customs, or administrative matters. It will, however, apply to a contract by which A agrees to reimburse B for discharging customs duties for which A was liable, as the obligation on which the claim is based, the *ius actionis*, is a plain vanilla contractual obligation, which relies on no principle of customs law to create or define it.[60]

The Regulation makes no claim to apply to the matters set out in Article 1(2), and for these the appropriate conflicts rule must be found by other means. Many of these matters would not have been seen as contractual in any event, so Article 1(2) largely confirms what would in any event have been deduced without it. They are: status and the capacity of natural persons;[61] obligations arising out of family and analogous relationships, including maintenance;[62] obligations arising out of matrimonial property regimes, also wills and succession;[63] obligations arising from bills of exchange and promissory notes and other negotiable instruments where the obligations arise from their negotiable character;[64] questions governed by the law of companies, such as creation, capacity, and winding-up;[65] the question whether an agent can bind a principal, or an organ bind the company, in relation to a third party;[66] the constitution and internal relationships of trusts;[67] obligations arising out of

---

[60] Case C–266/01 *Préservatrice Foncière TIARD SA v Netherlands* [2003] ECR I–4867.
[61] Article 1(2)(a); though this is subject to Art 13; see p 212.
[62] Article 1(2)(b).
[63] Article 1(2)(c).
[64] Article 1(2)(d). But contracts pursuant to which these instruments are issued are not excluded: [1980] OJ C282/1, 10.
[65] Article 1(2)(f): in many cases these issues will be referred to the *lex incorporationis*.
[66] Article 1(2)(g). But in so far as they are contractual, relations between principal and agent and agent and third party are not excluded.
[67] Article 1(2)(h).

dealings prior to the conclusion of the contract;[68] a very specific category of insurance contracts;[69] and evidence and procedure.[70]

Where a question of conflict of laws arises for any of these issues, the applicable law will be found elsewhere. While the United Kingdom was a Member State of the European Union it might have applied other European Regulations dealing with some of these matters, but after Exit Day, except where any such legislation has been retained, the common law conflicts rules will apply. As to these rules, and as will be seen in the chapters where they arise, the *lex domicilii* has a dominant role in relation to wills, succession, and family matters; the *lex situs* is dominant in relation to negotiable instruments; the *lex incorporationis* in relation to companies; the proper law of the trust in relation to trusts; and the *lex fori* over issues of evidence and procedure. In fact, none of these is contractual in nature, and their express exclusion from the Rome I Regulation is more confirmatory than anything else. The exclusion of the power of an agent to bind a principal to a third party from the Regulation was probably the result of the complexity of the issue and the deep differences between the common law and civilian analyses of agency; but an English court may still refer this issue to the law which governs the contract of agency, which may have been identified by the Rome I Regulation. This is because although the Regulation makes no claim to apply to issues excluded from its scope, it does not prohibit a national law taking that step in the exercise of its own legal authority.

The same approach will be taken to agreements on arbitration and choice of court, which are excluded by Article 1(2)(e).[71] There are several probable reasons for this exclusion. Arbitration agreements are substantially regulated by the New York Convention, and some jurisdiction agreements by the (former) Brussels Convention, (former) Lugano Convention, Hague Convention, and so forth. In some systems these agreements are understood as regulating purely procedural matters, or as dealing with an aspect of public law, namely the jurisdiction of courts, but are not seen as contractual obligations in civil or commercial matters. However issues, such as validity and interpretation, may arise and need to be resolved in the way in which

---

[68] Article 1(2)(i): the Rome II Regulation will apply. This may now be a better place for claims of breach of warranty of authority: cf *Golden Ocean Group Ltd v Salgaocar Mining Industries Pvt Ltd* [2012] EWCA Civ 265, [2012] 3 All ER 842, decided under the Rome Convention which did not contain a specific exclusion in these terms.

[69] Article 1(2)(j).

[70] Article 1(3).

[71] Although they may be taken into account in the determination of the governing law.

contractual issues are resolved. The English approach is to proceed on the basis that such agreements are usually terms of a larger contract, even though being for some purposes severable from it, and that as such, questions concerning their validity, meaning and interpretation should be answered by reference to the law governing that larger contract:[72] their *effect* on the jurisdiction of a court will, however, be governed by the laws on jurisdiction of courts or on arbitration, as the case may be. In those cases in which the agreement is freestanding and not part of a substantive contract, the law governing the agreement may be found by applying the Regulation or the traditional doctrine of the proper law: it will be for the common law to decide which is correct, but it has not done so yet.

Because the status of a person is predominantly the concern of the law of the domicile, so generally is her capacity. So far as contractual obligations are concerned, the requirement of contractual capacity in terms of age, marital status, and mental capacity is generally considered to be satisfied if the person had capacity either by the law of the country with which the contract was most closely connected or by the law of her domicile.[73] The Rome I Regulation intrudes on this analysis in only one respect. Article 13 provides that where two individuals make a contract in the same country, and one later relies on a personal incapacity according to some other law to plead the invalidity of that contract, she may do so only if the other party was, or should have been, aware of it: it is a policy choice to limit the effect of hidden or 'lurking' personal incapacity, but a sensible one. For corporations, the existence and extent of contractual capacity is a matter for the *lex incorporationis*.[74] But the legal effect, if any, of a contract made by a corporation without capacity to do so is a matter for the *lex contractus*: the answer may depend on the nature of the particular incapacity.

2. *LEX CONTRACTUS*: CHOSEN BY THE PARTIES

Article 3 of the Regulation provides that a contract is governed by the law chosen by the parties, provided that this choice is express or may be clearly

---

[72] May be does not mean must be: see *Sulamérica Cia Nacional de Seguros SA v Enesa Engenharia SA* [2012] EWCA Civ 638, [2013] 1 WLR 102. Where a jurisdiction clause falls within the scope of the 2005 Hague Convention on Choice of Court Agreements, some issues will be dealt with by that Convention.

[73] *Charron v Montreal Trust Co* (1958) 15 DLR (2d) 240 (Ont CA).

[74] *Haugesund Kommune v Depfa ACS Bank* [2010] EWCA Civ 579, [2012] QB 549.

demonstrated[75] by the terms of the contract or the circumstances of the case. In the Recitals, the Regulation refers to the parties' freedom to choose the law as 'one of the cornerstones' of the conflicts rules for matters of contractual obligation.[76] It is important to observe that Article 3 requires an actual choice, the existence of which can be shown in two (or three) ways. It makes no reference to, and gives no encouragement, still less authority, to look for, an 'implied' or 'inferred' choice.[77]

(a) Choice of law expressed by the parties
In every contract falling within the domain of the Regulation the parties are free to choose the law which will govern it, and in every case except contracts for the carriage of passengers[78] and certain kinds of contract of insurance,[79] for which, as we shall see, the menu of available laws is a limited one, they may choose a law which has no objective connection to themselves or to the facts of the contract: in this sense the commitment to party autonomy is completely clear (and the encouragement to choose English law almost as clear).[80]

The only qualification, stated in Article 3, is that where all other elements relevant to the situation at the time of choice are located in a country other than that which has been chosen the choice of the parties shall not prejudice the application of provisions of the law of that country which cannot be derogated from by agreement. This, though, is not a restriction on freedom of choice, for it does not question or contradict the choice which the parties have made, simply overlaying it in a very limited way; and it will only rarely be satisfied. The meaning of 'relevant to the situation' is malleable;[81] but in

---

[75] The Rome Convention had referred instead to this version of choice being 'demonstrated with reasonable certainty', which may mean that the test has become slightly more stringent.
[76] Point 11 of the Recitals.
[77] *Lawlor v Sandvik Mining and Construction Mobile Crushers and Screens Ltd* [2013] EWCA Civ 365, [2013] 2 Lloyd's Rep 98.
[78] Article 5(2).
[79] Article 7(3). In the negotiations leading to the conclusion of the Regulation, it had also been proposed that a free choice of law should not be possible for consumer contracts, but this was not agreed to.
[80] Case C-184/12 *United Antwerp Maritime Agencies NV v Navigation Maritime Bulgare* EU:C:2013:663, [2014] 1 Lloyd's Rep 161; Case C-135/15 *Hellenic Republic v Nikiforidis* EU:C:2016:774, [2017] ICR 147.
[81] Cf *Banco Santander Totta SA v Companhia Carris de Ferro de Lisboa SA* [2016] EWCA Civ 1267, [2017] 1 WLR 1323. For a slightly different approach, see the Opinion in Case C-54/16 *Vinyls Italia SpA v Mediterranea di Navigazione SpA* EU:C:2017:164, [2018] 1 WLR 543 (disposed of by the Court on other grounds).

principle, as Article 3(3) is equivalent to a restriction on, an exception to, party autonomy it is liable to be construed in a restrictive way.

The Regulation allows a choice of law actually made to be decisive except only in relation to limited and clearly specified matters;[82] but it associates this freedom with two requirements: the choice must actually be made, and that choice must be expressed or be so clearly demonstrable from the contract or the circumstances of the case that it did not require further expression. This will preclude the argument that the parties, as reasonable people, 'must have' made a choice but which they did not trouble to express, or that they 'would have been bound to agree' on the governing law. It is unlikely that the Regulation allows for an 'implied' or 'inferred' choice of law: the common law would have done so, but it cannot be correct to frame the question whether the parties made a choice of law in language which the Regulation does not use as terms of art. In principle, the freedom to choose a law is a freedom which must be affirmatively exercised; like all freedoms, if it is not exercised it will be lost.

A choice expressed in the form 'this contract shall be governed by the laws of France' will make French law the governing law. A less artful choice, such as 'this contract shall be construed in accordance with French law', will probably be taken the same way. There is little room for doubt when parties take advantage of the freedom to choose and express that choice clearly: Article 3 helps those who help themselves. The trouble is that choices of law, or what the parties may have thought were choices of law, are sometimes made by those who do not have English (still less, private international legal English) as their mother tongue, and it is hard to see why the law should penalize them for it.

Article 3 may validate a purported choice which is expressed formulaically, such as when the contract is expressed to be governed 'by the law of the place where the carrier has its principal place of business'. If there is no dispute about these identifiers, the expression of choice will be effective. But there may be genuine disagreement about who (ship owner, charterer) is the carrier, or which is the principal place (of day-to-day decision-taking, of supervision and overall direction) of business.[83] If ever it were to matter, the task of answering these questions would fall to the governing law, for they go to the interpretation[84] of a term of the contract; the problem arises

---

[82] Examined below (Section (B)(6)).
[83] *The Rewia* [1991] 2 Lloyd's Rep 325 (CA).
[84] Article 12(1)(a).

where answers to these questions are required in order to identify the governing law in the first place. Although the European Court held, in the context of the (former) Brussels I Regulation, that an analogous provision in such terms may be effective as an agreement on jurisdiction,[85] it presupposed that the court seised had been able to identify the geographical place which had been referred to. If instead one asks the simple question whether these words choose a law, either expressly or in a way which can be said to be clearly demonstrated from the terms of the contract or the circumstances of the case, the answer may be that they might appear to but do not. It is no help to say that, as a matter of English law, the carrier will be regarded as the charterer, or the principal place of business is that from which day-to-day control is exercised: the Rome I Regulation is meant to operate independently of national law, and to be a full, complete, and sufficient code for the identification of the governing law. From that point of view, some forms of words, although superficially intelligible, do not achieve it, and when this is so, Article 3 will not give effect to the choice made.

A choice of the laws of the United Kingdom, or of British law, for example, cannot be given effect according to its terms, because there is no such law to be chosen. An English court will interpret this as being an express choice of English law, on the basis of an assumption which is as factually correct[86] as it is delicate: what a court in Scotland would make of such a thing is not for us to say. A choice of 'English or French law' cannot be considered to be an effective choice of law, as it is not a choice of the laws of a country; Article 4 will apply instead. A choice of 'English law as it stood on the day on which the contract was concluded', or of 'English law as it stood immediately before leaving the European Union', or 'English law save insofar as inconsistent with the principles of Sharia law' will also be rejected: as choices of law, none of these is for 'the law of a country'. Parties who choose the law of a country have neither power nor authority to pick and choose the content of that law except to the extent that a law, if chosen, allows them to exclude the provisions of a particular statute, as English law does with the Contracts (Rights of Third Parties) Act 1999. Choices of 'religious laws' are plainly ineffective.[87]

---

[85] Case C–387/98 *Coreck Maritime GmbH v Handelsveem BV* [2000] ECR I–9337.
[86] cf *The Komninos S* [1991] 1 Lloyd's Rep 370 (CA).
[87] See further below, p 219.

(b) Choice of law clearly demonstrated by the terms or the circumstances

The alternative hypothesis in Article 3(1) is that the parties chose the law to govern the contract but did not express it as such. For Article 3(1) to be satisfied on this basis, it must be shown that the parties did actually choose the law to govern the contract; it is not enough to show that they would have chosen a particular law if they had been invited to do so. This will not happen very often, for a choice which was actually made but which was not expressed is not easy to understand unless it is argued that the written contract was inaccurate as a record of the agreement actually made, which is not what Article 3(1) has in mind. The real question is what evidence will be likely to satisfy this version of choice of law by the parties.[88]

We may first ask whether if the parties expressly choose the jurisdiction of a court this may also be seen as a choice of law, albeit one which they did not express. The answer which the common law principles would have given was that it counted as a choice of law unless substantially all the other factors in the case coalesced in pointing to another law.[89] A Latin maxim makes a similar point: *qui elegit iudicem elegit ius* (who chooses the court chooses the law), and this may one day be held to indicate the way in which the Regulation works. However, the context in which the common law arrived at this conclusion was almost always from a choice of English jurisdiction, and it is hard to dispel the suspicion that this is what encouraged an English court to conclude that there had been a choice of English law. And so far as the Regulation is concerned, all it actually says in Point 12 of the Recitals is that a contractual choice for the courts of a Member State, giving them exclusive jurisdiction, 'should be one of the factors taken into account in determining whether a choice of law has been clearly demonstrated', which is not very illuminating. In truth, there are decent arguments on both sides. If the parties set out a choice of jurisdiction, but said nothing about law, some will see in that clear evidence of a deliberate non-choice of law. On the other hand, it may be that commercial parties who chose London for the resolution of future disputes assumed, without troubling to think about it, that English courts would simply apply English law, and that there was no need for them to state the obvious; this may be thought of as a tacit choice of law:[90] after all, if obligations

---

[88] See *Lawlor v Sandvik Mining and Construction Mobile Crushers and Screens Ltd* [2013] EWCA Civ 365, [2013] 2 Lloyd's Rep 98 (a case on the Rome Convention).

[89] *Compagnie Tunisienne de Navigation SA v Compagnie d'Armement Maritime SA* [1971] AC 572.

[90] *Lawlor v Sandvik Mining and Construction Mobile Crushers and Screens Ltd* [2013] EWCA Civ 365, [2013] 2 Lloyd's Rep 98.

may be assumed tacitly, the idea of a tacit choice of law is not shocking. And finally, if the parties contract on the basis of a standard form, which is known in the trade as being founded on, and designed to be interpreted in the light of, English law, this may be a case in which the parties' actual choice may be deduced from the terms of the contract or the circumstances of the case. It may be that each case has to be considered on its own merits, and each contract interpreted against its own background of fact and circumstance.

By contrast, where an unexpressed choice of law is said to be demonstrable from an express choice for arbitration, it is impossible to see even a tacit choice of law to govern the substance of the contract. No doubt there is some sense in which the parties have chosen the law which will govern the procedure of the arbitration if one takes place, but that is a wholly different thing from the law which governs their substantive contract. The characteristic aim of arbitration is to keep the dispute between the parties as far away from the courts, and the rules which judges use to adjudicate, as possible. Arbitral panels are usually chosen for their institutional independence and technical knowledge; they are not usually selected for their expertise in a particular law, or, where they are, it is usually because the 'law' which the parties wish to have applied is not that of a state. The proposition that parties who agreed to arbitrate in London if things went wrong actually chose English law to govern their substantive contractual rights and duties is wholly unconvincing.

(c) Split, deferred, and altered choices of law

Although it allowed the parties to choose the law to govern their contract, the common law was very reluctant to permit two laws to be chosen to govern different parts of it, no doubt to avoid the risk of incoherence which might arise from allowing it. And it flatly denied the legal validity of an agreement to defer choosing the law until after the making of the contract:[91] such a choice of law was said to be 'floating', but, floating or not, the common law sank it. This was justified on doctrinal and on pragmatic grounds: the former reasoning that a contract, as a source of legally binding obligation, must have a law to make it binding from the very beginning; the latter, on the basis that conscientious parties intending to perform their contractual duties must have a point of reference to work out or check what those duties are. But there appeared to be nothing, in principle at least, to stop the parties changing the

---

[91] *Armar Shipping Co Ltd v Caisse Algérienne d'Assurance* [1981] 1 WLR 207 (CA).

proper law: if it was open to them to vary the contract, it must also have been possible for them to amend their choice of law as well.[92]

The position under the Regulation is simpler and more complex. Proceeding from the view that the parties are permitted to exercise freedom of choice, it is provided that they may agree to have separate parts of the contract governed by different laws.[93] They may also agree at any time to alter the governing law.[94] It is implicit, perhaps even explicit, that because such a variation is permitted and validated by the Regulation itself, this will override any contrary indication from the law originally chosen to govern and which, therefore, cannot be 'locked in'.[95] It appears to follow that the parties cannot fetter their right to change the governing law: if the parties agree today to alter the governing law for a contract made some time ago, there is no reason to impugn their exercise of choice. Where by contrast they do not act together in this way, and one of them acts pursuant to a power conferred by the contract to nominate a replacement law to govern the contract, the nomination must obviously comply with the conditions laid down in the contract itself.

It is not clear from the Regulation whether the parties may choose not to have a law at the outset. Logic may appear to suggest a negative answer, for a contract without a law makes no more sense under the Regulation than it did under the common law;[96] but if in default of choice made by the parties the governing law is initially supplied by Article 4, there will be no problem: if they agree at a later date to change the original law, they may;[97] and if they cannot agree to do that, the contract will remain governed by whatever Article 4 provided as governing law. All problems are thus solved or avoided.

(d) Choice of law made outside a contract

Although the point has not yet arisen directly, there appears to be no reason why a choice of law needs to be expressed in, or recorded as, one of the terms of the contract. It ought to be possible to show that parties agreed upon the law which would govern any contract which might result from their

---

[92] *Whitworth Street Estates (Manchester) Ltd v James Miller & Partners Ltd* [1970] AC 583.
[93] Article 3(1).
[94] Article 3(2); *Mauritius Commercial Bnak Ltd v Hestia Holdings Ltd* [2013] EWHC 1328 (Comm).
[95] A 'no variation' term in the contract would not, therefore, prevent variation of the governing law, as the authority to make the variation is contained in a higher law than the contract itself.
[96] *Amin Rasheed Shipping Corpn v Kuwait Insurance Co* [1984] AC 50.
[97] Regardless of whether the original law was chosen by them: Article 3(2).

negotiations, in just the same way as, as we shall see, they may choose the law to govern the obligations arising from the negotiations themselves. If the parties are permitted to agree after a contract is made to alter the law which governs it, it ought to be possible to show that the parties agreed in advance of concluding the contract that a particular law would govern it. After all, Article 3 does not require the choice of law to be expressed in the contract.

(e) The meaning of 'law'

According to the Regulation, 'law' indicates the domestic law of a country.[98] This has a number of consequences. First, certain choices which the parties may have wished to make are not available, and if made will be ignored. The Regulation excludes the possibility of choosing the *lex mercatoria*, as well as the rules or principles, whether or not regarded by their adherents as law, of a religion or cult. The parties may have what they conceive to be sound personal or business reasons for wishing their contractual obligations to be governed by Jewish 'law',[99] or sharia 'law',[100] or the *lex mercatoria*, or whatever else, but even if this is the choice which they express, a court has no power to give effect to it. If the parties want adjudication in accordance with such ideas they are free,[101] but also need, to provide for arbitration before a tribunal of their designation which may be directed to give them what they want. Quite apart from the fact that the courts are not likely to be equipped to deal with the proof and reliable application of material of this kind if it were chosen, it is hard to see how the admission of non-state 'law' would work in the context of Article 4. Take for example a contract made in England between two members of the same religious group, in circumstances in which both were keen to comply with its teachings in relation to business, ethics, and finance. The contract may be closely connected to England, as the country in which they reside, and to the system of religious values to which they adhere. Given that the contract could not be governed by both 'laws', which of these would govern it? Could the contract be said to have a closer connection to the one than to the other? The awkwardness of the question, and the impossibility of answering it, means that the Regulation has to exclude the possibility of

---

[98] The provision in Article 23 which would have allowed the parties to choose a set of rules made by the Community as an 'optional instrument' was excluded from the Regulation as retained.

[99] *Halpern v Halpern* [2007] EWCA Civ 291, [2007] 2 Lloyd's Rep 56.

[100] *Beximco Pharmaceuticals Ltd v Shamil Bank of Bahrain EC* [2004] EWCA Civ 19, [2004] 1 WLR 1784.

[101] *Jivraj v Hashwani* [2011] UKSC 40, [2011] 1 WLR 1872.

a non-state law governing the contract, while leaving the parties free, if they wish, to incorporate the principles (assuming these to be sufficiently clear to serve as terms) of a non-state body of rules as terms of the contract.[102] It is not a bad solution; all others would be far worse.

In this context, law means domestic law: the possibility of *renvoi* to the law of another country is precluded by Article 20. The justification lies in the pragmatic argument that if the parties went to the trouble of choosing a law, it would be unlikely, to the point of perversity, for them to have chosen anything other than the rules of domestic law; and if they were so perverse as to choose anything else the law is not bound to indulge them. One might question the wisdom of excluding *renvoi* in the case where the parties have not chosen a law but have chosen the court for adjudication. Common law orthodoxy would consider this a pretty clear indicator of choice for the domestic law of the court chosen. This looks odd, for what it more clearly is is an inevitable choice for whatever law the court at the place of trial would itself have applied. But this pattern of reasoning is apparently precluded by Article 20.

3. *LEX CONTRACTUS*: NOT CHOSEN BY THE PARTIES

Leaving aside for the moment the four categories of contract for which particular provision is made, and which are considered below, Article 4 provides the rules by which the court will identify the governing law where this has not been chosen by the parties in accordance with Article 3. By contrast with its predecessor in the Rome Convention, which had operated on the basis that the governing law was that of the country with which the contract was most closely connected, Article 4 of the Regulation provides a more detailed scheme which identifies the governing law by reference, in the first instance, to types of contract. This is designed to make the identification of the governing law more predictable than it would have been under the Rome Convention and, though the solution is not perfect, it is really rather sensible.

The default rules are set out in Article 4(1). The contracts to which it applies are listed by type; insofar as it is helpful to explain the principle by which these cases are dealt with, it appears to be that the person whose performance

---

[102] *Halpern v Halpern* [2007] EWCA Civ 291, [2007] 2 Lloyd's Rep 56. But there is nothing to prevent a choice of the law of a country which has chosen to incorporate into it the principles of a non-state system, whether secular, conventional, or superstitious.

under the contract will name or identify the contract is the person whose country of habitual residence identifies the governing law.[103] So for example, contracts for the sale of goods,[104] contracts for the provision of services, franchise contracts, and distribution contracts[105] will be governed by the law of the country in which the seller, supplier, franchisee, and distributor has his habitual residence, these being the parties who perform for payment by another: the problems arising from the fact that these categories appear to overlap is dealt with below. For contracts concerning land, the *lex situs* will apply. So a contract relating to a right *in rem* in land, or a tenancy of land, is governed by the law of the country in which the land is situated, though, by way of exception, a short private letting taken by a tenant who is a natural person is governed by the law of the country in which landlord and tenant have their habitual residence; if this condition is not met, the earlier rule applies.

A partial definition of habitual residence, which therefore plays a significant part in the identification of the governing law, is provided by Article 19. The starting point is that habitual residence is assessed on the date on which the contract was concluded. For a natural person not acting in the course of business, no further definition is given. For a natural person acting in the course of his business activity, it means his principal place of business; for a company or other body, it is the place of central administration; and where the contract is concluded in the course of operation of a branch or agency (or if, under the contract, performance is the responsibility of a branch or agency), it means the place where the branch or agency is located.

Where the contract is more complex, in the sense that it would fall within two of the categories in Article 4(1), such as a contract for the supply and installation of goods, or where it falls within none of these rules, such as with a contract of barter, or a licensing agreement, Article 4(2) provides that it will be governed by law of the country in which the person whose performance is characteristic of the contract is habitually resident. Even so, if the contract falls into two of the listed categories but in each case the answer is the same, there will be no problem; where this is not so, the identification of a performance as characteristic of the contract in its entirety may be challenging.

---

[103] It may be argued that the contract is (in English at least) named after, or designated by, the party whose performance is stated in Art 4(1).

[104] But where the sale is by auction, the governing law will be the law of the place of the auction if this is capable of being determined.

[105] For discussion of these in a jurisdictional context, see Case C–9/12 *Corman-Collins SA v La Maison du Whisky SA* EU:C:2013:860, [2014] QB 431.

Article 4 then makes two further provisions. It provides a default clause for where Articles 4(1) and 4(2) have failed to identify a governing law, and an escape clause for when they have but the answer which they give does not feel right. As to the former case, where Articles 4(1) and 4(2) have failed to point to a governing law, Article 4(4) provides that the contract shall be governed by the law of the country (not, if this is different, law) with which it is most closely connected.[106] As to the latter case, if Article 4(1) or 4(2), as the case may be, has pointed to a governing law, but the contract is manifestly more closely connected to another country, Article 4(3) provides that the law of that other country shall apply as the governing law. Although these two provisions serve quite distinct functions, they have a common thread.

The framework within which the governing law is identified in the absence of a choice by the parties is firmly based on the identification of connections and points of contact to *countries*, rather than on connections to *laws*: once the connection to a country has been ascertained, the domestic law of that country applies to govern the contract.[107] This may mean that although a contract might be seen to be most closely connected to English *law*, it may still be more closely connected to another *country*, and it will be the latter which identifies the governing law. However, in relation to these two clauses, point 21 of the Recitals to the Regulation tells the court that it may properly examine whether the contract has a close relationship with another contract, the law of which may exercise a gravitational pull.[108] So in a situation in which there are connected contracts, such as a bill of lading and contracts made in accordance with it,[109] or letters of credit or of comfort, issued as part of a larger financial transaction,[110] or contracts of reinsurance made back-to-back with contracts of insurance,[111] in which an express choice of law is made in some but not all contracts, common sense would say that all were probably

---

[106] Case C–133/08 *Intercontainer Interfrigo SC v Balkenende Oosthuizen BV* [2009] ECR I–9687; Case C–305/13 *Haeger & Schmidt GmbH v Mutuelles de Mans assurances IARD SA* EU:C:2014:2320, [2015] QB 319.

[107] *Crédit Lyonnais v New Hampshire Insurance Co* [1997] 2 Lloyd's Rep 1 (CA). The fact that the parties 'would have chosen' a different law if they had made a choice, which they did not, should not trigger the application of Art 4(3): *Lawlor v Sandvik Mining and Construction Mobile Crushers and Screens Ltd* [2013] EWCA Civ 365, [2013] 2 Lloyd's Rep 98 (a case on the Rome Convention).

[108] Point 20 of the Recitals; *British Arab Commercial Bank plc v Bank of Communications* [2011] EWHC 281 (Comm), [2011] 1 Lloyd's Rep 664.

[109] *The Mahkutai* [1996] AC 650 (PC).

[110] *Bank of Baroda v Vysya Bank Ltd* [1994] 2 Lloyd's Rep 87.

[111] cf *Forsikringsaktieselskapet Vesta v Butcher* [1989] AC 852, where the contracts were governed by different laws.

intended to be governed by the same law, to prevent the dislocation which would otherwise be risked. The statement in the Recitals now provides some justification for a court which wishes to follow that line of reasoning.[112]

The 'escape clause' in Article 4(3) is seen by some as liable to undermine the systematic predictability of Article 4(1). The general question is what is meant by the contract's being, in all the circumstances of the case, 'manifestly more closely connected' to another country. In a case dealing with the predecessor rule in the Rome Convention, the European Court,[113] in apparent rejection of a more stringent view found in Dutch[114] and Scottish[115] case law, stated that the escape clause would apply when there was good reason for it to apply,[116] and that a finding that another country was more closely connected to the contract was all that was required. No doubt this decision will, in the interests of legal certainty, continue to be taken seriously, though as Article 4(3) now includes the word 'manifestly', and as the rules in Article 4(1) and 4(2) of the Regulation which are to be escaped from are formulated in rather more detail than was the case before, the escape clause may be expected to be available only rarely.

At common law it was occasionally said that a presumption of validity meant that where the issues were finely balanced a contract should be governed by a law under which it would be valid.[117] The legitimacy of such a presumption was always debatable, but it could perhaps be defended as reflecting the presumed intention of the parties. It does not appear that there is room to accommodate it within Article 4 of the Regulation.

4. *LEX CONTRACTUS: LEX SPECIALIS* FOR CERTAIN CONTRACTS

There are four kinds of contract for which the identification of the governing law is not left to the general rules in Articles 3 and 4. For these particular

---

[112] Cf Case C–305/13 *Haeger & Schmidt GmbH v Mutuelles de Mans assurances IARD* SA EU:C:2014:2320, [2015] QB 319.

[113] Case C–133/08 *Intercontainer Interfrigo SC v Balkenende Oosthuizen BV* [2009] ECR I–9687.

[114] *Soc Nouvelle des Papéteries de l'Aa v BV Machinefabriek BOA* (25 September 1992).

[115] *Caledonia Subsea Ltd v Microperi Srl* 2003 SC 70.

[116] Which actually came close to saying nothing at all: see *Samcrete Egypt Engineers and Contractors SAE v Land Rover Exports Ltd* [2001] EWCA Civ 2019, [2002] CLC 533; *Ennstone Building Products Ltd v Stanger Ltd* [2002] EWCA Civ 916, [2002] 1 WLR 3059.

[117] For example, *Coast Lines Ltd v Hudig and Veder Chartering NV* [1972] 2 QB 34 (CA) 44, 48.

contracts, the point of departure is that an express choice of law by the parties will be effective in all cases,[118] though the operation of the law chosen may, in some respects and more than is otherwise the case, be overlaid by provisions from the law which would have been applicable to the contract if the law had not been chosen. Where the parties have not chosen the law, the governing law may be identified by provisions which are more intricate than those contained in Article 4. Given the intricacy of the law, only an outline can be provided here.

(a) Contracts for carriage

Article 5 makes modifications to the general rules for the identification of the governing law in a contract of carriage. If the contract is one for the carriage of goods, the parties are free to choose any law to govern their contract, but if they do not exercise that freedom, a carrier-oriented rule applies.[119] So far as choice by the parties is concerned, if the contract is one for the carriage of passengers, the range of laws which may be chosen is limited to five: the country of the habitual residence of passenger or of carrier, the country in which the carrier has his or its central administration, or the countries of the place of departure and of destination.[120] No doubt the purpose of this limitation is to prevent the selection of the law of a country which allows carriers to evade their responsibilities. If no such choice of law is made, the law of the country of the passenger's habitual residence will apply if either the place of departure or of destination was in that country; if that is not so, the country where the carrier has its habitual residence will apply. If the contract is manifestly more closely connected to another country, the law of that other country shall apply.

It is obvious that there may be contracts which do not fit tidily into this framework, such as contracts which contain multiple obligations, such as a cruise-and-hotel package,[121] or a contract for carriage by sea and rail. It seems that such cases will be approached as though each element in the contractual package is discrete for the purposes of finding the applicable law, at least if they can be regarded as independent obligations;[122] if they are not

---

[118] Save for certain prohibited choices in the context of contracts for the case of carriage of passengers and certain contracts of insurance, considered below.

[119] Article 5(1); Case C–305/13 *Haeger & Schmidt GmbH v Mutuelles de Mans assurances IARD SA* EU:C:2014:2320, [2015] QB 319.

[120] Article 5(2). In addition, a significant amount of legislation regulating carriage of passengers by air, package travel, etc was made by the European Union.

[121] cf Article 6(4)(b).

[122] cf Case C–133/08 *Intercontainer Interfrigo SC v Balkenende Oosthuizen BV* [2009] ECR I–9687.

independent, then in principle the law which governs the contract of carriage will govern the whole of the contract. But it would be wrong to be too clear or confident as to how this will actually work in practice.

(b) Contracts made by consumers

Article 6 makes modifications to the general rules for the identification of the governing law in certain consumer contracts. It is probably fair to say that the wording of Article 6 is as untidy and problematic as it is because it was a negotiated compromise between views and interest groups which were sharply polarized. Although it is expressed in slightly grudging terms, the parties are free to choose any law to govern their contract even though it is a consumer contract within the scope of Article 6. The legal protection for the consumer, which is at risk if the parties—which of course means the professional—choose the law to govern the contract and which is considered to be appropriate, is secured by other means.

The first task is to define the contracts which fall within Article 6. The definition is inclusive and exclusive. It includes a contract concluded between a natural person for a purpose outside her trade or profession with another person who is acting within his or its trade or profession; and the parties to such a contract are designated as consumer and professional respectively.[123] It is obvious that cases in which the customer makes the contract for more purposes than one will be problematic: for the purposes of jurisdiction under the (former) Brussels I Regulation such contracts did not confer jurisdictional advantage on the consumer unless the non-consumer element of the contract was negligible; however, the European Court may have more recently moved away from this narrow view towards a test of predominant purpose,[124] which would be better suited for use in the context of the Rome I Regulation. However that may be, Article 6(4) then excludes from the scope of Article 6 contracts of carriage[125] and contracts of insurance, for which special rules are provided elsewhere.[126] Also excluded are a contract for sale or rent of land other than a timeshare-use contract, as well as a contract for the supply of services to a consumer exclusively in a country other than that in which he has his habitual residence.

---

[123] Case C–110/14 *Costea v SC Volksbank România SA* EU:C:2015:538, [2016] 1 WLR 814.
[124] Case C–498/16 *Schrems v Facebook Ireland Ltd* EU:C:2018:37, [2018] ILPr 147.
[125] Other than a package holiday: Art 6(4)(b). Certain financial contracts are also excluded: Art 6(4)(d) and (e).
[126] This exclusion is explained in point 32 of the Recitals.

Assuming the contract is still within the scope of Article 6, the next question is whether the professional pursues his commercial or professional activities in the country of the consumer's habitual residence, or if he by any means—which will increasingly include electronic means—directs his activities to that country or to several countries including that country. If the professional does so direct his activities, and if the contract falls within the scope of such activities, then unless a law has been chosen to govern it, the contract will be governed by the law of the country in which the consumer has her habitual residence. Indeed, if a law has been chosen by the parties to govern such a contract, that choice may not deprive the consumer of legal protection which would have been afforded to her by the law which would have applied if there had been no such choice: for this to be so, the protective rule in question must be one which may not be derogated from by agreement, or contracted out of, as one might say.[127] If the professional does not so direct his activities, the applicable law is determined in accordance with Articles 3 and 4.

It is necessary to say something more about this plausible, but actually rather troublesome, notion of 'targeting' or 'directing' professional activities into the country of the consumer's habitual residence as this is elaborated in points 24 and 25 of the Recitals.[128] First, for these provisions to apply, the contract must be concluded within the framework of the targeting. This appears to mean that there must be a connection of some sort between, rather than a bare geographical coincidence of, the targeting and contracting, though it is evidently not a 'cause-and-effect' requirement that the consumer respond specifically to identified targeting.[129] Second, the simple accessibility of an internet site will not by itself establish that there has been targeting of the person who connects with it, but if the internet site solicits the conclusion of distance contracts, that will be different. It has also been said that the language used on a website, or currency referred to, is not to be taken as a relevant factor, but this must be open to question. It is very hard to see how an internet site which is readable in Finnish or Hungarian is not targeted at consumers from those countries: who else could even hazard a guess

---

[127] Consumer Rights Act 2015 contains the principal provisions of English law.

[128] See also Joined Cases C–585/08 *Pammer v Reederei Karl Schluter GmbH & Co KG* and C–144/09 *Hotel Alpenhof GmbH v Heller* [2010] ECR I–12527 on the former Brussels I Regulation.

[129] The position remains unstable, on account of the slight divergence between the former Brussels I Regulation and the Rome I Regulation: see Case C–190/11 *Mühlleitner v Yusufi* EU:C:2012:542, [2012] ILPr 571; Case C–218/12 *Emrek v Sabranovic* EU:C:2014:666, [2014] ILPr 571; Case C–297/14 *Hobohm v Benedikt Kampik Ltd & Co* EU:C:2015:844, [2016] QB 616.

at what the words actually mean? If a website has a page in Portuguese, to whom, apart from Portuguese residents, can it credibly be said to be directed at? Is it really aimed generally at the world at large, just in case any of them has Portuguese as a working language? One may understand that a website in French or German might be seen to speak to consumers in several countries but none in particular, or if in English, to practically the whole world, but to exclude language and currency from the list of factors which are material to the question whether the professional has targeted consumers in a particular country is misguided. One does not need to be much of a sleuth to suspect that special interest groups ganged up and got their way by predicting the death of the internet unless the scope of the pro-consumer rule were cut back as far as possible.

(c) Contracts of insurance

Article 7 makes modifications to the general rules for the identification of the governing law for certain insurance contracts. They do not apply to reinsurance, to which the ordinary rules of the Regulation apply.[130]

For insurance, a primary distinction is drawn between insurance of large risks other than life insurance, and the rest. In the case of such large risks, no matter where the risk is situated,[131] the law governing such insurance may be chosen in line with Article 3; in default of such choice it will be governed by the law of the insurer's habitual residence.[132] In the case of insurance of non-large risks, if the risk is not situated in a Member State, the rules for choice of law are those of Articles 3 and 4; but if the risk is situated in a Member State, an express choice of law may be made from a restricted list, the broad justification for which is to protect the policyholder from outlandish choices of law, and in default of such choice, the governing law shall be the law of the Member State in which the risk is situated at the time of the conclusion of the contract.

(d) Individual employment contracts

Article 8 makes modifications to the general rules for the identification of the governing law for individual contracts of employment.

The question of how to identify a contract as of employment, as distinct from some other relationship according to which work is done for the benefit

---

[130] Article 7(1).
[131] The location of the risk is dealt with in Art 7(6).
[132] Article 7(2).

of another, or provided to a third party, can be a problem. In the case of senior individuals with management responsibilities, in particular, it evidently depends on demonstrating a sufficient degree of 'subordination', though as employees are usually encouraged to show initiative and take responsibility, this can be a rather imprecise tool.[133] More generally, 'the essential feature of an employment relationship, however, is that for a certain period of time a person performs services for and under the direction of another person in return for which he receives remuneration'.[134] However, as new forms of labour exploitation, conveniently described as 'fake self-employment', are imposed on those whose institutional vulnerability is even greater than that of the typical employee, there is work to be done in policing the limits of provisions such as Article 8. Whether any such thing will take place in English law, outside the EU, remains to be seen.

A choice of law by the parties—which really means the employer—which conforms to Article 3 is effective, but the choice of law may not deprive the employee of legal protection which would have been afforded to him by the law which would have applied if there had been no such choice. For this provision to apply, the protective rule in question must be one which may not be contracted out of.[135] If the law which is to govern the contract has not been chosen by the parties, the contract will be governed by the law of the country in which (or failing that, from which) the employee habitually carries out his work in performance of the contract;[136] if no such single country can be determined, it will be governed by the law of the country in which is situated the place of business which engaged him,[137] unless (in any case) the contract appears to be more closely connected to another country in which case the law of that country shall apply.[138] The interpretation of Article 8 will be aligned as far as possible with that of the corresponding jurisprudence of the Brussels I Regulation.

---

[133] See for example Case C–47/14 *Holterman Ferho Exploitatie BV v Büllesheim* EU:C:2015:574, [2016] ICR 90; Case C–603/17 *Bosworth v Arcadia Petroleum Ltd* EU:C:2019:310.

[134] Case 66/85 *Lawrie-Blum v Land Baden-Württemberg* [1986] ECR 2121.

[135] Article 8(1).

[136] Article 8(2) For cross-border cases, and the recourse to a centre-of-gravity approach, see Case C–29/10 *Koelzsch v Luxembourg* [2011] ECR I–1595; Case C–64/12 *Scheckler v Boedeker* EU:C:2013:551, [2014] QB 320; Case C–168/16 *Nogueira v Crewlink Ireland Ltd* EU:C:2017:688, [2018] ICR 344.

[137] Article 8(3). See Case C–384/10 *Voogsgeerd v Navimer* [2011] ECR I–13275;

[138] For cases in which the duties are carried on outside the territorial jurisdiction of any state (such as on an oil rig) see [1980] OJ C282/1, 26.

5. ISSUES TO WHICH THE *LEX CONTRACTUS* IS APPLIED

Having dealt with the question how it is to be identified, it is now necessary to examine the issues to which the governing law, identified by Articles 3 to 8, will be applied. When we have done so, we will mention again the treatment of some core contractual issues to which the law that governs the contract may not apply.

Subject to the reservations which we have mentioned above, Article 12 of the Regulation lists five items 'in particular' to which the governing law is to be applied. These are: the interpretation of the contract; the performance of the contract; the consequences of a partial or total breach of obligations, including the assessment of damages so far as this is governed by rules of law; the various ways of extinguishing obligations, including limitation and prescription; and the consequences of nullity of the contract. The fact that the list in Article 12 is introduced by the expression 'in particular' means that it is not exhaustive. After we have considered those five listed items we will be in a position to examine other issues in which laws other than the governing law may play a part.

(a) Interpretation

So far as interpretation is concerned, it is obvious that the meaning of the contract, and of its terms, must be referred to the governing law. In addition to the interpretation of the express terms, the question whether terms may be (and if so, on what conditions) implied or otherwise read or written into the contract will be answered by the governing law. The principle is clear, but the implementation of it may be more tricky. A court, called upon to interpret the contract, may need to address some fundamental questions: whether questions which need to be asked and answered are framed subjectively or objectively; whether it may imply terms which contradict express terms; whether it should read the terms of a contract literally, or in a way which makes the most 'business sense', or in any other way; whether oral or other evidence may be permitted to modify or override the apparent meaning of the terms of a written contract, and so forth. The system of law which governs the contract may have its own answers to questions of this type, but as evidence and procedure is governed by the *lex fori*,[139] there is a preliminary, question-framing,

---

[139] Article 1(3) excludes it from the scope of the Regulation; the application of the *lex fori* is the result of doing so.

decision to be taken. In principle the court should probably apply the rules of the governing law to the extent possible, but if it considers that the issue before it is within the autonomous definition of 'procedure', it is not required to apply the relevant provision of the governing law but should apply its own. That may mean that an English court will feel free to exclude, in accordance with English domestic law, certain kinds of evidence, such as superseded drafts of the contract, even though the governing law would not do so; but the sense that it goes against the overriding principle of uniformity of interpretation, which applied to the Regulation as an instrument of European law, is palpable. After Exit Day, such considerations will be less persuasive.

The correction or rectification of a contract must surely be considered to be an aspect of the interpretation of the contract. If it were to be suggested that there is a difference between the interpretation of what the contract says, and the alteration of what the contract says, the sensible response is that these are all part of the single and indivisible task of interpreting the agreement which the parties actually made.

(b)   Performance

The question when a party must perform, the order in which the parties must perform, the time and manner and place of performance, and so forth, are all defined by the governing law. What counts, and does not count, as performance of the contract is determined by the governing law. The question whether time is of the essence, whether the duties must be performed personally or may be delegated, and so on, are all issues for the governing law to answer if the terms of the contract have not already done so. Whether a party must act in a particular way to perform, or need only make reasonable endeavours to bring about a particular result, or may 'substantially' perform while leaving a few details undone, or must make a substitute act if the primary duty cannot be performed (such as delivering so much of the crop as was not destroyed by the drought, or delivering to an alternative place, for example), and so forth, are all questions for the governing law to answer.

The question whether performance is required despite, or is affected or is untouched by, illegality is in principle a matter for the governing law. This will be true for illegality arising under a rule of the governing law itself as well as when the illegality arises under a foreign law in a way which has an impact on the performance of the contract. It will be for the governing law to determine the effect, if any, of that foreign-arising illegality on the duty to perform. However, on this issue the answer given by the governing law may sometimes be supplemented or overridden by other laws; the point is considered below.[140]

(c) The consequences of a total or a partial breach

Whether conduct counts as performance or a breach is a matter for the governing law; and if it is a breach, the consequences are also referred to the governing law. So for example, the question whether the innocent party may terminate the contract, or may rescind the contract and treat it as void, or may refuse to release the other party from the duty to perform what he had promised to do, will be referred to and answered by the governing law. So also will be the consequences of breach which are more usually thought of as remedies: the rules which govern the availability of damages, and the rules which form the basis for their assessment, will be taken from the governing law, though the duty of the court is to reach its own decision on the basis of those principles, rather than to seek to impersonate the foreign judge in the application of them to the facts of the case.[141] In other words, the rules which govern the assessment of damages will be taken from the governing law, but the arithmetical computation of the result to which they lead will still be a procedural exercise, done by the court itself. Evidence should not therefore be given of the sum which a foreign court would award, just of the rules and principles by which the foreign law would determine what the court is required to do.

If the governing law would award damages for breach, but would not order performance in specific or substituted form, an English court should probably refrain from offering its own, different, remedy for breach of contract. If the *lex contractus* would not provide for or permit an injunction to restrain conduct said to amount to a breach, it is at least arguable that an English court should refrain from ordering the injunction which English law would otherwise have permitted, on the basis that if the parties make a contract governed by a particular law, they probably expect the enforcement of that contract to reflect, in some sense at least, what that law would have provided.[142] However, if the exclusion of procedure is read up, not down, the question whether to grant relief of this kind, which is indissociable from questions governing its control and supervision, will be left to the law of the forum.

---

[140] See p 239.
[141] *Vizcaya Partners Ltd v Picard* [2016] UKPC 5, [2016] 1 All ER (Comm) 891; *Deutsche Bank AG v Comune di Savona* [2018] EWCA Civ 1740, *BNP Paribas SA v Trattamento Rifiuti Metropolitani SpA* [2019] EWCA Civ 768.
[142] *OJSC TNK-BP Holding v Lazurenko* [2012] EWHC 2781 (Ch).

(d) The extinguishing of obligations, including limitation and prescription

To the extent that breach had not been dealt with as an aspect of performance, it would fall within this heading instead. The ending of obligations—the
when, the why, and how of it—is determined by reference to the governing
law. So points which in domestic law would be seen to fall under the law of
frustration, force majeure, the effect of supervening illegality, and termination on account of breach, are governed by the *lex contractus*, as is the question of how long it takes for the innocent party to lose by inaction the right to
bring proceedings in respect of an obligation which has not been performed.

An obligation may also be extinguished by the rescission, or setting aside,
or avoiding of the contract or of a term within it. In all such cases the contract
may be considered as voidable, which is to say, valid and binding unless and
until something is done to alter that. It is obvious that in such cases, if the
governing law provides that a party who has been the victim of one of these
vitiating factors may rescind, annul, avoid the contract, this will extinguish
the obligation in a very fundamental way. The question whether the victim
has any recourse when the governing law denies the availability of such relief
is considered below; there may be cases in which a party who was unaware
that the governing law gave him no right to rescind a contract which had
been performed, for example, is able to satisfy the court that he should not be
left without relief. A question of similar type arises when the governing law
would refuse the innocent party the possibility of rescinding the contract by
pointing to a contract term or disclaimer by which it was agreed that the innocent party had not relied on anything said, expressly or otherwise, by the
other party.

(e) The consequences of nullity of the contract

If a supposed contract was a nullity, or if a voidable contract has been rescinded, the consequences are referred to the governing law. The extent of the
duty to make restitution, or to make other payment, or to return (from the
perspective of the other party, accept the return of) property which changed
hands is all for the governing law to determine. It may be argued that where
a supposed contract was a nullity from the beginning, because of a truly fundamental mistake or something of that kind, the consequences cannot be
contractual at all. However, the two immediate answers to that are that the
Rome I Regulation provides that they are contractual by providing the conflicts rule for them;[143] and that even if it did not, and one were to look to the

---

[143] Cf Case C–366/13 *Profit Investment Sim SpA v Ossi* EU:C:2016:282, [2016] 1 WLR 3832.

Rome II Regulation instead—there being nowhere else to look—the instruction which its Article 12 would give is to look to the law of the contract or supposed contract from which the enrichment derives.

(f) Other issues for the governing law to deal with

In addition to the matters listed in Article 12, the governing law will also determine the location and nature of the burden of proof and the operation of any presumptions.[144] In relation to formal validity, compliance with the governing law is sufficient; otherwise compliance with the law or laws of the place where the parties were when they made the contract will also suffice.[145]

In addition to these issues for which the Regulation makes an express reference to the governing law, it seems to follow that particular questions which the common law would regard as quintessentially contractual must be referred to the governing law. For example, whether there was a need for consideration (and if there was, whether there was consideration) for a promise must be referred to the governing law. The question whether a non-party can enforce the promises of the contract, in spite of not being privy to it, must be answered by the governing law, along with the question whether a non-party can be bound by the obligations of a contract to which he was not privy but of which, for example, he was well aware and which he realizes he may impair if he acts in a particular way. The question whether parties are jointly, or severally, liable is for the governing law, as is the question whether performance by one party discharges the obligation of another.

The question whether liability can be restricted or excluded by a term or notice is, at least at first sight, a matter for the governing law. However, in the case of contracts made by consumers which fall within Article 6, if the governing law allows the exclusion, Article 6 may allow another law to override it in order to secure the protection of the consumer; and outside that context, the law of the forum may superimpose its own view of the matter.[146]

(g) Formation disputes: not exclusively for the governing law

Subject to the fact that the formal validity of a contract is, by Article 11, assessed by a rule of alternative validating reference, the governing law will, in general, determine whether the contract is valid. But the concept of 'validity' covers a range of possible objections, ranging from breakdowns in formation

---

[144] Article 18.
[145] Article 11.
[146] See below, p 238.

to the effect of a change in the law making performance illegal; and disputes about contractual validity are sometimes difficult to deal with.

The point of departure is that the contention that there was, or that there is now, no binding contract by which the parties are bound is one which will be resolved by the law which would govern the contract if it were taken or found to be valid. So for example, if X enters into negotiations with Y, and at the point where these terminate, X's law would say that no contract had been concluded, while Y's law would say that a contract had been, the prevailing view is that one should ask what law would govern the supposed contract if there really were one, and to use this law to go back and determine whether the parties had reached contractual agreement. This, at any rate, is the effect of Articles 3(5) and 10(1) of the Regulation,[147] and it is (the point being made just for curiosity's sake) broadly in line with what some took to be the solution given by the common law. When reference is made to the 'putative' governing law, or the governing law of the putative contract, they are references to this 'law'.

It does not take much to see that the methodology involved in this approach is open to serious objection. If we suppose that Y will be contending that there was a valid and binding contract, while X says that there never was any such thing, it is hard to explain why a court should proceed by assuming, conditionally but still with significant effect, that Y's submission is correct and that the decision should be taken on the basis of the law which would have governed the contract if it were, as Y says it is, valid; the idea that a judge should begin the process of adjudication by taking sides is not one which appeals to the rational mind.[148] The reverse proposition, which respects another, equal, aspect of the autonomy of parties, namely the right to walk away from negotiations which have not reached agreement, appears equally convincing.

But alternative solutions are not attractive, either. One possibility might have been to characterize the facts to see whether they disclose, or have the feel of, an issue falling within a broad understanding of what counts as a contract; but this is liable to degenerate into little more than a judicial sniff test; and on these facts, never mind any more commercially complex ones, that

---

[147] Which also provides that whether a particular term is valid is determined by the law which would govern it on the footing that it was valid: a proposition which is particularly challenging where each party has proposed a contract term, including a choice of law, which contradicts that of the opposite party.

[148] For common law judicial confirmation of this point of view, see *Trina Solar Australia Pty Ltd v Jasmin Solar Pty Ltd* [2017] FCAFC 6, (2017) 247 FCR 1.

is not good enough. Another might have been to apply the *lex fori* to decide whether there is a contract and, if there is, to use the proper law which it must necessarily[149] have to decide whether there was a valid contract. That would mean that if according to the *lex fori* there is no contract, that would be an end of it: but why should the *lex fori*, which might have no real connection to either party, have even that much of a role?

The Regulation adopts a more satisfying, targeted, solution. It refers the issue to the governing law, but with a saving provision made for parties whose own domestic law would have told or reassured them that they had not consented and were therefore not bound and were therefore free from contractual obligation.[150] Article 10(2) qualifies the approach in Article 10(1) by allowing the party who contends that he (it appears to be worded as a concession extended to individuals which is not extended to companies) should not be bound to rely on the law of his habitual residence 'to establish that he did not consent' if it would be unreasonable to apply the governing law, and it alone, to the question.[151] But if he has dealt by reference to the foreign law before, or maybe simply because he was prepared to make an international contract, he may be found to have taken a known risk, and to have forfeited a protection which was designed for the innocent abroad.[152]

It is apparent that, by contrast with all the possible rules of single reference, the rule of dual reference in Article 10 has a lot to be said for it. It is, after all, quite hard to come up with a set of facts for which it will produce a result which is plainly unsatisfactory: in this context, that is saying something. And leaving aside the case of the novice, for whom Article 10(2) is sufficient, perhaps there is something in the idea that if the parties have engaged with each other and have come so close to the point where one arguably closely connected law would say they had made a contract, they have only themselves to blame if that law holds that they did so and the court accepts its answer. After all, if issues of obligation arising from pre-contractual fault can be referred to the law which would have governed the contract if one had been concluded, as Article 12 of the Rome II Regulation says, it is not surprising that that same law is used to determine, in principle, whether the parties did conclude a contractual obligation in the first place.

---

[149] *Amin Rasheed Shipping Corpn v Kuwait Insurance Co* [1984] AC 50.
[150] Foreshadowed by Jaffey (1975) 24 ICLQ 603.
[151] It is unclear whether this reference to habitual residence excludes parties who are not natural persons, for whom the corresponding point of reference is the place of business.
[152] cf *Egon Oldendorff v Libera Corpn* [1995] 2 Lloyd's Rep 64.

The question of which issues, or objections, are liable to be brought under the protective umbrella of Article 10 is not completely clear. The most obvious is where a party argues that he is not bound and cannot be liable because there was no binding *offer and acceptance*. This plea is a matter for the governing law, for it goes to the validity of the contract; but an individual may in a proper case rely on his own law to demonstrate that he did not consent, by reference to Article 10(2). So for example, if he discards a letter making an offer, he may rely on Article 10(2) in circumstances in which the governing law would have considered him to be bound.[153] If he argues that there was no *intention to create legal relations*, the effect of this plea will primarily be a matter for the governing law. But if he formulates the argument to say he did not consent to, nor had any reason to suppose that he was, entering into legal relations at all, because under his own law such an agreement would not be legally enforceable, Article 10(2) may avail him.

More difficult is the case in which the individual party argues that the alleged contract cannot be enforced because the price was never agreed, and there was therefore no sufficient *certainty of contractual terms*. It is not impossible, but it is hard, to see that the governing law, which will certainly apply to the interpretation and validity of the contract, should be displaced or qualified by the argument that the individual cannot be held to have consented to something which, as a matter of his own law, he could never have been bound by and that, if this were made good, Article 10(2) would in principle be available to him. The essence of his argument is that he did consent, even though it may not be to something which all laws would consider to be enforceable.

If a party argues that his agreement was procured by *fraud*, or *negligent or innocent misstatement*, or by *material non-disclosure*, or by *duress*, or by the exercise of *undue influence*, the legal effect of his plea is that his consent was given, but was vitiated and, subject to conditions, is liable to be taken back. If the governing law would nevertheless regard these pleas as insufficient to allow relief, could Article 10(2) be invoked to establish that the individual party did not consent so as to be not contractually bound? It seems likely

---

[153] For illustration, see the Japanese Commercial Code, Art 509: (1) When a merchant has received, from a person with whom he makes transactions ordinarily, the offer of a contract in the line of the business in which he works, he shall dispatch a notice of acceptance or refusal of the offer of the contract without delay. (2) When a merchant fails to dispatch a notice as set forth in the preceding paragraph, he/she shall be deemed to have accepted the offer of the contract set forth in said paragraph.

However, the rule only applies where there is an existing relationship between the parties, and this will almost lock the door to the possible application of Article 10(2).

that the answer is no: the victim of these wrongs would not say that he had not consented, but had consented only because of a trick or other wrong. In other words, even under his law it would be said that he did consent, and that makes Article 10(2) unavailable.[154] On the other hand, a person may know that under his own law it is not incumbent on him to check the accuracy of representations made by another, so that he will not have to be bound if he relies on misrepresentations; and he may have relied on the security of his own law as a result, just as he does when he throws away an offer letter, knowing that he cannot be bound by it. When the issue is presented in this way, it is more arguable that Article 10(2) should be allowed to operate here too, for an alleged consent which does not bind a party, and which he is right to assume does not bind him, is not really consent at all. Arguable, perhaps, but as Article 10(2) is an exception to the application of the governing law, doubtful.

For further example, if a party argues that the alleged contract was void on the basis of a mutual *mistake*, or his own unilateral mistake, this is, in effect, a confusion which prevents consensus, and Article 10(2) is in principle applicable. But if he argues that the alleged contract was void on the basis of fundamental common mistake, he is not arguing that he did not consent, but that his full and free consent was to something which a court may be unable to enforce; Article 10(2) will not assist him.

6. DISPLACING THE GOVERNING LAW

In addition to the instances which have been mentioned as part of the analysis of what law governs the contract or an issue arising within it, of which Article 3(3) was the one of general application,[155] there are three further circumstances in which the law identified as governing the contract will be overridden or displaced by the provisions of another law so that it will, to that extent, not apply. In the first two cases which we examine, the Regulation describes these laws as 'overriding mandatory provisions' which Article 9(1) defines as laws, the respect for which is regarded by a country as so crucial for safeguarding its public interests (political, social, or economic organization)

---

[154] *Lupofresh Ltd v Sapporo Breweries Ltd* [2013] EWCA Civ 948, [2013] 2 Lloyd's Rep 444.
[155] And on which see *Banco Santander Totta SA v Companhia Carris de Ferro de Lisboa SA* [2016] EWCA Civ 1267, [2017] 1 WLR 1323.

that they are applicable to any contract falling within their scope, regardless of the law which might otherwise be applied.[156] Where such a law has been identified and is made applicable (the grounds on which this arises will be seen shortly), the governing law is not annulled but is, to this extent, over-ridden by and subordinated to the rules of another system of law. It may be appropriate to think of 'mandatory laws' as being contained in directions given by the legislator directly to the judge, as distinct from laws which are made relevant because, but only because, of the way a party makes a contract or puts its case. However they are pictured, their definition is deliberately restrictive;[157] it is intended to define a category of laws narrower than those which cannot be contracted out of by agreement.

(a) Mandatory laws of the forum

Article 9(2) provides that a mandatory law of the forum will be applicable notwithstanding any other provision of the Regulation. The operation of this provision is therefore entirely determined by the court in which the trial takes place, though it has to work within the principles of interpretation es-tablished by the European Court. Its inclusion in the Regulation recognizes that it is inevitable that a court must be free to apply provisions of its own law which are considered to be of truly fundamental importance. In the context of a trial in England, examples *may* include legislation controlling contract terms which purport to limit or exclude liability. Other examples would be those provisions of the Financial Services and Markets Act 2000 or similar and successor legislation, which make an investment agreement made through an unauthorized person unenforceable;[158] presumably some-thing similar would apply to the provision of professional services by others who may lawfully do so only if they are registered or regulated.[159] Legal pro-visions of this kind cannot be sidelined by the simple expedient of choosing a law other than English to govern the contract; they are necessary, and need to be applied, to stop unauthorized sellers of pyramid[160] and Ponzi schemes from running wild. If a judge concludes that Parliament has made a law and

---

[156] Article 9(1); Case C–184/12 *United Antwerp Maritime Agencies NV v Navigation Maritime Bulgare* EU:C:2013:663, [2014] 1 Lloyd's Rep 161; Case C–135/15 *Hellenic Republic v Nikiforidis* EU:C:2016:774, [2017] ICR 147.

[157] Point 37 of the Recitals.

[158] Financial Services and Markets Act 2000, ss 26, 27.

[159] In addition, the Consumer Rights Act 2015.

[160] The nomenclature of 'pyramid' for these frauds is bafflingly inapt. Pyramids are the epitome of architectural stability. What these schemes are is the inverse: a funnel, into which much is poured, and from which everything runs out and is lost.

directed the judge to stop any attempt to contract out of it, then even if the wording of Article 9(1) appears to be out of reach it is very hard to see that an English judge could properly ignore what he has been told to do. Article 9(1) should probably be seen as an exhortation, but not more.

(b) Mandatory laws of the place of performance

A court cannot be expected to apply the laws of a foreign country simply because the law or legislature of that foreign country regards them as being of overriding importance to the organization of itself as a state:[161] in principle, and as a fundamental matter of territorial sovereignty, a legislator is understood to speak directly, and to give instructions, to his own judges, but not to anyone else. The Regulation, therefore, does not impose a similar obligation upon a judge to apply the overriding mandatory laws of any old foreign country.[162] But insofar as a contract requires[163] performance in a foreign country, and the overriding laws of that country would make performance there unlawful, Article 9(3) allows a court to give effect to those laws: the rule is entirely permissive.[164] In this respect, the Regulation recalls, perhaps not surprisingly, a rule of common law conflict of laws to the effect that an English court would neither enforce nor order performance of a contract where that performance would be illegal—in a more than technical or administrative sense[165]—under the law of the country in which performance was due.[166] The common law could never have countenanced an English court enforcing a contract to smuggle alcohol into the United States during prohibition[167] (or, for that matter, into some other country which has the same outlook), or to export from India goods which were destined for the ghastly regime in power in South Africa,[168] for example; and it would not make the tiniest

---

[161] For a telling illustration, Case C–135/15 *Hellenic Republic v Nikiforidis* EU:C:2016:774, [2017] ICR 147.

[162] Case C–135/15 *Hellenic Republic v Nikiforidis* EU:C:2016:774, [2017] ICR 147.

[163] If the common law is to be taken as any guide, it must be *required* rather than intended or expected: *Libyan Arab Foreign Bank v Bankers Trust Co* [1989] QB 728.

[164] Article 9(3).

[165] It will depend on the nature and degree of the illegality, and probably on the awareness of the party prepared to make a contract to perpetrate it; see also *Royal Boskalis Westminster NV v Mountain* [1999] QB 674; *Ryder Industries Ltd v Chan* [2016] 1 HKC 323.

[166] A different view, that the non-enforcement rule was confined to contracts whose proper (governing) law was English law, is indefensible. It is not the function of Her Majesty's judges to make orders which require the commission of crimes on the territory of foreign friendly states, or the payment of compensation for the failure to commit such crimes.

[167] *Foster v Driscoll* [1929] 1 KB 470.

[168] *Regazzoni v KC Sethia (1944) Ltd* [1958] AC 301. See also *Lemenda Trading Co Ltd v African Middle East Petroleum Co Ltd* [1989] QB 728; *Euro-Diam Ltd v Bathurst* [1990] 1 QB 30.

difference that the *lex contractus* considered this fact to provide no defence to the demand for performance. It is inconceivable that the Regulation would have taken a different view, and it does not.

(c) Non-application of the governing law on grounds of forum public policy

Although it is not exactly a case of the *lex contractus* being overridden by another law, a provision of the governing law will be set aside where its application would be manifestly contrary to public policy of the adjudicating court.[169] The relationship between this rule, stated in Article 21, and Article 9 is clear enough. Article 9(2) provides for the governing law to be overlaid by a specific provision of domestic law contained in the law of the forum, and Article 9(3) allows notice to be taken of a law of the country in which performance was due: both superimpose something on the provisions of the governing law. Article 21, by contrast, simply blanks out a provision of the governing law whose application by the court to the case before it would be unbearable, with the result that the governing law applies as if that rule were not part of it. For example, a rule of the *lex contractus* which considered a contract to be valid even though forced on a victim by duress should be disregarded.[170] A rule of foreign law which upheld as valid a contract term that restrained a person's freedom to trade or perform services for a period of years, which would be found to be illegal as a restraint of trade as a matter of English domestic law, could properly be refused application—with the consequence that there was no binding restraint—on this ground;[171] the same might conceivably be said of a rule of the *lex contractus* which provided for the payment of a sum which would in English law be seen as an unconscionable and unjustifiable penalty. It is likely that in some cases at least, the question whether English public policy is engaged will depend on the degree of connection to England, but in others, the rule of foreign law will be regarded as unfit for application in all and any circumstances.

---

[169] Article 16.

[170] *Royal Boskalis Westminster NV v Mountain* [1999] QB 674 (contract to secure release of hostages held as human shields by Iraqi authorities).

[171] The common law certainly said so: *Rousillon v Rousillon* (1880) 14 ChD 351.

C. CONTRACTS CONCLUDED BEFORE 18 DECEMBER 2009

Though it will eventually fade away, litigation concerning contracts made prior to 18 December 2009, but after 1 April 1991, which were within the temporal scope of the Rome Convention, will continue for a little while yet;[172] and decisions of the European Court on the interpretation of the Rome Convention will remain informative in any event. It is therefore necessary to say something brief about the principal[173] respects in which the provisions of the Convention differed or differ from the corresponding provisions of the Rome I Regulation.

The power of the parties to choose and express a law to govern their contract set out in Article 3 of the Convention was for all practical purposes the same as in the Regulation, but the provisions of Article 4, which identified the governing law in the absence of such choice, were significantly different. The point of departure was that the contract would be governed by the law of the country with which it was most closely connected; but it was then presumed that this would be the country of habitual residence of the party whose performance was characteristic of the contract.[174] The difficulty of this general and unparticularized rule was considerable, for it required one side of a contractual agreement to be identified as the 'characteristic' one, while the other side was not. The paradigm was, no doubt, the contract of sale, for which sale was characteristic, on the footing that all that the buyer was obliged to do was to pay the price. Even if this was a fair representation of most contracts of sale (which it was not; the obligations of the buyer in respect of delivery are almost as significant as those of the seller; and anyway, such a contract is more accurately referred to as one of sale and purchase), it will not have been true for all; and for contracts which were more complex than the sale of sweets in a corner shop, a template in which one party performs while the other pays would not necessarily fit. Contracts of distribution and

---

[172] By contrast, it does not seem appropriate to discuss the common law rules of private international law as, in the field of contracts in civil and commercial matters, these can only apply to contracts made over 20 years ago.

[173] It should also be noted that the provisions for consumer, employment, and carriage contracts were slightly different, and that the Rome Convention did not apply to insurance or risks situated in the Member States of what was then the EEC. These points are not dealt with here. Nor is the requirement in Art 18, that the Convention be given a uniform interpretation, for the replacement of the Convention by a Regulation has ensured that this does not need to be separately and specifically enacted.

[174] Article 4(1).

distributorship, for one, were hard to deal with, for each side does something more significant than simple payment,[175] as were barter, and reinsurance; and it came to be understood that the notion of a characteristic and a 'non-characteristic' performance was not as helpful as it may have seemed when it was first invented. Not only that: for contracts made in the course of a trade or profession the governing law was presumed to be the country of the principal place of business, except where, under the terms of the contract, performance was to be effected through a place of business other than the principal place of business, which led to a complication in cases in which it was implicit, but was not contractually obligatory, that performance be through a secondary place of business.[176] The escape clause in Article 4(5) of the Convention applied if the characteristic performance could not be determined, or if the contract as a whole was more closely connected to another country than that indicated by the rules on characteristic performance; it was held in England,[177] and in Luxembourg,[178] that this escape clause was not intended to be restrictive or particularly narrow, for if the contract really was more closely connected to another country, it would be surprising for the law of that country not to govern it: but Article 4(5) was not satisfied by showing that the parties 'would have chosen' a different law if they had made a choice. It bears repetition that the less satisfactory the default rule, the more work the escape clause would have to do. If one takes the view, as one now should, that Articles 4(1) and 4(2) of the Rome I Regulation are more likely to produce a sensible choice of law to begin with, it would be justifiable for Article 4(3) of the Regulation to have a narrower sphere of operation than Article 4(5) of the Convention.

The Rome Convention provided for the permissive application of the mandatory[179] laws of a country other than that of the forum or of the applicable

---

[175] For which the supplier, rather than the distributor, was the party whose performance was held, by courts in England (*Print Concept GmbH v GEW (EC) Ltd* [2002] CLC 382) and France (*Optelec SA v Soc Midtronics BV* [2002] Rev Crit 86) to be characteristic. This was an odd way of looking at a contract generally called 'distribution', rather than 'supply for the purpose of distribution by another'.

[176] *Iran Continental Shelf Oil Co v IRI International Corpn* [2002] EWCA Civ 1024, [2004] 2 CLC 696; *Ennstone Building Products Ltd v Stanger Ltd* [2002] EWCA Civ 916, [2002] 1 WLR 3059.

[177] *Samcrete Egypt Engineers & Contractors SAE v Land Rover Exports Ltd* [2001] EWCA Civ 2019, [2002] CLC 533.

[178] Case C–133/08 *Intercontainer Interfrigo SC v Balkenende Oosthuizen BV* [2009] ECR I–9687.

[179] The definition of 'mandatory' which is now in Art 9(1) of the Regulation had not appeared, in terms at least, in the Convention.

law. The power to apply such laws, picked up from the law of a country 'with which the situation has a close connection', was provided for by Article 7(1), but the contracting states were permitted to enact the Convention without this provision, and the United Kingdom did so.[180] It was thought, and probably rightly, that the principle was as unsound as the drafting of Article 7(1) was woolly. The odd result was that the question whether an English court might apply the provisions of a law other than the applicable law was left to be determined by the conflicts rules of the common law, on the footing that where a hole had been cut in the fabric of the Convention as enacted in English law the common law conflicts rules remained intact. Accordingly, provisions of the law of the place of performance could be given effect to the extent that they rendered performance of the contract unlawful;[181] it is gently ironic that such a provision was, in substance, made and incorporated as part of the Rome I Regulation.[182]

The Rome Convention also gave contracting states the power to not enact the provision which stated, as the Rome I Regulation also provides, without licence to exclude it, that the governing law was to be applied to the consequences of nullity of the contract. Why the United Kingdom took advantage of this was a mystery, for it was obvious[183] that if the governing law was used to reach the conclusion that a supposed contract was void, the same law would—however one understood the theoretical[184] basis for the conclusion—determine the restitutionary or other consequences. But the point is now just a wrinkle in the blanket of legal history, which description may, in time, be extended to the Convention itself.

---

[180] Article 23 of the Convention; Contracts (Applicable Law) Act 1990, s 2(2).
[181] *Ralli Bros v Compania Naviera Sota y Aznar* [1920] 2 KB 287.
[182] Article 9(3) of the Regulation.
[183] To the English, at least; for a rather odder and decidedly arid-looking view from the romanist perspective of Scots law, see *Baring Bros & Co Ltd v Cunninghame DC* [1997] CLC 108.
[184] That is, that the issue of recovery is contractual, or that the issue of recovery is not contractual but still governed by the law which governed or would have governed the contract.

6

NON-CONTRACTUAL OBLIGATIONS

On Exit Day, and unless any further legislative provision is made, the provisions of EU law set out in the Rome II Regulation, Regulation 864/2007, will be retained as the law of the United Kingdom. The adjustments necessary to allow the Rome II Regulation to operate as English private international law are made by the Law Applicable to Contractual Obligations and Non-Contractual Obligations (Amendment etc) (EU Exit) Regulations 2019, SI 2019 No 834: these adjustments are of no substantial importance. It follows that we will be able to refer in this Chapter to the Rome II Regulation without needing to draw attention to its precise status as EU legislation (as it was prior to Exit Day) or as retained EU legislation (as it is on and after Exit Day).

A. INTRODUCTION

If the obligation or alleged obligation with which the court is concerned is not contractual in the sense of the Rome I Regulation which was examined in the previous chapter, and if it is a civil or commercial matter which arose out of events which occurred on or after 11 January 2009, the conflicts rules which identify the applicable law are those set out in the Rome II Regulation. As was explained in the previous chapter, the two Rome Regulations cover and divide the whole of the field of obligations arising in civil and commercial matters into contractual and non-contractual obligations.[1] It is neither necessary nor helpful to ask, in terms of English domestic law, whether the matter before the English court is one of tort, or unjust enrichment, or equitable obligation, or for money had and received, or any such thing. Although these may be terms of art, and useful, if the Regulation directs the court to apply English domestic law, they play no role in the determination of the law

---

[1] If authority is needed, Case C–359/14 *Ergo Insurance SE v If P&C Insurance AS* EU:C:2016:40.

The Conflict of Laws. Fourth Edition. Adrian Briggs, Oxford University Press (2019). © Adrian Briggs
DOI: 10.1093/oso/9780198838500.003.0006

applicable to the obligation: the days when these familiar terms would have been helpful to a private international lawyer have been and gone, and the retention of the Regulations after Exit Day as the law of the United Kingdom means they are not coming back.

It is not necessary to repeat the points which explain the technique of interpretation and application of the Rome II Regulation where these follow directly from what was said about the Rome I Regulation which must be read so as to be consistent with it.[2] However, the matters excluded from the scope of the Rome II Regulation are in some respects wider and more significant than the exclusions from Rome I. In particular, it does not apply to non-contractual obligations arising out of violations of privacy and rights relating to personality, including defamation, which means that a significant body of material is left outside the Regulation within whose natural scope it would otherwise have fallen: to this the non-Rome conflicts rules of English law continue to apply. As privacy and defamation cannot be regarded as peripheral to the law of non-contractual obligations, it is necessary to say something about the rules preserved and reserved for such cases. It is, however, a misfortune that the conflicts rules of English law which have hung on for these cases, and which are dealt with at the end of this chapter, are as unsatisfactory as they are.

The Rome II Regulation applies to non-contractual obligations in civil and commercial matters which fall within its scope in terms of subject-matter[3] and time; but it goes on to draw its own internal distinction between what *it* calls 'tort and delict' on the one hand, and what one might call 'other, non-tortious', non-contractual obligations on the other. It is convenient to start with those aspects of the rules for determining the applicable law which are common to these two categories, and to deal with the tort/delict and 'other' cases of non-contractual obligation in the light which it shines.

The Rome I and Rome II Regulations were designed as a seamless whole, to make a complete and coherent statement of the conflicts rules for obligations arising in civil and commercial matters. This is achieved, in part at least, by channelling the analysis for those issues which are positioned where the Regulations may appear to overlap towards the *lex contractus* as identified by the Rome I Regulation. This does not mean that in every case in which the litigants in a tort matter are also parties to a contract the law

---

[2] Recital 7 to the Rome II Regulation. And, no doubt, vice versa.
[3] See Case C–359/14 *Ergo Insurance SE v If P&C Insurance AS* EU:C:2016:40.

applicable to the tort will be the law which governs the contract, but often it will, and in those cases in which the tort and contract are intertwined there will be little reason to seek to formulate the claim by reference to the one Regulation rather than the other. The Regulation methodology is refreshingly clear. One asks whether the matter raised before the court is civil or commercial. If it is, one asks whether it is based on the law of obligations. If it is,[4] one asks whether the obligation in question is contractual or non-contractual, there being no third option; if is it non-contractual the applicable law will be found by applying the rules set out in this chapter. These questions are framed and answered by reference to the autonomous definition of terms used in the Regulation; national law plays no part in it. We will consider or reconsider below the relationship or interface between the two instruments and the two species of the genus of 'obligation' in order to better understand what counts as a non-contractual obligation.

B. THE ROME II REGULATION

The Rome II Regulation[5] was adopted by the European Union in 2007, as part of the larger project to establish uniform rules to determine the applicable law for obligations in civil and commercial matters. Though the negotiations started from scratch, in the sense that there was nothing analogous to the Rome Convention which had prepared the ground for the Rome I Regulation, the curious characteristic of the law applicable to torts or non-contractual obligations is that almost all solutions found in national laws are unsatisfying. An understanding of the law put in place by the Regulation must acknowledge that basic truth, for it shows that the Regulation may have succeeded in crafting a set of rules which works sufficiently well that courts and commentators just leave it alone while refining the details. For this reason, though, a digression into the history of the conflict of laws in matters of tort may be instructive, but it is strictly optional. A proper understanding of the modern law does not depend on reading it.

---

[4] And assuming that it is not an obligation specifically excluded from the material scope of the Regulation under which it would otherwise have fallen.
[5] [2007] OJ L199/40.

1. BACKGROUND

A contract is an agreement, and if the law to be applied to it is not one which the parties chose, it will still be deduced from points of connection which the parties knew or should have known about from the start: the core principles which identify the law applicable to contracts are easy and uncontroversial, with only the detail calling for debate. Torts, by contrast, are the law's accidents, messy and usually unplanned, and covering a far more diverse range of interests and duties. A single or uniform law conflicts rule may struggle to deal convincingly with personal injury, negligence, economic torts and conspiracies, unfair competition, liability for the escape of fires and animals, defamation, nuisance, conversion and other interference with goods, patent infringement, invasion of privacy, and damage to reputation; but when causes of action arising under foreign laws of tort and delict are added in, a universal conflicts rule, whether very flexible or very inflexible, will be difficult to devise. The parties to a contract know of each other, and the range of persons with a potential claim will be predictable; by contrast, the parties to a tort claim, as often as not flung together or strewn about by the tort, will not always be known to each other in advance. In devising appropriate conflicts rules, this has to be borne in mind.

As a matter of history, the focus of the conflicts rules for tort tended to centre on the *lex fori* or the *lex loci delicti commissi*. A justification for the *lex fori* was sometimes said to lie in the similarity between torts and crimes, but a better view was that the imposition of legal duties and civil obligations without regard to the agreement of the parties was a matter on which each court was entitled, and perhaps bound, to prefer the civil liberty and civil liability standards of its own law. Justification for the *lex loci delicti commissi* was the homely advice that when in Rome one should generally do as Romans do. At this level of generality each has an attraction, which may even be the reason English law wove them into a rule of 'double actionability'; a requirement that the claimant make good his claim under English law and under the relevant foreign law.[6] But that placed an unusual burden on a claimant, and could also require the application of a law which had little real connection with the parties or the facts of the claim; and this prompted the suggestion that, just as a contract was governed by a proper law, so also should a tort be.[7] However,

---

[6] *Boys v Chaplin* [1971] AC 356.
[7] Originating in Morris, 'The Proper Law of a Tort' (1951) 64 Harv LR 881.

in England, the judicial response to hard cases was to allow a 'flexible exception' to the basic rule of double actionability to cater for cases with unusual facts.[8] The United States saw a more fundamental recasting of the rules, whereby the uniform application of the *lex loci delicti commissi* was largely given up for a variety of alternative techniques. They took root there, mainly because the application of the law of the place of the tort is less attractive within a federation in which each of the states is legally foreign but not noticeably geographically so: whereas it may be obvious that one is in Rome, it may not be so apparent in the United States that one is not in Kansas anymore. Borderless inter-state trade and traffic make a rigid application of the law of the place where the tort occurred less attractive than it might otherwise be. A range of alternatives were developed to deliver the elusive goal of an intuitively right answer derived nevertheless from scientific theory. The New York Court of Appeals[9] toyed with a test of close or closest connection, and with a more complex approach which asked (and sought to answer) which state or states had laws which were intended, or 'interested', to apply to the particular issue before the court for decision: a method oddly entitled 'governmental interest analysis'.[10] The debate later extended to inquire which state's law might be the most impaired if not applied;[11] to the use of a 'better law' approach,[12] a technique tending to make it difficult for a court not to apply its own domestic law; and whatever else all this experimentation may have achieved, the overall result really does resemble, in a disconcerting way, a wilderness of single instances. But the American jurisprudence certainly demonstrated that a uniform conflicts rule did not fit all torts equally well, and in that, at least, it did a useful job.

In Canada and Australia, by contrast, the fact that many of the torts litigated before the courts have taken place elsewhere within the federation moved the courts in precisely the opposite direction. The Supreme Court of Canada opted for a rigid and uniform *lex loci delicti* rule;[13] the High Court of Australia also opted for a rigid *lex loci delicti* rule,[14] being critical of both

---

[8] *Boys v Chaplin* [1971] AC 356; *Red Sea Insurance Co Ltd v Bouygues SA* [1995] 1 AC 190.
[9] *Babcock v Jackson* 191 NE 2d 279 (1963), [1963] 2 Lloyd's Rep 286 (NY CA).
[10] Currie, *Selected Essays on the Conflict of Laws* (Durham: Duke University Press, 1963).
[11] *Bernard v Harrah's Club* 546 P 2d 719 (1976).
[12] *Cipolla v Shaposka* 262 A 2d 854 (1970); *Clark v Clark* 222 A 2d 205 (1966).
[13] *Tolofson v Jensen* [1994] 3 SCR 1022.
[14] *John Pfeiffer Pty Ltd v Rogerson* (2000) 203 CLR 503; *Régie Nationale des Usines Renault v Zhang* (2003) 210 CLR 491.

the path taken in the United States and the English common law amalgam of rule and exception. Even so, even if it is possible to pinpoint the place where the tort occurs—and it sometimes is not—experience shows that the need to make an exception in the interests of flexibility becomes irresistible when the facts are sufficiently unusual; and the courts in Canada and Australia may yet have to think again.[15]

England was not immune to the winds of change blowing from America. Parliament eventually abolished the rule of double actionability and the undue burden it placed on the claimant. But it opted neither for a *lex loci delicti* rule, nor for a proper law approach. It took its cue from the acute observation of the Law Commission[16] that to search for the place of the tort may be to look for something that is not there:[17] after all, the elements making up the cause of action may be widely dispersed, and the notion that the tort has a location is, perhaps in the cases most likely to result in litigation, a fiction: perhaps a useful fiction, but the law should do better than that. Parliament therefore made a rule which placed its main focus on the place of the damage, which law would generally apply, and supplemented this with a rule of exception where this initial general rule did not yield the intuitively right solution.[18]

Those who drafted the Rome II Regulation were not able to draw on an established consensus, and still less on one in which a single conflicts rule could be devised and applied across the board. Their solution was to adopt a general rule (*lex generalis*) with as much certainty as possible, but allowing for a clear and measured exception where the facts called for it. This would work alongside particular conflicts rules (*lex specialis*) for torts or contexts whose particular concerns and framework meant that the general rule would not suit them. By and large that is exactly what the Rome II Regulation delivers, and the decision to retain it as law in the United Kingdom after departing the European Union was plainly correct. It is far superior to anything which preceded it.

---

[15] It can be argued, although it is not convincing to do so, that the adoption of the principle of *renvoi* into the Australian *lex loci* rule, in *Neilson v Overseas Projects Corp of Victoria* (2005) 233 CLR 331, was a surrogate for the flexibility which the Court was at pains to reject. This does not appear to be based on a fair or accurate reading of the analysis contained in the judgments.

[16] Law Commission Report 193 (1990).

[17] The point is made in more prosaic form in Recital 12 to the Regulation.

[18] Private International Law (Miscellaneous Provisions) Act 1995, Part III. See also (in New Zealand) Private International Law (Choice of Law in Tort) Act 2017.

2. ROME II REGULATION: APPLICATION AND SCOPE

(a) Time and date

The Rome II Regulation was adopted in July 2007. There was some initial confusion as to its temporal scope: by contrast with the law of contract, for which the date on which the contract is concluded serves as a neat and comprehensible starting date, torts and other non-contractual obligations do not always start so cleanly. Article 31, as amended, provides that the Regulation applies to events giving rise to damage which occur on or after 11 January 2009.[19] This is fine as far as it goes, though where the events which give rise to damage occur both before and after that date it is not so helpful. Take a case of product liability, for example. If a pharmaceutical drug or surgical implant is manufactured before 11 January 2009, but sold and used on or after that date, would the Regulation apply to a claim by an injured user? In the context of the Brussels I Regulation, which gave special jurisdiction to the courts for the place where the harmful event occurred, the European Court said that in cases of product liability the event which gave rise to the damage was the manufacture, rather than the sale, acquisition, or use, of the product.[20] It seems legitimate to argue, therefore, that the Regulation will apply to claims based on products manufactured on or after 11 January 2009 but not manufactured before. For other kinds of tort, such as tortuously caused asbestosis or mesothelioma, such clarity is unavailable. With time the problem will be forgotten, as the commencement date recedes into history. But as one cannot write with certainty where the law offers no basis for it, it suffices to identify the issue and to wait for judicial assistance.

(b) Material scope

The Regulation applies to non-contractual obligations in civil and commercial matters: to all obligations which derive from one of the events listed in Article 2, which is to say, 'any consequence arising out of tort/delict, unjust enrichment, *negotiorum gestio* or *culpa in contrahendo*'.[21] It applies whenever there is a conflict between the laws of states, including, in the case of the United Kingdom, a conflict between the laws of the parts of the United Kingdom.[22] It applies to non-contractual obligations in the nature of torts,[23]

---

[19]   cf Case C–412/10 *Homawoo v GMF Assurances SA* [2011] ECR I–11603.
[20]   *Kainz v Pantherwerke AG* EU:C:2014:7, [2015] QB 34.
[21]   Case C–359/14 *Ergo Insurance SE v If P&C Insurance AS* EU:C:2016:40, [2016] ILPr 451.
[22]   Article 3 of the Retained Regulation will stand in place of Article 25(2) of the original Regulation.
[23]   From this point, the reference to 'tort and delict' is used in this short form.

it being quite irrelevant whether liability arises from statute law or case law. It applies also to non-contractual obligations which, as far as the Regulation is concerned, are not torts, which is to say, to obligations arising from unjust enrichment, from *negotiorum gestio*, and from pre-contractual fault. Assuming that the events complained of took place after the start date of the Regulation, the law which the court is to apply to the non-contractual obligation will, unless excluded by the Regulation from its material scope, be identified by the rules set out in the Regulation.

Some of the exceptions from the material scope of the Regulation are similar to those of the Rome I Regulation. It excludes non-contractual obligations arising out of: family relationships, including maintenance;[24] matrimonial property regimes, also wills and succession;[25] bills of exchange, cheques and promissory notes, and other negotiable instruments to the extent that the obligations arise out of their negotiable character;[26] the law of companies such as creation, capacity, and winding up;[27] and the relations between settlors, trustees, and beneficiaries.[28] It does not apply to evidence and procedure,[29] and, for all of these, what needs to be said was said in the previous chapter.

Other exclusions from its material scope are more obviously peculiar to the Rome II Regulation and, in several cases, respond to particular interests and issues recently exposed. The Regulation does not apply to the liability of the State for acts and omissions in the exercise of State authority (*acta jura imperii*).[30] This may have been prompted by a case under the Brussels I Regulation in which a Greek claimant sought to bring proceedings in tort against Germany for loss and damage caused by its armed forces when they were Nazis. Though the European Court ruled that the matter did not arise in a civil or commercial matter,[31] on the basis that acts of war were not civil or commercial in nature and the obligations arising from them were not either, the legislation is now clear. The Rome II Regulation will not apply to any non-contractual obligations said to arise from such acts; the exclusion extends to those who claim against those who act on behalf of states in such excluded activity. Next, the Regulation

---

[24] Article 1(2)(a).
[25] Article 1(2)(b).
[26] Article 1(2)(c).
[27] Article 1(2)(d).
[28] Article 1(2)(e).
[29] Article 1(3).
[30] Article 1(1).
[31] Case C–292/05 *Lechouritou v Germany* [2007] ECR I–1519.

does not apply to non-contractual obligations which assert the personal liability of auditors to a company or to its members in the statutory audit of accounts.[32] No explanation is given as to why this should be, but again, the common law rules will apply in such cases. Third, it does not apply to non-contractual obligations arising out of nuclear damage:[33] no doubt the rule in the Regulation for non-contractual obligations in respect of environmental damage was unattractive to those states whose nuclear activities are liable to cause catastrophic damage in other countries. Fourth, it does not apply to non-contractual obligations arising out of violations of privacy and rights relating to personality, including defamation.[34] The explanation for this exclusion of this lively and topical area of non-contractual liability appears to lie in the particular sensitivities raised by privacy and self-esteem, on the one hand, and the freedoms of speech and of the press, on the other. For there are some states in which the dignity and self-esteem of persons in public life appears to outweigh the so-called right of the press to publish and of the prurient to poke their noses in; in other states the freedom of the press is considered to be a vital part of the struggle against mendacity in high places. It was little surprise that agreement on applicable law was not attained at the first attempt; the result is that non-contractual obligations arising out of these matters are governed by the conflicts rules considered at the end of this chapter.

3. ROME II REGULATION: GENERAL AND COMMON PROVISIONS

(a) Habitual residence

As is the case with the Rome I Regulation, the principal point of reference between a person and a law is defined in terms of habitual residence. Article 23 defines this in terms which are functionally identical to those in Article 19 of the Rome I Regulation. The main difference is that the Rome II Regulation does not specify the date for the assessment of habitual residence, but it seems reasonable to suppose that it will be the date of the accrual of the cause of action rather than the date on which legal proceedings are begun.

---

[32] Article 1(2)(d).
[33] Article 1(2)(f).
[34] Article 1(2)(g).

(b) Choice of law by the parties

Whether the non-contractual obligation in question is a tort or not, Article 14 of the Regulation sets out the circumstances in which the parties may submit or subject it to the law of their choice. This means that they may[35] make an agreement as to the applicable law, and in confirming or conferring the autonomy of the parties in this way the Regulation makes a mighty improvement on the rules which previously held sway in England, where the notion that parties could choose the law (as distinct from the jurisdiction) to resolve their dispute insofar as it involved a tort was never seriously developed. The freedom conferred on the parties by Article 14 is not, however, unfettered. The parties' choice of law may be made by an agreement entered into after the event giving rise to the damage, but if the agreement is made before the occurrence of the event giving rise to the damage, it will be binding only if all parties are pursuing commercial activity and the agreement was freely negotiated. In any event, it must be expressed, or demonstrated with reasonable certainty by the facts of the case. Where the agreement is contained in a contractual term, any question of construction of the scope of that agreement will, no doubt, be answered by giving the parties' choice of law as broad a construction as reasonably possible, the better to achieve uniformity of governing law.

Limiting this freedom to those engaged in commercial activities makes sense if the aim is to prevent choice of law 'agreements' being imposed on parties whose non-contractual obligations are the equivalent of contracts made by consumers: there being no such thing as 'consumer torts', this was probably the best way to produce an analogous rule. Where all the elements relevant to the situation at the time of the event giving rise to the damage are in a country other than that whose law has been chosen, the parties' choice cannot prevent the application of rules of law of that country which cannot be derogated from by agreement.[36] As far as English law is concerned, this power to choose the law was long overdue.

So much may have been expected. But because the Regulation also applies to non-contractual obligations which are not torts, it opens the door to the possibility, in principle at least, that parties negotiating towards a possible contract may agree upon the law which will apply to any non-contractual obligations which may arise from their pre-contractual dealings. This freedom is likely to be most useful in commercial relationships, for the idea

---

[35] Subject to specific exceptions: Art 6(4), Art 8(3) (and by implication, Art 13).
[36] Article 14(3).

of agreeing after the breakdown of relations upon a specific law to govern pre-contractual obligations is improbable; but it opens the door to the selection of a law which limits, or perhaps extends, the duties which each negotiating party owes to the other: duties of disclosure, care, truthfulness, good faith, and so on. While this law will not of itself govern the validity of the contract,[37] it offers an opportunity to parties to manage the risks to which each is exposed in the negotiation phase of their relationship.

(c) Scope of applicable law

According to Article 22, the applicable law applies to determine who bears the burden of proof; it also determines the application of any presumption, such as may relate to causation, of fault. Article 20 provides that the *lex causae* will govern the extent to which a debtor, who has himself satisfied a claim which existed against several debtors, may recover compensation or contribution from the other debtors.[38]

In addition, Article 15 sets out a long list of issues which will be governed by the *lex causae*; this long list is not exhaustive. The *lex causae* will govern the basis and extent of liability, including the determination of who may be held liable for acts done, including the imposition of vicarious liability for the acts of another; also, the grounds for exemption from liability, including any limitation of liability and division of liability, such as the effect of contributory negligence and the apportionment of liability as between multiple tortfeasors. So also, the existence, nature, and assessment of damage or the remedy claimed: in other words, it will govern all the component parts of the remedies. There is therefore no reflection of the awkward division apparently drawn by the corresponding provision of the Rome I Regulation;[39] the rules governing the assessment and calculation of damages will be taken from the applicable law which for this purpose includes the tariffs, guidelines, and similar quasi-legal ingredients of that system of law.[40] It will govern the measures which a court may take to prevent or terminate injury or damage or to ensure the provision of compensation, though, in this case, there is a necessary limitation in that the court is not required to go beyond an exercise of

---

[37] Because the Rome II Regulation applies only to non-contractual obligations.
[38] The view that this is always governed by the Civil Liability (Contribution) Act 1978, which apparently operates as a statute of mandatory application (see *Roberts v SSAFA* [2019] EWHC 1104 (QB)), cannot prevail in a case to which the Rome II Regulation applies.
[39] Article 12(1)(c) of the Rome I Regulation; also the common law: *Cox v Ergo Versicherung* [2014] UKSC 22, [2014] AC 1379.
[40] *Wall v Mutuelle de Poitiers Assurances* [2014] EWCA Civ 138, [2014] 3 All ER 340.

the powers which it has under its own procedural law. It will also answer the question whether a right to damages or other remedy may be passed on or inherited, which appears to include the assignment of rights even where this would be considered champertous; and it will determine who are the persons entitled to compensation for damage sustained personally and liability for the acts of another person: a point which seems to have been provided for previously but which is made with double force. And it will determine the manner in which an obligation may be extinguished, as well as prescription and limitation, which includes the rules relating to the commencement, interruption, and suspension of time.[41]

There will be some cases in which the application of a provision of the applicable law, say the *lex delicti*, is difficult to the point of being impossible; where that is so, the court will simply have to apply its own law by default. This may be significant if a tort is found to be governed by a law under which the assessment of damages would simply involve leaving the issue to a civil jury. In such a case an English court may consider that it cannot apply the applicable law, for its rule is either that the measure of damages is whatever the trier of fact feels to be the right figure, or it takes the form of a procedural mechanism rather than a rule of substantive law capable of being proved and applied as such. Though not unthinkable, it is not very attractive to try to show the court that a 'typical' jury award would fall within a particular range, for this would not be the application of a rule of law so much as a prediction as to the bare and unreasoned result of applying it, which is not the same thing at all. If the quantification of loss and damage, in accordance with rules of foreign law, means that the court informs itself of the principles by which the foreign court would make its decision, and then applies these to come to its own conclusion,[42] then if this does not allow the English court to produce a figure the court will be discharged from its duty to apply foreign law.

Nevertheless, the basic scheme of the Regulation is clear enough to see: it is to refer practically all issues to the law identified by the Regulation as applicable, and to leave to public policy or to mandatory laws of the forum, considered below, the making of necessary exceptions. In other words, the technique is to establish a broad general rule controlled by an exception formulated by reference to the particular needs of the individual case.

---

[41] For illustration (only) of the technique of applying foreign limitation or prescription rules, see *Iraqi Civilians v Ministry of Defence* [2016] UKSC 25, [2016] 1 WLR 200.

[42] cf *Iraqi Civilians v Ministry of Defence* [2016] UKSC 25, [2016] 1 WLR 200 [14].

(d) Overriding the applicable law

Just as is the case with the Rome I Regulation, the law identified as applicable by the Rome II Regulation may be displaced, and this may be done positively (by the superimposition of a rule of the domestic *lex fori* which is considered mandatory) or negatively (by the non-application of a provision of the applicable law where its application would be manifestly contrary to public policy). We may take them in turn.

Article 16 provides for the application of overriding mandatory provisions of the *lex fori* where that law requires their application irrespective of the law otherwise applicable. The definition of 'overriding mandatory provisions' which is given by Article 9(1) of the Rome I Regulation is not reproduced in Rome II, but the European Court has explained that it is to be read as though it was there: consistency of interpretation requires the two overriding provisions to be treated as essentially the same.[43] Insofar as the issue is whether the application of a provision of the *lex fori* is simply imperative, there is no reason to suppose that it matters whether it will displace the provisions of a contractual or a non-contractual applicable law; but it will not be sufficient to show that the rule of the *lex fori* is, in the opinion of the court, simply a better rule or one which, within domestic law, may not be excluded by the parties.

Article 26 allows a provision of the applicable law to be refused application where its application would be manifestly incompatible with the public policy of the forum.[44] As the Regulation applies to non-contractual obligations governed by any law, it is not difficult to imagine that there will be some instances in which a legal system contains a rule which an English court finds to fall outside the wide range of foreign laws which are very different but not intolerable. If the Regulation were to have extended to privacy and defamation, the public policy objection to the application of foreign law might have been expected to have a rather more prominent role.

Point 32 of the Recitals indicates that a rule of the *lex causae* which would lead to the recovery of 'non-compensatory exemplary or punitive damages of an excessive nature' may be found to be objectionable in this way. The primary aim of this provision is awards of damages which are excessively large, though if the approach of the Canadian courts were to be at all instructive,

---

[43] C–149/18 *Silva Martins v Dekra Claims Services Portugal SA* EU:C:2019:84.
[44] Article 26. It is the application, rather than the rule itself, which has to be found to offend.

damages would need to be truly astronomic[45] before some judges would be shocked into reaching for their own sense of public policy. There is no reason, however, to confine the operation of this provision to cases in which the applicable law would lead to very high damages. It must be open to a court to find that a rule of the applicable law capping damages at a level regarded as unfeasibly low to be contrary to public policy, especially in circumstances in which the claimant had only a transient connection with the state in which the damage occurred.[46]

(e) The meaning of law

Law, in the context of the Rome II Regulation, means the domestic law of the country whose law is identified as applicable. Article 24 means that there is no place for *renvoi* in the law of non-contractual obligations.

Only in one sense is this a pity. The High Court of Australia, in a thoughtful judgment concerning the law to be applied to torts committed overseas, concluded 'that the law of the place of the tort' should mean the law, including foreign law where it was sufficiently proved that the foreign judge would apply it, which would be applied by the judge holding court at the place of the tort.[47] Not only would this remove the incentive to practice forum-shopping, but it was also the best and fairest understanding of what 'the law of the place of the tort' actually meant, for it is perfectly rational to consider that 'law' actually is what a judge would apply to resolve the matter before him. This common law thinking, however, is not relevant to a scheme cut from very different cloth. The Regulation does not look to 'the place of the tort' in order to apply its law as a rule of single reference. It specifies a specific element within the framework of the obligation, and uses its location as an applicable law rule of first reference, supplementing this with a series of measured exceptions for cases in which this rule of first reference does not or would not yield a satisfactory answer. It is so different a technique for finding the applicable law that the observations of the High Court of Australia upon common law technique can have no part to play in it.

---

[45] cf *Beals v Saldanha* [2003] 3 SCR 416, where the damages ordered by a foreign court were not contrary to Canadian public policy despite their truly extraordinary size in relationship to the original loss.

[46] *Harding v Wealands* [2006] UKHL 32, [2007] 2 AC 1 (where the cap was inapplicable in any event as being a procedural rule going to quantification).

[47] *Neilson v Overseas Projects Corp of Victoria* (2005) 223 CLR 331.

(f) Insurance and other third party issues

The question whether the victim of damage may bring his or her claim directly against the insurer of the wrongdoer is answered benevolently: Article 18 provides that a direct claim may be brought if this is permitted by the law which governs the non-contractual obligation *or* by the law which governs the insurance contract.

In truth, this is a tricky issue to analyse, and the answer given by Article 18 has the great virtue of steering clear of it. The issue is tricky because it is hard to decide whether the victim's claim against the tortfeasor's insurer is to establish something analogous to vicarious liability for the wrong done by the insured, or to make a claim as third party to the contract of insurance which may arise under the *lex contractus* or be granted by the statute law of the forum. The best way of dealing with such puzzles is sidestep them, and that is what Article 18 does;[48] insofar as it shows favour to the victim and disfavour to an insurer, its impact can be priced by the insurance industry which is well able to look after itself.[49]

A rather cumbersome provision in Article 19 deals with subrogation. In effect, if an insurer has discharged a liability of its insured, the law which governs the insurer's duty to satisfy the claim also determines whether it may exercise against the debtor (wrongdoer) the rights which the insured party had against the wrongdoer.

4. ROME II REGULATION: GENERAL RULE FOR TORTS

(a) Scheme of Chapter II

The general approach taken to the applicable law in Chapter II of the Regulation, which applies to non-contractual obligations which are torts and delicts, is to establish a rule for general cases, and to provide special rules for particular kinds of tort for which the general rule is either not appropriate or not sufficient. The conflicts rules in Chapter II of the Regulation apply to torts which have occurred as well as to those which are likely to occur.[50] Given the

---

[48] Case C–240/14 *Prüller-Frey v Brodnig* EU:C:2015:567, [2015] 1 WLR 5031; *Keefe v Mapfre Mutualidad Compania de Seguros y Reaseguros SA* [2015] EWCA Civ 598, [2016] 1 WLR 905; *The Yusuf Cepnioglu* [2016] EWCA Civ 386, [2016] 3 All ER 697.

[49] The same observation may be made in relation to rights/claims given in relation to motor accidents caused by uninsured drivers, the cost of bearing which is imposed on the Motor Insurers' Bureau and similar organisations.

[50] Article 2(2).

wide variety of torts, and the correspondingly wide variety of geographical connections displayed by some tort cases, it is unsurprising that the regime is sometimes complex; but it is entirely satisfactory that there be a general rule as well as specific ones.

There is a need to distinguish between torts, to which Chapter II applies, and other non-contractual obligations which fall under Chapter III; and this may[51] be problematic in cases which English domestic law might simply see as tortious while other national laws do not. The cases which call most obviously for the application of this line of distinction are causes of action for damages which arise from being wrongfully induced to enter into a contract, such as (in English law, simply for the purposes of illustration) fraud, negligent misrepresentation, and the strict-ish liability imposed by Misrepresentation Act 1967; and causes of action in which the claimant decides to treat the wrongdoer as unjustly enriched without legal cause by the profit which he has gained, so by-passing the tort which has been committed. As to the first, it seems pretty clear that the Regulation intends these cases to fall within Article 12, and therefore to be regarded as falling outside Chapter II. As to the second, it may be better not to worry, for if the claim alleging unjust enrichment arises as the consequence of a tort, Article 10(1) will be likely to mean that it will be governed by the *lex delicti* in any event; and if that is so, no further analysis is called for.

(b) General rule

Article 4 establishes the rule for general cases in slightly complicated form. The point of entry depends on whether the defendant and victim are habitually resident in the same country when the damage occurs. If they are, the law of that country will be the applicable law for the non-contractual obligations arising out of the tort;[52] but if they are not so resident, the applicable law will be that of the country in which the damage occurs, irrespective of the country in which the event giving rise to it occurred, and further irrespective of the country in which the indirect consequences of the event giving rise to the damage occur.[53] Despite what is said in point 18 of the Recitals to the Regulation, there is no reason to treat one of these as an exception to the other: they are each starting points, and the claim goes through whichever

---

[51] However, according to Art 13, where the non-contractual obligation results from the infringement of an intellectual property right, it falls under Art 8, and not within Chapter III.

[52] Article 4(2).

[53] Article 4(1).

door is provided for it.[54] For the purposes of Article 4, it is not helpful to frame the questions which have to be asked by reference to particular torts or particular causes of action, but by types of loss and damage. For the applicable law will generally be found by focusing on the damage, not on the tort.

(c) Damage, and where it occurs

According to Article 2(1), damage covers 'any consequence arising out of tort/delict, unjust enrichment, *negotiorum gestio*, or *culpa in contrahendo*'. The 'where the damage occurs' version of the general rule reflects a distinction, which originates in case law under the (former) Brussels I Regulation, between the place where damage occurs, which is significant, and the place or places where it is (otherwise, and especially afterwards) suffered, felt, written up, or recorded, or where it produces a 'ricochet' effect, to use a civilian term. It follows that the relevant jurisprudence of the European Court on that instrument will drift across to the Rome II Regulation. The scheme of Article 4(1) requires the damage to be located: it does not allow for the possibility that the relevant damage cannot be pinned down to a place of occurrence. In some cases it may be permissible to 'centralize' the occurrence of damage in a single place, but hard cases are bound to arise.

The challenge of ascribing a location to the occurrence of damage has proved to be considerable, and the work is far from complete. It may be helpful to examine bodily injury, damage to tangible property, damage to intangible property, moral or reputational damage, and (which will prove to be the most important, and the most difficult) financial loss. We will then be in a position to make a proper analysis of secondary or consequential loss and damage.

For damage taking the form of bodily injury, the place of its occurrence is not usually difficult to locate. But not always: in poisoning and asbestos cases, for example, is the place where the damage occurs the place where the malign substance is ingested, or the place where the victim is when symptoms of a hitherto invisible harm first manifest themselves? There appears to be no firm basis for preferring one view over the other, though the latter may be easier to work with. Cases of asbestosis and mesothelioma are topical examples, but other slow-acting impairments of the body present the same challenge. Impairment of mental wellbeing may be seen as immediate personal harm: if

---

[54] If for example, Art 4(2) were a true exception to Art 4(1), it would be liable to restrictive interpretation, so as not to jeopardise the general rule. That approach makes no sense in this context.

bullying or intimidation causes damage to mental wellbeing, Article 4(1) should look to the place of the occurrence of this immediate consequence, rather than to the loss of earnings which results from the time off work. But where this anxiety is the consequence of, or reaction to, physical (or, indeed, economic) damage it will be irrelevant to the applicable law.

For damage to tangible property, the place where the thing was when it was damaged will usually be easy to locate. But not always. If for example a garage fails to reconnect the brakes of a car which it has serviced, so that a traffic accident takes place on the way home, it would seem strange to say that the damage to the car occurred in the garage and that everything else was a consequence of it: one must suppose that a court will have to be guided by common sense rather than by over-thinking the analysis. For damage to intangible property, the place where the intangible is located will be likely to be the place where the damage done to it occurs. Damage to intellectual property is dealt with by a *lex specialis*, and is best considered in that context. Damage taking the form of wrongful depletion of a customer's credit balance with his bank is better analysed under the broader head of financial loss, though it will also feature in our analysis of loss or damage which is consequential upon some other loss or damage.

So far as moral or reputational damage is concerned, as the Regulation stops short of obligations arising from privacy, personality, and defamation, the problem of locating the place where such damage occurs will rarely arise. However, in its jurisprudence on the Brussels I Regulation, from which these obligations were not excluded, the European Court was driven to accept that the ubiquity of the internet and of social media which operate in disembodied form made a 'place where the damage occurs' rule very difficult to operate. Its pragmatic solution was to allow the place where the victim has the centre of his or her interests as the place where (all) the damage occurred. Outside this context, loss or damage of this kind will often be the consequence of a damage which has already been done, and it will not therefore be relevant to the identification of the applicable law.

Financial loss is the most problematic. If one takes as example losses caused by acting in reliance on misinformation, it might be argued that the loss occurs where the thing which is acquired at an overvalue is acquired, or at the place of the bank account from which the funds are sent and lost. In the context of the Brussels I Regulation the European Court was concerned that the place of the depleted bank account was either unknowable in advance to the defendant, or susceptible to manipulation by the claimant, or both, and that such a solution would be inconsistent with the principle of legal certainty. It therefore suggested that the place at which the claimant made the legal commitment which meant that financial loss was now unavoidable—the place where she concluded the contract, for example—was the place where the loss or damage occurred.[55] Granted that if this is the act by which it occurred, the place where the act was done will appear to be the place where the loss occurred; but having clarified the law in this way the Court re-muddied the waters by appearing to accept that the place where a claimant held her bank account could be the place where loss occurred if this was known to the other party.[56] In the Court's defence it may be said that to read 'in which the damage occurs' as meaning 'in which the contract was made' is to substitute one problematic rule with another which may be even more unpredictable as methods of contracting multiply. The result is a bit of a mess; it now falls to the Supreme Court to sort it all out for us.

The real difficulty lies in distinguishing 'immediate' from 'consequential' loss and damage. Tort lawyers are familiar with the idea that financial loss may be the consequence of damage to tangible property, and they may sometimes need to decide whether it is directly or indirectly consequential on damage done to a thing. But for our purposes, it is the bare fact that it is consequential which makes it irrelevant to the identification of the applicable law. So for example, if I damage a colleague's car so that he has to pay for a taxi to get home, the cost of his doing so can be seen as the indirect consequence of the event which has already occurred. But what of the simple fraud in which a person takes another's bank card or bank details and misuses it or them to withdraw money from the other's bank account? What of the case in which she takes another person's mobile telephone to make use of it for which the other will have to pay? Is the financial loss which is caused to the victim an indirect consequence of the event, or is the financial loss the first and only loss which occurs, the anterior steps being merely events giving rise to it? It seems inevitable that a degree of roughness and readiness will be needed to make this rule work in some cases, even if the general principle is clear enough.

The proposition that certain kinds of loss and damage are the indirect consequences of an event which has already occurred extends to loss or damage which impacts on secondary victims of a tort. A person who suffers—so far as she is concerned, immediate—traumatic shock or bereavement from,

---

[55] Case C–12/15 *Universal Music International Holding BV v Schilling* EU:C:2016:449, [2016] QB 967; *AMT Futures Ltd v Marzillier* [2017] UKSC 13, [2018] AC 439.
[56] Case C–304/17 *Löber v Barclays Bank plc* EU:C:2018:701.

or from observing or learning of, the death or injury of another sustains loss which is the consequence of an event which has already occurred. The claimant may argue that the trauma is a direct consequence, not a consequence which is indirect, and that it is therefore not rendered irrelevant to the identification of the applicable law by Article 4(1). But this is not the view which the European Court has taken: it distinguishes between the direct occurrence of damage, which is that done to the victim who is injured or killed, and the adverse impacts on others which may be described, in a slightly unsympathetic turn of phrase, as 'after-effects of the accident'.[57] If, for example, a road traffic accident kills a person whose relatives in another country suffer bereavement or mental trauma, the location of those relatives plays no part in the identification of the law which will govern the non-contractual obligations arising out of the tort, including any such obligations owed to the relatives.[58] The Regulation requires us to find the law identified by Article 4, and to use this as the basis for all the non-contractual obligations which arise; it does not enquire into the location of the damage done to the secondary victim, even though that person may fairly say that the damage done to him feels very direct indeed and did not occur in the place where[59] the car came off the road.

(d) Escape clause

Whichever initial version of the general rule applies, Article 4(3) provides that if from all the circumstances of the case it is clear that the tort is manifestly more closely connected with another country, the law of that other country shall apply instead. This 'escape clause'[60] is not directly available in the case in which the location of the damage is just too difficult. It applies only if the tort as a whole is manifestly more closely connected to another country than that which has been indicated by Article 4(1) or 4(2), as the case may have been. By contrast with what the common law allowed,[61] it does not permit one specific issue within the tort to be hived off and referred to a different law. It is also provided that the requisite degree of closer connection may be seen in the existence of a pre-existing relationship between the

---

[57] cf *Brownlie v Four Seasons Holdings Inc* [2017] UKSC 80, [2018] 1 WLR 192 [20]. The claim of the bereaved widow in such a case would in principle be governed by Egyptian law as the place of the damage, even though her connection to Egypt was purely for a few days' family holiday.

[58] Case C–350/14 *Lazar v Allianz SpA* EU:C:2015:802, [2016] 1 WLR 835.

[59] Or even when, if the event which causes their trauma is their hearing of the earlier accident.

[60] Point 18 of the Recitals. An escape clause will probably be regarded as an exception to the rule from which it escapes, and as such given a restrictive interpretation.

[61] Perhaps under the influence of American thinking: *Boys v Chaplin* [1971] AC 356.

parties, such as a contract. Where, therefore, the contract is governed by a law which the parties have chosen and expressed, it would be rational for a tort associated with the contractual relationship to be governed by the same law, though whether this can be explained as there being a connection linking the tort to a country, as distinct from a system of law, is debatable. This does not contradict Article 14, which lays down fairly strict conditions for the validation of a choice of law made by the parties to govern a tort. That is a separate and distinct process from what is involved when Article 4(3) directs a court to consider whether there is a pre-existing relationship between the parties, governed by a law which they may have chosen, which has a manifestly close relationship with the tort.

Apart from cases in which Article 4(3) is triggered by a pre-existing relationship between the parties, recourse to the exception will be rare, but it will be more likely to arise in relation to Article 4(1) than Article 4(2). For the latter, the cases in which a tort will be manifestly more closely connected to a country other than that of the parties' shared habitual residence will presumably be where the fact that the parties have the same habitual residence is unplanned and purely coincidental. In relation to Article 4(1), by contrast, the country of the occurrence of the damage may not be the country which lies, intuitively, at the heart of the obligation. In cases in which this is so, the reference to Article 4(3) will allow a more suitable law to be chosen. However, the abstract debate about how strict or restrictive is the permitted recourse to Article 4(3) is not illuminating, for there are no objective units of measurement, and, in any event, every case will turn on its own set of facts.

5. ROME II REGULATION: RULE FOR SPECIFIC TORTS

In five types of case or context, the rules for determining the applicable law are not the general rules in Article 4, but a special rule, which may or may not be self-contained, which has been designed to better reflect the structure of the particular tort or context.

(a) Product liability

Article 5 provides a partial *lex specialis* for non-contractual obligations arising from damage caused by a product. The principle which underpins the rules is sensible enough, but the drafting is problematic. The point of departure is that if claimant and defendant are habitually resident in the same country, the law of that country shall apply. If they are not, the focus shifts to the country or countries in which 'the product' was 'marketed', which leads to three possibilities, which must be taken in turn. The law of that country in which the victim was habitually resident will apply if the product was marketed there; failing which, the law of the country in which the product was acquired will apply if the product was marketed there; failing which, the law of the country in which the damage occurred will apply if the product was marketed there. However, the answer derived from this process may be displaced in favour of the law of the country in which the *tortfeasor* is habitually resident if he could not reasonably foresee the marketing the product, or a product of the same type, in the country whose law had been identified according to the provisions described. And finally, where Article 5(1) has given its answer, if the tort is manifestly more closely connected with a country other than that derived from the series of questions just described, Article 5(2) requires that law to apply instead.

The proposition that it is appropriate to apply the law of a country in which the product was marketed if there is a defined connection to that country is reasonable. It is fair to the defendant for it will apply only if he knew or should have known of the marketing there; if a manufacturer[62] releases his product he cannot really complain when the law of that country applies so long as he knew or should have known of the marketing there: if it is marketed by a downstream retailer of whose activity the defendant[63] had no means of knowing, it would be unfair to say that having released the product into the stream of commerce he simply has to live with the consequences, wherever they are; it makes no difference that he may have tried to prevent its being marketed in a particular country. And as a product may be marketed in many countries, it is necessary to identify a singular market(ing) whose law will apply by reference to the series of questions set out above.

But the devil is in the detail: the operation of the rule will depend on the true meaning of the phrase 'the product was marketed', and on this the Regulation does not provide the clarity which we need. As to the meaning of 'the product', does it mean the actual one, or the specific model, or products which are part of the same family?[64] And what counts as 'marketing' in a world in which advertising, sales promotion, the raising of 'brand consciousness', and opportunities to purchase by telephone or computer are

---

[62] Though Article 5(1) is not necessarily confined to claims against a manufacturer.
[63] As to who the defendant must be for the purpose of this Article, no indication is given.
[64] For example, 'the iPhone' would describe a very large number of different versions of the same thing.

everywhere and nowhere? All answers would be speculative, and principle does not seem to point clearly to any particular conclusion.

And if none of these hypotheses applies, then in spite of the fact that the opening words of Article 5 indicate that it is exhaustive, leaving no room for any other law to deal with non-contractual obligations arising out of product liability, the court must still decide on the claim before it. It will, it appears, fall back on the *lex generalis* in Article 4(1), and apply the law of the place where the damage occurred. If one were to ask whether the net effect of Article 5 is superior to what Article 4 would have yielded, the answer is not easy to give.

(b) Unfair competition; acts restricting free competition

Article 6 deals with non-contractual obligations arising out of unfair competition[65] and acts which restrict free competition. For these torts, the general solution provided by Article 4 is excluded altogether, except for the single case in which unfair competition affects exclusively the interests of a specific competitor.[66]

For unfair competition, Article 6(1) provides that the applicable law is that of the country in which competitive relations or the collective interests of consumers are likely to be affected; it remains to be seen how this rule is to work where the tort has this effect in more countries than one. For cases of restriction of competition, the basic orientation of the rule set out in Article 6(3) is to apply the law of the country where the market is, or is likely to be, affected: this reflects the broader general rule in Article 4(1) in favour of the place where the damage occurs. If the effect of the unlawful activity is conspiracy which leads to a loss of sales, the relevant market will be where the sales would have taken place;[67] if it is unlawful cartel activity causing an increase in cost it will be where the increased costs were incurred. However, if the restriction affected more than one market, a pragmatic solution is called for to avoid complexity and the fragmentation of claims. It is most convenient to set it out exactly as the Regulation does in Article 6(3)(b): 'When the market is, or is likely to be, affected in more than one country, the person seeking compensation for damage who sues in the court of the domicile of the defendant, may instead choose to base his or her claim on the law of

---

[65] Including claims by consumer organisations to restrain the use of unfair terms in contracts with consumers: Case C–191/15 *VfK v Amazon EU* EU:C:2016:612, [2017] QB 252.

[66] Article 6(2).

[67] cf Case C–27/17 *AB flyLAL-Lithuanian Airlines v Starptautiskā lidosta Rīga VAS* EU:C:2018:533, [2019] 1 WLR 669; Case C–451/18 *Tibor-Trans Fuvarozó és Kereskedelmi Kft. v DAF TRUCKS N.V.* EU:C:2019:635.

the court seised, provided that the market in that Member State is amongst those directly and substantially affected by the restriction of competition out of which the non-contractual obligation on which the claim is based arises; where the claimant sues, in accordance with the applicable rules on jurisdiction, more than one defendant in that court, he or she can only choose to base his or her claim on the law of that court if the restriction of competition on which the claim against each of these defendants relies directly and substantially affects also the market in the Member State of that court.'

The result will be that where, for example, a cartel has engaged in a price-fixing conspiracy, and has put this into practice across several national or regional markets, the claimant may be able to choose to base his claim on the law of the country in which proceedings are brought. It is a pragmatic solution for cases which are almost inevitably complex. Indeed, it has been suggested that the applicable law rule in Article 6(3)(b) could provide the model for an improved rule of special jurisdiction under the (former) Brussels I Regulation.[68]

No choice of law by the parties is permitted for torts falling within Article 6.[69]

(c) Environmental damage

For non-contractual obligations arising out of environmental damage,[70] including damage sustained by persons or property as a result of such damage, Article 7 specifies as applicable the law of the country in which the damage occurs unless the victim opts to found his claim on the law of the country in which the event giving rise to the damage occurred. In other words, the only two possible laws to be applied are that of the occurrence of the damage and that of the event giving rise to it: there may be a closer connection with a third country, but that country's law is shut out from potential operation.

Once again, at first sight the rule, and in particular the option which it gives to the claimant (who may be but need not be a personal victim), reflects the special jurisdictional rule given by the former Brussels I Regulation for cases of tort. But this rule opens up the possibility that when toxic emissions escape from an industrial plant just across the border, a claimant may ask the courts for the place of the defendant's domicile to apply the law of the

---

[68] See the Opinion of the Advocate-General in Case C–352/13 *CDC Hydrogen Peroxide SA v Evonik Degussa GmbH* EU:C:2014:2443. The point was not addressed by the Court in its judgment: EU:C:2015:335.
[69] Article 6(3).
[70] See also Recital 24 for the amorphous definition of 'environmental damage'.

place where the fish or birds were killed. No doubt the possibility that something similar might be done accounts for the exclusion of non-contractual obligations arising out of nuclear damage, for Member States using these terrifying machines for generation of electric power tend to site them on the remotest edges of their territory, whence it is hoped that wind and tide will carry the consequences away. The idea that Irish residents might bring proceedings against the company running a nuclear power plant on the coast of Cumbria, complaining of radiation escaping into the Irish Sea, and be entitled to have the English court apply Irish law,[71] for example, will not have been an attractive one.

(d) Infringement of intellectual property rights

For non-contractual obligations arising from the infringement of intellectual property rights, Article 8 provides that the applicable law is the law of the country for which the protection is claimed;[72] where the non-contractual obligation arises from the infringement of a unitary Community right, the 'country in which the act of infringement was committed' is located at the place of the initial act of infringement at the origin of the conduct complained of.[73]

Article 8 does not allow the parties to depart from it by an Article 14 agreement.

(e) Industrial action

Non-contractual obligations arising from industrial action are governed by the general rule in Article 4, but with one modification: in place of Article 4(1), with its reference to the law of the place where the damage occurs, Article 9 makes its reference to the law of the country where the action is to be or has been taken. The rule applies whether the claim lies against a worker or a workers' organization, and whether the action is past, or pending. It is a sensible enough rule, for two among many reasons. First, there is a closer association between criminal law and civil law in the area of industrial relations than in most other areas: the idea that the law of the place determines the presence or absence of criminal liability for organizing strikes and other campaigns of industrial warfare is so well entrenched that it is natural to allow the law of the place where the action is taken to determine the civil law

---

[71] In fact, the problem is liable to be even more acute in mainland Europe.
[72] See Case C–170/12 *Pinckney v KDG Mediatech AG* EU:C:2013:635; [2014] FSR 354.
[73] Case C–24/16 *Nintendo Co Ltd v BigBen Interactive GmbH* EU:C:2017:724.

consequences as well. Second, there will be cases in which the place of the damage would in any event be hard to discern. If one considers the long campaign of industrial action organized by or on behalf of the maritime trade unions against ship owners and ship operators who flag or re-flag their vessels in convenient places, the industrial action has its employer-damaging effects in several countries at the same time: indeed, it would be liable to fail if it did not. This is more than enough to justify the terms of Article 9.

6. ROME II REGULATION: OBLIGATIONS WHICH ARE NOT TORTS

(a) Scheme of Chapter III

Chapter III of the Rome II Regulation provides the rules for non-contractual obligations arising in three contexts which evidently are not at home within a chapter dealing with torts.[74] Their appearance in Chapter III is a matter of organizational convenience, and that Chapter III should simply be regarded as *sui generis*. There is no reliable relationship to the special jurisdictional rules in Article 7 of the (former) Brussels I Regulation. For example (and it is only one example), a claim made for the recovery of sums paid under a failed contract falls under the special jurisdictional rule for matters relating to a contract in Article 7(1) of the Brussels I Regulation, but if the location of unjust enrichment in Chapter III of the Rome II Regulation were to suggest that this kind of claim was based neither on a contractual nor on a non-contractual obligation in the nature of a tort, it is hard to see how it could have fallen within Article 7 of the Brussels I Regulation at all. For this among other reasons, it is suggested that point 7 of the Recitals to the Rome II Regulation, which calls for consistency in interpretation, should not be pressed beyond the limit of what is sensible. With the United Kingdom no longer bound by the Brussels I Regulation, any argument which calls for consistency of this kind is not liable to be persuasive.

The three cases placed within Chapter III share two characteristics. First, they arise, or are liable to arise, in territory adjacent to or overlapping with other categories of case for which an applicable law rule is separately prescribed. Unjust enrichment claims may arise in connection with a contract which has been rescinded, or with a 'contract' which was mistakenly

---

[74] For the problems of locating knowing receipt within Chapter III or Chapter II, see fn 1 above.

supposed to have been made, or with a payment made on the misunderstanding that the person paid was the contractual counterparty when he was not, or when it was not realized that the contract had been discharged. They may arise in connection with a tort, such as the misappropriation of another's property to make a gain; and they may arise without any such connection. Uninvited intervention in another's affairs may take place between contracting parties, or in the circumstances in which a tort is committed, such as where the claimant intervenes to prevent a fire carelessly started from doing damage to another's property, or in response to an Act of God for which no one is to blame.[75] And pre-contractual fault almost always arises in connection with a contract, even though in some cases the fault prevents the conclusion of the valid and binding contract which was foreseen.

In other words, these three causes of action are not as free-standing and insulated from the rest of the world as some others may be. This could have been problematic, but the excellent practical sense of the Regulation is to provide conflicts rules for these cases which mean that in these adjacent cases, the applicable law takes its colour from the relationship to which it is proximate.

Second, the three cases are dealt with by a series of sub-rules, addressed in sequence, and finishing up with a default sub-rule. It is not exactly elegant, but it seems to offer the best opportunity for connecting the issue to a law which might rationally have been expected to govern it, which is a virtue in its own right.

And the freedom of the parties to choose the law to govern their non-contractual obligation, which is conferred by Article 14, applies also to Chapter III. All things considered, the result is pretty satisfactory.

(b) Unjust enrichment

The applicable law for non-contractual obligations arising out of unjust enrichment, which includes obligations arising from the payment of amounts wrongly received (or, perhaps more correctly, anyhow received but wrongfully retained), is covered by a four-part rule set out as Article 10. If the obligation concerns a relationship between the parties, such as a contract or a tort, it will be governed by the law which governs that prior relationship. Otherwise, if the parties had their habitual residence in the same country when the event giving rise to the unjust enrichment occurred, the law of that

---

[75] There is, no doubt, a theological point to be made here; it is better ignored.

country will apply, failing which the applicable law will be that of the country in which the unjust enrichment took place. And whichever of those rules provided the answer, if the non-contractual obligation is manifestly more closely connected to another country, the law of that country shall apply instead.

If one accepts that unjust enrichment is little more than a label applied to a motley collection of individual cases in which a law might properly require payment or repayment, but which fit neither individually into another legal category nor together as an integrated whole, an applicable law scheme of alternate reference is rational. The effect of the scheme in Article 10 is that those non-contractual obligations closely connected to contracts[76] or torts will be governed by the *lex contractus* or the *lex delicti*, with the result that there is no need to worry whether they should be regarded 'as' contractual or tort claims: that may have been, as said above, a controversial issue in the interpretation of the Brussels I Regulation,[77] but it has been taken care of and put to bed for the purpose of applicable law. As to the escape clause which allows reference to the law of another country, this will most likely arise in the case for which the applicable law would otherwise be selected as the place of the enrichment. For the place of enrichment may be difficult to locate or artificial where the 'enrichment' takes the form of electronic crediting of bank or other accounts: particularly in the case in which funds are instantaneously transferred—except that nothing except data, whatever that is, is actually transferred—from one account to another (and all the more so if the true beneficiary of the bank account is cloaked in mystery), it may hard to say where 'the' unjust enrichment took place, and harder to believe that it should actually matter.[78] Even so, the fact that this default rule resembles what the common law rules would have said on the same question simply goes to show that this rather uncomfortable rule of last resort may be the least bad option.

(c) *Negotiorum gestio*

The applicable law for non-contractual obligations arising from acts performed without due authority in connection with the affairs of another (*negotiorum gestio*, benevolent interference, or necessitous intervention)

---

[76] A claim for repayment on the annulment of a contract is contractual: Case C–366/13 *Profit Investment Sim SpA v Ossi* EU:C:2016:282, [2016] 1 WLR 3832 (a case on special jurisdiction under the (former) Brussels I Regulation).

[77] See p 71.

[78] cf *Fiona Trust & Holding Corp v Privalov* [2010] EWHC 3199 [179].

is, according to Article 11, framed in the same general way. The first rule is to apply the law which governs the relationship existing between the parties if there is one; if not, the law of the shared habitual residence when the event giving rise to the damage occurred, if there is one; if not, the law of the country in which the intervener's act was performed; and in any event, an escape clause allows the application of the law of the country with which the obligation is manifestly more closely connected.

(d) *Culpa in contrahendo*

Article 12 of the Rome II Regulation deals with non-contractual obligations arising from dealings prior to the conclusion of a contract, whether or not a contract was concluded. The Regulation labels this *culpa in contrahendo*, though pre-contractual fault, which will include misrepresentation and non-disclosure, would be more familiar to English ears. As was said above, this conflicts rule deals with the non-contractual obligations which arise from such dealings. It does not apply to the contractual obligations which arise, so it will not apply to the question whether the contract is valid, voidable, or non-existent, for those are issues of contractual obligation (or not) to which the *lex contractus* as identified by the Rome I Regulation will usually apply.[79] The rule in Article 12 is left to deal with the applicable law for claims for compensation for fraud, misrepresentation, non-disclosure, failure to negotiate or to contract in good faith, and so forth, where these arise from dealings prior to the making or possible making of a contract. Insofar as there was an obligation to do or to refrain from doing any of these things, the obligation is a non-contractual one: adjacent to contractual, perhaps, but non-contractual.

The principal rule enacted by Article 12 is that the non-contractual obligation in such cases is governed by the law which applies to the contract or would have applied to it had it been entered into. Where the applicable law cannot be determined on that basis—presumably where it is just not possible to say or predict with sufficient certainty which law would have governed a contract which never came into being—the applicable law is determined on the basis of a three-part rule which reflects the three-part rule in Article 4. Presumably, if this process results in an applicable law which seems completely unfair to the court, public policy will serve as the rule of last resort.

---

[79] If the contract was concluded on or after 17 December 2009.

C. OBLIGATIONS OUTSIDE THE ROME II REGULATION

Left outside the scope of the Rome II Regulation, and governed by the rules of the common law and Parliamentary statute—which the Regulation displaced for non-contractual obligations falling within its scope—are non-contractual obligations arising from events occurring before 11 January 2009; obligations arising otherwise than in civil and commercial matters; and all non-contractual obligations arising out of violations of privacy, and rights relating to personality, including defamation.[80] It is likely that the European Union will extend the Rome II Regulation to cover such cases but, if it happens after Exit Day, any such thing will not affect the United Kingdom unless Parliament considers that such a change would improve English law and acts accordingly.

1. DEFAMATION

The conflicts rule for claims in the nature of defamation, whenever committed, is found in the common law, because defamation was excluded from the Private International Law (Miscellaneous Provisions) Act 1995.[81] Though what is said in relation to defamation describes the conflicts rule which once applied to all torts, we will limit ourselves to its application to defamation.

The principal problem is not with the conflicts rule as such, but with defamation as a tort. This is because the common law regarded every communication of defamatory material to another as an individual tort, separate and distinct from every other communication of the same information: for conflicts purposes there is no 'aggregation' of the publication or of the complaint. So far as the conflicts rule is concerned, the first step is to work out where the tort, or torts, occurred. This is done by enquiring where the cause of action 'in substance' arose;[82] in the context of defamation, that place will be where the information was received. If that was in England, English domestic

---

[80] It is not certain, but claims which allege economic loss resulting from negligence, for example by carelessly writing a 'kiss of death' job reference (cf *Spring v Guardian Assurance plc* [1995] 2 AC 296), will not be excluded from the Rome II Regulation, as the basis of liability is not defamation, and the damage is economic rather than moral, reputational, or personal.

[81] Section 13 of the 1995 Act. The Defamation Act 2013 places limitations on the jurisdiction of the court to hear defamation claims, but does not appear to affect the conflict of laws rules which will apply in those cases which the court does have jurisdiction to hear.

[82] *Metall und Rohstoff AG v Donaldson Lufkin & Jenrette Inc* [1990] QB 391, CA.

law applies, no matter how otherwise foreign or otherwise exceptional the facts may be, because every tort committed in England is invariably governed by English law.[83] For torts committed outside England, the claimant must satisfy the rule of double actionability: he must show that the facts and matters relied on would give rise to tortious liability under the domestic law of England, and would establish civil liability for the same head or heads of damage according to the law of the place where the cause of action arose, though here, if the factual connection with one or the other of these laws is remote, the claimant may be dispensed from the requirement of satisfying it.[84] But in principle the requirement of double actionability means that for overseas defamation the claimant must win twice to win once.

The problem, as was said, arises from the rule that each publication, each copy, is a separate and self-contained tort. The logic is impeccable; the bad outcomes are legendary. It meant, among other things, that an individual who fancied himself to have been defamed in a newspaper might pick and choose the 'publications' to complain of. If, for example, the principal place of publication is in the United States, under the laws of which there would be limited civil liability for publishing material about a person in the public eye, the claimant may decide to complain only of the sales of the newspaper in England. Whilst this might limit the size of the damages, the science by which damages for defamation are assessed is obscure, and it is far from clear that the practice ever reflected the theory of the arithmetic. In one ridiculous case a deranged German aristocrat, in exile in Paris, sent his manservant to purchase in London a seventeen-year-old copy of a magazine in the pages of which he claimed to have been defamed. The servant having obeyed his orders, it was held that the sale was a fresh publication by the magazine, for which a claim could be brought.[85] Claimants have since trodden shamelessly in the footsteps of the mad duke.[86] Defamation claims having no rational connection to England routinely turned up in the Strand,[87] it being alleged in all pantomime seriousness that readers or listeners in England would now hold the claimant in ridicule and contempt, and that the court should treat

---

[83] *Metall und Rohstoff AG v Donaldson Lufkin & Jenrette Inc* [1990] QB 391, CA.

[84] *Red Sea Insurance Co Ltd v Bouygues SA* [1995] 1 AC 190.

[85] *Duke of Brunswick v Harmer* (1849) 14 QB 185. He was awarded £500, on any view of the matter a ludicrous sum for a single sale to the claimant's own servant sent to make the purchase.

[86] *Berezovsky v Michaels* [2000] 1 WLR 1004, HL. The same principle has been applied to defamation by internet publication: *Dow Jones Inc v Gutnick* (2003) 210 CLR 575.

[87] 'Libel tourism', as it was pejoratively known.

the case between two foreigners as though it involved two members of the Tunbridge Wells Lawn Tennis Club.

When Parliament enacted the Defamation Act 2013, it focused on the jurisdiction of the court. Section 9(2) provides that the court has no jurisdiction to hear the claim unless it is satisfied that, of all the places in which the statement[88] complained of has been published, England is clearly the most appropriate place in which to bring the action. The court does not appear to have any discretion; it does not appear that the parties may, by consent, create a jurisdiction where the Act has forbidden it. The Act did not touch the conflicts rules for defamation but the problem which called for legislative attention was not one created by the conflict of laws in the first place.

2. OTHER WRONGS

(a) Privacy and rights of personality (1996–present day)

Save for defamation, malicious falsehood, and similar causes of action arising under foreign laws, for which the rules were not changed, the conflicts rule of double actionability was replaced by Part III of the Private International Law (Miscellaneous Provisions) Act 1995, which came into effect in 1996. After the coming into force of the Rome II Regulation, the Act now applied only to causes of action based on a violation of privacy and other rights relating to personality apart from defamation. It will also apply, of course, to causes of action where the events giving rise to liability occurred before 11 January 2009.

The general rule in Section 11 of the Act is (or was) to apply the law of the place where the events constituting the tort in question occurred. Where these events are not entirely located within a single country, the applicable law will be the law of the place where the person was when she sustained the injury or was killed; the law of the place where the property was when it was damaged; and in cases not falling within either of these, the law of the country in which occurred the most significant element or elements of the events comprising the tort.[89] Where the court finds that the answer given by Section 11 is not persuasive, because the tort, or the issue, in question is so much more closely connected to another country that it is substantially more

---

[88] Including references to any statement which conveys the same, or substantially the same, imputation as the statement complained of: s 9(3).

[89] See *VTB Capital plc v Nutritek International Corp* [2013] UKSC 5, [2013] 2 AC 337.

appropriate for the law of that other country to be applied to determine the issue or question, Section 12 allows that other law to be applied instead.[90] The applicable law will determine most aspects of liability, but it will not be applied to the quantification of damages, which is a procedural matter on which an English court always applied English domestic law.[91]

For torts which complain about the violation of privacy,[92] therefore, the applicable law will be either that of the place where the events constituting the tort occurred, or if they are not all located in the same place, the law of the country in which occurred the most significant element or elements of the events comprising the tort. It seems inevitable that this rule lends itself to a degree of manipulation by a claimant, who may identify the invasion of his personal space, or the disclosure or broadcasting of material acquired, as the element of the events which has the greatest significance, framing the claim so as to take advantage of the rule in general and the way it will operate in particular. But so long as the claim can be made good, there is nothing to prevent the claimant putting it as he pleases.

(b) Equitable wrongs (prior to 2009)

The conflicts rule of the common law for torts was not considered to apply to equitable wrongs which were not torts. What the conflicts rule for such wrongs was, however, was much harder to say. On one view the court simply applied the *lex fori*, taking account of foreign points of contact simply as data to inform the assessment, in accordance with English equitable principle, of what conscience required. Another view sought to analogize the particular equitable wrong with one for which there was an established conflicts rule, such as contract, tort, company law, and unjust enrichment. Yet another, at least where equitable remedies were sought, was to look to the *lex causae* to determine whether the obligation which arose under it was sufficiently similar to a fiduciary duty to justify treating it as an equitable wrong for which local equitable remedies were appropriate.[93]

The better view always was that 'equitable wrong' was a meaningless term in the conflict of laws, and that all such cases had to be accommodated within

---

[90]   See *VTB Capital plc v Nutritek International Corp* [2013] UKSC 5, [2013] 2 AC 337.

[91]   *Harding v Wealands* [2006] UKHL 32, [2007] 2 AC 1; *Cox v Ergo Versicherung* [2014] UKSC 22, [2014] AC 1379.

[92]   For these purposes, the misuse of private information should be regarded as a tort: *Vidal-Hall v Google Inc* [2015] EWCA Civ 311, [2016] QB 1003. So, surely, should a claim alleging breach of confidence.

[93]   For example, *First Laser Ltd v Fujian Enterprises (Holdings) Co* [2013] 2 HKC 459.

a traditional common law conflicts rule. It is a relief that insofar as the claim is based on an obligation which is not contractual it will now fall under the Rome II Regulation, with the result that the patchy history which preceded it can be mostly forgotten.

(c) Unjust enrichment (prior to 2009)

The common law never developed a robust conflicts rule for claims based, more or less precisely, on the idea of unjust enrichment: the formulation that it was governed by the proper law of the obligation to make restitution raised more questions than it answered. It was suggested that where the enrichment was closely connected to a contract (real, terminated, rescinded, frustrated, supposed, intended, void) the *lex contractus* would be used,[94] and in cases concerned with land, the *lex situs* was liable to be applied. It was suggested by academic authority, though rarely confirmed by judicial decision,[95] that other cases were liable to be governed by the law of the place of the enrichment, but the uncertainty which this was bound to create, as the very notion of enrichment became ever more delocalized, means that its passing into history is no regret.

---

[94] cf *Baring Bros & Co v Cunninghame DC* [1997] CLC 108 (Outer House).
[95] *Barros Mattos Jr v Macdaniels* [2005] EWHC 1323 (Ch), [2005] ILPr 630; *First Laser Ltd v Fujian Enterprises (Holdings) Co* [2013] 2 HKC 459.

7

PROPERTY

Insofar as any question of jurisdiction arises in this chapter (it does particularly in relation to immovable property), the general situation of English private international law after Exit Day is set out in the introduction to Chapter 2; any question of the effect of foreign judgments likewise in Chapter 3. Insofar as any question arises in this chapter (it does particularly in relation to the assignment of intangible movables) as to the law applicable to matters of contractual and non-contractual obligation, the general situation of English law after Exit Day is set out in the introductions to Chapters 5 and 6.

The private international law of property is a large topic, or perhaps several large topics. Its range is diverse: immovable and movable property, tangible and intangible property, as well as intellectual and family property. It has to deal with a variety of transactions: commercial and domestic, voluntary and involuntary, *inter vivos* and as a consequence of death, marriage, and divorce. It can raise difficult questions about the relationship between jurisdiction and applicable law, and between property and the law of obligations. In many cases in which a court is called upon to adjudicate it is asked to settle a dispute about title, and to make an order which is good and reliable against the world, not just as between the parties to the action. In England, at any rate, most of the conflicts rules are established by the common law. Although the European Union intervened to harmonize private international law in the fields of succession to property and matrimonial property, those Regulations did not extend to the United Kingdom.

Where the conflicts rules are found in the common law, a court may be entitled[1] to apply the law selected in its *renvoi* sense: that is to say, to apply the law (including any conflicts rules) as it would be applied by a judge sitting in the foreign country and hearing the case himself. Even though parties may establish a common position that *renvoi* is not being relied on in their case, this cannot be taken as a decision that the doctrine is inadmissible in the context of property law.

---

[1] If the rules of foreign law are pleaded and proved to the satisfaction of the court.

The Conflict of Laws. Fourth Edition. Adrian Briggs, Oxford University Press (2019). © Adrian Briggs
DOI: 10.1093/oso/9780198838500.003.0007

The private international law of property traditionally divides into immovable and movable property, and movables sub-divide into tangible things and intangible property. Whether property is an immovable is determined by the law of the place where it is, the *lex situs*.[2] It may be thought that this offends against the principle that characterization is a matter for the *lex fori*, and that in cases of potential disagreement, such as where the property is an oil rig, the interest of a mortgagee in the property mortgaged, the interest of a beneficiary under a trust of land, and so on, this question should be answered by the law of the forum whose conflicts rules are in issue, after all. But where the *lex situs* is broadly applicable, and *renvoi* applies also, it would be somewhat self-defeating to distort the very law which a court is seeking to apply. The result is that the question whether property is movable or immovable is determined by the *lex situs*.

A. IMMOVABLE PROPERTY

For present purposes, immovable property is probably confined to land. The traditional view that it included patents, and perhaps also copyrights, has fallen out of favour, though proceedings to establish the validity of a patent should, for reasons of their own, also be confined to the courts where the patent was granted: not, perhaps, because the patent is immovable, but because this is the only answer that makes any real sense. We will return to this when we look at intellectual property more generally.

1. JURISDICTION

Although we have dealt with jurisdiction in a previous chapter, the private international law of immovable property requires us to re-visit the topic here.

(a) Common law
The long-established rule of the common law was and is that an English court has no jurisdiction to determine questions of title to land situated outside England, and had no jurisdiction to entertain tort claims in which the claim depended on title to land outside England.[3] So for example, where a claim

---

[2] *Re Hoyles* [1911] 1 Ch 179, 185.
[3] *British South Africa Co v Companhia de Moçambique* [1893] AC 602; *Hesperides Hotels Ltd v Aegean Turkish Holidays Ltd* [1979] AC 508.

was brought which alleged trespass to a hotel and its furniture, in the northern part of the island of Cyprus by defendants claiming authorization by the authorities of something calling itself the 'Turkish Republic of Northern Cyprus', the court could not entertain the action concerning trespass to the land, though it could hear the claim alleging wrongful interference with the chattels. The decision shows the width of the rule, for under the *lex situs* (which, as an English connecting factor, acknowledged only the laws of the Republic of Cyprus), there was no question about title, as the ordinances of the illegal non-state were not law. But the exclusionary rule still operated, because the claim advanced depended on title to foreign land, even where there was no dispute about it.

In the immediate aftermath of the Cypriot hotel case, the common law rule was modified by statute to remove the bar to jurisdiction in tort claims where the issue of title was not the principal issue;[4] but otherwise the common law rule remains in place,[5] even in the face of judicial scepticism. Its historical basis may have been that such actions were 'local', and had to be tried in the place where the land was situated, but a more pragmatic reason is that most laws impose similar limitations for reasons of public policy. And as titles to land are increasingly recorded on a register, only the court with personal jurisdiction over the registrar has any sensible basis for taking a case which may result in the registrar being directed to amend the register of title. It follows that, so far as the common law is concerned, disputes about title to foreign land must be tried in the courts of the *situs*, no matter how inconvenient this is, and notwithstanding that the parties would be willing to submit to the personal jurisdiction of an English court. It probably follows that foreign judgments which purport to rule on title to English land will not be recognized in England.[6]

There is a very important common law qualification to this rule. There is nothing to prevent a court exercising jurisdiction over a claim based on a personal obligation, even if that obligation relates to a foreign immovable, and even though it may appear to the untrained eye that the court is doing indirectly what it cannot do directly. It derives from the ancient case of *Penn v Baltimore*.[7] A boundary dispute arose between the proprietors of the proto-states of Pennsylvania and Maryland. They made a contract to go

---

[4] *Re Polly Peck International plc (in administration) (No 2)* [1998] 3 All ER 812 (CA) 828.
[5] Civil Jurisdiction and Judgments Act 1982, s 30.
[6] Although there is the possibility that they may be recognized between the parties as judgments binding them *in personam*, see *Pattni v Ali* [2006] UKPC 51, [2007] 2 AC 85.
[7] (1750) 1 Ves Sen 444.

to arbitration to settle the boundary, but one of them then refused to proceed. Though the court admitted that it had no legal power to determine colonial boundaries, which was within the exclusive jurisdiction of the Privy Council, it had jurisdiction to order parties to act in accordance with their contracts and their consciences, and in ordering specific performance it did just that.[8] Despite these colourful origins, the principle is plain enough: if the claim is brought to enforce a contract, or in respect of a pre-existing equitable obligation, such as a trust, between the parties, the court does not lack jurisdiction to enforce it, even if the obligation derives from, or is created by, a transaction relating to land;[9] a similar principle applies if a court is administering an estate which includes foreign land. Indeed, it is because there is no contract or equity between trespasser and proprietor that legislation was required to align the law of tort with this general principle. So if it is claimed that the vendor has failed to perform his contract for sale of land,[10] or that a bare trustee should convey legal title to the claimant beneficiary, the court does not lack jurisdiction[11] to enforce the personal obligation against the defendant, which it may back up with its considerable coercive powers, requiring the conveyance of the land; or awarding damages for the breach, for example. Likewise, a court should have jurisdiction to assess shares in the equitable ownership of foreign land to the purchase of which the parties claim to have contributed, and to decree the performance of the duties of any resulting or constructive trust. The court is not doing something indirectly which it cannot do directly; it is doing, directly, exactly what it is asked to do.

(b) The (former) Brussels I Regulation

Common law principles of jurisdiction were inapplicable when jurisdiction in a civil or commercial matter was governed by the Brussels I Regulation. As we saw above, proceedings which had as their object rights *in rem* in, or tenancies of, land in another Member State were within the exclusive jurisdiction of the courts of that state.[12] This meant that a claim founded on and seeking to enforce the claimant's existing legal title was subject to exclusive jurisdiction, but that proceedings to enforce or dissolve personal obligations

---

[8] The line which was drawn became known as the Mason-Dixon Line.
[9] cf Case C–294/92 *Webb v Webb* [1994] ECR I–1717: a case on what became Art 24(1) of the Brussels Regulation.
[10] *Stevens v Hamed* [2013] EWCA Civ 911, [2013] ILPr 623.
[11] That is to say, it will still need to have jurisdiction in accordance with the rules in Ch 2.
[12] See p 58; and Chapter III of the (former) Brussels I Regulation requires the non-recognition of judgments which conflict with this rule.

undertaken in respect of that land were not, even though (albeit the case law was untidy) the effects of the judgment might well have an impact on third parties. Where the land was in a non-Member State, but the proceedings otherwise reflected those to which Article 24(1) applied, the Article itself was obviously inapplicable as it could not give exclusive jurisdiction to a non-Member State. Less clear was whether the rule could be applied by analogy, or such cases be left to the application of the common law rule (or, indeed, neither). Though it was much debated in the literature, the issue was studiously avoided by the courts.[13]

2. APPLICABLE LAW

(a) To the issue of title to land

Where the court does have jurisdiction, the inevitable conflicts rule for questions concerning title to land is to apply the *lex situs* as this would be applied in a court at the *situs*: this may, of course, result in the application of the domestic law of country other than that of the *situs* via the principle of *renvoi*. The usual justification for this result is the futility of doing anything other than what a local judge would do, for she alone has control of the immovable, and her view on the correct answer is inevitably destined to prevail: even those whose distaste for *renvoi* sends the needle off the scale accept that it has a proper role in questions of title to immovable property. It is rather ironic that this justification is not as convincing as it may seem. The real question for the foreign judge (as, were the roles reversed, it would be for an English judge) is whether to accept that a judge in another country had the right to make an order concerning local land at all, rather than asking whether that judge arrived at the right substantive answer: she may still refuse to recognize a foreign judgment, even though its reasoning and the result appear to her to be unimpeachable; and the recognition of a judgment does not usually depend on the conclusion that the adjudicating judge decided correctly. Having said that, it is impossible to maintain a credible argument for the application of anything other than the *lex situs*, and in its *renvoi* sense if the parties raise it, where the question is properly one of determining title to the land.[14]

---

[13] See generally at p 91 above.
[14] *Bank of Africa v Cohen* [1909] 2 Ch 129 (CA).

(b) To the obligation which relates to the land

Matters are completely different where the court has jurisdiction over an obligation relating to land: there is no reason to suppose or insist that the law governing the obligation must be the *lex situs* of the land. Although the application of the *lex situs* may be presumed to be the governing law, in the absence of choice, for contracts concerning land,[15] it is not difficult to see, for example, that two people in England, making a contract for sale and purchase of a pied-à-terre in Paris, or a beachside villa in Barbados, will expect, and may certainly choose, the contract to be governed by English law. Likewise, the fact that one of the assets of a trust is land in a foreign country provides little reason to suppose that the law governing the trust is the law of that foreign country: all the more so if the law of that country does not provide for trusts, or the trust contains a diverse range of assets. The law of that foreign country may decide whether the land is, for example, capable of being owned by a foreigner or held in trust for another, or whether the proprietor has personal capacity to deal with it or to create a charge over it; but all this is merely data taken into account by the law which governs the obligation in question, which is governed by its own law.[16] So for example, if the vendor fails to complete the sale, or the purchaser the purchase, because the *lex situs* provides that land may not be owned by a foreigner, the law applicable to the contract will determine the effect, if any, of that fact on the legal validity, and if valid, enforceability, of the contract. If, for example, it decides that the vendor is in breach, for having failed to perform what he promised, the court will not order specific performance, but there is no reason whatever to object to an award of damages.

B. MOVABLE PROPERTY

The reason for applying the *lex situs* in the case of title to immovables is that, because the land cannot be moved, the application of the *lex situs* combines expectation with reality. By contrast, movables move: the clue is in the name. True as this is, it does not affect the approach to the conflict of laws, only the justification for the answer which it gives. Private international law treats tangible and intangible movable property separately.

---

[15] Rome I Regulation, Art 4(1)(c).
[16] *Akers v Samba Financial Group* [2017] UKSC 6, [2017] AC 424.

1. TANGIBLE THINGS

Questions of title to, or the right to possession of, tangible movable property are governed by the *lex situs* of the thing at the date of the event which is alleged to have affected title to it.[17] In the leading classic case, when goods rescued from a shipwreck on the coast of Norway were auctioned and sold by the local magistrate, the buyer acquiring a good title under Norwegian law, it was held that the title of the former owner was lost: Norwegian law held that the local auction gave title to the purchaser, and removed it from the former owner, and that was pretty much that. Certainty and security of title are paramount, and are best achieved by the general application of the *lex situs*: if you take a title which is good according to the law of the place where the thing is, that really should be conclusive against the world. Recognizing this, and understanding that hard cases will inevitably make bad law, the courts have been resolute in refusing, as well they might, to admit exceptions to the *lex situs* rule. So for example, if the parties are together in one place but the thing is elsewhere, the law of the place of the transaction, the *lex loci actus*, will not be applied but the *lex situs* will;[18] if an artwork is stolen from England and purchased from the thief in a country which considers the purchaser to get good title, the *lex situs* of the thing when sold will apply.[19] Of course, if the parties have made a contract which specifies when property will pass, this may be effective, but only if its validity and effect are acknowledged by the *lex situs* applying (one presumes[20]) its own conflicts rules to assess the effect of the contract. The *lex situs* prevails.

As to whether *renvoi* does so as well, the answer is unclear. One view of the principle of security of title would suggest that our concern is with law as a local judge would apply it to the matter at hand; and if it is pleaded, *renvoi* should be admissible, the better to support the policy underpinning the conflicts rule itself.[21] An opposite view[22] holds that recourse to the principle of *renvoi* may actually weaken the reliability of local advice (which tends to be

---

[17]   *Cammell v Sewell* (1860) 5 H & N 728.

[18]   *Glencore International AG v Metro Trading Inc* [2001] 1 Lloyd's Rep 283.

[19]   *Winkworth v Christie, Manson & Woods* [1980] Ch 496.

[20]   The argument to the contrary is that the Rome I Regulation, Art 20, does not allow for this. One response might be that as the Regulation does not apply to proprietary issues, it does not affect the operation of the *lex situs* in its full, *renvoi*, sense.

[21]   In this respect the methodology is that of *Neilson v Overseas Projects Corpn of Victoria* (2005) 223 CLR 331.

[22]   *Iran v Berend* [2007] EWHC 132 (QB), [2007] 2 All ER (Comm) 132; *Blue Sky One Ltd v Mahan Air* [2010] EWHC 631 (Comm). *Dornoch Ltd v Westminster International BV* [2009] EWHC 889 (Admlty), [2009] 2 Lloyd's Rep 191, is open-minded on the issue.

sought and given in relation to domestic law) and the expectation that local law will be applied and that titles obtained in accordance with local domestic law will be indefeasible. As matters currently stand, the arguments are balanced and law is not settled.

It is possible for there to be a succession of transfers of, or other dealings with, a movable, and for these to take place in a series of countries with conflicting laws. There are two basic possibilities which may have been used to justify the law by which title will be determined. Suppose that X delivers a car to Y on terms of hire purchase, according to which X remains owner during the period of hire, but that Y drives the car to a second country where he sells the car to Z. Suppose also that under the law of the second country, a person in possession of a chattel with apparent ownership of it can sell and confer a good title on a buyer in good faith, but that under the law of the first country, the governing principle of *nemo dat quod non habet* would mean that Y had no title to give. Under the law of the first country X had an indefeasible title, which could not be affected by a purported sale by a non-owner. Under the law of the second country, the principle of indefeasible titles does not prevail, and a buyer in good faith, Z, may acquire a title which was better than that of his seller. It is clear that the law considers the principal question to be whether Z obtained a good title. Once that is known, the status of earlier titles falls from view, though if it is alleged that Y committed a tort against X when he did an act which destroyed X's title, the law applicable to non-contractual wrongs will deal with the question of liability.

It is obvious that it can be very difficult: in one truly memorable case, the judge had to follow the trail of a painting which disappeared from its home in Germany at the end of the war and then passed from hand to grubby hand before re-appearing at Sotheby's. So murky was the evidence of where the painting was, or who may have transferred it (never mind how or why they might have done so) there was no transaction which, applying the *lex situs* rule and the need to establish sufficient facts to make it do anything, overrode the title of the claimant state.[23] Ironically, perhaps, the one event which may have altered its title was the dissolution of the foundation which had owned the painting in the first place, and the vesting of its assets by succession '*in universum jus*' by another legal body: and for the purposes of that succession, it does not matter where the assets of the entity are, for they are not subject to a transaction or a transfer, but to the consequences of a process.

---

[23] *City of Gotha v Sotheby's* (9 September 1998). It is one of the most fascinating judgments ever written.

The rule as it applies to transfers allows for one exception. If the goods are in transit and[24] their *situs* unknown there is an argument that the case for applying the *lex situs* has gone, and that it makes better sense to apply instead the law which governs the transaction which is alleged to have affected title.[25] By contrast, where a disposition of goods is effected by document, it is not yet, and may never be, accepted that the *lex situs* of the goods can be overlooked in favour of (say) the law of the place of the documents, or the law of the place of the handing over or endorsing of the documents. In principle, the answer should be that if the *lex situs* of the goods considers the purported disposition by dealing with the documents as effective, that will be conclusive; but that if it does not, that is conclusive also.[26] Any uncertainty in the minds of those involved in the trade or transaction will presumably be reflected in the price or in the taking of insurance.

Although the conflicts rule was originally established in the context of derivative titles, that is, transfers, it also applies to original modes of acquisition, to establish the claim of title to things found (*occupatio*), to new things made (*specificatio*), to things incorporated into something else (*accessio*), and to things mixed and blended (*commixtio* and *confusio*).[27] But the simple moving of a chattel from one country to another will not have any effect upon its title; to hold otherwise would be most inconvenient. If goods are transported across several countries, and under the law of one of them an existing title is for some reason not recognized, it would be unhelpful for the thing thereafter to be regarded as ownerless and as available for *occupatio*. It may be necessary to adapt the exception, described in the last paragraph, to produce this result.

We may draw the following conclusions. The question whether A obtained good title to a camera which he bought in Ruritania is governed by Ruritanian law, even if the camera had been delivered on hire purchase terms or under a conditional sale to A's seller in England; whether B lost his title to a painting stolen from him in England and sold by auction in Italy to another is governed by Italian law, even though the theft took place in England;[28] whether

---

[24] In its established form, this is conjunctive, not disjunctive. Although there is a case for restating the exception in disjunctive form, the increased scope for uncertainty which this would create will make it unlikely to be adopted.

[25] Dicey, Rule 133, exception.

[26] There will naturally be consequential contractual claims.

[27] *Glencore International AG v Metro Trading Inc* [2001] 1 Lloyd's Rep 283. The *situs* rule also applies to seizure by way of nationalization or confiscation of property by governments; see Section (D)(1), below.

[28] *Winkworth v Christie, Manson & Woods Ltd* [1980] Ch 496.

C succeeded in reserving and retaining title to steel after its use or on-sale by D is answered by the *lex situs* of the steel at the time of D's use of or dealing with it, which law will also decide whether it is still steel or is a completely different thing;[29] whether E became owner of something he found while on holiday in Greece will be answered by Greek law, even if the original owner had never given up hope of finding it.

Actions to recover movable property, or to obtain damages for its wrongful loss, are brought in the form of tort actions: in the domestic common law, as claims alleging the tort of conversion; in foreign systems as claims which allege usurpation, interference, trespass, and so on. In terms of private international law, one supposes, these are claims based on the non-contractual obligation of the defendant to the claimant, and therefore as claims which fall within the material scope of the Rome II Regulation. Of course, this does not mean that the law which governs the obligation relied on by the claimant, and probably governed by the law of the place where the damage occurred, also determines the question of title. Title still has to be determined—where it is material to the obligation relied on by the claimant or the defence raised in answer to the claim—by the common law conflicts rules. This is because the Rome II Regulation applies only to the obligation, not to answer the questions of property law upon which that obligation may depend.

The conflicts rule for tangible movables also applies to negotiable instruments.[30] As the instrument, being negotiable, is as good as the right to which it is the key, transfers of the document are, in effect, transfers of the thing. The same principle applies to bearer shares, which are treated as tangible things, and where transfer of the instrument is effective to transfer all rights or property inherent in it.

2. INTANGIBLE PROPERTY

(a) General

The conflicts rules which apply to dealings with intangible property—the rights arising from a debt owed by a bank to an account-holder, the rights under a policy of insurance, the rights of an investor in a unit trust, shares

---

[29] *Re Interview Ltd* [1975] IR 382; *Armour v Thyssen Edelstahlwerke AG* [1991] 2 AC 339; but both cases are only weak authority for the proposition advanced in the text.

[30] Whether the document is negotiable is determined by its *situs* at the time of its purported negotiation.

in companies, bonds and complex financial securities, and so forth—have traditionally raised issues of complexity, for three among many reasons. First, it was sometimes difficult to see why or on what basis intangibles which derived from simple contracts were characterized under the common law as property at all, rather than as the simple contractual or analogous right/obligation which they often are. If the question is who is now entitled to the benefit of a debt or other contractual obligation, this is really to ask little more than who stands in a relationship equivalent to privity with the debtor or obliged party. From this perspective there will be no substantial distinction between owning a debt and being owed a debt. This analysis would tend to suggest that the issues which arise are really only facets of the law of contract, albeit with a particular gloss supplied by laws regulating finance, security, and insolvency, but which may allow them to be got up to look like something else as well. It would follow from that that, whatever the common law might have thought, one would expect to find the answer to questions of the conflict of laws in the Rome I Regulation.

Second, the universe of intangible things is almost certainly too wide for a uniform conflicts rule to be comfortably applied to everything in it. A rule developed in the 19th century for the assignment of spousal insurance policies or of interests under family trusts and dynastic settlements, was not designed for, and may not adapt to, dealings with interests in financial instruments held in indirect holding systems; and it may really, really struggle with delocalized or dematerialized 'securities' of the sort which now serve to underpin or undermine the global financial system. Either a conflicts rule has to allow for pragmatic exceptions, so that doctrinal dogmatism does not defeat the expectations of commerce, or the law must develop new (sub-)rules.

Third, the common law authorities on dealing with debts or intangible property were remarkably opaque. As editor of Dicey, Dr Morris asserted, in the face of some really useless case law, that the law governing the underlying obligation would determine its assignability; the law governing the actual or purported transaction of assignment would govern the effect of the relationship between assignor and assignee; and when the two answers were combined, the answer would emerge. Article 14 of the Rome I Regulation provides a statutory rule for voluntary assignments of contractual obligations which is similar in effect to the common law as declared by Dr Morris. Article 14(2) states that the law governing the right or claim assigned, which really means the law under which the obligation was created, determines its assignability, the relationship between assignee (or, one supposes, assignees if there are more than one) and debtor, the conditions for invoking the assignment against the debtor, and the discharge of the debtor. Article 14(1) states that the mutual obligations of assignor and assignee are governed by the law applicable to the contract between them. In other words, issues involving the debtor and enforcement against him are governed by the law which governs the debt; any residual or consequential issues between the creditors, or between those trading in the debt owed by the debtor, are for the law governing their bilateral relationship.

This has the basic elements of good sense about it, for it accords due weight to the law which created the thing being dealt with. It protects the legitimate expectation of the parties who created the obligation that it has all, but only, the characteristics with which they endowed it, thereby reflecting the essentially contractual nature of the thing assigned; and it invites the conclusion that, as Article 14 embraces these matters within the Rome I Regulation as matters relating to contractual obligations in the autonomous sense, it precludes any argument that they are, in any exclusionary sense, proprietary. It also means that there is no need, at this stage, to enquire into the location of a debt. That question does arise, however, if there has been an involuntary seizure (governmental, judicial) of the debt, and it is therefore touched on in relation to governmental seizure of property.[31]

Having said that, there remains a persistent argument that, while Article 14 regulates contractual issues properly so called, it should not apply to 'the proprietary aspects of intangibles', by which is meant the relative rights of one assignee against another assignee. The difficulties with this argument were many, but for reasons set out in the discussion of the meaning of contractual obligations, it is not currently tenable.[32] On the other hand, the Rome Regulation analysis causes problems for those who trade in bundles of debts (receivables), and for whom the task of ascertaining the law under which each separate debt was created (or will in the future be created) is discouraging. From this perspective it may be argued that the property which is passed from one to another may be seen not as the debt (which really means the credit) as such, but as the right to tell the debtor whether to discharge the debt by paying to A or to B or to C as the case may be. If an 'assignment of the debt' is understood as a passing of the right to give instructions to the debtor, giving the assignee the right to tell the assignor to direct the debtor to pay the

---

[31] Below, p 294.
[32] *Raiffeisen Zentralbank Österreich AG v Five Star Trading LLC* [2001] EWCA Civ 68, [2001] QB 825; see p 207 above.

assignee, it is then less obvious that this 'property' is the same 'property' as the debt itself.

The differences in approach are serious and fundamental, and it is hard to see how they may be reconciled. For practical purposes, however, the 'contractual' approach seems to be more easily reconciled with the Rome I Regulation as it is currently framed; and if it has to be concluded, as it does have to be, that the particular issue now has a legislative solution, then until legislative amendment there is little more to be usefully said about it.

Article 14 will be applicable where a contract is made to assign a contractual right or claim. Where the assignment is not by way of contract, the rule still applies, for Article 14(3) extends the meaning to outright transfers (which must include gifts), and transfers by way of security. It is less clear that Article 14 can apply where the right assigned is not a contractual one, for it will appear that in such a case, the Rome I Regulation is simply not engaged. Certainly, where the right assigned is a right to sue another in respect of a non-contractual obligation, its transferability will be determined by the law governing that non-contractual obligation;[33] but in principle, in any case in which the Regulation does not apply, there is no objection to the common law using it to help give shape to the common law. In any case, as Article 14 is probably a reflection of the state of the common law as it was best understood, in the cases in which the common law rules on assignment of intangible property continue to apply, they may well be indistinguishable from those set out in Article 14.

(b) Special cases

Transfers or assignments of registered shares are governed by the *lex incorporationis* for the obvious practical reason that any solution which departs from the law applicable to the share register is futile. In such cases, the general rule in Article 14 of the Rome I Regulation is inapplicable.[34] This may be deduced from the exclusion in Article 1(2)(f) or, perhaps more persuasively, from the argument that it is inaccurate to say that shares are ever assigned: as they comprise a bundle of duties and obligations as well as rights, simple assignment of them is impossible, and the process misdescribed as 'share transfer' is in fact the surrender and new-grant of rights in the company. For shares and other instruments held in systems according to the terms of which a 'shareholder' has only an interest as co-claimant with others

---

[33] Rome II Regulation, Art 15(1)(e).
[34] *Macmillan Inc v Bishopsgate Investment Trust plc (No 3)* [1996] 1 WLR 387 (CA).

in relation to a pool of similar assets registered in the name of someone else (a process which may be replicated upwards through several levels of holding), it seems inevitable that a mechanical solution, derived from a rule made for cases of much less complexity, is not going to work, especially where it would, for no compelling reason, defeat the expectations of all those who participate in the system. On the footing that private international legal science was unlikely to produce a universal solution suitable to those whose business is founded on such activities, a Convention was concluded at The Hague in 2003 which would, if ever adopted, apply a dedicated, if rather complicated, conflicts rule. The proposed rule would not 'look through' to find and apply the law under which the ultimate or original intangible was issued, but would treat the rights of an investor against the entity with which he holds a securities account as being the property, or thing, with which dealing is done, which seems fair enough. But the Convention has been mostly ignored.[35]

(c) Intellectual property

In relation to intellectual property rights, to the extent that a question is not governed by convention or statute, and is not outside the jurisdiction of an English court, issues concerning patents, copyright, and trade mark rights will be governed by the law of the place of the right of protection, or the law of the place for which protection is claimed (*lex protectionis*); and that law will determine whether and on what terms they are assignable. This seems inevitable. Contracts which deal with intellectual property are, of course, just contracts, and they obviously fall within the domain of the Rome I Regulation.

Where jurisdiction is governed by the residual rules of common law, there was thought to be a complication resulting from the view that an English court had no jurisdiction to adjudicate the validity of a foreign intellectual property right. But though said over and again, it was not supported by significant English[36] authority; and in relation to copyright, at least, the Supreme Court concluded that there never had been any such exclusionary common law rule.[37] As the issue of validity of the right would frequently be raised by a defendant sued in proceedings alleging infringement, it was inconvenient that a court could be deprived of jurisdiction over a tort claim,

---

[35] It is in force in relation to Mauritius, Switzerland, and the United States.

[36] *Potter v Broken Hill Pty Co* (1906) 3 CLR 479. But this was reinterpreted, and doubt cast on the width of the proposition as a matter of Australian law, in *Habib v Commonwealth of Australia* (2010) 183 FCR 62.

[37] *Lucasfilm Ltd v Ainsworth* [2011] UKSC 39, [2012] 1 AC 208. The rule may therefore survive for patents; though if it does, the exception in *Penn v Baltimore* (fn 7) will apply to it as well.

especially in relation to a defendant over whom it had personal jurisdiction under the Brussels I Regulation. Certainly, where the right in question was granted under the law of a Member State, and the question of validity had to be determined, Article 24(4) of the Brussels I Regulation gave exclusive jurisdiction, even where the issue simply arose as a defence to a claim alleging infringement, to the Member State of deposit or registration.[38] But where the right arises under the law of a non-Member State, the question whether a court may apply Article 24(4) by analogy, or may look over its shoulder and apply what remains of the common law exclusionary rule, or do neither, remains unsettled. However, the idea that the courts in England are equipped to determine, and can be called upon to determine, the validity of a Japanese or Argentine patent, when the Brussels Regulation provided that they could not determine the validity of a French or German patent, is far from obviously right.

As to conflicts rules for infringement and other non-contractual claims, the Rome II Regulation applies the *lex protectionis* to non-contractual obligations arising from the infringement of intellectual property rights, and excludes the right of the parties to choose another law to govern them.[39]

C. TRUSTS

As hard to pin down in domestic law (are they structures of property or of obligation?) as they are in private international law, trusts throw up some sharp problems to which the common law, for a very long time, managed to avoid giving answers. Today, the private international law of trusts is found in part in legislation made to give effect to The Hague Convention on the Recognition of Trusts.[40] From the perspective of English law, however, the Convention has more to do with the identification of the governing law than with the recognition of foreign trusts for which the common law needed little assistance. The Convention defines a trust as the legal relationship, created, *inter vivos* or on death, voluntarily, and evidenced in writing, when the settlor places assets under the control of a trustee for the benefit of a beneficiary or for a specified purpose.[41] The Act goes further, extending this Convention definition to encompass trusts of property arising under the law of any part of

---

[38] Case C–4/03 *GAT v LüK* [2006] ECR I–6509.
[39] Article 8.
[40] Recognition of Trusts Act 1987.
[41] Article 2.

the United Kingdom, and to trusts created by judicial decision;[42] and applies it to trusts falling within its definition whatever the date of their creation.[43] Its application to implied, resulting, and constructive trusts is therefore clear. Accordingly, the implied or constructive trust arising from the joint purchase of property will fall squarely within the scope of the Act; but where a constructive trust is sought against or imposed upon a defendant found answerable to what the common law would regard as an equitable claim, the relevant conflicts rules are probably those examined under the law of obligations in the previous two chapters.

A trust is, for practical purposes, governed by the law chosen by the settlor; in default of such a demonstrable choice it is governed by the law with which it is most closely connected.[44] In identifying the latter, regard is to be had to the place of administration of the trust, the *situs* of the assets of the trust, the place of residence of the trustee, and the objects of the trust and the places where they are to be fulfilled, but the manner in which these are weighed up is not specified. The governing law regulates the trust, its construction, effect, and administration,[45] but is liable to be displaced or overridden by mandatory and conflicts rules of the *lex fori*, and by public policy.[46] It follows, though, that is it perfectly possible to establish a trust (for example, governed by English law) over property located in a state whose law does not provide for trusts.[47]

It is probable that the law which governs the trust also defines the nature and extent of the liability of trustees. As a matter of English domestic law, a trustee who undertakes a liability on behalf of the trust remains personally liable to the outsider with whom he has dealt—his having acted or contracted 'as trustee' does not affect the contractual or other liability which he assumes to the counterparty, even if it gives him a distinct hope of indemnification—other systems may see the dynamic relationships created by the trust differently. If the law governing the trust limits the personal liability to outsiders of a trustee acting as such, recognition of the trust probably extends to

---

[42] Recognition of Trusts Act 1987, s 1(2).

[43] Article 22.

[44] Articles 6, 7. Note that it is the connection to a law, and not to a country, which is the determining factor. See also *Gómez v Gómez-Monche Vives* [2008] EWCA Civ 1065, [2009] Ch 245.

[45] Article 8.

[46] Article 18.

[47] *Akers v Samba Financial Group* [2017] UKSC 6, [2017] AC 424. Even so, some may wonder how a trust can exist over property which cannot be the subject of a trust, any more than one can have a contract to sell things which are not saleable, such as children. To say that the personal obligations arising from the relationship can be enforced without regard to the property may not be enough.

recognizing this as well.[48] Otherwise it is hard to see that 'the trust', as distinct from a distorted reflection of it, is being recognized at all.

D. EVENTS WHICH AFFECT TITLE TO PROPERTY

We have already examined the conflict of laws rules applicable to acquisition or loss of title by transfers, and the other ordinary transactions of daily life. It is now necessary to consider the effect, on title to property, of other life-changing events.

1. GOVERNMENTAL SEIZURE OF PROPERTY

The seizure or confiscation of property by governments allows us to see the fundamental rules of the conflict of laws in action. The effect of nationalization, or other expropriation or seizure of property by governments, takes as its point of departure the general *lex situs* rule which was considered above.

(a) Property within the territorial jurisdiction of the state

If the property is within the territorial jurisdiction of the state, both the *lex situs* rule and the respect which comity requires to be given to the acts of sovereigns fully executed within their territory will lead to the recognition of the title acquired by this legislative or executive act according to local law:[49] the reference to 'territorial' is important, for it excludes the possibility that the nationality of the owner is in any way relevant. There is no question of an English court being called upon to 'enforce' the foreign law: once that law, the *lex causae* according to the rules of the English conflict of laws, has done what it set out to do and has vested title to the property in the state, there is nothing else left in the foreign law to need enforcing,[50] and the title acquired under it can be enforced as such. So if property is seized by a state pursuant to a confiscatory law, and is then sold by state authority to a buyer who takes good title under that law and

---

[48] *Investec Trust (Guernsey) Ltd v Glenalla Properties Ltd* [2018] UKPC 7, [2019] AC 271. The decision makes perfect sense in the context of the Guernsey and Jersey statutory regimes; its extension to English law is not uncontroversial.

[49] *Luther Co v James Sagor & Co* [1921] 3 KB 532 (CA); *Princess Paley Olga v Weisz* [1929] 1 KB 718 (CA).

[50] *Williams & Humbert Ltd v W & H Trade Marks (Jersey) Ltd* [1986] AC 368.

who then brings the property to England, the former and dispossessed owner has no claim for its delivery up from the person who, as a matter of the English conflict of laws, has an indefeasible title;[51] he has no claim for damages for conversion or other wrong because his dispossession was in accordance with the law of the place where it was done. The transfer of ownership and loss of possession and of any right to possession were all completed under the *lex situs* of the property at the time of the act, and any claim which asserts a right which follows from the claimant's lost ownership will be defeated by the good new title and the lawful taking of possession: after all, if you keep your chattels in a particular place, you can hardly claim to be immune from the laws in force at that place from time to time. Likewise, if a government passes a decree to take ownership of shares in a company incorporated and registered under its law, it may, as new controlling shareholder, direct the management of the company to recover debts and property abroad: the reasoning is the exactly the same.[52] It is only if the confiscating law were so abhorrent that it should be refused even recognition as law,[53] and title acquired by reference to it and the *lex situs* rule treated to a complete ignoral, that the result will be different. But, for example, a rule of Iraqi law which purported to dissolve the state of Kuwait and bodies created under its law, and which vested the property in the Iraqi state, was so monstrous that a court was required to disregard it utterly and completely, no matter where the property was.

Something similar may be true where the Human Rights Act 1998 directs an English court not to apply its laws, which expression certainly includes its conflicts rules, in a way which would contradict the requirements of the European Convention on Human Rights. One would expect that an English court was precluded from giving a judgment which had the effect of condoning behaviour (and giving it effect in the English legal order), wherever committed, which violated the standards of the European Convention. But when faced with a submission substantially in those terms, the House of Lords wobbled, requiring instead that the offending conduct amount to a 'flagrant' breach of the standards of the Convention.[54] This does not feel convincing; it will need to be reconsidered. In the meantime, unless the Convention

---

[51] *Luther Co v James Sagor & Co* [1921] 3 KB 532 (CA).

[52] ibid.

[53] *Kuwait Airways Corpn v Iraqi Airways Co (Nos 4 and 5)* [2002] UKHL 19, [2002] 2 AC 883, refusing to recognize an Iraqi law dissolving Kuwait and assuming ownership of Kuwaiti-owned property.

[54] *Barnette v United States of America* [2004] UKHL 37, [2004] 1 WLR 2241.

is found to be the source for one, there is no rule of English private international law which withholds recognition from a foreign expropriatory law unless compensation is paid for the acquisition;[55] the fact that there may be such an obligation in public international law is of no general relevance in private law.

(b) Property beyond the territorial jurisdiction of the state

By contrast, and perhaps rather obviously, had the decree laid claim to property situated outside the territory state, the ordinary application of the *lex situs* rule would mean that title to the property in England, at least, would be unaffected or unchanged by this legislative act. Any action in the English courts would be founded on a law which was not part of the *lex situs* at the time of the relevant act, and it will follow that such a claim must fail. It follows, of course, that if a foreign state purports to confiscate English copyright, its law will have no effect on title to it.[56] It follows that any action brought to complete what the foreign law had sought to accomplish would have to be seen as seeking the enforcement of that law; and if that is so, the rule against the enforcement of a foreign penal, revenue, or other public law will, as was shown above,[57] defeat the claim on that ground too.

(c) Recovery proceedings brought by a state

It is sometimes suggested that the analysis is more complicated if the property in question was within the territory of the seizing state at the time of the legislative act, but that before being taken into the state's possession it is spirited away. In cases where the *lex situs* itself requires possession to be taken as a precondition to the acquisition of title under it, title will not have been acquired while the property was within the territory of the state, and title cannot be acquired by legislative decree once the property is outside it.[58] There is, however, no wider justification for imposing such a requirement that possession must have been taken as a condition which limits the ability of the state to enforce its title when title has been acquired and vested according to its own law. At the very least, there is no such limitation where the property in question was ownerless when the state legislated to vest title in itself: where the state legislates to acquire title to ownerless property within its territory,

---

[55] *Williams & Humbert Ltd v W & H Trade Marks (Jersey) Ltd* [1986] AC 368.
[56] *Peer International Corp v Termidor Music Publishers Ltd* [2003] EWCA Civ 1156, [2004] Ch 212.
[57] See Ch 4.
[58] *AG for New Zealand v Ortiz* [1984] AC 1.

English private international law will regard the title as good, perfect, and reliable; after all, the acquisition of title to ownerless property is something which anyone can achieve,[59] even if a state can do it in special ways.

By contrast, where the state has legislated for and demanded and acquired its title by expropriating a person who was, until then, the owner, or has nationalized the property of an individual—vesting by divesting, so to speak—the approach will be different. The rule which prevents an English court enforcing foreign public laws will mean that unless the state has already taken possession of the property (in which case it can simply rest upon its lawful acquisition of possession followed by unlawful dispossession), an application for delivery up will be understood as the state calling on the English court to order that it be given the possession which it had not hitherto obtained. It will therefore be seen as asking the English court to enforce a right of divestment, which is peculiar to a state. That makes it a foreign public law; the court will consider that it is being asked to enforce it, and it will not.[60]

The rules about seizure apply easily to immovable property, and to tangible property. In relation to intangible property they certainly apply to shares situated where the company is incorporated, seized, and acquired, in accordance with the law of that country.[61] It is less obvious how it will apply to simple contractual intangibles, but the *situs* of a debt is in general the place of residence of the debtor,[62] for it is there that she may generally be sued, and the *situs* rule will probably apply to it in this sense. Article 14 of the Rome I Regulation, dealing as it does only with voluntary assignments, is irrelevant to the issue.

(d) Judicial seizure of property

Although its function is obviously very different, judicial seizure of property as part of the enforcement of judgments reflects governmental seizure, in that it is assumed that a court can properly order the seizure of, or seize, property within the territorial jurisdiction of the court.[63] Where the property in question is a debt, an English court may make a 'third party debt order' in

---

[59] *Islamic Republic of Iran v Barakat Galleries Ltd* [2007] EWCA Civ 1374, [2009] QB 22.

[60] ibid explaining *Brokaw v Seatrain UK Ltd* [1971] 2 QB 476 (CA); *AG for New Zealand v Ortiz* [1984] AC 1, 20 (CA); aff'd on different grounds, 41.

[61] *Williams & Humbert Ltd v W & H Trade Marks (Jersey) Ltd* [1986] AC 368.

[62] See Section (D)(1)(d) in relation to judicial seizure.

[63] Where the property is not within the jurisdiction of the court, it may still appoint a receiver who is directed to go and try to obtain it (indirectly doing what cannot directly be done?): *Masri v Consolidated Contractors (UK) Ltd (No 2)* [2008] EWCA Civ 303, [2009] QB 450; *Tasarruf Mevduati Sigorta Fonu v Merrill Lynch Bank & Trust Co (Cayman) Ltd* [2011] UKPC 17, [2012] 1 WLR 1721.

favour of a judgment creditor in respect of an existing debt due to the judgment debtor so long as the debt is within the jurisdiction of the court. This means that the third party, against whom the order is made, must be resident within the jurisdiction of the court, it being assumed that that is the proper place to sue him and hence that this is the *situs* of the debt in respect of which the order is to be made.[64]

Such is the law, though its foundations are rather less strong than the courts seem to suppose. The answer to the question where a person can be sued is today more complex than simply asking where he is resident; and the question whether a debt is discharged (the court should not make the order unless it is satisfied that its doing so will discharge the debt, and will not leave the third party liable to pay over again, for the third party will have been brought, against its will, into a dispute between others) is governed by the *lex contractus*,[65] rather than *lex situs*, of the debt.

2. MARRIAGE AND PROPERTY RIGHTS

The impact of marriage on property rights is only a piece of a larger picture. When a marriage is annulled or dissolved, most systems of law authorize the court to make orders in relation to the property of the spouses which may override property rights created or existing prior to or independently of the marriage, or which would arise if there had been no marital regime to supervene;[66] and where a marriage is terminated by death, many systems employ rules of succession, perhaps modified by restricting the testamentary freedom of a deceased, to provide for those left behind. Others employ the institution of a matrimonial property regime, often but not always community of property, to regulate the property rights of the quick and the dead. Our concern at this point is simply with the effect which marriage has on the property rights of spouses up to the point when an event such as divorce or death may displace or even override the matrimonial regime.

Where the parties to a marriage enter into a matrimonial contract to govern their property rights *inter se*, the proper law of that contract obviously governs its creation, validity, interpretation, and effect, including the

---

[64] *Soc Eram Shipping Co Ltd v HSBC* [2003] UKHL 30, [2004] 1 AC 260; *Taurus Petroleum Ltd v State Oil Marketing Co of the Ministry of Oil, Republic of Iraq* [2017] UKSC 64, [2018] AC 690.

[65] Rome I Regulation, Art 12.

[66] For example, Matrimonial Causes Act 1973, s 24(1)(c); cf *Radmacher v Granatino* [2010] UKSC 42, [2011] 1 AC 534.

identification of the property which does[67] and does not fall within it,[68] and including whether foreign land, for example, is intended to fall within it.[69] Such contracts were excluded from the material scope of the Rome I Regulation: partly because they are intimately connected with status, which is also excluded, but also because it was intended that they would be dealt with in a dedicated Regulation. It follows that the private international law of matrimonial property rights is a matter of common law, the principal characteristic of which is that the proper law may be chosen by the parties. In the absence of such choice, the proper law will be the law with which the marriage contract has its closest and most real connection, which may also be referred to, unhelpfully, as 'the law of the matrimonial domicile'.[70] There was a historical preference for this law being that of the husband's domicile, but this has been indefensible at least since the abolition of the wife's dependent domicile at the end of 1973. The capacity of a person to make a marriage contract is governed by the law of his or her domicile at the date of marriage.[71] It is consistent with principle that once a matrimonial contract has been made, a change in domicile cannot alter its content and the rights created under it;[72] but there is nothing in principle, or probably in law, to prevent the spouses exercising their joint autonomy to vary their contract by agreement.

Where the parties do not make a matrimonial contract it was once thought that the factual and legal basis of the proprietary aspect of their relationship was different, and that a distinct set of answers was applicable. According to this view, the law by reference to which they married (the law with which the marriage had its closest connection; the matrimonial domicile) applied to determine the proprietary consequences of marriage,[73] but this original property regime, because not contractual, did not necessarily survive a change of spousal domicile. By far the better view always was,[74] however, that on marriage the spouses simply expect, receive, and adopt the scheme which is imposed or implied by the law of the original matrimonial domicile.[75] This may be a system of community of property, or separation of property, or some other variant. Whether this is conceptualized by the law

---

[67] *Re De Nicols (No2)* [1900] 2 Ch 410; *Murakami v Wiryadi* (2010) 268 ALR 377.
[68] *Re Fitzgerald* [1904] 1 Ch 573 (CA).
[69] *Murakami v Wiryadi* (2010) 268 ALR 377, following *Re De Nicols (No2)* [1900] 2 Ch 410 and followed by *Slutsker v Haron Investments Ltd* [2013] EWCA Civ 430.
[70] *Duke of Marlborough v AG* [1945] Ch 78 (CA). The connection is to a law, not to a country.
[71] *Re Cooke's Trusts* (1887) 56 LT 737; *Cooper v Cooper* (1888) 13 App Cas 88.
[72] *De Nicols v Curlier* [1900] AC 21.
[73] *Re Egerton's Will Trusts* [1956] Ch 593.
[74] Goldberg (1970) 19 ICLQ 557.
[75] It might be better to refer to this as the proper law of the marriage, but little turns on that.

of the matrimonial domicile as a tacit contract or as the default provision is immaterial, though as the regime will be held to continue to apply after a change in personal domicile, and for the same reasons, as where there is an express contract, the idea of a tacit contract makes sense. So for example, when two Indonesian parties married in Indonesia, they expected without fuss or bother that the joint property regime of Indonesian law would apply to any acquisition of real property outside Indonesia. It followed that land acquired by them in New South Wales was subjected to a regime which, so far as Australian private international law was concerned, should be regarded as assumed by means of a tacit contract.[76]

A seeming problem may arise when two systems of proprietary provision come into contact and become entangled. If spouses marry into a system of community, when one dies the community rules will determine what portion of the marital property accrues to the survivor, and what falls into the estate of the deceased. But if the deceased dies domiciled in a country where the basis of the law is the separation of property and particular provision for inheritance, that law may give the survivor a claim to a portion of the estate of the deceased, with the result that, in principle at least, the survivor can claim more than either system would have provided. A practical solution would be for characterization of the issue or issues to lead to the result that only one of these schemes applies, but if the court is unable to see past the analysis that tells it, correctly enough, that there are two, sequential, issues—what did the deceased own when he died? who succeeds to the estate of the deceased?— each having its own conflicts rule, this will be hard to achieve.

3. DISSOLUTION OF MARRIAGE AND PROPERTY RIGHTS

The private international law rules for (post-)matrimonial property orders, which, as a matter of domestic law, give a court very wide powers to adjust and override property rights, and which, for the purposes of private international law, are closely related to the dissolution of marriage, are best examined as part of family law. It is nevertheless telling that when the Supreme Court had to consider the validity and effect of an express matrimonial contract upon the parties at the date of their divorce, it simply subsumed the

---

[76] *Murakami v Wiryadi* (2010) 268 ALR 377, following *Re De Nicols (No2)* [1900] 2 Ch 410 and followed by *Slutsker v Haron Investments Ltd* [2012] EWHC 2539 (Ch).

contract, the intrinsic validity of which it did not question, within the set of data to be taken into account within the statutory regime for dealing with financial relief on divorce.[77]

4. BANKRUPTCY AND PROPERTY RIGHTS

The private international law rules for personal bankruptcy form an important part of the law on change of status and property rights. However, because of the tendency of states to legislate for bankruptcy and corporate insolvency together, it is best examined as part of the law of corporations. It is not logical, but for convenience of exposition, it will appear in the final chapter of this book.

5. DEATH AND PROPERTY RIGHTS

When someone dies and the question arises of the ownership and devolution of his or her property, it is necessary, at least for the purposes of English private law, to deal separately with two issues, each having its own conflicts rules, as well as jurisdiction and the recognition of foreign orders and judgments.

The first stage is the administration of the estate of the deceased: the interim process during which the assets are identified and collected, the proven debts paid according to their priority, and the balance of the estate calculated. If the deceased was subject to a regime of community of property, the effect of this on his estate will be calculated at this stage of administration. During this period, legal systems differ on the question of who owns the property: in some, the property vests immediately in those who will ultimately take it, but in England it vests in those charged with the administration of the estate.

The second stage is the substantive devolution of the estate: once the administration is complete, a further set of rules determines who actually takes which property. Substantive devolution sub-divides into three kinds: testate succession, where devolution is governed by a will left by the deceased and proved in the administration; intestate succession, where the deceased left no valid will or a will which left some of his estate ungifted, and the law steps in to allocate the property according to a formula which usually incorporates a

---

[77] *Radmacher v Granatino* [2010] UKSC 42, [2011] 1 AC 534.

descending scale of relationship; and *bona vacantia* where, because there is no succession (because there is no will and according to the rules on intestacy there is no relative to whom the property will pass by operation of law), the property is regarded as truly ownerless and will be taken by the state as a matter of last resort.

(a) Administration of deceased estates

The administration of estates is the process by which the estate of a deceased person is organized and settled prior to its distribution to those to whom the assets will pass by way of succession. As a matter of English law, administration requires an order of the court to empower a person to deal with the assets of a deceased, whether this is done by proving a will in order to appoint an executor or by obtaining a grant of letters of administration of an intestate estate.[78] Although the court may make a grant of representation of any deceased, only rarely will it do so if there is no property of the deceased in England. Whichever is done, the grant confirms or vests the property of the deceased in the grantee. Where the deceased died domiciled in a foreign country, the court will usually make a grant to the person who, under the law of the domicile, has been or is entitled to be appointed to administer the estate.[79] Once appointed, the representative may take all steps to get in all property, wherever situated, of the deceased. The substance of the administration is governed by the law of the country under which the grant of representation was made.[80] As a matter of English law, in the paying of the deceased's debts foreign creditors and English creditors are treated alike; the admissibility of and priority between claims is governed by English law as *lex fori*.

A foreign grant has no direct effect in England: the person appointed overseas must also obtain an English grant.[81] This stands in curious contrast to the fact that the status of a foreign-appointed trustee in bankruptcy is recognized without the need for further order. Although it has been said that the current English system is the best way to secure the interests of English creditors, it is hard to see how this can explain the difference in treatment between different types of representation.

---

[78] *New York Breweries Co v AG* [1899] AC 62.
[79] Senior Courts Act 1981, s 25(1).
[80] *Re Kloebe* (1884) 28 Ch D 175; *Re Lorillard* [1922] 2 Ch 638 (CA).
[81] *New York Breweries Co v AG* [1899] AC 62.

(b) Succession to property

Except where its rules lead to the conclusion that there was no valid will and no relative of the deceased to take on the intestacy, it is the law of succession which determines who takes the property of a deceased who may have died with or without leaving a will.[82] When disputes about succession arise, if a duly appointed representative is before the court, an English court has jurisdiction to determine a question of succession.[83] A foreign court is regarded as having jurisdiction to determine succession to the property, wherever situated, of a deceased dying domiciled in that country, and its decision will in principle be recognized in England;[84] it will also be recognized as having jurisdiction to determine the right of succession to all property within its territorial jurisdiction, regardless of the domicile of the deceased. The potential overlapping of decisions will require the principles of estoppel by *res judicata* to regulate it.

Where the deceased died having left a will, any question of her testamentary capacity is governed by her domicile at the date of making the will,[85] and the capacity of a legatee to take is conferred by the law of either his own or the testator's domicile. The formal validity of the will is satisfied if it is formally valid according to the law of the place when and where it was executed, or by the law of the place (at the time of either execution or death) where the deceased died domiciled or habitually resident or of which she was a national.[86] The same laws govern the formal validity of a will revoking an earlier will.[87] Wills of immovables are formally valid if they conform to the *lex situs*.[88] The material validity of a will is governed by the law of the testator's domicile at death,[89] except for immovables, for which it is governed by the *lex situs*.[90] It follows that if it is argued that the testator was limited as regards the fraction of her estate over which she had testamentary freedom, as is the case in systems which provide a statutory portion for spouses and children, this question will be treated as one going to the material validity of the will. But the interpretation of the will is governed by the law of the domicile at the date

---

[82] Dicey, Morris, and Collins, *The Conflict of Laws* (15th edn, Sweet & Maxwell, 2012) Ch 27.

[83] *Re Lorillard* [1922] 2 Ch 638 (CA).

[84] *Re Trufort* (1887) 36 Ch D 600; *Ewing v Orr-Ewing* (1883) 9 App Cas 34; *Ewing v Orr-Ewing* (1885) 10 App Cas 5.

[85] *Re Fuld's Estate (No 3)* [1968] P 675.

[86] Wills Act 1963, s 1.

[87] ibid, s 2(1)(c).

[88] ibid, s 2(1)(c).

[89] *Whicker v Hume* (1858) 7 HLC 124; *Re Groos* [1915] Ch 572; *Re Ross* [1930] 1 Ch 377.

[90] *Nelson v Bridport* (1846) 8 Beav 547; *Freke v Carbery* (1873) LR 16 Eq 461.

of making the will.[91] The validity of an act of revocation is governed by the domicile of the testator at the date of revocation.[92] So the question whether subsequent marriage, or the tearing up or burning of a will, revokes an earlier will is determined by the *lex domicilii* of the testator at the date of the marriage or other revoking event.

Where the deceased dies without leaving a valid will or fails to will a part of her estate, the intestate succession is governed by the domiciliary law of the deceased at the date of her death, except that succession to immovables is governed by the *lex situs*.[93] It is inherent in the nature of intestate succession that it means the taking of property, by operation of law, but by a relative of the deceased who did not make a will.

Where there is no will and no person to take by way of intestate succession, the property still has to pass. In this case the principles can no longer be those of succession, for there is no one to succeed to it. Instead, a state will assume title to ownerless property within its territorial jurisdiction as *bona vacantia*. An illusory problem arises when the law of the deceased's domicile would vest the property of an intestate in the state as 'final heir' of a deceased. It has been said that in this context it is necessary to characterize the rule of law relied on by the claiming state to determine whether it is a succession rule or a rule about *bona vacantia*, and that this is a matter of ascertaining the substance of the foreign rule rather than being persuaded by its form.[94] This is the product of muddled thinking. Quite apart from the fact that the process of characterization is directed at issues as distinct from rules of law, the conflict of laws requires a characterization line to be drawn between intestate succession and the acquisition of *bona vacantia*, to which a different conflicts rule, the *lex situs*, applies. The court must first decide whether the issue concerns property which is owned by way of succession, or is ownerless for failure of succession: only in the latter case does an issue arise of its devolution as *bona vacantia*. It is a matter of substance, not form. A state may claim to be an heir if it wishes, but the substance of its law is to make provision for property which has no other owner, *bona vacantia*; and an English court should not characterize this as succession.

---

[91] *Ewing v Orr-Ewing* (1883) 9 App Cas 34.
[92] *In bonis Reid* (1866) LR 1 P & D 74; *Curati v Perdoni* [2012] EWCA Civ 1381.
[93] *Balfour v Scott* (1793) 6 Bro PC 550.
[94] *Re Maldonado's Estate* [1954] P 233 (CA).

8

Persons

In this chapter, and prior to Exit Day, the private international law of matrimonial causes, parental responsibility, and maintenance was covered in part by two European Regulations: the Brussels II Regulation, Regulation 2201/2003, and the Maintenance Regulation, Regulation 4/2009. According to the Jurisdiction and Judgments (Family) (Amendment etc) (EU Exit) Regulations 2019, SI 2019 No 519, regulations 3 and 4, these two European Regulations will be revoked. For this reason they are in this chapter sometimes referred to as '(former)' Regulations, to convey the message that until Exit Day they are in full force and effect, but unless further legislative arrangements are made they will not apply to proceedings commenced before an English (or, where recognition is concerned, other Member State) court on or after Exit Day.

SI 2019 No 519 makes consequential alterations to English law, which will come into effect on Exit Day. In summary these may be summarized as follows.

First, the jurisdiction of an English court in respect of divorce or nullity proceedings. If the court was seised prior to Exit Day, the Brussels II Regulation will remain in force.

If the court was seised after Exit Day, the jurisdictional rules will be set out in the Domicile and Matrimonial Proceedings Act 1973, section 5 (as amended by SI 2019 No 519, Sched, para 7), which will closely follow the substance of the former Regulation. Accordingly, the English court will have jurisdiction if (a) both parties to the marriage are habitually resident in England and Wales; or (b) both parties to the marriage were last habitually resident in England and Wales and one of them continues to reside there; or (c) the respondent is habitually resident in England and Wales; or (d) the applicant is habitually resident in England and Wales and has resided there for at least one year immediately before the application was made; or (e) the applicant is domiciled and habitually resident in England and Wales and has resided there for at least six

The Conflict of Laws. Fourth Edition. Adrian Briggs, Oxford University Press (2019). © Adrian Briggs
DOI: 10.1093/oso/9780198838500.003.0008

months immediately before the application was made; or (f) both parties to the marriage are domiciled in England and Wales; or (g) either of the parties to the marriage is domiciled in England and Wales.

Second, the recognition of matrimonial decrees from the courts of a Member State. If the decree was obtained by means of judicial proceedings in the court of a Member State which was seised before Exit Day, the Brussels II Regulation will remain in force for the purpose of recognition of the decree. For foreign decrees obtained by means of judicial proceedings in the court of a Member State which was seised after Exit Day, the rules will be those set out in the Family Law Act 1986.

Third, so far as concerns matters of maintenance and parental responsibility, if the court in question (English or Member State) was seised before Exit Day, the relevant European Regulation will continue to apply to the proceedings. If it is seised after Exit Day, English proceedings will be governed by the laws which applied before the relevant European Regulation came into effect. No major amendment was made to those laws as they applied in the United Kingdom.

A. ADULTS

Family law, and the private international law of marriage in particular, is the one area in which the *lex domicilii*, the law of the domicile, still has a significant role to play. Not every issue is answered by recourse to it, and statutory reform has made inroads into its territory. But family law, so far as it concerns adults, is substantially about status; status is traditionally determined by the personal law; and as far as the common law conflict of laws is concerned, the personal law is the *lex domicilii*, the law of the domicile.

It should not be supposed, however, that this means that there will be international agreement on the status of an individual. For although most systems agree that status is a matter for the personal law, there is no agreement about which law—domicile, habitual residence, nationality, law of a religious group, and so on—actually is the personal law; and even as between legal systems which use the *lex domicilii* as the personal law, there are differences between legal systems in the way it is defined. In the context of family law, the reference to *law* is liable to indicate the whole law, including the rules of the conflict of laws, which would be applied by a judge hearing the case in his own court: the principle of *renvoi* is generally taken to be relevant to those family law cases in which it is pleaded and proved.

It is sensible to raise at the outset an issue which follows from this, but which also lurks deeply[1] in the private international law of persons, for if it is unaddressed the law risks being found to lack the coherence for which it claims to strive. The issue is whether 'personal status' remains useful in formulating the rules of private international law.

One possible approach would have been to refer the issues to be discussed in the first part of this chapter to the personal law, that is, to the law of the domicile. If that law were to determine the validity of marriage, the effect of a divorce or nullity decree, and so on, it would be easy to defend the view that status was an issue in its own right, governed by a single law of general application. But, as we shall see, the rules of private international law do in fact make reference to several of these potentially applicable laws, so weakening the idea that 'the' personal law is the determinant of status. It has been accepted, first by the common law and then by legislation, that the validity of a divorce (and later, also the validity of an annulment of marriage) could be referred to a number of possible laws in addition to, or in place of, the law of the domicile, and that as long as it could be found to be valid by reference to one of them, that would be sufficient to make it valid for the purpose of English private international law. Such a development in the law of matrimonial causes instantly means that the view of status which might be taken by the personal law is not reliable: if the divorce is recognized as effective by reference to one of the laws available for its validation, but the *lex domicilii* would not share that view, the idea of having a single law to determine status is illusory. Indeed, if life is a length of time during the course of which marriage, divorce, annulment, and so on, are regarded as milestones, transactions, each tested by reference to the law or laws to which it seems sensible to refer them, personal status is simply what results from these events from time to time.

If that is so, the idea that adults may choose the law by which these transactions are to be governed, or to which these transactions are to be referred, becomes more plausible. The common law never countenanced such a thing (save in the tragically under-appreciated sense that parties with the means may choose where to go to marry or to petition for divorce); but if these

---

[1] Though as will be shown, coming much closer to the surface than it has previously done.

processes really are the contracts and engagements one makes to get through life, why should the right to choose the law associated with them be available only to those with the means to travel? Legislation and proposals for legislation coming from the European Union would have opened the door to a rather greater choice of law to govern the effect of life-changing events; but the common law should have recognized this for itself. If these are just events, mostly entered into by choice, whether happily or unhappily, why on earth should adults of sound mind not be allowed choose the law to determine the legal effects of what they are doing? Does personal autonomy and respect for private life not entail the right to choose the law to govern these major events? Would it not be sufficient for public policy to be used as the means to override the unpalatable consequences of a choice of law which has been made, but to intervene no further than that? Perhaps the idea of a progression of law from status to contract has a part to play here too; perhaps the idea that one should be able to choose how to make one's private life is one to be taken more seriously.

But one must take the law as it currently is. The plan of this chapter is therefore to examine adult relations: marriage, matrimonial causes, and financial provision; but for reasons which will be explained, to deal only very briefly with the extraordinarily complex law relating to children.

1. MARRIAGE

Assessment of the validity or invalidity of marriage requires a preliminary distinction to be drawn between formal validity, capacity to marry, and other impediments to marriage.[2] The first is concerned with the ceremony and its components, the second with whether the person is in law free to marry the other person, and the third with a miscellany of unhappy factors not falling within the scope of the other two. An advantage of this division is that it reflects the plausible and legitimate interest of a number of countries in the validity of marriage, but seeks to limit that interest to those particular issues with which they are most closely concerned. On the other hand, the disadvantage of making reference to a number of laws may lead to complexity; and the greater the number of laws referred to, the greater the chance of finding that one of them grounds an objection. If this were fair criticism, it might be

---

[2] Dicey, Morris, and Collins, *The Conflict of Laws* (15th edn, Sweet & Maxwell, 2012) Ch 17.

better to refer the validity of marriage to a single law, such as the law of the place where it is celebrated. But this is not how English law has developed.

From time to time it is said that English law makes a presumption of the validity of marriage.[3] All this appears to mean is that where there is room for any flexibility in the rules of the conflict of laws, and the parties believe that they have gone through a valid ceremony of marriage, any remaining doubt should probably be resolved in favour of validity. This is not because marriage is a superior state of human existence, but reflects the pragmatic view that where there has been a wedding ceremony, and reliance has been placed on its validity, there needs to be good reason to surprise the parties and any interested third parties by finding it to have been invalid all along.

Once the particular issue has been characterized, and the relevant conflicts rule identified, it is necessary to decide how precisely to frame the question which is to be answered by reference to the chosen law. Suppose, for example, facts in issue before the court are characterized as raising an issue of formal validity, and that this requires reference to the law of the place of celebration. The question to be referred to the foreign law for answer will be either 'is this marriage formally valid despite . . .?' or 'is this marriage valid despite . . .?', the difference being whether the characterization which led to the choice of law remains in place as a constraint on the formulation of the question. It was proposed above[4] that it does not: that where the English court is trying to decide the case as the foreign judge would, there is no sense in pre-empting the foreign law on the first stage of the analysis which it would have to undertake. The question is therefore whether the alleged defect makes the marriage invalid, not whether it makes it formally invalid.

(a) Formal validity of marriage

The formal requirements of a marriage ceremony and the effects of non-compliance are governed by the law of the place of celebration of the marriage, the *lex loci celebrationis*.[5] The question whether there is need for a public, civil, or religious ceremony,[6] whether particular words need to be read or spoken in the course of the ceremony, whether the ceremony must be held in temple, registry, or out in the fresh air, whether it need take place within certain hours, who may celebrate the marriage, whether a religious

---

[3] For example, *Radwan v Radwan (No 2)* [1973] Fam 35; *K v A* [2014] EWHC 3850 (Fam), [2015] 2 FLR 461.

[4] At p 20 above.

[5] *Simonin v Mallac* (1860) 2 Sw & Tr 67; *Berthiaume v Dastous* [1930] AC 79 (PC).

[6] *Taczanowska v Taczanowski* [1957] P 301 (CA).

practitioner need be present, whether it is necessary for either spouse to be present in person or by proxy,[7] or whether it is necessary for the parents or other third parties to give their consent,[8] are all characterized as issues of formal validity. They are all referred to the *lex loci celebrationis*, and the consequences in terms of nullity or otherwise are determined by it as well. If the marriage would be invalid by the domestic law of the place of celebration, but would be valid by reference to the law to which a judge at the *locus celebrationis* would look if he were trying the issue, the marriage will be formally validated via the principle of *renvoi*.[9] Although it may be theoretically possible, it is improbable that the reverse proposition would invalidate a marriage, for it is hard to believe that there is a system of family law anywhere which would not regard compliance with its own forms as sufficient.

There are two exceptions to the proposition that a marriage is formally valid only if it complied with the *lex loci celebrationis*: in each case a marriage will be formally valid by virtue of having met the rudimentary formal requirements of the English common law as this stood prior to 1753. This extraordinary proposition is only a little less startling if the point is made that this is in substance a reference to the canon law which prevailed across much of Europe, and in England until 1753. All that is required is the public declaration of intention to marry in the presence of witnesses, with no need for a priest,[10] which comes close to saying that there are no formal requirements at all. In any event, this will establish formal validity where it was impossible for the parties to comply with local forms, or where the place of celebration was under belligerent occupation and the parties belonged to or were associated with those occupying forces.[11] As to the first of these, impossibility may be invoked where two persons wish to marry in a place where civil order has wholly broken down or where there is no human population. Less clear is how it applies if parties have rational objections to the form (if, for example, marriage requires a declaration of religious faith) or are shut out *tout court* (if for example no provision is made for same sex marriage) of local marriage ceremonies. Not everyone will accept that parties should be able to opt out of or override local law; but if the parties are effectively excluded from the

---

[7] *Apt v Apt* [1948] P 83 (CA); *McCabe v McCabe* [1994] 1 FLR 257 (CA).

[8] *Simonin v Mallac* (1860) 2 Sw & Tr 67; *Ogden v Ogden* [1908] P 46 (CA) (both parental consent); cf *Sottomayor v De Barros (No 1)* (1877) 2 PD 81 (CA) (papal consent, although this may instead be a question of personal capacity).

[9] *Taczanowska v Taczanowski* [1957] P 301 (CA).

[10] *Wolfenden v Wolfenden* [1946] P 61; *Penhas v Tan Soo Eng* [1953] AC 304 (PC).

[11] *Taczanowska v Taczanowski* [1957] P 301 (CA); *Preston v Preston* [1963] P 411 (CA).

local formality criteria for marriage, it is hard to deny that marriage is impossible for them there, and we are, after all, only dealing with formalities. As regards belligerent occupation, it would have been obscene to require persons who wished to marry while serving in forces in the occupation of enemy territory in 1945, or in civilian groups associated with them, to comply with the formal requirements of German or other fascist laws: the exception was a pragmatic one in the interests of common decency. Statutory provision is made for members of HM forces to marry while serving abroad, and for consular marriages.[12]

(b) Capacity of persons to marry

Each party is required to have capacity to marry the other according to the law of his or her ante-nuptial domicile, the *lex domicilii*.[13] The reason is said to be that who, whether, and when someone is capable of marrying is best determined by the law of the society in which he or she has roots. It was once suggested that the law of the intended matrimonial home might be a more appropriate test, but the inherent uncertainty of such a test makes it difficult to support, at least when the question arises prospectively.[14] Even so, there is much to be said for the view that the law of the society in which the would-be spouses are going to live has the most obvious interest in saying whether they have what it takes to live there as spouses.

The category of capacity includes the age at which matrimony is possible[15] and the prohibited degrees of relationship.[16] It also covers the question of whether a person may marry someone of the same sex, though the problems thrown up by this justify its separate treatment. The distinct issue of the effect of a previous marriage arguably dissolved or annulled by decree is also examined separately below, as it deals with a more complex conflict of laws and judgments.

The concurrent role of the *lex loci celebrationis* in the regulation of capacity is also a bit of a puzzle. The first question is whether it is necessary to comply with the capacity rules of the *lex loci* as well as with those of the personal law or laws. If the marriage takes place in England it is natural that the parties must also satisfy the capacity requirements of English law,[17] at least if the

---

[12] Marriage (Same Sex Couples) Act 2013, s 13.
[13] *Brook v Brook* (1861) 9 HLC 193; *Sottomayor v De Barros (No 2)* (1879) 5 PD 94.
[14] For its use retrospectively, see *Radwan v Radwan* [1973] Fam 35.
[15] The Marriage Act 1949, s 2 applies to any marriage in England and requires that neither party be under 16.
[16] *Brook v Brook* (1861) 9 HLC 193.
[17] There is no judicial authority to this effect, however.

issue arises prior to the celebration of the marriage, in the form of judicial review of a registrar's refusal to license the marriage. So if the registrar refuses to permit the marriage of two foreign-domiciled persons, one of whom is under 16, he will not be ordered to marry them even if each has domiciliary capacity. But if the marriage has taken place in England, the parties having had capacity by the relevant personal laws, and subject to what is said below about marriages celebrated overseas, it is less easy to see the proper interest of English law in then regarding it as invalid. If the marriage takes place overseas, the dominant view is that the parties do not need capacity under the *lex loci* in addition to satisfying their personal laws.[18]

Even so, there is a respectable argument that capacity by the *lex loci*, whether English or foreign, ought generally to be required for a marriage to be valid. It feels unconvincing to say that the law of the place of the ceremony is uniquely concerned with formal validity, and that it is completely unconcerned with personal capacity. Moreover, if the law under which the celebrant is vested with authority considers that, on account of the parties' lack of capacity to marry, his purported act of marriage was a nullity, is it really right to ignore it? If it is correct to understand marriage as something which is brought into existence by a marriage officer, rather than as something done by the parties themselves, the law which defines the officer's powers appears to be uniquely interested in the question whether he or she has altered the status of the parties, even though making a reference to an additional law will tend to increase the invalidity of marriages.

By contrast with the possibility that the *lex loci* may invalidate a marriage, otherwise valid, for lack of capacity, it may also validate a marriage even though one of the parties lacks domiciliary capacity. If the marriage takes place in England and one party is domiciled in England, it suffices for the other to have capacity according to English domestic law, even though that other party lacks capacity under the foreign domiciliary law.[19] This principle is justified on the slightly shaky footing that injustice would otherwise be done to an English domiciliary. The principle has always been controversial: the original case concerned a party whose personal law forbade marriage without the consent of the head of the Roman Catholic Church. This, and the examples of prohibition on inter-racial marriage also discussed by the court, could and should have been dealt with as rules which should be disregarded

---

[18]   *Breen v Breen* [1964] P 144.
[19]   *Sottomayor v De Barros (No 2)* (1879) 5 PD 94; *Ogden v Ogden* [1908] P 46 (CA) (alternative ratio).

as being offensive to English public policy, rather than by making a more general exception to the need for domiciliary capacity. And it did seem odd that the rule was not generalized: it was never held that capacity was satisfied if the marriage was celebrated in the domicile of one party and the other had capacity under that law. But for good or ill, the exception for English domiciliaries marrying in England remains good law.

(c) Other issues affecting the validity of marriage

A number of other factors have a bearing on the validity or invalidity of marriage. Some of them may be seen as, or as very close to, issues of capacity. Others are not; but they are not the subject of a uniform conflicts rule. They are grouped together here for convenience rather than for coherence.

First, each party must consent to marry, or to become married to, the other. Any argument that there was no consent, whether this is said to be the result of mistake, fraud, concealment, or duress, will in principle be governed by the *lex domicilii* of the party said not to have consented, as though this were a question of his or her personal capacity.[20]

Second, it is rational, though not clearly established by law, that physical impediments such as inability or refusal to consummate the marriage by sexual intercourse are referable to the law of the allegedly incapable party,[21] although contrary views are not untenable: it may be argued that the willing-and-able party has no capacity to marry a person who will refuse to consummate and that the former's law should apply instead. However that may be, as absence of consent and refusal both render a marriage voidable rather than void, and as the evidence is likely to be problematic, there is certainly room for the further alternative view that the case should be treated as though it were one of divorce, for which the court always applies the *lex fori*.

Third, special rules apply to the validity of polygamous marriages in so far as polygamy is alleged to be an impediment. A marriage will count as polygamous[22] if the marriage was celebrated in polygamous form[23] and was contracted by a man whose *lex domicilii* gave him personal capacity for polygamy.[24] The first of these means that a marriage lawfully celebrated in England is inevitably monogamous. The second needs no further

---

[20] *Szechter v Szechter* [1971] P 286, but cf *Vervaeke v Smith* [1983] 1 AC 145.
[21] *Ponticelli v Ponticelli* [1958] P 204.
[22] Subject to the Private International Law (Miscellaneous Provisions) Act 1995, s 5, a marriage is polygamous if actually or potentially so.
[23] *Lee v Lau* [1967] P 14.
[24] *Hussain v Hussain* [1983] Fam 26 (CA).

explanation, save that if the husband loses his personal capacity for polygamy, for example by changing his domicile, the nature of the marriage will be changed to monogamy.[25] When the matter was regulated by the common law, the second condition meant that a marriage celebrated overseas by an English-domiciled man was not polygamous, for he had no personal capacity for polygamy, but if celebrated by an English-domiciled woman it could be polygamous, and would on that account be invalid. It is now provided[26] that if a potentially polygamous marriage is actually (in the sense of arithmetically) monogamous, an English woman does not lack capacity to enter it, and the domiciliary incapacity of English law is limited to actually polygamous marriages. Moreover, while a woman domiciled in a country which permits polygamy may contract a polygamous marriage, and an Englishwoman has no personal capacity for actual polygamy,[27] it has been held, in a decision ostensibly designed to uphold the validity of a marriage which had endured for 20 years, that her personal capacity to have contracted a polygamous marriage should be governed by the law of what was the intended matrimonial home.[28]

Fourth, if a previous marriage has been dissolved or annulled by a decree recognized by English law otherwise than under the (former) Brussels II Regulation,[29] the subsequent remarriage of either party is not invalidated by the refusal of some other system of law to recognize the decree.[30] So if an Irish domiciliary is divorced by a decree recognized by the Family Law Act 1986 but denied recognition under Irish law, the remarriage will be valid even though Irish law, as the law of the domicile, would regard the first marriage as subsisting and the second marriage as bigamous and void: this result is brought about by the Family Law Act and the judicial deduction that one can hardly say that a divorce has been recognized, in accordance with Parliament's instruction, if it leaves a spouse incapable of remarriage.[31] This reverses the understanding of the common law which, although recognizing

---

[25] *Ali v Ali* [1968] P 564; *Parkasho v Singh* [1968] P 223. This still seems rather odd. After all, if the husband to a monogamous marriage changes domicile and by doing so acquires personal capacity for polygamy, it is improbable that the marriage changes its nature and risks becoming invalid.

[26] Private International Law (Miscellaneous Provisions) Act 1995, s 5.

[27] Private International Law (Miscellaneous Provisions) Act 1995, s 5.

[28] *Radwan v Radwan (No 2)* [1973] Fam 35.

[29] Regulation (EC) 2201/2003, [2003] OJ L338/1. It replaced the original Brussels II Regulation, Regulation (EC) 1347/2000, and is on that account sometimes known as Brussels II*bis*; it will be revoked on Exit Day. It is discussed at p 325 below.

[30] Family Law Act 1986, s 50.

[31] *Lawrence v Lawrence* [1985] Fam 106.

that a divorce would break the bonds of matrimony, regarded capacity to remarry as a distinct issue for which there was a different, domiciliary, conflicts rule. The inverse position, where the *lex domicilii* recognizes the validity of a decree which English legislation does not, is not legislated for. But if the *lex domicilii* regards an individual as capable of remarriage it is hard to see the rational interest of English law in contradicting it just because English private international law would not recognize the matrimonial decree.[32]

However, where recognition of the decree of a court in a Member State is mandated by the (former) Brussels II Regulation,[33] the provisions of the Family Law Act 1986 do not apply,[34] and the impact of the decree on the parties' capacity to remarry is even more uncertain. As the Regulation governs the dissolution of matrimonial ties, and disclaims any effect on related issues,[35] the conclusion that the right to remarry is a consequence of recognition may not follow if the personal law of the (former) spouse refuses to recognize the decree. The issue is whether to regard the question as one governed by the law of the state which granted the decree and to give it the effect it had under that law;[36] or to discern the answer from the text of the Regulation; or to revert to the common law;[37] or to pretend that the Family Law Act 1986, section 50, had not been made inapplicable to such cases.[38] The correct answer has yet to be identified and explained.

Fifth, public policy may intervene at the point when a rule of the *lex causae*, even after making due allowance for different cultural and social traditions, offends the English conception of marriage, freedom to marry, and the equality of the sexes. For example, if the personal law of one of the parties denies marital capacity to a person on grounds which are capricious, penal, or discriminatory,[39] such an impediment will, or at any rate should, be ignored. And if the personal laws were to confer marital capacity at the age of five, or allow marriage to a dead person,[40] it may be that English public policy would deny recognition to the marriage. But it is well understood that English law draws the limits of public policy tightly, with the result that

---

[32] *Schwebel v Ungar* (1963) 42 DLR (2d) 622 (Ont CA) supports the application of the *lex domicilii* over the non-recognition of the *lex fori*.

[33] Regulation (EC) 2201/2003; SI 2001/310, as amended.

[34] SI 2001/310, reg 9, amending the Family Law Act 1986.

[35] Recital 10.

[36] cf Case 145/86 *Hoffmann v Krieg* [1988] ECR 645.

[37] Giving primacy to the personal law: *Schwebel v Ungar* (1963) 42 DLR (2d) 622 (Ont CA).

[38] Despite the wording of SI 2001/310, reg 9.

[39] *Scott v AG* (1886) 11 PD 128; cf *Sottomayor v De Barros (No 2)* (1879) 5 PD 94.

[40] Certain laws allow a person to marry, *post mortem*, a fiancé(e) who was killed in war service.

marriages which are considerably different from the English domestic law model may be recognized.

Sixth, English law now treats the marriage of same-sex couples as a species of the genus of marriage; but the effect in private international law of the language by which the Marriage (Same Sex Couples) 2013 implements this policy is not completely clear. The marriage of same sex couples in England 'is lawful'.[41] What this means if either or both spouses are domiciled in a country which does not allow such marriage is unclear. If one of the parties is English, the incapacity of the other under foreign law will be ignored by reason of the injustice which its application would inflict on the English party.[42] If neither is English, the old common law exceptional rule cannot apply; the question is whether section 1 of the 2013 Act overrides a personal incapacity in a law which makes such marriage unlawful. It is hard to be sure of the answer. A similar problem arises from section 10, which provides that if such a marriage is celebrated outside England, the marriage is not prevented from recognition 'only because' it is the marriage of a same sex couple. Suppose a couple, who are domiciled in a country which would deny their capacity to marry each other, marry in a country which pays no attention to what English law would regard as being their personal laws. If an English court applies the usual domiciliary rules governing capacity, it will still consider the marriage to be void; but if section 10 requires an English court to disregard any and every rule of foreign law which denies validity on the ground that it is a same-sex marriage, then the marriage will be valid.[43]

2. MATRIMONIAL CAUSES

The private international law of matrimonial causes[44] has to juggle a number of laws which may all be thought to have some interest in the issues which arise; the results are untidy. The laws which determine the initial validity of marriage may not be those which apply on its annulment or dissolution; the

---

[41] Marriage (Same Sex Couples) Act 2013, s 1.

[42] *Sottomayor v De Barros (No 2)* (1879) 5 PD 94.

[43] The separate institution of civil partnership, created under the Civil Partnership Act 2004, is not discussed here, for although it continues in existence, its use (unless extended to non-same-sex couples, in the light of *R (on the application of Steinfeld and Keidan) v Secretary of State for International Development* [2018] UKSC 32, [2018] 3 WLR 415) will presumably now diminish, and existing civil partnerships may, if the civil partners wish it, be converted to marriages.

[44] The rules also cover judicial separation, but the infrequency of this form of decree justifies its omission from a book of this size.

laws which determine the effectiveness of an annulment or dissolution may not be, as has been seen, the ones which regulate the right to remarry. There are two parties who, by the time matters come to court, may have separate domiciles and different residences; there will be laws which had, laws which have, and laws which will have, a connection to the facts and to the parties themselves. There may be third parties with personal laws which also have an interest in being taken into account. Decrees of nullity and divorce may be obtained by civil proceedings which may or may not also be fully judicial, but may also be obtained in accordance with religious 'law'. A local policy of being disposed to grant recognition to divorces may clash with a foreign law's policy of not doing so; and all in all there is plenty of scope for a conflict of laws. Perhaps because of this, the *lex fori* features more prominently than one might expect it to; and the rules on jurisdiction and recognition are inevitably complex. Painting the picture by reference to principle is, therefore, rather difficult.

Outside the context of the law which is applied in matrimonial causes, the law does not draw a sharp distinction between divorce and annulment, for although the two forms of decree are conceptually distinct, the law is complicated enough without having entirely separate sets of rules for jurisdiction, applicable law, and recognition. They may be considered together as matrimonial causes.

Part of the law was contained in the Brussels II Regulation.[45] The original version of the Regulation[46] was made to govern, if only partially, the jurisdiction of Member States to grant matrimonial decrees, and to deal with the recognition and enforcement of decrees granted in other Member States: if one asks why the European Union considered this to be a proper matter for its intervention, the answer lies in the problems which arose when a divergence of national laws on the (non-)recognition of divorces and remarriages impinged on those who wished to exercise their right of free movement. The Regulation was amended in 2003.[47] Even though its territorial scope is limited, its rules on jurisdiction to grant decrees were made to be comprehensive.

---

[45] Regulation 2201/2003, [2003] OJ L338/1. Consequential amendments to English statutes are made by SI 2001/310, as itself amended by SI 2005/265. In some books, 'Brussels II' is used to refer to the original Regulation, and 'Brussels IIa' or 'Brussels II*bis*' for the amended Regulation. This distinction is unnecessary.

[46] Regulation (EC) 1347/2000, [2000] OJ L160/19.

[47] The amendments are mainly concerned with provisions dealing with parental responsibility for children.

(a) Obtaining decrees from an English court

The jurisdiction of an English court to grant a decree of divorce, legal separation, or annulment is governed in the first instance by rules contained in the Brussels II Regulation. In cases in which the Regulation applied or applies, the point of departure is to ask questions about the respondent: whether the respondent is habitually resident in a Member State[48] or is a national of a Member State other than the United Kingdom or Ireland, or is domiciled[49] in England, Scotland, Northern Ireland, or Ireland. If he or she were, jurisdiction might be taken only in accordance with Articles 3–6 of the Regulation.[50] According to these, the court has jurisdiction if both spouses are domiciled in England.[51] Alternatively, it has jurisdiction if England is where the spouses are habitually resident; or England is where they were last habitually resident, so long as one of them still resides there; or England is where the respondent is habitually resident or is where (in the event of a joint application) either of the spouses is habitually resident; or England is where the applicant is, and for a year immediately before the application was made was, habitually resident; or England is the country of domicile of the applicant who was also habitually resident there for six months immediately prior to the application.[52] If none of these provisions gives jurisdiction to the court, there is no jurisdictional basis for English proceedings; where they give jurisdiction to the English courts and those of another Member State, Article 19 provides for a first-seised rule to settle any problem of *lis alibi pendens*.[53]

If, but only if, Articles 3–6 failed to confer jurisdiction on the courts of *any* Member State, Article 7 of the Regulation provided that the 'residual' jurisdiction of the court was a matter for its national law to determine.[54] Accordingly, an English court would have jurisdiction if either party to the marriage was domiciled in England on the date the proceedings were begun.[55] Jurisdiction over proceedings for nullity was substantially the

---

[48] A state of the European Union excluding Denmark: Art 1(3).

[49] As a matter of the law of the United Kingdom: Art 41(b).

[50] Article 7.

[51] Article 2(1)(b). The corresponding rule for the other Member States except Ireland is framed in terms of nationality rather than domicile. 'Domicile' has its common law meaning: Art 4(2); and England is treated as if it were a Member State by reason of Art 41.

[52] Article 2(1)(a).

[53] *Bentinck v Bentinck* [2007] EWCA Civ 175, [2007] ILPr 391; *Prazic v Prazic* [2006] EWCA Civ 497, [2007] ILPr 381.

[54] Article 8. Even if the respondent was neither resident in nor citizen of a Member State, if a court identified by any of the criteria listed in Arts 3–6 could nevertheless have jurisdiction, Art 7 is inapplicable: Case C–68/07 *Lopez v Lizazo* [2007] ECR I–10403.

[55] Domicile and Matrimonial Proceedings Act 1973, s 5(2) as amended by SI 2001/310, reg 3(4).

same,[56] save that a decree of nullity might also be granted if one party had died but at death was domiciled, or had for a year been habitually resident, in England.[57] Again, where proceedings are based on Article 7, other proceedings may also be brought in a foreign court. If that court were in another Member State, Article 19 applied a first-seised rule to remove the jurisdiction of the second court, but the Regulation otherwise makes no provision for and takes no account of principles of *forum conveniens* in relation to matrimonial causes. Subject to that overriding rule an English court has a statutory[58] power to stay proceedings. Accordingly, when jurisdiction is taken under Article 7, a stay may be obligatory if there are prior divorce proceedings in another part of the United Kingdom,[59] and is discretionary in all other cases. Although this statutory power may be distinct from the inherent power to stay on grounds of *forum non conveniens*, any distinction between the two mechanisms is more technical than substantial. It follows that if the foreign court is clearly and distinctly more appropriate than England for the resolution of the dispute, the argument that the petitioner will be disadvantaged by having to proceed in the foreign jurisdiction will not ward off a stay if substantial justice may still be done there.[60] Given the peculiar pressures in matrimonial cases, there is, and should be, no[61] hard and fast rule that a stay should be granted if the foreign proceedings were begun first, but there will be a rational disinclination to allow later-begun proceedings to continue in a way which simply duplicates earlier ones and which seem to have no proper purpose.

In proceedings for divorce an English court applies English domestic law.[62] There is much sense in this. Whenever proposals are made to alter the

[56] Domicile and Matrimonial Proceedings Act 1973, s 5(3) as amended by SI 2001/310, reg 3(5).
[57] ibid.
[58] Domicile and Matrimonial Proceedings Act 1973, Sch 1, para 9, as amended by SI 2001/310, reg 4. Whether a court may stay its proceedings if jurisdiction is founded on Art 2 of the Regulation but the natural forum in a non-Member State may be debatable, but the clear answer given in *JKN v JCN* [2010] EWHC 843 (Fam), [2011] 1 FLR 826 was that a stay was permissible, and that authority derived from the Brussels I Regulation, which would have suggested the contrary, was inapplicable. The decision was approved in *Mittal v Mittal* [2013] EWCA Civ 1255, [2014] Fam 102.
[59] Domicile and Matrimonial Proceedings Act 1973, Sch 1, para 8. But see also *Villiers v Villiers* [2018] EWCA Civ 1120.
[60] *De Dampierre v De Dampierre* [1988] AC 92.
[61] By contrast, the High Court of Australia does appear to have such a view: *Henry v Henry* (1996) 185 CLR 571. It appears to be more European than the Europeans.
[62] It was so assumed in *Zanelli v Zanelli* (1948) 64 TLR 556, and the question was not raised again.

grounds upon which a divorce may be obtained as a matter of domestic law, there is public debate and often sharp disagreement, for divorce seems to raise issues of public as well as of private concern. If the English court has jurisdiction to entertain the proceedings, it would be hard to justify a divorce being granted on grounds which would be insufficient in English domestic law, and perhaps even harder for a petitioner to be denied a divorce although satisfying the criteria of English law for dissolution of a marriage which has failed. The general application of English domestic law to everyone, equally, is, from this pragmatic vantage point, just what the equal protection of the laws seems to require.

That said, one may ask whether there is room for another point of view. The automatic application of English law was established when the jurisdictional rules which defined when an English court would act at all were very restrictive: as a court could not dissolve a marriage unless both parties were domiciled in England,[63] what else but English law could be applied to the petition? But as these jurisdictional rules were loosened, first in consequence of the change in the law which meant that a married woman no longer had her husband's domicile foisted on her as one of dependency,[64] and then becoming very liberal, the question whether it was still appropriate to apply only English law to the dissolution should perhaps have been asked again. If it was asked, it was not done loudly enough for anyone to hear. When the jurisdictional connection to England is relatively weak, some will be tempted to think that the case for applying English law to the substance of the proceedings is less obviously strong; and if a sensible structure for an alternative conflicts rule could be devised to deal with the issues raised by the possible termination of a failing marriage, perhaps it should be considered. The fact that it has not been may, however, suggest that there is no real alternative to the present position that English law always applies. The Regulation did not address the question of applicable law.

For decrees of nullity, the applicable law will be deduced from the grounds of invalidity examined in relation to the original validity of marriage: allegations of personal incapacity will be governed by the *lex domicilii*, and so on. If the marriage is plainly void, as distinct from being voidable or dissoluble, there is no need to obtain a decree to this effect, although it will often be

---

[63] *Le Mesurier v Le Mesurier* [1895] AC 517.
[64] Domicile and Matrimonial Proceedings Act 1973, which altered the law of domicile and set out jurisdictional rules for the grant of divorces.

possible, and prudent, to do so.[65] Where the alleged defect relied on is one which is in substance unknown, either precisely or by analogy, to English law, no reported authority exists to confirm or deny that the court may still annul the marriage.[66] Such cases will doubtless be rare, and the chances must be that to grant a decree on such grounds would offend English public policy in any event.

(b) Foreign decrees recognized under the Family Law Act 1986

A decree from Scotland, Northern Ireland, the Channel Islands, or the Isle of Man will be recognized on the same basis as an English decree, that is, that it was granted by a court.[67] In other words, if divorces obtained in England and the rest of the British islands are to be recognized as having legal effect, they must be obtained by judicial proceedings.[68] 'Religious divorces' purportedly obtained in England, whether unilaterally or from some 'religious court', will therefore be ineffective in English law.

For decrees from outside the British islands (and leaving aside the (former) Brussels II Regulation, which we will deal with below), recognition is governed by the Family Law Act 1986.[69] The Act, which has a number of drafting curiosities, draws a fundamental distinction according to where the decree was obtained: they are either divorces obtained in the British islands[70] or are overseas divorces. The distinction appears to assume that divorces were always obtained in a single country; as will be seen, reality does not always conform to that template.

'Overseas divorces', which means divorces obtained in a country outside the British islands, will be recognized, according to section 45(1), only in accordance with sections 46–49; and according to section 46 it is necessary to decide whether they were obtained by means of proceedings (whether judicial or otherwise) or not.[71] The separate treatment of divorces obtained with

---

[65] Some very strange law draws a distinction between void marriages and non-marriages, which appear to be 'even more void than void marriages': see *A v A* [2012] EWHC 3763 (Fam), [2012] 2 FLR 387; *Akhter v Khan* [2018] EWFC 54, [2019] Fam 247. Matrimonial decrees may be granted in relation to the former, but cannot be given in respect of the latter.

[66] cf *Vervaeke v Smith* [1983] 1 AC 145.

[67] Family Law Act 1986, s 44.

[68] Family Law Act 1986, s 44.

[69] The legislation draws no distinction between divorces and annulments, and the term 'decrees' is used to encompass both. But for convenience of explanation, 'divorce' is used to include divorce and nullity.

[70] This expression includes England, Scotland, Northern Ireland, the Channel Islands, and the Isle of Man. Nevertheless, for convenience we will refer to English and overseas divorces.

[71] ibid, s 46.

and without proceedings requires the drawing of a peculiarly unpersuasive line of division. Had any distinction really been thought to be necessary, separate treatment of civil-judicial, and religious-non-judicial, divorces would have reflected the rather different procedures and assumptions underpinning each kind of case. But this was not done and, for the recognition of foreign divorces, all now turns on whether the divorce was obtained by 'proceedings'.

There is another problem. The scheme put in place by sections 44 and 45(1) appears to be based on the assumption that every divorce or annulment can be said to have been obtained in a single country. Problems therefore arise when a decree is obtained by means of proceedings whose component parts occur in more countries than one. In relation to decrees presented for recognition as overseas divorces, the leading cases[72] were both ones where part of the proceedings leading to the divorce—in each case a divorce obtained outside court and pursuant to 'religious law'—had taken place in England. In holding that this precluded recognition of the decree, the court did not limit its reasoning to a case where part of the process had taken place in England.[73] Instead, it deduced from the statutory definition of an overseas divorce that, to be recognized as such, all the elements required for it to be obtained must be located in one foreign country. It would follow that a Jewish divorce requiring the elaborate writing and delivery of a bill of divorce, or a form of Muslim divorce obtained by the writing of the words of repudiation and sending them both to the wife and to a statutory agency, would be denied recognition if any of the elements—often the sending of notice or service of a document—was geographically separated from the rest; and it appears to be irrelevant that the divorce would be recognized as effective in all of the countries in which a part of it happened. Why English law would deny recognition to a divorce which is effective under the laws of each and all of the countries which had a factual connection, on the ground that it did not all happen in the one geographical place, is impossible to explain.

If this is right, and if it applies, as the court suggested, to all overseas divorces, it leads to absurd results. The first is that such a trans-national divorce, being excluded from the definition of an overseas divorce, is not one which section 45(1) requires to be recognized under the Family Law Act 1986 or not at all: that dichotomy is applied only to overseas divorces, which means those

---

[72] *Berkovits v Grinberg* [1995] Fam 142, applying *R v Secretary of State for the Home Department, ex p Fatima* [1986] AC 527 (a case on earlier legislation).

[73] If the court can persuade itself that the divorce is obtained (only) in the place of the act immediately after which the marriage is dissolved, it will be obtained in only one place: see *Solovyev v Solovyeva* [2014] EWFC 1546, [2015] 1 FLR 734.

obtained in *a* country. No provision of the Act proscribes the recognition of divorces which are not, in this particular sense, mono-territorial overseas divorces. As all other statutory schemes for recognition have been repealed, it appears to follow that such decrees fall to be recognized under the rules of the common law thought to have been abolished 40 years ago.[74]

The second is that a judicial divorce, obtained from a foreign court, could not be recognized as an overseas divorce if any of the procedural essentials— such as the service of the petition on the respondent—took place outside that state: it would no longer be a divorce obtained (only) in one state and it will no longer fall under section 45. If it were possible to treat judicial divorces separately, this conclusion could be avoided,[75] but the legislation is not framed that way. Indeed, the corollary would be that where service of an English petition is made outside England, the divorce will, by parity of reasoning, not be seen as a divorce obtained in England, with the restrictions which the law places on such divorces. None of this makes any sense, but it all follows from the legislative categorization of divorces according to where they were obtained, and the judicial deduction that this requires all elements of the procedure to be concentrated in the one place. The law needs to be re-thought.

If the decree was obtained in a single country outside the British islands, and is not covered by the (former) Brussels II Regulation, the rules governing its recognition depend on whether it was obtained by judicial or other proceedings.[76] Judicial proceedings are not hard to identify as such, but 'other proceedings' have been held to require the involvement of an agency of or recognized by the state whose role is more than merely probative.[77] Quite why this was considered to be a line worth drawing is also a mystery,[78] and it can call for some intricate analysis of religious and foreign law. For example, a 'religious' divorce conforming to the (Pakistani) Muslim Family Law Ordinance 1961 is obtained by proceedings,[79] because the requirement to

---

[74] The Recognition of Divorces and Legal Separations Act 1971, which abolished them, was itself repealed by the Family Law Act 1986. The rules recognized a divorce if granted by a court which had a real and substantial connection to the case.

[75] *Solovyev v Solovyeva* [2014] EWFC 1546, [2015] 1 FLR 734.

[76] Family Law Act 1986, s 54(1).

[77] *Chaudhary v Chaudhary* [1985] Fam 19 (CA).

[78] Indeed, it may not have been intended as a line at all: its appearance in the Recognition of Divorces and Legal Separations Act 1971 may have been intended to clarify that *all* divorces, whether judicial or not, were within the Act. Only after it had been held that 'judicial or other proceedings' were not inclusive, but served to exclude some forms of divorce, did the idea take root that there was a line to be drawn, and this understanding, or maybe misunderstanding, was subsequently taken up into the Family Law Act 1986.

[79] *Quazi v Quazi* [1980] AC 744.

notify a statutory agency and the imposition of a statutory timetable may be seen as amounting to proceedings. The same conclusion was arrived at, but on rather less convincing grounds, in the case of a Jewish divorce, which was obtained by proceedings because, it seems, of the elaborate or costly ceremonial involved in writing the bill of divorce.[80] But a purely religious Muslim divorce, commenced and completed in three words of repudiation spoken by the husband,[81] is not obtained by means of proceedings.[82]

If the decree was obtained by proceedings and is to be recognized as such, it must be obtained where either[83] party was domiciled (according either to English law or to the law of the place of the obtaining)[84] or was habitually resident or was a national. The decree must be effective under that law to dissolve the marriage.[85] Where domicile or habitual residence is relied on as the jurisdictional connection, the decree must be effective in the relevant law district, such as Nevada as distinct from the United States; but in the case of nationality, it must be effective throughout the entire national territory,[86] a fact which may raise issues of foreign constitutional law. Recognition of the decree may be denied[87] on grounds of lack of notice or of the right to be heard, or if the matter is already *res judicata*. It may also be denied on grounds of public policy, and the claim of that policy to be applied may vary according to whether the marriage or the spouses had a significant connection to England.[88] Although the grounds upon which the decree was obtained are not specified as a ground of objection, they will, in an extreme case, be relevant, such as where a marriage is judicially[89] annulled for racial or religious reasons. Some may read the cases dealing with 'religious' divorces and wonder how it can be correct for the law to recognize a form of divorce in which one spouse has no right to be consulted, never mind represented and heard. Perhaps Article 6 of the European Convention on Human Rights[90] will provide the answer that recognition

---

[80]   *Berkovits v Grinberg* [1995] Fam 142.
[81]   'Talaq, talaq, talaq' ('I divorce you, I divorce you, I divorce you').
[82]   *Chaudhary v Chaudhary* [1985] Fam 19 (CA).
[83]   Husband or wife, petitioner or respondent.
[84]   Family Law Act 1986, s 46(5).
[85]   ibid, s 46(1); though not necessarily to reattribute marital capacity: s 50.
[86]   ibid, s 49(3)(a).
[87]   ibid, s 51.
[88]   cf *Chaudhary v Chaudhary* [1985] Fam 19 (CA). If the parties agreed to the procedure taking place overseas, objections to the outcome on grounds of public policy will be very hard to advance: *Lachaux v Lachaux* [2019] EWCA Civ 735.
[89]   If a marriage is said to be dissolved by operation of law when one of the parties changes religion, this should not be seen as done by divorce.
[90]   cf *Pellegrini v Italy* [2001] 8 *Reports of Judgments and Decisions* 353 (ECHR).

of such practice is hardly consistent with the human rights supposed to be secured by the Convention. The proposition that such mistreatment is warranted by religious discrimination is painfully insufficient, and the fact that the law of another country may tolerate it or be in thrall to it is nothing to the rational point.

If the decree was obtained without proceedings, its recognition requires that it be obtained where both parties were domiciled when it was obtained; or obtained where one was domiciled, with the country of domicile of the other party recognizing the decree. But it will be denied recognition in any event if either party had been habitually resident in the United Kingdom throughout the year prior to its being obtained.[91] The statutory grounds of non-recognition include those which may be raised against decrees obtained by proceedings but recognition may also be denied if there is no official document certifying the effectiveness of the decree under the law of the foreign country.[92] The sense of this is baffling.

(c) Decrees recognized under the Brussels II Regulation

The rules of the Brussels II Regulation provided for decrees from other Member States. In effect, such decrees must be recognized. The rules governing recognition are set out in Chapter III of the Regulation. A divorce, legal separation, or annulment pronounced by a court[93] in a Member State is recognized without any procedure or formality.[94] Non-recognition is permitted[95] where recognition is manifestly contrary to public policy; where the judgment was given in default of appearance and there was no due and timely service, unless the respondent has unequivocally accepted the judgment; where the judgment is irreconcilable with a local judgment in proceedings between the same parties; or where it is irreconcilable with an earlier judgment from a non-Member State in proceedings between the same parties which qualified for recognition. But the jurisdiction of the adjudicating court may not be reviewed or subjected to the test of public policy;[96] recognition

---

[91] Family Law Act 1986, s 46(2).

[92] ibid, s 51(4), a requirement read minimally in *Wicken v Wicken* [1999] Fam 224.

[93] Which includes all authorities with jurisdiction in these matters, so that non-judicial decrees are treated as if they were judicial decrees: Art 2(1). By way of derogation, it appears from recital 7 that 'purely religious procedures' are excluded from the scope of the Regulation, and decrees granted in such circumstances are therefore recognized, if at all, under the Family Law Act 1986.

[94] Article 21.

[95] Article 22, on which see Art 45(1) of the Brussels I Regulation.

[96] Article 24.

may not be withheld on the basis that the recognizing court would not it-self have granted the decree;[97] and the substance of the judgment may not be reviewed.[98] Unexpectedly, perhaps, recognition is said not to affect the property consequences of the marriage, maintenance obligations, or other ancillary measures,[99] although it is hard to see how that could be completely observed. As was observed above, the Regulation does not explain whether it is implicit in the obligation to recognize a decree that the parties to the former marriage recover their capacity to marry, even if the personal law of one of them would refuse to acknowledge it. Recital 8 to the Regulation might suggest that recognition of the decree extends only to the dissolution of matrimonial ties, but there is English authority, vouched for by common sense, for the proposition that a decree can hardly be said to have been rec-ognized if it does not carry with it the freedom to remarry unencumbered by the previous marriage.[100]

(d) Financial provision and maintenance

The court has power on the granting of a divorce, or on the recognition of an overseas divorce obtained by means of proceedings, to make an ancillary order for financial provision.[101] Originally the power to do so was confined to cases in which the English court had granted the divorce, but the power was extended. The legislation contains jurisdictional limitations which re-quire, in effect, that there is a genuine connection with England. The power of the court to act is not excluded, though, by the fact that the foreign court has made an order of its own. The court has to strike a balance between (on the one hand) not allowing a claimant who feels that the foreign court was not generous enough to have a free second bite at the cherry and (on the other) the fact that the court should make its own assessment of what is appropriate, and that this may differ significantly from the foreign court's assessment.[102] The court applies English law to substantive claims for finan-cial provision,[103] though the extent to which it takes account of factors which connect the claim with foreign countries is, as one might expect, delicate and

---

[97] Article 25.
[98] Article 26.
[99] Recital 8 to the Regulation.
[100] *Lawrence v Lawrence* [1985] Fam 106 (CA); Family Law Act 1986, s 50. But s 50 does not apply to decrees recognized under the Regulation: Family Law Act 1986, s 45(2) as inserted by SI 2001/310, reg 9.
[101] Matrimonial and Family Proceedings Act 1984, Part III.
[102] *Agbaje v Agbaje* [2010] UKSC 13, [2010] 1 AC 628.
[103] *Sealey v Callan* [1953] P 135 (CA).

contentious. In exercising its statutory powers a court may give dominant effect to a pre- or post-nuptial agreement, but no principle of private international law appears to be involved in calibrating the role which is given to the agreement in question.[104]

The jurisdictional rules governing maintenance applications are complex, and the law provided several bases for the exercise of jurisdiction. The complexity reflects two broad facts: the first is that there are many and diverse reasons why, or circumstances in which, an English court ought to be able to make such orders, which in any event would make for an untidy list, the content of which would not be susceptible to an organization which will lay bare the principle which made it rational. Second, the European Union adopted Regulation 4/2009 to deal with jurisdiction, applicable law, recognition and enforcement of decisions, and judicial cooperation in matters relating to maintenance obligations. The Regulation was certainly welcome, and the United Kingdom opted into it. According to Article 1(1), its scope is 'maintenance obligations arising from a family relationship, parentage, marriage, or affinity', and apart from the obligation to interpret this autonomously,[105] it is left at that. It will presumably include proprietary legal relations arising directly from the marriage or its dissolution, and exclude those which have no connection with the marriage.[106]

According to Article 3 of the (former) Maintenance Regulation,[107] the English court has jurisdiction if either the creditor or the defendant is habitually resident in England, or if the English court has jurisdiction over proceedings concerning status or parental responsibility and the matter relating to maintenance is ancillary to those proceedings: this provides the formal basis for the English court to continue to be able to make orders for ancillary financial relief as part of the divorce or annulment proceedings before it.[108] Article 4 confers or recognizes a restricted right for the parties to choose a court, the choice being required to be in writing, though there is no power to make a choice of court if the maintenance obligation is in respect of a child under 18. Jurisdiction may also be based on voluntary appearance.[109] Where

---

[104] *Radmacher v Granatino* [2010] UKSC 42, [2011] 1 AC 534.

[105] Recital 11.

[106] cf Case 143/78 *De Cavel v De Cavel* [1979] ECR 1055.

[107] Regulation (EC) 4/2009, [2009] OJ L7/1; see also SI 2011/1484.

[108] For the English court's power to grant financial relief after a foreign divorce, see Matrimonial and Family Proceedings Act 1984; *Agbaje v Agbaje* [2010] UKSC 13, [2010] 1 AC 628. But the jurisdictional rules of the Maintenance Regulation will prevail to the extent that they conflict with those of the 1984 Act (eg insofar as the application is for maintenance as opposed to some other property adjustment order).

[109] Article 5.

those provisions do not give jurisdiction to the courts of any Member State, the courts of the Member State of the parties' common nationality (which in England means common domicile) have 'subsidiary' jurisdiction.[110] And where none of these provisions serves to give jurisdiction to the courts of any Member State, all that remains is an exceptional power to take jurisdiction as a matter of necessity.[111] It will therefore be seen that the jurisdictional provisions of the (former) Maintenance Regulation are exhaustive, and do not provide for any 'residual jurisdiction' over defendants who have no domicile in a Member State.

A foreign divorce, even if recognized in England, does not automatically terminate an English maintenance order.[112] A foreign maintenance order which is final and conclusive[113] may be recognized and enforced in England at common law and under statute,[114] for it is a civil judgment *in personam*. The provisions for recognition are largely reciprocal with the grounds of jurisdiction exercised by English courts. Otherwise, orders from Member States may be enforced under Chapter IV of the (former) Maintenance Regulation; the registration is made in the magistrates' court for the place where the respondent is resident for the purposes of this instrument, or where assets against which enforcement may be made are situated. The permissible objections to registration are few.

3. PERSONAL BANKRUPTCY

The law on corporate insolvency is discussed in the following chapter, as part of the law of corporations. A substantial part of it will also be seen to apply to individual bankruptcy, but something needs to be said of it here.

The (former) EU Insolvency Regulation[115] dealt with jurisdiction, applicable law, and recognition and enforcement of judgments, and applied this to personal bankruptcy as well as to corporate insolvency. But because it is, in

---

[110] Article 2(3) read together with Art 6.

[111] Articles 3–7. *Lis alibi pendens* is regulated by Art 12.

[112] *Macaulay v Macaulay* [1991] 1 WLR 179.

[113] Though as the court which made the order usually has the power to vary the figures, it may be that its decision is only really final in relation to payments the due date for which has already passed.

[114] Maintenance Orders Act 1950, Part II; Maintenance Orders (Facilities for Enforcement) Act 1920; Maintenance Orders (Reciprocal Enforcement) Act 1972; Civil Jurisdiction and Judgments Act 1982.

[115] Regulation (EC) 1348/2000, [2000] OJ L160/1; recast as Regulation (EU) 2015/848, [2015] OJ L141/19 (in force from 26 June 2017), but with little real change.

practice, most commonly applicable in corporate insolvency, the summary of its provisions which properly belongs in the following chapter, but which will be equally applicable to personal bankruptcy, will not be pre-repeated here. The account which follows in this section is, therefore, the law as it applies to bankruptcies to which the (former) Regulation does not apply, which principally means cases where the centre of the debtor's main interests is outside the territory of the Member States.

The English courts have jurisdiction to declare bankrupt any debtor who is domiciled or present in England on the day of presentation of the petition.[116] They also have jurisdiction if he was ordinarily resident, or had a place of residence, or carried on business (or was a member of a partnership firm which carried on business) in England at any time within the three years prior to the presentation of the petition.[117] A debtor who has subjected himself to a voluntary arrangement submits to the jurisdiction by doing so.[118] In deciding whether to exercise their discretion to make the order, the courts will consider the location of assets, any foreign bankruptcy, and other issues of general convenience.[119] The bankrupt may be examined by order of the court, but the private examination of any other person is probably limited to those who are present within the jurisdiction to be served with the summons requesting their attendance.[120]

As to the law which is applies in the proceedings, an English court applies English law, the *lex fori*, to the bankruptcy.[121] The making of the order operates as a statutory assignment of the debtor's property, wherever situated, to his trustee;[122] the bankrupt may be ordered to assist the trustee in recovering property which lies outside the control of the court. A creditor who is or who has made himself subject to the personal jurisdiction of the court may be restrained from taking proceedings overseas, in order to safeguard the principle of equal division.[123] Foreign debts must be shown to be due and owing by reference to the law under which they arise, but the court will use its own rules to secure, as best it may, equality between creditors of the same class.[124] The power of the court to set aside an antecedent transaction is not subject

---

[116] Insolvency Act 1986, s 265.
[117] ibid, s 265.
[118] ibid, s 264.
[119] *Re Behrends* (1865) 12 LT 149; *Re Robinson, ex p Robinson* (1883) 22 Ch D 816 (CA).
[120] cf *Re Seagull Manufacturing Co Ltd* [1993] Ch 345 (CA).
[121] *Re Kloebe* (1884) 28 Ch D 175; *Re Doetsch* [1896] 2 Ch 836.
[122] Insolvency Act 1986, ss 283, 306, 436.
[123] *Barclays Bank plc v Homan* [1993] BCLC 680 (CA).
[124] *Re Scheibler* (1874) 9 Ch App 722.

to express limitation, but the defendant against whom reversal of the transaction is sought must be (or, by service out with leave of the court, be made) subject to the jurisdiction of the court, and the test is whether it is just and convenient in all the circumstances of the case to make the order.[125]

An English discharge operates in relation to all the debts provable in the bankruptcy, irrespective of the law which governed the debt.[126] The position in relation to foreign bankruptcies is, however, quite different: a foreign bankruptcy will not discharge a debt or other contract which is governed by a different law, such as English law, as the discharge of debts is considered to be a matter for the *lex contractus*.[127] The principle has been established for over a century, but it has been a cause of complaint for almost as long.

A foreign bankruptcy will be recognized if the debtor was domiciled[128] in or submitted[129] to the jurisdiction of the foreign court; and the bankruptcy will vest English movables (though not land) in the assignee if this is the effect it has under the foreign law.[130] The result may be that the debtor no longer has property in England, and this will tell strongly against making an English order. A discharge from a foreign bankruptcy is effective in England only if it is effective under the law which governed the debt.[131] A court may not question the bankruptcy jurisdiction of a Scottish or Northern Irish court; and the effect of such an order extends to all property in England, not excluding land.[132]

B. CHILDREN

Previous editions of this book contained a summary of the rules of private international law relating to children. Leaving aside questions of legitimacy, which today are archaic and offensive, and adoption which is comparatively straightforward, the modern law of children is principally concerned with parental responsibility, guardianship, and custody. The complexity of fact

---

[125] *Re Paramount Airways Ltd* [1993] Ch 223 (CA); *Bilta (UK) Ltd v Nazir* [2015] UKSC 23, [2016] AC 1.
[126] Insolvency Act 1986, s 281.
[127] *Gibbs and Sons v Soc Industrielle et Commerciale et des Métaux* (1890) 25 QBD 399 (CA); *Re OJSC International Bank of Azerbaijan* [2018] EWCA Civ 2802.
[128] *Re Hayward* [1897] 1 Ch 905.
[129] *Re Anderson* [1911] 1 KB 896.
[130] *Re Craig* (1916) 86 LJ Ch 62.
[131] *Gibbs and Sons v Soc Industrielle et Commerciale et des Métaux* (1890) 25 QBD 399 (CA); *Re OJSC International Bank of Azerbaijan* [2018] EWCA Civ 2802.
[132] Insolvency Act 1986, s 426.

and law in this area, and in particular the possibility that several courts may be entangled in a dispute relating to children, has given rise to a substantial amount of legislation, in international conventions, European regulations, and parliamentary acts. It is apparent that the way in which this all fits together is neither perfect nor obvious;[133] the disentangling of the law operating in the United Kingdom as a result of the (former) Brussels II Regulation and patching it up again is, inevitably, only going to make things worse. In any event, the volume of case law which it has generated in recent years bears witness to the complexity and the anxiety which these cases, particularly concerning the abduction and (non-)return of children, are always liable to generate. The conclusion to which all this tends is that a book of this intended size cannot do justice to the private international law of children, and that as a result its detailed operation will not be discussed further. This is not because is not important, but because it is too important for it to be compressed into what would otherwise be the available space.

It is worth reflecting, though, on the root cause of the difficulty in coming to a satisfactory statement and understanding of the private international law of children as currently configures. The dominant factor in the law, and the principal basis of the power to make an effective adjudication, is the habitual residence of the child. In principle this makes perfect sense: the court at the place where the child is most closely integrated into society is, most people would accept, best placed to make orders about welfare and custody. The law of the place of the child's habitual residence is, for the same reason, usually the most appropriate law to apply. However, it will not always be so straightforward: 10 points are mentioned here, but the list could be much longer than that. First, there may be divergent views about whether a child's habitual residence is automatically, or presumptively, or independent of, that of its parents or parent. Second, there may be divergent views about the age (or other definitional identifiers) of a child whose habitual residence is to be assessed independently of a parent , or about the age at which this ceases to be so. Third, it may appear, if one focuses on the child, that the child has settled into a particular place even though the relevant parent has not decided whether to settle down in that place. Fourth, quite apart from any impact brought to bear by the habitual residence of the parents, there may still be divergent views about where the child's habitual residence is. Fifth, it may be argued that the relevant habitual residence should make special provision

---

[133] It will not be significantly easier to understand or to operate if the Brussels II Regulation is revoked by the European Union (Withdrawal) Act 2018 s 8 and SI 2019/519.

for the case in which the child would have been habitually resident in a place if only he or she had not been removed, or wrongfully removed, to another place. Sixth, it may be argued that the relevant habitual residence should make special provision for the case in which the child would have been habitually resident in a place if only his or her mother had not been coerced against her will into being somewhere else before the birth of the child and prevented from leaving with the child after its birth. Seventh, it may be argued that the child may have been habitually resident in a particular place when proceedings were instituted, but that the child is now more obviously integrated into surroundings and society somewhere else. Eighth, it may be argued that the child is now more integrated into surroundings and society only because of abduction, of failure to comply with an order for return, and that this should somehow count for less than it would if it were not tainted by parental misconduct. Ninth, it may be argued, perhaps only in extreme cases (but these are the ones which need the greatest care), that the country or law of habitual residence is liable to make orders, or to allow parental conduct, which is in the eye of the court significantly detrimental to the best interests of the child, or worse. Tenth, the idea that there should be a jurisdictional fight over the habitual residence of a child, possibly through three levels of national courts and a stay while a reference is made to the European Court, simply multiplies the difficulties.[134] And there is more, much more, which could be said. The circumstances of children born and living within less traditional family structures, which are subject to differing degrees of legal acceptance, are bound to raise new factual and legal complexities for domestic law, never mind private international law.

For all that, it may very well be that the dominance[135] of the habitual residence of the child is liable to be unsatisfactory, but that all the alternatives are

[134] The starting point would be *Re J (A Minor) (Abduction: Custody Rights)* [1990] 2 AC 562 and *Re S (A Minor) (Abduction: European Convention)* [1998] AC 750. But these authorities are now mostly eclipsed: see for example *A v A (Children: Habitual Residence)* [2013] UKSC 60, [2014] AC 1; *Re S (A Child) (Habitual Residence and Child's Objections: Brazil)* [2015] EWCA Civ 2, [2015] 2 FLR 1338; *Re R (A Child) (Jurisdiction: Habitual Residence)* [2015] EWCA Civ 674, [2016] 1 FLR 1119; *Re R (Children)* [2015] UKSC 35, [2016] AC 76; *Re B (A Child)* [2016] UKSC 4, [2016] AC 606; *Re J (A Child)* [2017] EWCA Civ 80, [2017] Fam Law 496; *Re C (Children)* [2018] UKSC 8, [2019] 1 AC 1. See also, from the European Court, Case C–523/07 *Re A* [2009] ECR I–2805; Case C–497/10 PPU *Mercredi v Chaffe* EU:C:2010:829, [2012] Fam 22; Case C–499/15 *W v X* EU:C:2017:118, [2017] Fam 305; Case C–111/17 PPU *OL v PQ* EU:C:2017:436; Case C–521/17 *Re HR* EU:C:2018:513, [2018] Fam 385; Case C–85/18 PPU *CV v DU* EU:C:2018:220; Case C–393/18 PPU *UD v XB* EU:C:2018:835, [2019] 1 WLR 3083.
[135] Dominance certainly does not mean sole application. All systems, certainly including English law, make alternative, and in some respects last-ditch, provisions for exercising jurisdiction where the welfare of a child is concerned.

worse. The challenges for a court are not really those of private international law, or are not challenges which the rules of private international law are capable of solving. The behaviour and misbehaviour of parents complicates to an almost impossible degree the orderly and sensitive resolution of disputes; the ability of obstructive or defiant parents to create 'new facts' is something which private international law cannot control. As can be seen from the statute book and the law reports, an immense amount of labour has been devoted to trying to make the law relating to children better. It is not readily apparent that it has done any good at all. It may be that a court should simply be instructed to make orders which appear to it to be in the best interests of the child, and to leave it at that: dealing with the matter as one of domestic, not private international, law, for which the special expertise of the family courts and their practitioners, rather than the abstraction of private international law, is the least bad solution.

9

Corporations

In this chapter, and prior to Exit Day, the private international law of insolvency and bankruptcy was covered in part by two European Regulations: the Insolvency Regulation 1346/2000, and the recast Insolvency Regulation 2015/848. According to the Insolvency (Amendment) (EU Exit) Regulations 2019, SI 2019 No 146, a fragment of Regulation 2015/848 is retained as English law, but otherwise it is not retained as English law. The principal effect of this is that the court will continue to have jurisdiction to open insolvency proceedings when the debtor's centre of main interests is in the United Kingdom. Otherwise Part 1 of the Schedule to SI 2019 No 146 provides that the recast Insolvency Regulation shall not have effect in the United Kingdom. Consequential amendment is made to secondary legislation. Transitional provisions are made to provide for the continued application of the Regulations after Exit Day in the case of insolvency proceedings opened before Exit Day.

Insofar as any rule of company law was derived from the fundamental principles of European law, particularly the four freedoms, these principles, and the law derived therefrom, will cease to be part of English law on Exit Day.

A. INTRODUCTION

Although a corporation is a person—a legal[1] rather than a natural person, but never mind—it has been the tradition of English private international law to treat corporations separately from the law of natural persons, and instead to examine the private international law of corporations alongside corporate insolvency, presumably on the basis that insolvency is a significant fact of corporate life and litigation. That tradition is observed here. Less

---

[1] Otherwise a '*persona ficta*'.

The Conflict of Laws. Fourth Edition. Adrian Briggs, Oxford University Press (2019). © Adrian Briggs
DOI: 10.1093/oso/9780198838500.003.0009

traditional, though, is the scope of this chapter, which focuses on a number of general principles of private international law as they operate in relation to corporations and insolvency, rather than on the immense and highly technical details of the law.

The conflicts rules of the common law used, and still use, the *lex incorporationis* to govern many of the issues raised under the law of corporations. This made sense when the link between a company and its place of incorporation was natural. It makes rather less sense, or a rather different sense, when the company is created,[2] technically but for the purpose of avoiding tax, supervision, and liability, under the law of some remote island (whether or not surrounded by sea), or 'registry of convenience'. The common law also takes very seriously the principle of (separate) corporate personality, being very reluctant to treat nominally separate corporate entities as though they were, or were part of, the same economic unit.[3] Whether this approach is still suitable for dealing with modern corporate structures is therefore open to serious question. Even so, the challenge for those who would wish the law to be different is to find a stable principle which will allow such distortions and perversions to be disregarded. If it sometimes seems that the English common law has barely tried, it may be that such problems require legislative, rather than judicial, attention.

Insolvency, by contrast, was dominated by the application of *lex fori*. This made perfect sense when insolvency was a predominantly local affair, but it was not suited to dealing with a problem which grew in recent times to be one of alarming size. When the financial structures which have led to corporate insolvency have substantial cross-border components, the cross-border elements cannot be ignored. Rules designed for local insolvencies would be bound to need something extra. Even where they were receptive to the idea, which did not always appear to be the case, there was only so much that judges could do to manage the proceedings before them in a way which was sensitive to the fact that other courts were liable to be involved in the same work and in relation to the same failed business: comity is all very well, but it provides little justification for not applying laws laid down by Parliament.[4]

---

[2] Or re-created, if it runs away from the law and place of its incorporation to one of these stinking tax havens and pretends to be re-created there.

[3] *Adams v Cape plc* [1990] Ch 433; *Prest v Petrodel Resources Ltd* [2013] UKSC 34, [2013] 2 AC 415.

[4] For a creative suggestion of what a court proposed to do under its inherent jurisdiction, see *Cambridge Gas Transportation Corp v Committee of Unsecured Creditors of Navigator Holdings plc* [2006] UKPC 26, [2007] 1 AC 508. The case is now regarded as having gone too far.

Though domestic legislation made modest provision for rendering assistance in relation to foreign insolvency proceedings, the first serious attempt at cross-border cooperation took the form of a European Regulation,[5] which applied to corporate insolvency as well as to personal bankruptcy; it was recast in 2015,[6] though making only minor changes to the original scheme. In a parallel development, a Model Law on cross-border insolvency, developed at the United Nations,[7] was given effect in English law in 2006. It has the aim, and certainly offers the prospect, of further developing the cross-border co-operation and coordination of insolvency procedures outside the context of the European Union. These statutory steps taken to bring order to the administration of cross-border insolvency have been far more successful than anything which national parliaments or individual judges could ever have achieved. Although the detail of the law is complex, the field of cross-border insolvency is an excellent example of when legislation to improve the state of the law is the only way ahead.

B. CORPORATIONS

It makes sense to look first at the private international law of corporations, and then at the law of insolvency: as to this latter, what is said about corporate insolvency will apply also to personal bankruptcy, the outline of which was briefly mentioned in the previous chapter. The sources of private international law are principally those of the common law, though European law on the freedom of movement and establishment made a significant contribution to the private international law of corporations as it applied in English courts.

1. THE ROLE OF THE *LEX INCORPORATIONIS*

A corporation is an artificial creation, a legal person. The question whether, and with what powers, a body corporate has been created is determined by the law under which its creation took place, which the common law

---

[5] Council Regulation (EC) 1346/2000, [2000] OJ L160/1.
[6] Regulation (EU) 2015/848, [2015] OJ L141/19. In effect from 26 June 2017.
[7] UNCITRAL, 30th session, 1997. For the implementing legislation, see Insolvency Act 2000, s 14(4) and SI 2006/1030.

still considers to be the *lex incorporationis*. Likewise, the question who is empowered or authorized to act on its behalf is a matter for the *lex incorporationis*, though the legal consequences of an act[8] which an officer or organ was not entitled to perform may also be referred to another law. The question whether an individual is personally liable for the acts or engagements of a corporation is also governed by the *lex incorporationis*; and, in principle, all issues having to do with the internal government and management of a corporation are referred to that law.[9] It is perfectly obvious that this offers an incentive to incorporate under a law which offers advantages to those who may wish to create a corporation with wide powers but restricted liabilities, or to incorporate with no significant risk of allowing liability to affect individual officers or corporators: there are times when one wonders whether onshore[10] or offshore[11] havens of this kind actually have any other purpose.[12] This is, however, little more than a consequence of the doctrine of separate corporate personality[13] and the fact that some laws offer more than others to the self-serving corporator. Though it is sometimes suggested that the place of incorporation should not be decisive, and that the law of the place of daily or central management and control should assume a more prominent role;[14] or that the doctrine of separate corporate personality really needs to be balanced by an analysis based on the economic realities of life and the need to assert effective control over multi-national enterprises,[15] these arguments have tended to be directed at jurisdiction over companies rather than at the hegemony of the *lex incorporationis* as the law applicable to issues of legal personality, power, and responsibility.

---

[8] Say the making of a contract or the commission of a tort: the *lex contractus* and the *lex delicti* would play the dominant role in determining the existence and location of liability resulting from the acts in question.

[9] *Bonanza Creek Gold Mining Co v R* [1916] 1 AC 566 (PC); *Lazard Bros v Midland Bank* [1933] AC 289; *National Bank of Greece and Athens SA v Metliss* [1958] AC 509; *Carl Zeiss Stiftung v Rayner & Keeler Ltd (No 2)* [1967] 1 AC 853; *JH Rayner (Mincing Lane) Ltd v Department of Trade and Industry* [1990] 2 AC 418.

[10] Delaware, for example.

[11] The Channel Islands and the Isle of Man are obvious examples, but British possessions in the western Atlantic are notorious as well.

[12] Although it is possible that the question whether the corporate veil will always protect whoever is behind it will not necessarily be answered by the *lex incorporationis*. See *VTB Capital plc v Nutritek International Corp* [2013] UKSC 5, [2013] 2 AC 337.

[13] For the strictness with which English law defends the principle of separate corporate personality, and refuses to look behind the veil of incorporation, see *Prest v Petrodel Resources Ltd* [2013] UKSC 34, [2013] 2 AC 415.

[14] Drury [1998] CLJ 165.

[15] Muchlinski (2001) 50 ICLQ 1; cf *Vedanta Resources plc v Lungowe* [2019] UKSC 20, [2019] 2 WLR 1051.

(a) Recognition of corporations

English law recognizes the creation of corporations, and the acquisition of legal personality by them, and the protection from legal liability of those who incorporate them, by reference to the *lex incorporationis*. The untidy reality of life has required that the recognition of corporations be extended to those which are created under the ordinances of a semi-state, such as Kosovo or Taiwan, or the altogether illegal 'Turkish Republic of Northern Cyprus'.[16] Moreover, although English law does not recognize the legal personality of an international organization in the absence of domestic legislation to confer such status, where a foreign law has conferred such personality under its law, the legal personality which results from it may be recognized in England.[17] So the Arab Monetary Fund, an international organization of states of which the United Kingdom is not a member, had been given legal personality under the laws of the United Arab Emirates, and was accordingly recognized as a person under English law. What would have happened if it had been given personality under the laws of more states than one raises questions to which no easy answers exist and which it is better not to ask.

(b) Dissolution of corporations

What the law creates the same law can also destroy, so the question whether a corporation has been dissolved is also referred to and answered by the *lex incorporationis*[18] alone. The validity of a corporate dissolution may raise difficult questions when the law under which the corporation was created ceases to exist and in its geographical place a new law arises. But corporations created under the law of the Russian Empire were recognized as having been dissolved under the laws of the Soviet Union, and, at the end of the same century, in a satisfying piece of legal and political symmetry, vice versa.[19]

(c) Amalgamation of corporations

A combination of the rules for creation and dissolution means that the amalgamation of corporations, the recognition of the new corporation, and whether it assumes at birth the rights and liabilities of the dissolved

---

[16] Foreign Corporations Act 1991, s 1.

[17] *Arab Monetary Fund v Hashim (No 3)* [1991] 2 AC 114; *Westland Helicopters Ltd v Arab Organisation for Industrialisation* [1995] QB 282.

[18] *Lazard Bros v Midland Bank* [1933] AC 289; *Russian and English Bank v Baring Bros* [1932] 1 Ch 435 (and if there is a branch in England it cannot sue after the corporation has been dissolved; it should be wound up).

[19] *The Kommunar (No 2)* [1997] 1 Lloyd's Rep 8.

corporation(s), are in principle all questions for the *lex incorporationis*,[20] although the issue whether this process also discharges liabilities incurred by the original corporation is a distinct and contractual one, governed by the law applicable to those obligations.[21] An English court will naturally seek, for pragmatic reasons, to give effect to a corporate succession, and will do what it can to ensure that it is effective in English private international law. But corporate reconstruction may be a process rather than an event, and it can leave loose ends untied: for example, the old corporations may remain undissolved for a period after the creation of the new, which may make business sense but is not really how succession works in everyday life and death.[22] In a proper case, a court may come to the conclusion in a particular case that the process is not a true succession or amalgamation notwithstanding the language used by the foreign legislator.[23]

(d) Migration of corporations

The fact that a corporation's residence may determine its liability to pay tax provides an incentive to companies, who wish to avoid the taxes which they doubtless expect[24] others to pay, to try to migrate from one state to another. National laws variously put obstacles in their way, limiting or removing the power of a corporation established under their laws to remove their residence or central management and control to another country while remaining incorporated under the original law. These restrictions are challenged from time to time for their compatibility with European Union law on freedom of establishment; and the challenges usually fail. It has been generally been held that European law does not object if the *lex incorporationis* itself prevents a company moving its central management and control to another country, or requires ministerial consent to do so, if the company is to remain

---

[20] *National Bank of Greece and Athens SA v Metliss* [1958] AC 509; if the two corporations are incorporated in different countries the *lex incorporationis* of each must recognize the amalgamation. See also *Adams v National Bank of Greece and Athens SA* [1961] AC 255 for cases where there may not be a true and complete succession to the rights and liabilities of the former companies. For an analogous principle in relation to insolvency, where a foreign bankruptcy does not discharge a contract governed by a different law, see *Gibbs and Sons v Soc Industrielle et Commerciale des Métaux* (1890) 25 QBD 399 (CA); *Re OJSC International Bank of Azerbaijan* [2018] EWCA Civ 2802.

[21] *Adams v National Bank of Greece and Athens SA* [1961] AC 255.

[22] This is the reason why the imagery of 'succession' has at times been questioned.

[23] *The Kommunar (No 2)* [1997] 1 Lloyd's Rep 8.

[24] And if they are newspapers, stridently insist that everyone else should pay, which is one of the ironies of Case 81/87 *R v HM Treasury and the IRC ex p Daily Mail.*

incorporated in the original state.[25] In the same way, the *lex incorporationis* may prevent the transfer of a company's seat to another Member State while retaining its original incorporation.[26] But it will be otherwise if the company migrates and simply converts itself into a company governed by the law of the migrated-to Member State, always assuming that the law of the migrated-to state does not require the incoming company to be wound up in the state from which it is migrating.

(e) Domicile of corporations

As a matter of common law, a corporation is domiciled at the place of its incorporation.[27] This, for example, means that the capacities[28] of the corporation are governed by its *lex incorporationis* and the general principle that legal capacity is governed by the law of the domicile is preserved. It also means that, as far as the common law is concerned, a corporation has, and can only ever have, only one domicile.

In other contexts, however, a 'statutory domicile' may be conferred, which is separate and wholly distinct from the common law determination of domicile.[29] In the context of jurisdiction in civil and commercial matters which were within the domain of the Brussels I Regulation, a corporation was domiciled where[30] it had its statutory seat or its central administration or its principal place of business.[31] It is obvious that this could be seen as 'the' domicile which determines corporate capacity, for a corporation may, under this slightly inelegant provision, have as many as three domiciles for jurisdictional purposes. It is right that this is possible, for the function and purpose of domicile in the Brussels I Regulation is to define and describe a connection with a Member State sufficient to expose the defendant to the general jurisdiction of the courts of that place; a company or corporation

---

[25]   Case 81/87 *R v HM Treasury and the IRC ex p Daily Mail* [1988] ECR 5505; Case C–208/00 *Überseering BV v NCC* [2002] ECR I–9919. How (if at all) this will be regulated after the United Kingdom leaves the EU is not known.

[26]   Case C–210/06 *Cartesio Oktató és Szolgáltató bt* [2008] ECR I–9641.

[27]   *Gasque v Inland Revenue Commissioners* [1940] KB 80.

[28]   To some extent this will also determine its liability to pay taxes.

[29]   *Ministry of Defence and Support of the Armed Services of Iran v FAZ Aviation Ltd* [2007] EWHC 1042 (Comm), [2008] 1 All ER (Comm) 372. See also *Young v Anglo American South Africa Ltd* [2014] EWCA Civ 1130.

[30]   In the sense of 'wherever'.

[31]   See Art 62 of the recast Regulation, 1215/2012. For the purposes of the United Kingdom, 'statutory seat' means the registered office or, where there is no such office anywhere, the place of incorporation or, where there is no such place anywhere, the place under the law of which the formation took place: Art 62(2).

may certainly have more than one of these. It follows that the two varieties of corporate domicile—the common law domicile of the *lex incorporationis*; the Brussels domicile or domiciles for the purpose of jurisdiction in civil and commercial matters—have nothing in common but their unfortunate use of the same word.

2. TAKING JURISDICTION OVER CORPORATIONS

As with individual defendants, a corporation can be sued in England when process can be served on it. In one respect, service on a corporation is more complex than service on individual defendants, for there can hardly be personal service on an artificial person. But the changes to the methods of service brought in by the Civil Procedure Rules simplified matters considerably, and the Companies Act 2006 has made statutory service on companies less complicated.[32]

A company registered under the Companies Acts may be served by leaving the document at, or by posting it to, the company's registered office. An overseas company[33] which has registered statutory particulars with the registrar of companies may be served by leaving the document at, or sending it to, the address of the person authorized to accept service; but if that is not possible it may be left at 'any place of business of the company in the United Kingdom'.[34] In this context a place of business will be taken to mean somewhere fixed and definite and from which the business of the company is carried on. A good starting point may be to ask whether it makes contracts there. If the answer is yes, this will constitute a place of business; and if that is so, the court will have jurisdiction over the company generally: its jurisdiction is not limited to issues arising out of activity at that place.[35] If contracts are not made at the particular place, a court may certainly still find that the activity carried on at the place in question constitutes the carrying on of business, for the statutory rule is

---

[32] For the separate nature of the schemes, see *Sea Assets Ltd v PT Garuda International* [2000] 4 All ER 371.

[33] One incorporated outside the United Kingdom: Companies Act 2006, s 1044. The extent of the obligation on such a company to register particulars is governed by ss 1045–48.

[34] Companies Act 2006, s 1139.

[35] *Okura & Co Ltd v Forsbacka Jernverks AB* [1914] 1 KB 715; cf *Adams v Cape Industries plc* [1990] Ch 433 (CA).

not defined in terms of a principal place of business; and there is more to business than the making of contracts.[36]

As indicated above, in addition to statutory service under the Companies Acts, a company, including an overseas company,[37] may be served in accordance with Part 6 of the Civil Procedure Rules, at any place within the jurisdiction where it carries on its activities, or at any place of business within the jurisdiction. Service is made by leaving the document with a person holding a senior position[38] within the company.

Service is one thing; jurisdiction is another. Where the company is domiciled in a Member State for the purposes of the (former) Brussels I Regulation, Article 24(2) gives exclusive jurisdiction to the courts of the seat[39] of the corporation in proceedings having as their object the validity of the constitution, the nullity or dissolution of companies, or decisions of their organs. This reflects the fact that the birth and death of a company, and the inherent legal validity of acts of its organs, can really only be dealt with in the one place. Of course, the consequences of acts which were based on decisions of corporate organs which were not valid are not within this jurisdictional rule.[40]

3. CONTRACTS MADE BY CORPORATIONS

The two main issues which arise when dealing with contracts made by corporations are those of capacity (of the corporation to make the contract at all) and authority (of the organ or officer to bind the corporation). As the private international law of agency is apparently immune to reform by convention, these questions are still principally left to be resolved by common law conflicts rules.

---

[36] *South India Shipping Corp Ltd v Export-Import Bank of Korea* [1985] 1 WLR 585 (CA); cf *SSL International plc v TTK LIG Ltd* [2011] EWCA Civ 1170, [2012] 1 WLR 1842 (holding occasional board meeting not enough).

[37] Service under CPR Pt 6 may be made as an alternative to statutory service: CPR 6.3(2).

[38] CPR 6.5(3)(b); for the definition of 'senior position', see the Practice Direction 6A. But not if the company does not carry on business within the jurisdiction: *SSL International plc v TTK LIG Ltd* [2011] EWCA Civ 1170, [2012] 1 WLR 1842.

[39] As this seat is specially defined, for the purposes of this rule, by the national law of the court seised, and not as defined by Art 62 of the Regulation: Art 24(2).

[40] Case C–144/10 *BVG v JP Morgan Chase Bank NA* [2011] ECR I–3961; see also *Grupo Torras SA v Sheikh Fahad Mohammed Al-Sabah* [1996] 1 Lloyd's Rep 7 (CA); *Speed Investments Ltd v Formula One Holdings Ltd (No 2)* [2004] EWCA Civ 1512, [2005] 1 WLR 1936.

If there is no dispute that the corporation had capacity under the *lex incorporationis* to enter into the contract, no problems arise. But where it is alleged that it did not, the contract may be *ultra vires* the corporation, and this may well lead to the *lex contractus*—the validity of a contract made by a party without legal capacity is a matter for the law which governs the contract, after all—considering the contract to be void.[41] Even so, the corporation may in a proper case be precluded by its own conduct from relying on its own incapacity and the consequences which would follow from it,[42] although it is debatable whether the applicable principles should be those of the *lex fori* or of the *lex contractus*.[43] Where the corporation had capacity to enter the contract, but the person purporting to act on its behalf did not have authority to so act, the question whether the contract made between the agent and the third party binds or may be relied on by the company is a tricky one, though the orthodox view is that it is a matter for the *lex contractus* of that contract which was created.[44] The case law is notoriously difficult though. It seems right that where an agent acts on behalf of a principal, a third party is generally entitled to assume that the agent has such power and authority as he would have under the law which governs the contract which they make. It is true that where the agent is the representative of a company, a third party will or should be aware that the *lex incorporationis* may place limits upon the extent to which a company can be bound, but this deemed awareness applies more obviously to the legal capacities of the company than to the powers which it has chosen to vest in a particular officer. It follows that there is no strong reason to make a special rule for contracts made by corporate agents who acted outside their authority: the extent to which the company is bound and entitled should be a matter for the law of the contract brought into being between the agent and the third party.

If a corporation has been dissolved and amalgamated with, or to create, another, the question whether this dissolution terminates the contract as a source of obligation is, as has been said, a matter for the *lex contractus*. So although the amalgamation may provide for the vesting of all liabilities in the new corporation, it cannot discharge those liabilities, then or later, unless it is also the law applicable to them.[45] The result may, however, be that

---

[41] *Haugesund Kommune v Depfa ACS Bank* [2010] EWCA Civ 579, [2012] QB 549.

[42] *Janred v ENIT* [1989] 2 All ER 444 (CA).

[43] If there would be estoppel under the one but not the other, there is a conflict of laws; principle suggests that the *lex fori* should defer to the *lex contractus*.

[44] *Chatenay v Brazilian Submarine Telegraph Co* [1891] 1 QB 279; *Maspons v Mildred* (1882) 9 QBD 530 (CA); *Ruby SS Corpn v Commercial Union Assurance Co Ltd* (1933) 150 LT 38 (CA).

[45] *Adams v National Bank of Greece and Athens SA* [1961] AC 255.

the contract is not discharged but there is no counterparty against which to enforce the obligation.

4. WINDING UP OF COMPANIES

The dissolution of companies under the *lex incorporationis* is one thing, but the winding up of companies is more complex. European legislation required a distinction to be drawn between solvent and insolvent companies when dealing with their winding up.[46] So far as solvent companies are concerned, English courts may wind up a company registered in England.[47] But the Brussels Regulation provided that a solvent company may not be wound up if it had a seat in another Member State and no seat in England.[48]

The regimes which apply to insolvent companies are more complex. The law on the winding up of insolvent companies has been made that way, albeit for good reason, by three principal developments. The first was probably the original EU Insolvency Regulation,[49] which took effect in 2002 and which was latterly recast.[50] It applies when the 'centre of main interests' of the debtor is in a Member State; its aim was to coordinate, to the extent possible, the insolvency of entities which have their centre of main interests in a Member State. Second, and in approximate parallel to the Regulation, is a statutory scheme made under the auspices of the United Nations as a Model Law, which also aims to enshrine the policy that insolvency should be concentrated in and organized around procedures conducted at the centre of main interests of the debtor. Each of these instruments has produced a significant quantity of case law in a rather short time. The third development is that the common law has discovered or rediscovered powers to assist or cooperate with a foreign court exercising insolvency jurisdiction. These powers appear to have lain dormant for a long time, but have been reawakened to uncertain effect, with the result that they appear to exist in uneasy parallel with statutory powers conferred by Parliament under the Insolvency Act 1986. We cannot hope to deal with the entirety of the law, much of which is more properly seen as domestic rather than private international law; but there are

---

[46] See Fletcher, *Insolvency in Private International Law* (2nd edn, Oxford University Press, 2005).
[47] Insolvency Act 1986, s 117.
[48] Regulation 1215/2012, Art 24(2).
[49] Regulation (EC) 1346/2000, [2000] OJ L160/1.
[50] Regulation (EU) 2015/848, [2015] OJ L141/19: in effect from 26 June 2017.

issues of broader significance for private international law on which it will be proper to concentrate.

(a) Centre of debtor's main interest not in a Member State: common law and statute

Where the matter is not one governed by the (former) Insolvency Regulation, an English court may wind up a company formed under the Companies Acts:[51] when it does it may make orders which are necessary or desirable to protect the integrity and efficiency of the process, including injunctions to restrain those having recourse to courts overseas.[52] Less expected, perhaps, is the fact that the court may wind up a company not formed under the Companies Acts so long as the company has a 'sufficient connection' with the jurisdiction and is insolvent, and it is not otherwise inappropriate to make the order.[53] A 'sufficient connection' will exist if there are persons in England who could benefit from a winding-up order and there is enough connection with England to justify making the order.[54] Perhaps most unexpected of all is that an insolvent company which has been dissolved under its *lex incorporationis* may be revived for the purpose of being wound up.[55] As Parliament can make any provision it cares to, the creation of a zombie company in the exercise of a statutory power to act is not a legal impossibility. But it represents a significant victory for pragmatism over the principle that dissolution is the exclusive concern of the *lex incorporationis*.

When the English court makes the order, the assets of the company are bound by a trust for the benefit of those interested in the winding up.[56] The liquidator appointed is under an obligation to get in all the assets to which the company appears to be entitled, and is obliged to use them to discharge English and foreign liabilities. If there is also a foreign liquidation he is obliged to seek to secure equal treatment for all claimants, not just for English creditors.[57] Many provisions of the Insolvency Act 1986 dealing with orders

---

[51] Insolvency Act 1986, s 117.

[52] *Stichting Shell Pensioenfonds v Krys* [2014] UKPC 41, [2014] 1 WLR 4482.

[53] ibid, ss 220, 221; *Re A Company (No 00359 of 1987)* [1988] Ch 210; *Re Paramount Airways Ltd* [1993] Ch 223 (CA).

[54] *Re A Company (No 00359 of 1987)* [1988] Ch 210; *Re A Company (No 003102 of 1991), ex p Nyckeln Finance Co Ltd* [1991] BCLC 539; *Stocznia Gdanska SA v Latreefers Inc* [2001] BCC 174 (CA).

[55] Insolvency Act 1986, s 225.

[56] This may also mean that a creditor who brings (or continues: *Stichting Shell Pensioenfonds v Krys* [2014] UKPC 41, [2014] 1 WLR 4482) proceedings in a foreign court, in order to improve his position at the expense of the other creditors, may be restrained from doing so.

[57] *Re Bank of Credit and Commerce International SA* [1992] BCLC 570.

which may be made in the course of administration or liquidation are silent about what their international scope is intended to be, but they will probably be interpreted as applying where there is a sufficient connection with England,[58] which may not be very much more helpful, but which probably reflects the common sense of the view that if something cannot be defined well, it is better that it not be defined at all.

So far as concerns a foreign winding up, a liquidator appointed under the *lex incorporationis* is recognized by English private international law,[59] because the question of who is authorized to act on the company's behalf is a matter for the *lex incorporationis*. There appears to be no authority on the recognition of a liquidator appointed under the law of a third country, though if the company can be seen to have submitted to the jurisdiction of the foreign court, there is a good case to be made for the recognition, in principle at least, of the person appointed by the submitted-to court.

The courts of the United Kingdom have, as one would expect, a statutory obligation to assist each other in a winding up.[60] In relation to countries outside the United Kingdom the Secretary of State may designate and has designated certain countries whose laws may be applied in an English insolvency, and whose courts (though not liquidators acting on their own authority[61]) may request cooperation from an English court.[62] This means, for example, that an Australian court can request cooperation from the English courts, though the critical question for the English court will be what form that cooperation may be allowed to take. If an Australian court should request the remission to Australia of assets in England, with the intention that these will be distributed in the Australian insolvency which has rules of priority between creditors which are not the same as those which would have been applied in English proceedings, there will be a tension between giving effect to the statutory rules provided for English insolvency and the fact that the main insolvency is in Australia. Though the Insolvency Act would allow the English court to apply Australian law, it does not clearly authorize it to not apply English statutory rules which would govern the case;[63] and in any event, if the assets are remitted to Australia, not everyone will consider

---

[58] *Jetavia SA v Bilta (UK) Ltd* [2015] UKSC 23, [2016] AC 1; *Re Paramount Airways Ltd* [1993] Ch 223 (CA).

[59] *Bank of Ethiopia v National Bank of Egypt and Ligouri* [1937] Ch 513.

[60] Insolvency Act 1986, s 426(4).

[61] *Re BCCI SA (No 9)* [1994] 3 All ER 764.

[62] Insolvency Act 1986, s 426(4); and see at Section (4)(c)below the reference to the Cross-Border Insolvency Regulations 2006.

[63] *Re BCCI SA (No 10)* [1997] Ch 213.

this to mean that the English court is 'applying Australian law' as distinct from applying English law in order to allow an Australian court to apply Australian law.[64]

The United States has not been designated under the Insolvency Act, so the manner and form of cooperation with a US insolvency, for example, is principally a matter for the 2006 Regulations implementing the Model Law, which are considered below. But from one point of view these are incomplete in their coverage,[65] in the rather special sense that there may be some measures which the foreign court may ask for (such as the enforcement of one of its judgments) but which the Regulations do not bind the requested court to provide. The question whether in these circumstances the English court may do anything, and, if so, what, has exercised the courts in recent years. It does not simplify matters too much to say that one strand of judicial thinking accepts that if English law recognizes the foreign proceedings as brought in the proper place,[66] it should go as far as it can, according to 'a common law principle of modified universalism',[67] to grant the assistance requested, whereas another strand is apprehensive about a judicial free-for-all in which the rules of private international law are trampled by a result-oriented, but otherwise ill-defined, principle of insolvency law.

Nevertheless, if a court is asked to assist a foreign court in its administration of an insolvency, the point of departure for the common law is to enquire whether the legislation under which a court has a statutory power to cooperate with or assist a foreign insolvency precludes, explicitly or implicitly, the possibility of a common law power to make the order asked for. It is a good question, but the usual answer is that legislation which provides that X may be done does not preclude the doing of Y if there is a distinct legal basis for Y to be done.[68] Indeed, a related (and even more obvious) principle would explain that if a statute provides that a court may do Z, there is no basis for the contention that another court—say in a foreign country—is forbidden to do Z.[69] But establishing that legislation does not preclude the exercise of

---

[64] Re HIH Casualty & General Insurance Ltd, McGrath v Riddell [2008] UKHL 21, [2008] 1 WLR 852; New Cap Reinsurance Corp v Grant [2011] EWCA Civ 971, [2012] QB 538 (appeal dismissed without reference to this point, sub nom Rubin v Eurofinance SA [2012] UKSC 46, [2013] 1 AC 236).

[65] In fact, they are very incomplete when compared with the Insolvency Regulation, particularly on the treatment of jurisdiction and lis pendens.

[66] In the place of incorporation as far as the common law is concerned; at the centre of main interests so far as the Regulations are concerned.

[67] UBS AG New York v Fairfield Sentry (in liq) [2019] UKPC 20 [19].

[68] Singularis Holdings Ltd v PricewaterhouseCoopers [2014] UKPC 36, [2015] AC 1675.

[69] UBS AG New York v Fairfield Sentry (in liq) [2019] UKPC 20.

a common law power is only the first step. It does not answer the question of what principles define or restrict the exercise of that common law power.

In one case in which a (Manx) court had been asked to exercise what appeared to be a common law power to cooperate with a US insolvency, the Privy Council agreed that an order may be made, reflecting Manx statute law, which would remove a shareholder's interest in a Manx company and transfer its value to a committee of unsecured creditors.[70] Manx statute law allowed such an order to be made in the context of Manx insolvency proceedings, but said nothing to suggest that this same power could be deployed in aid of foreign proceedings; still less did it say that this could be done more or less on the say-so of a US court and without the procedural apparatus which would have applied in a purely Manx case. This is the reason why the order made in the case itself must have been based on the common law. It has since been held that the decision was wrong:[71] either because it was arrived at by 'interpreting' a statute as if it said something which it did not say,[72] or because it violated other settled principles of private international law (such as the rules for the enforcement or not of foreign judgments) without a proper basis for so doing.[73]

A more conservative, and currently more reliable, position would be that the court may respond to a foreign request by making an order which it would have power to make in a domestic case, but that it should only do so if the order is (or very closely corresponds to) one which the foreign court could have made under its own law. This rule of double reference is evidently designed to prevent a liquidator getting access to legal powers which the law under which he was appointed did not confer on him. Some will see this as sound and principled; others will wonder why, if the law under which the liquidator was appointed did not forbid his seeking such assistance, and especially if a foreign court authorized the liquidator to ask for this particular form of assistance, this should be a bar to his doing so.[74] It can appear that the interests of the creditors are subordinated to an abstract, and rather unattractive, dogma.

---

[70] *Cambridge Gas Transport Corp v Official Committee of Unsecured Creditors of Navigator Holdings plc* [2006] UKPC 26, [2007] 1 AC 508. See also, for a very interesting discussion, *Re OJSC International Bank of Azerbaijan* [2018] EWCA Civ 2802.

[71] *Rubin v Eurofinance SA* [2012] UKSC 46, [2013] 1 AC 236; *Singularis Holdings Ltd v PricewaterhouseCoopers* [2014] UKPC 36, [2015] AC 1675.

[72] *Singularis Holdings Ltd v PricewaterhouseCoopers* [2014] UKPC 36, [2015] AC 1675.

[73] *Rubin v Eurofinance SA* [2012] UKSC 46, [2013] 1 AC 236.

[74] *Singularis Holdings Ltd v PricewaterhouseCoopers* [2014] UKPC 36, [2015] AC 1675. The decision appears to misread *Credit Suisse Fides Trust SA v Cuoghi* [1998] QB 818, where the Court of Appeal ordered relief which a Swiss court had no power to make.

In a very significant case,[75] the English court was asked to assist a US court by giving effect to a judgment of the US court against corporate officers who were said to have defrauded the company but who had not themselves personally submitted to the jurisdiction of the US court.[76] When the majority of the Supreme Court refused to make the orders applied for, it pointed out that the enforcement of foreign judgments is governed by the ordinary rules of private international law which were not liable to be circumvented, which really means contradicted, when a request from or on behalf of a foreign court arrives in its inbox. It made no difference that the circumvention was asked for by a court exercising insolvency jurisdiction: it was simply inadmissible. The judgment did not say so openly, but the court may well have wondered how, if it had assisted the US court by making the order applied for, it would be able to deal properly with a request from, say, a Russian court, asking it to make similar orders against those said to have siphoned funds from a Russian company (whose patron-oligarch had become an outlaw) in administration in Moscow. The conclusion to which one comes is that cooperation with foreign insolvencies and their officers is a fine and proper thing, but there may be contexts in which it should be left to governments to identify those to whom cooperation is and is not to be extended, and for Parliament to enact the law in exhaustive form. The common law is not well equipped to conduct a quality audit of foreign insolvency courts; and a common law power to cooperate beyond the terms authorized by a recent statute may prove to be a dangerous thing to have discovered.

All that being said, the rule of the common law that a judgment *in personam* may be recognized if the person against whom the judgment is to be enforced submitted to the jurisdiction of the foreign court has been held to be satisfied by a creditor submitting a claim in the insolvency to the liquidator, with the consequence that an English court could then enforce a foreign judgment ordering the return of preferential or other improper payments. Not everyone will be immediately persuaded that the simple filling in of a form by a creditor-claimant, and its posting to a liquidator, is the legal equivalent of the issue of a writ by a claimant exposing him, there and then, to the full range of judicial power of the supervising court.[77] However, if this is regarded as a sufficient submission to the insolvency jurisdiction of a foreign court, why should the principle not extend to a shareholder, or office-holder, in a company which submits to the insolvency jurisdiction of a foreign court?

[75] *Rubin v Eurofinance SA* [2012] UKSC 46, [2013] 1 AC 236.
[76] *Rubin v Eurofinance SA* [2012] UKSC 46, [2013] 1 AC 236.
[77] *Rubin v Eurofinance SA* [2012] UKSC 46, [2013] 1 AC 236.

There is still much work for the common law to do if this power to assist a foreign insolvency court is to be developed.

(b) Centre of debtor's main interests in a Member State: Insolvency Regulation

In insolvencies to which the Insolvency Regulation was applied, the Regulation prescribes and limits the jurisdiction of the courts of Member States in relation to the opening of insolvency proceedings; the identification of the law to be applied in the insolvency proceedings; and the recognition of judgments from other Member States ordering the opening, conduct, and closure of such proceedings. Its purpose is (or was) to bring order to an area which was excluded from the original jurisdictional scheme of what became the Brussels I Regulation, and for which the coordination of the judicial function had been particularly problematic. The position if or when the United Kingdom withdraws from the European Union is complex: the rules under which the courts of the United Kingdom may exercise jurisdiction will be substantially retained, but the effect which the Regulation requires an English court to give to connections with or proceedings in another Member State (and vice versa, which is rather more serious) will be dissolved.[78]

The Insolvency Regulation was made to apply to debtors wherever domiciled, but the critical requirement is that the centre of the debtor's main interests be in a Member State. In the nature of things, this test, or connecting factor, is likely to be hardest to use in the cases in which its guidance is the most needed, for the kind of business for which it is a crucial definitional tool is likely to be cross-border in the first place; and there is more than a trace of suspicion that some companies, faced with the prospect of insolvent winding up, may try to migrate the centre of their main interests to a Member State whose insolvency law is more forgiving of bad business, and more prepared to allow a fresh start, than are some others.[79] Still, the general rule is that for a company the centre of main interests is presumed to be the place of the registered office,[80] although it seems inevitable that scrutiny of the whole of a company's activities may be required where the issue of location is contested.

---

[78] SI 2019/146.

[79] See Art 3 of the recast Regulation for a limited measure to counter such shifting.

[80] Article 3. The expression has an autonomous meaning. The presumption applies even though the debtor is a subsidiary of a company incorporated elsewhere, on the broad footing that it is the appearance to those dealing with the debtor which is the principal concern: Case C–341/04 *Re Eurofood IFSC Ltd* [2006] ECR I–3813. See also Case C–396/09 *Interedil srl v Fallimento Interedil srl* [2011] ECR I–9915; Case C–191/10 *Rastelli Davide e C Snc v Hidoux* EU:C:2011:838, [2013] BCLC 329.

The Regulation applies to collective insolvency proceedings which involve the complete or partial divestment of a debtor and the appointment of a liquidator,[81] whether the debtor is an individual or a corporate body. It excludes insurance undertakings and credit institutions.[82] The overall aim was to ensure that, within the European Union, the lead role is given to a single court, and that proceedings in all other courts are relegated to a subordinate role. Accordingly, 'main proceedings' may be opened only in the Member State in which the centre of a debtor's main interests is situated at the date of the request to open the proceedings.[83] 'Secondary' or 'territorial' proceedings may be opened in any Member State in which the debtor has an 'establishment'.[84] Though their effect is confined to assets situated[85] in the Member State in which the secondary or territorial proceedings are opened, they may be opened before main proceedings are. The law which is generally applicable to insolvency proceedings and their effects is the *lex fori*,[86] which governs most issues,[87] but exceptions are made for a list of other matters for which this would not be the appropriate law.[88] An order from a court in a Member State opening insolvency proceedings must be recognized, from the time it becomes effective, in all other Member States, and be given the same effect as it has in the state of origin.[89] Judgments relating to the conduct and closure of insolvency proceedings are recognized in all other Member States,[90] and enforcement of orders takes place under the Brussels I Regulation. A liquidator appointed in the main proceedings is to be recognized in all other Member States[91] and accorded the powers which he has under the law of the state of his appointment. If there are secondary proceedings in another Member State, his powers are limited in relation to those assets; but the various liquidators are under an obligation to share information and to cooperate with each other.[92]

---

[81] Including a trustee or an administrative receiver appointed under a floating charge: Art 1.
[82] Article 1.
[83] Even if it moved its centre after the date of the request: Case C–1/04 *Re Staubitz-Schreiber* [2006] ECR I–701. For very recent prior movements of the COMI, see Recitals 29–32, and Art 3.1.
[84] Any place of operations where the debtor carries out a non-transitory economic activity with human means and assets: Art 2(10).
[85] Defined in Art 2(9).
[86] Article 7.
[87] Article 7. See Case C–594/14 *Kornhaas v Dithmar* EU:C:2015:806, [2016] BCC 116.
[88] Articles 8–18.
[89] Articles 13 and 20. See Case C–444/07 *Re MG Probud Gdynia sp zoo* [2010] ECR I–417.
[90] Article 32.
[91] Article 21.
[92] Article 41.

From time to time a court has had to determine whether proceedings brought or intended to be brought before a court fall within the material scope of the (former) Brussels I Regulation or under the (former) Insolvency Regulation. The guiding principle is that the right or duty relied on in the proceedings is part of the ordinary civil law, the fact that proceedings are brought by or against a liquidator does not remove them from the material scope of the Brussels I Regulation; but if they seek to establish rights or obligations which are peculiar to insolvency, then they will fall within the Insolvency Regulation, and therefore outside the Brussels I Regulation.[93]

(c) Centre of main interests not in a Member State: the 2006 Regulations

In a development reflecting that established by the Insolvency Regulation, the UNCITRAL produced a Model Law on cross-border insolvency which was given effect in the United Kingdom in the form of the Cross-Border Insolvency Regulations 2006.[94] The Model Law, as given effect in England, does not provide a comprehensive scheme to regulate every aspect of cross-border insolvency, but does aim to pave the way for states to enact legislation to provide for the recognition of foreign insolvency procedures (though not the recognition of foreign judgments *in personam*),[95] the right of foreign representatives to have access to courts, requests for cooperation, and judicial coordination of concurrent proceedings. Its guiding principle is that an insolvency organized at the centre of main interests of the debtor should be recognized and given priority, and that the role of the English courts in such a case is a secondary and supplementary one.[96] It is unsurprising that the extent to which this will require an English court to make orders which it would not have made as part of an English insolvency is yet to be fully mapped.

---

[93] For example, Case C–111/08 *SCT Industri AB v Alpenblume AB* [2009] ECR I–5655; Case C–292/08 *German Graphics Graphische Maschinen GmbH v van der Schee* [2009] ECR I–8421; Case C–157/13 *Nickel & Goeldner Spedition GmbH v 'Kintra' UAB* EU:C:2014:2145, [2015] QB 96; Case C–295/13 *H v K* EU:C:2014:2410; Case C–641/16 *Tünkers France v Expert France* EU:C:2017:847; Case C–649/16 *Valach v Waldviertel Sparkasse Bank AG* EU:C:2017:986; Case C–535/17 *NK v BNP Paribas Fortis NV* EU:C:2019:96.

[94] SI 2006/1030. For an excellent discussion, see *Re OJSC International Bank of Azerbaijan* [2018] EWCA Civ 2802.

[95] *Rubin v Eurofinance SA* [2012] UKSC 46, [2013] 1 AC 236.

[96] SI 2006/1030, Sch 1, Art 20.

Index

Note: *For the benefit of digital users, indexed terms that span two pages (e.g., 52–53) may, on occasion, appear on only one of those pages.*